Journalism: critical issues

Edited by Stuart Allan

Open University Press

Open University Press
McGraw-Hill Education
McGraw-Hill House
Shoppenhangers Road
Maidenhead
Berkshire
England
SL6 2QL

email: enquiries@openup.co.uk
world wide web: www.openup.co.uk

and Two Penn Plaza, New York, NY 10121–2289, USA

First published 2005

A catalogue record of this book is available from the British Library

ISBN 0 335 21475 4 (pb) 0 335 21484 3 (hb)

Library of Congress Cataloguing-in-Publication data
CIP data applied for

Typeset by RefineCatch Ltd, Bungay, Suffolk
Printed in the UK by Bell & Bain Ltd, Glasgow

Contents

PART III
Journalism's realities

PART IV
Journalism and the politics of othering

PART V
Journalism and the public interest

Contributors

Stuart Allan is Reader at the School of Cultural Studies, University of the West of England, Bristol. He is the author of *News Culture* (Open University Press, 1999; second edition, 2004) and *Media, Risk and Science* (Open University Press, 2002). His previous collections include, with co-editor Barbie Zelizer, *Journalism after September 11* (Routledge, 2002) and *Reporting War: Journalism in Wartime* (Routledge, 2004). He is the editor of the 'Issues in Cultural and Media Studies' book series for Open University Press.

Alison Anderson is Principal Lecturer in Sociology at the University of Plymouth. She is author of *Media, Culture and the Environment* (UCL, 1997) and co-editor of *The Changing Consumer* (Routledge, 2002). Recent articles on journalistic portrayals of environmental issues, genetics and war have appeared in *Sociological Research Online*; *Knowledge*; *Technology and Society* and *New Genetics and Society*. She is currently conducting research on nanotechnology and news media production with Alan Petersen, Stuart Allan and Clare Wilkinson.

Olga Guedes Bailey is a journalist, and Senior Lecturer in the School of Media, Critical and Creative Arts at Liverpool John Moores University, England. She was recently appointed Visiting Professor at the Shanghai University of Finance and Economics, Humanities College, China. She has published essays on global audiences, environmentalism and journalistic practice and the consumption of new technologies.

Steven Barnett is Professor of Communications at the University of Westminster and a regular columnist on broadcasting in the *Observer*. He is the co-author of *Westminster Tales: the 21st Century Crisis in Political Journalism* (Continuum, 2001) and *The Battle for the BBC* (Aurum Press, 1994) and has contributed to a number of books and journals on media policy, media and politics and public service broadcasting. He is an editorial board member of the *British Journalism Review*.

Oliver Boyd-Barrett is Professor of Communication at California State Polytechnic University, Pomona. Recent books include *Approaches to Media* (co-edited with Chris Newbold; Edward Arnold, 1995), *The Globalization of News* (co-edited with Terhi Rantanen; Sage, 1998) and *The Media Book* (co-edited with Chris Newbold and Hilde Van Den Bulck; Hodder Arnold, 2002).

Michael Bromley is Professor of Journalism at the University of Queensland, Brisbane, Australia. A former daily newspaper journalist, he has taught in a number of universities in the UK, the US and Australia. He has published widely on journalism and the news media, and is a founder co-editor of the journal *Journalism: Theory, Practice and Criticism* and a member of the editorial boards of *Australian Studies in Journalism* and *Media History*.

Cynthia Carter teaches in the Cardiff School of Journalism, Media and Cultural Studies, Cardiff University. Her books include the co-authored *Violence and the Media* (Open University Press, 2003) and the co-edited *News, Gender and Power* (Routledge, 1998), *Environmental Risks and the Media* (Routledge, 2000) and *Critical Readings: Media and Gender* (Open University Press, 2004). She also co-edits the refereed journal *Feminist Media Studies*. She is currently researching children's online responses to news reports of terrorism and the war in Iraq.

Simon Cottle is Professor and Director, Media and Communications Program at the University of Melbourne. His most recent book includes: *The Racist Murder of Stephen Lawrence: Media Performance and Public Transformation* (Praeger, 2004), and he was the editor of *Media Organization and Production* (Sage 2003) and *News, Public Relations and Power* (Sage 2003). He is currently writing *Mediatized Conflict* (Open University Press) and undertaking a major international study of the changing international forms, flows and frames of television journalism. Funded by the Australian Research Council, it is entitled: 'Television Journalism and Deliberative Democracy: A Comparative International Study of Communicative Architecture and Forms of Democratic Deepening.'

Chas Critcher is Professor of Communications at Sheffield Hallam University, UK. He originally studied at the Centre for Contemporary Cultural Studies at the University of Birmingham where he co-authored *Policing the Crisis* (Macmillan, 1979), a study of social reaction to mugging. He recently published *Moral Panics and the Media* (Open University Press, 2003), examining a series of case studies of moral panics in Britain.

Matthew David teaches Sociology at University of Plymouth. His research has addressed 'local environmental movements', IT in education, social exclusion, and constructions of property in science. He is author (with Carole Sutton) of *Social Research* (Sage, 2004) and *Science in Society* (Palgrave, 2005). Peer reviewed articles have appeared in *Sociological Research Online, New Genetics and Society, Telematics and Informatics*; *Critical Horizons*; *Current Sociology* and elsewhere.

Máire Messenger Davies is Professor of Media Studies and Director of the Centre for Media Research in the School of Media and Performing Arts, University of Ulster at Coleraine. A former journalist, her PhD is in psychology and she has written widely on the relationship between media, culture and the young. Her books include *Television is Good for Your Kids* (Shipman

1989, second edition, 2001); *Fake, Fact and Fantasy: Children's Interpretations of Television Reality* (Erlbaum 1997) and *Dear BBC: Children, Television, Story-telling and the Public Sphere* (Cambridge University Press, 2001). She is currently developing projects with colleagues at the University of Ulster on children's responses to media representations of political conflict.

Bob Franklin is Professor of Journalism Studies at the Cardiff School of Journalism, Media and Cultural Studies. He is co-editor of *Journalism Studies*. Recent books include: *Packaging Politics: Political Communication in Britain's Media Democracy* (Arnold, 2004); *British Television Policy: A Reader* (Routledge, 2002); *Social Policy, the Media and Misrepresentation* (Routledge 1999); *Making the Local News: Local Journalism in Context* (Routledge, 1998) and *Newszak and News Media* (Arnold, 1997). *Television Policy, The MacTaggart Lectures* and *Key Concepts in Journalism Studies* will be published in 2005.

Robert A. Hackett is Professor of Communication at Simon Fraser University, Vancouver. From 1993 to 2003, he co-directed NewsWatch Canada. His various publications on media and politics include *Sustaining Democracy? Journalism and the Politics of Objectivity* (with Y. Zhao; Garamond, 1998) and *Democratizing Global Media: One World, Many Struggles* (co-edited with Y. Zhao, Rowman & Littlefield, 2005). He has been active in several citizens' media reform groups, and is currently researching media democratization as a social movement.

Ramaswami Harindranath is Senior Lecturer in the Media and Communications Program at the University of Melbourne, Australia. He co-authored *The 'Crash' Controversy* (Wallflower Press, 2001), and is currently completing a manuscript entitled *Southern Discomfort* to be published in 2005. He has written on diverse topics such as audience research, 'race' and representation, social movements and cultural imperialism.

Ian Hutchby is Reader in the School of Social Sciences and Law at Brunel University, London. His research focuses on the development and application of conversation analysis in a range of areas, including broadcast talk, conflict and argumentation, institutional and therapeutic discourse and technologically mediated interaction. His principal publications are *Confrontation Talk* (Lawrence Erlbaum, 1996), *Conversation Analysis* (Polity, 1998) and *Conversation and Technology* (Polity, 2001). His articles have appeared in numerous international journals including *Sociology*; *Discourse and Society*; *Discourse Processes*; *Text*; *Discourse Studies* and the *Journal of Sociolinguistics*.

Richard Keeble is Professor of Journalism at the University of Lincoln and editor of *Ethical Space: The International Journal of Communication Ethics*. He was editor of the *Teacher*, the newspaper of the National Union of

Teachers, from 1980 to 1984 and has freelanced for a range of leftist journals. His publications include *The Newspapers Handbook* (Routledge, 2001, third edition).

Justin Lewis is Professor of Communication at the Cardiff School of Journalism, Media and Cultural Studies. He has written several books about media, culture and society. Among his recent books is *Constructing Public Opinion: How Elites Do What They Like and Why We Seem to Go Along With It* (Columbia University Press, 2001).

Minelle Mahtani is Assistant Professor in the Department of Geography, University of Toronto. She was a national television news producer at the Canadian Broadcasting Corporation and is also associate strategic counsel for IMPACS (the Institute for Media, Policy and Civil Society). She has published on media and minorities, critical 'race' theory and feminist geography. Her book on the experiences of 'mixed race' women in Toronto, Canada is forthcoming with University of British Columbia Press.

P. David Marshall is Professor and Chair of the Department of Communication Studies at Northeastern University in Boston. He is the author of many articles on media, new media, popular culture and public personalities and two books, *Celebrity and Power* (University of Minnesota Press, 1997) and *New Media Cultures* (Edward Arnold/Oxford, 2004). He is the co-author of *Web Theory* (Routledge, 2003; with Robert Burnett) and *Fame Games: the Production of Celebrity in Australia* (Cambridge, 2000/1 with Graeme Turner and Francis Bonner) and he is currently completing an edited collection entitled *Celebrity Culture Reader* for Routledge (2005). He is also the founder of one of the premier and most innovative Internet journals *M/c – a Journal of Media and Culture* (www.media-culture.org.au) and regularly contributes through interviews to many of the major radio and television networks nationally and internationally.

Brian McNair is Professor of Journalism and Communication at Strathclyde University. His previous books include *The Sociology of Journalism* (Arnold, 1998), *Journalism and Democracy* (Routledge, 2000), *News and Journalism in the UK* (Routledge, 2003, fourth edition) and *Mediated Access* (University of Luton Press, 2003; with Matthew Hibberd and Philip Schlesinger). He is currently working on a book length study of *Cultural Chaos*, for publication by Routledge in 2006.

Martin Montgomery teaches at the University of Strathclyde, Glasgow, where he is Reader in English Studies and Director of the Scottish Centre for Journalism Studies. His publications include a standard work of sociolinguistics, *An Introduction to Language and Society* (Routledge, 1995) and articles in journals such as *Media, Culture and Society, Language and Literature* and *Journal of Pragmatics*. He is currently working on a study of the language of broadcast news.

Alan Petersen teaches sociology at University of Plymouth. His research spans the fields of the sociology of health and illness, media and bio-technologies and gender studies. He is currently undertaking research on nanotechnology and news media production with Alison Anderson, Stuart Allan and Clare Wilkinson. His recent works include the co-authored book *The New Genetics and the Public's Health* (Routledge, 2002), the co-edited book *Consuming Health* (Routledge, 2002), *Engendering Emotions* (Palgrave, 2004) and the co-edited book *Genetic Governance* (Routledge, 2005).

Susanna Hornig Priest is Director of Research for the College of Mass Communications and Information Studies at the University of South Carolina in Columbia, South Carolina. Her research centres on public responses to risks associated with science and technology, including the media's role in framing risk issues. She is widely published on the subject of risk and the public, including recent articles in *Risk Analysis*; *Public Understanding of Science*; *Science Communication*; *Science and Engineering Ethics*; *Society* and *Nature Biotechnology*. Her book on media, biotechnology and public opinion, *A Grain of Truth*, was published by Rowman & Littlefield in 2001.

Jane Rhodes is Associate Professor of Ethnic Studies and an affiliated associate professor of communication at the University of California, San Diego. Her research focuses on the historical relationships between race, media and social movements. She is the author of *Mary Ann Shadd Cary: The Black Press and Protest in the Nineteenth Century* (Indiana University Press, 1998), which won the AEJMC award for best book in mass communication history. Her new book, *Framing the Black Panthers: The Spectacular Rise of a Black Power Icon* is forthcoming from The New Press in 2005.

Karen Ross is Reader in Mass Communication at Coventry University, England and visiting professor at the School of Politics, Queens University Belfast, Northern Ireland (2001–4). Previous publications include: *Women and Media* (with Carolyn Byerly; Blackwell, 2004); *Media and Audiences* (with Virginia Nightingale; Open University Press 2003); *Mapping the Margins: Identity Politics and Media* (Hampton Press, 2003); *Women, Politics, Media* (Hampton Press, 2002); *Women, Politics and Change* (Oxford University Press, 2001); *Black Marks: Minority Ethnic Audiences and Media* (Ashgate, 2001) and *Black and White Media* (Polity, 1996).

David Rowe teaches media and cultural studies and is Director of the Cultural Industries and Practices Research Centre (CIPS) at the University of Newcastle, Australia. His books include *Popular Cultures: Rock Music, Sport and the Politics of Pleasure* (Sage, 1995) and *Sport, Culture and the Media: The Unruly Trinity* (second edition, Open University Press, 2004); he co-authored *Globalization and Sport: Playing the World* (Sage, 2001) and edited *Critical Readings: Sport, Culture and the Media* (Open University Press, 2004).

Prasun Sonwalkar is a senior lecturer in journalism studies at the School of Cultural Studies, University of the West of England, Bristol. A former journalist, he has worked at various levels on *The Times of India*; *Business Standard*; *Zee News* and *Indo-Asian News Service*. He has contributed chapters to *Media, Violence and Terrorism* (Unesco, 2003), *Reporting War: Journalism in Wartime* (Routledge, 2004), *International News in the 21st Century* (University of Luton Press, 2004), *Issues and Challenges in Asian Journalism* (Times Press, 2005) and articles to *Media, Culture and Society*; *Gazette, Modern Asian Studies*; *Contemporary South Asia* and *Communicator*. He is currently co-editing a volume on political violence and the media for the Hampton Press.

Linda Steiner teaches journalism and media studies at Rutgers University, in New Brunswick, New Jersey. She is editor of *Critical Studies in Media Communication* and a former associate editor of *Journalism and Mass Communication Quarterly*. In 2004 she co-authored *Women and Journalism* (with Deborah Chambers and Carole Fleming; Routledge) and co-edited *Critical Readings: Media and Gender* (with Cynthia Carter; Open University Press).

Howard Tumber is Professor of Sociology in the School of Social Sciences, City University, London. Recent books include *Media at War: The Iraq Crisis* (with Jerry Palmer; Sage 2004); *Media Power, Policies and Professionals* (Routledge 2000); *News: A Reader* (Oxford University Press, 1999), *Reporting Crime: The Media Politics of Criminal Justice* (with Philip Schlesinger; Oxford University Press, 1994) and *Journalists at War* (with David Morrison; Sage 1988). He is a founder and co-editor of *Journalism: Theory, Practice and Criticism*.

Ingrid Volkmer, University of Otago, New Zealand, has published widely on issues concerning global communication. Her particular interests are the new worldwide media infrastructure and its impact on societies and cultures. She has been a visiting scholar at MIT and a fellow at the Shorenstein Center on the Press, Politics and Public Policy, Harvard. She is also Director of the Global Media Research Consortium, a group of 12 universities, which carries out internationally comparative research.

Karin Wahl-Jorgensen teaches in the Cardiff School of Journalism, Media and Cultural Studies. She is interested in the relationship between citizenship, democracy and mass media. Her work has appeared in more than 20 different journals, and she is currently working on two books. *Journalists and the Public* (Hampton Press) looks at how journalists deal with and discuss letters to the editor. *Citizens or Consumers? The Media and the Decline of Political Participation* (Open University Press), is co-authored with Justin Lewis and Sanna Inthorn, and examines how citizens are represented in the news.

Barbie Zelizer is the Raymond Williams Professor of Communication at the University of Pennsylvania's Annenberg School for Communication. A former journalist, Zelizer's books include *Covering the Body: The Kennedy Assassination, the Media and the Shaping of Collective Memory* (University of Chicago, 1992), *Remembering to Forget: Holocaust Memory Through the Camera's Eye* (University of Chicago, 1998), *Journalism After September 11* (with Stuart Allan; Routledge, 2002), *Taking Journalism Seriously: News and the Academy* (Sage, 2004) and *Reporting War: Journalism in Wartime* (with Stuart Allan; Routledge, 2004). She is a founding co-editor of the journal *Journalism: Theory, Practice and Criticism*.

Introduction

Hidden in plain sight – journalism's critical issues
Stuart Allan

> At any given moment there is a sort of all-pervading orthodoxy, a general tacit agreement not to discuss large and uncomfortable facts.
>
> George Orwell

These are troubled times for journalism. One commentator after the next is declaring the conviction that it is in a state of crisis, even in danger of losing its place at the heart of democratic society. Some of the voices raising the alarm are pointing to reportorial scandals – such as those involving Andrew Gilligan at the BBC, Jayson Blair at *The New York Times* or Jack Kelley at *USA Today* – as evidence of a deeper, more disturbing malaise.[1] Even certain noteworthy journalists are wondering aloud whether the fabric of a once proud profession is slowly coming unravelled, not least – they fear – by the relentless pull of populism, politics and profits on its rapidly fraying threads.

It was all too telling, some would suggest, that when the *Daily Mirror* conceded that its photographs purporting to depict the abuse of an Iraqi prisoner at the hands of British soldiers were actually fakes, few seemed genuinely surprised. The incessant drive to be first with the story, to scoop one's rivals whatever the cost, had claimed its usual casualty – the truth. The *Mirror*'s front-page apology read:

SORRY . . .
WE WERE
HOAXED

Iraqi PoW abuse pictures handed to us WERE fake

It is now clear that the photographs the *Mirror* published of British soldiers abusing an Iraqi prisoner were fakes.

The evidence against them is not strong enough to convict in a court but that is not the burden of proof the *Daily Mirror* demands of itself. Our mission is to tell the truth.

That is something this newspaper has been doing for more than 100 years and will always strive to do. If ever we fail, we are letting down the people who mean most to us. Our readers.

So to you today we apologise for publishing pictures which we now believe were not genuine.

We also say sorry to the Queen's Lancashire Regiment and our Army in Iraq for publishing those pictures.

The *Daily Mirror* printed the photographs in good faith . . .

(*Daily Mirror*, 15 May 2004; p. 1)

Much was made by critics of how the reputation of the country's troops in Iraq, and possibly even their safety, had been 'traded for what now appear to be cheap news headlines' (to quote the angry words of one Member of Parliament). Not surprisingly, however, there was every indication that it was back to business as usual in the newsroom soon after; albeit without the still defiant editor, Piers Morgan, who reportedly had been 'frog-marched' out the door of the Canary Wharf offices. The newspaper's corporate owner, Trinity Mirror, nervous about their shareholders' investments and advertisers' preferences, demanded his resignation with immediate effect. Still, as the *Guardian* observed in an editorial leader, 'Mr Morgan had edited a rumbustuously anti-war paper – uneven in tone, but often laudable in ambition.' Noting that there 'is some irony that the only people to have lost their jobs over the unhappy events in Iraq have been journalists', the leader nevertheless added that 'it would be foolish to deny that there are lessons for the British media in the downfall of Mr Morgan' (*Guardian*, 15 May 2004).

Lessons of a different sort were apparent to journalists in the US, where authentic photographs of torture in the notorious Abu Ghraib prison 20 miles outside Baghdad were at issue. Despite the concerted efforts of groups such as Amnesty International, the Red Cross and Human Rights Watch to draw news media attention to the disturbing allegations being made regarding the US military's mistreatment of Iraqi prisoners, their information was all but ignored by journalists for several months. The story finally broke, however, when the CBS News programme *60 Minutes II* went on air on 28 April 2004 with several of the horrific images in its possession. In the course of the ensuing furore, which engendered a major political crisis for the Bush administration, CBS was widely heralded for its shocking exclusive. Closer scrutiny of its handling of the story, though, revealed that the programme's producers had provided Pentagon officials with ample opportunity to prepare a 'media response' (some 11 pages in length) before the images were broadcast. Specifically, details emerged that eight days before the report was to air CBS anchor Dan Rather had been contacted by General Richard B. Myers, chair of the Joint Chiefs of Staff, requesting that the broadcast be delayed, if not suspended altogether. Myers reportedly expressed his concerns about the potential repercussions for US forces in Iraq, fearing that the release of the images might result in further deaths of soldiers.

Few would dispute that it was understandable for Pentagon officials to be making such a request of CBS News, given their interest in managing the situation to their advantage. Far less comprehensible, in the opinion of critics, was CBS's decision to grant it. Evidently when *60 Minutes II* finally went to air, their primary motivation was to pre-empt Seymour Hersh's (2004) report on the prisoner abuse – complete with photographs – which they had heard was about to be published by the *New Yorker* magazine. Many of those who had been dismayed by CBS's apparent willingness to bow to Pentagon pressure were quick to speculate about what might have happened otherwise. Had CBS not feared being scooped by Hersh, would it have broadcast a less substantive treatment of events, or even elected to hold the story back altogether? Rather himself had explained to viewers why the request was granted in a 'postscript' to the story:

> A postscript. Two weeks ago, we received an appeal from the Defense Department, and eventually from the chairman of the military Joint Chiefs of Staff, General Richard Myers, to delay this broadcast given the danger and tension on the ground in Iraq. We decided to honor that request while pressing for the Defense Department to add its perspective to the incidents at Abu Ghraib Prison. This week, with the photos beginning to circulate elsewhere and with other journalists about to publish their versions of the story, the Defense Department agreed to cooperate in our report.
>
> (Dan Rather, *60 Minutes II*, CBS TV, 28 April 2004)

Jeff Fager, executive producer of *60 Minutes II*, later insisted that he felt 'terrible' about the delay. 'News is a delicate thing,' he stated. 'It's hard to just make those kinds of decisions. It's not natural for us; the natural thing is to put it on the air. But the circumstances were quite unusual, and I think you have to consider that' (cited in the *Washington Post*, 4 May 2004). Many critics were less than convinced, to put it mildly, arguing that there was no justification for suppressing the story. Some believed that Defence officials' agreement to 'co-operate' signalled little more than a desire to 'spin' the story in a manner that would help contain adverse publicity. The scandal, according to the official line, revolved around the actions of some 'bad apples', and was not indicative of systemic policies and procedures. Evidence to the contrary was readily available elsewhere, of course, not least with respect to the abuses committed in Afghanistan and Guantánamo Bay. Meanwhile there could be no denying the sad reality that two weeks of CBS self-censorship must have had painful consequences for the Iraqi prisoners in question.

Less than a month following the broadcast, further questions were being raised about journalism's obligation to inform its publics while, at the same time, holding those in positions of power accountable for their actions. On 26 May 2004 the editors of the *New York Times* published a note to the daily's readers, under the Page A-10 header 'The *Times* and Iraq', which amounted to a remarkable *mea culpa* over its war coverage. While declaring themselves proud of 'an enormous amount of journalism' published about the prelude and early stages of the conflict, the editors nevertheless proceeded to admit that their review of the reporting:

> . . . found a number of instances of coverage that was not as rigorous as it should have been. In some cases, information that was controversial then, and seems questionable now, was insufficiently qualified or allowed to stand unchallenged. Looking back, we wish we had been more aggressive in re-examining the claims as new evidence emerged – or failed to emerge . . . Complicating matters for journalists, the accounts of [Iraqi] exiles were often eagerly confirmed by United States officials convinced of the need to intervene in Iraq. Administration officials now acknowledge that they sometimes fell for misinformation from these exile sources. So did many news organizations – in particular, this one . . . It is still possible that chemical or biological weapons will be unearthed in Iraq, but in this case it looks as if we, along with the administration, were taken in. And until now we have not reported that to our readers.
>
> (*New York Times*, 26 May 2004)

Of the Iraqi exiles who proved to be unreliable sources of information, the editors drew particular attention to Ahmad Chalabi (who had fallen out of favour with the Bush administration the week before, when his alleged links to Iranian intelligence interests were revealed). No journalists were identified in the note by name, however, although commentators promptly singled out star Pulitzer prize-winning reporter Judith Miller, a close confidant of Chalabi, as the main culprit. Much was made by critics of an e-mail she allegedly sent to the Baghdad bureau chief a few weeks earlier: 'I've been covering Chalabi for about 10 years, and have done most of the stories about him for our paper . . . He has provided most of the front-page exclusives on WMD [weapons of mass destruction] to our paper' (cited in *Editor and Publisher*, 26 May 2004). Despite what the *Times* later admitted was a 'deluge' of e-mails and letters criticizing Miller, demands for her resignation were resisted.

In acknowledging the newspaper's shortcomings, the *New York Times*' editors re-opened wounds inflicted by the Jayson Blair plagiarism scandal – wounds that had just begun to heal. Among the measures taken in the aftermath of that scandal, following editorial changes at the top, was the appointment of Daniel Okrent as Public Editor (effectively an ombudsperson). Okrent (2004), in a carefully crafted critique of the *Times*' 'flawed journalism' on Iraq, to use his phrase, contended that the 'failure was not individual, but institutional'. By way of clarification, he identified five 'journalistic imperatives and practices that led *The Times* down this unfortunate path' as follows:

- *The hunger for scoops.* Recognizing that 'newspaper people live to be first,' Okrent conceded that caution and doubt – especially important in times of war – can be 'drowned in a flood of adrenalin'. In the *Times* WMD coverage, he argued, 'readers encountered some rather breathless stories built on unsubstantiated "revelations" that, in many instances, were the anonymity-cloaked assertions of people with vested interests.'

- *Front-page syndrome.* For reasons which have much to do with personal egos, the desire for recognition – such as in the form of a byline on page 1 – can be incredibly intense. Stories declaring a direct link between Al Qaeda and Saddam Hussein, for example, were bound to attract attention, despite being seriously problematic. 'Other stories', Okrent added, 'pushed Pentagon assertions so aggressively you could almost sense epaulets sprouting on the shoulders of editors.'

- *Hit-and-run journalism.* 'The more surprising the story', the familiar newsroom maxim holds, 'the more often it must be revisited.' Time and again, according to Okrent, the *Times* did not re-examine assertions made by its sources. Insufficient efforts were made to follow them up, to track them, or to 'hold the officials publicly responsible if they did not pan out'.

- *Coddling sources.* Where responsible journalism is concerned, anonymous sources can be crucial – but they can also be toxic. A newspaper, Okrent believes, has an obligation to explain to its readers precisely why they should believe such a source is telling the truth, and then take appropriate action when this proves not to be the case. He wrote that the 'automatic editor defense, "We're not confirming what he says, we're just reporting it," may apply to the statements of people speaking on the record. For anonymous sources, it's worse than no defense. It's a license granted to liars.'

- *End-run editing.* In Okrent's view, based on discussions with current and former colleagues, 'a dysfunctional system enabled some reporters operating out of Washington and Baghdad to work outside the lines of customary bureau management.' Of concern here, among other issues, was the extent to which reporters were unable to raise substantive questions or reservations about stories. 'When a particular story is consciously shielded from such challenges,' he observed, 'it suggests that it contains something that plausibly should be challenged.'

In the course of highlighting these issues, Okrent took care to explain that it was not his intention to demand further acts of contrition. Rather, in sharp contrast, his aim was to help facilitate efforts to establish more aggressive forms of reporting for the newspaper. In his words, the 'aggressive journalism that I long for, and that the paper owes both its readers and its own self-respect, would reveal not just the tactics of those who promoted the WMD stories, but how the *Times* itself was used to further their cunning campaign.'

Okrent is not alone in yearning for this kind of reporting, of course. The issues he identifies are all too pertinent to public debates about the current state of journalism in an array of different national contexts. The WMD story is one of many where certain troublesome facts have been lost to the swirl of disinformation and 'background briefings', where the news media are widely perceived to have failed to provide an adequate basis for a diverse array of voices to be heard about the case (or, more to the point, lack thereof) for war. For those following these debates, there seems to be something of a consensus – regardless of their place on the political spectrum – that what counts as journalism needs to be recast anew.

Bottom-line pressures

In light of these sorts of concerns, it is hardly surprising that the language of 'crisis' is being increasingly used to describe journalism today. Still, efforts to characterize this crisis recurrently encounter difficulties when seeking to pinpoint its precise nature. Here it is necessary to look beyond the array of different incidents where lapses in journalistic integrity have come to the fore so as to determine, in turn, whether broader trends or patterns are discernible.

In its assessment of the current state of journalism in the US, for example, a recent Pew Research Center report makes for grim reading. 'Roughly half of journalists at national media outlets (51 per cent), and about as many from local media (46 per cent), believe that journalism is going in the wrong direction,' the report states. Its findings suggest that 'significant majorities of journalists have come to believe that increased bottom line pressure is "seriously hurting" the quality of news coverage' (some 66 per cent of national news people surveyed were of this view, and 57 per cent of local journalists). Moreover, it appears that concern among journalists about the 'deleterious impact of bottom-line pressures' is grow-ing, once these results are set in relation to polls taken by the Center in 1995 and 1999. The table 'Profit pressures hurting coverage' provides a brief overview below.

This survey, based on interviews with 547 national and local reporters, producers, editors and executives across the US in March and April 2004, similarly highlights other issues of importance.[2] Evidently, more journalists than ever are feeling alarmed about their profession's credibility problems with the public, due in part to their perception that standards of accuracy are in decline. At the same time, growing numbers of them (about half of those surveyed who work on newspapers or magazines) have witnessed reductions in the size of their newsroom staff in the past three years. 'Journalists are in a glummer mood than we've found them in the past', observed Andrew Kohut, director of the Pew Research Center. 'That view is much more prevalent where cutbacks have happened' (cited in *AP*, 23 May 2004).

It is this issue of 'bottom-line pressures' that warrants particular attention here. The survey's findings throw into sharp relief the ways in which these pressures underpin what the report's authors call the 'crisis of confidence' besetting journalism. Among those journalists surveyed who are concerned about growing financial pressure, the majority – 86 per cent – believes that

Profit pressures hurting coverage

Effect of bottom-line pressure on news coverage	National			Local		
	1995 %	*1999* %	*2004* %	*1995* %	*1999* %	*2004* %
Hurting	41	49	66	33	46	57
Just changing	38	40	29	50	46	35
Other/don't know	21	11	5	17	8	8
	100	100	100	100	100	100
Reporting is increasingly sloppy and error-prone						
Valid criticism	30	40	45	40	55	47
Not valid	65	58	54	59	42	52
Don't know	5	2	1	1	3	1
	100	100	100	100	100	100

Source: Pew Research Center (2004)

the news media pay too little attention to complex stories. Some 56 per cent of them said that the press is 'too timid' these days; 52 per cent that news reports are increasingly prone to factual errors and sloppy reporting; and 50 per cent that the 24-hour news cycle is weakening journalism. In an essay published in conjunction with the survey, Bill Kovach (of the Committee of Concerned Journalists), along with Tom Rosenstiel and Amy Mitchell (both of the Project for Excellence in Journalism), provide further insights. Their assessment of this data leads them to argue that there are 'alarming signs that the news industry is continuing the short-term mentality that some critics contend has undermined journalism in the past.' Pointing to the dramatic increase in the number of journalists surveyed who share the view that increased bottom-line pressure is seriously harming news quality, Kovach *et al.* make the additional observation that such pressure – not only from corporate owners but also from advertisers – is becoming more entrenched. 'If five years ago we saw the seeds of change', they write, 'today we see a trend toward fragmentation among all players involved: journalists, executives and the public. Not only do they disagree on solutions, they seem further apart on identifying the problems.'

This widening gap between problems and solutions becomes even more apparent in global contexts. Alarm bells have long been sounded about the dangers for independent journalism posed by the growing concentration, conglomeration and globalization of news media ownership. Some have aptly likened the control over information exercised by these companies as 'the new censorship', especially where the interests of public service collide with the private ones of shareholders. Drawing on recent figures, Alden (2005) describes the top ten global media companies (ranked by market capitalization) as follows:

1. General Electric
£182.6bn
Owns NBC Universal; several US regional channels; significant non-media interests
Web site: www.ge.com/en

2. Time Warner
£40.4bn
Owns HBO, CNN, Time, Warner Books, AOL
Web site: www.aoltimewarner.com

3. Viacom
£30.2bn
Owns CBS, MTV, Nickelodeon, Simon & Schuster, outdoor advertising
Web site: www.viacom.com

4. News Corporation
£28.2bn
Owns BSkyB, News International, HarperCollins, DirecTV (US), Star TV (Asia)
Web site: www.newscorp.com

5. Walt Disney
£26.7bn
Owns ABC, several US newspapers, Disney channels, Miramax, theme parks
Web site: http://disney.go.com

6. Comcast
£20.6bn
Owns E! Entertainment, Golf Channel
Web site: www.comcast.com

7. Vivendi
£15.1bn
Owns Canal Plus
Web site: www.vivendiuniversal.com

8. Bertelsmann[3]
£13.4bn
Owns Random House, Five, Ballantine, BMG
Web site: www.bertelsmann.com

9. Gannett

£12.0bn

Owns Newsquest, which has acquired hundreds of British local newspapers; US national newspaper *USA Today*.

Web site: www.gannett.com

10. Clear Channel

£11.7bn

Owns hundreds of US regional radio stations; outdoor advertising

Web site: www.clearchannel.com

Source: Alden (2005: 260); for information about their additional assets, see also *Columbia Journalism Review*'s 'Who Owns What' (www.cjr.org/tools/owners); FreePress (www.mediareform.net); MediaChannel (www.mediachannel.org/ownership), among others.

Even a glance at their respective financial statements (several of which are available online, hence my inclusion of Web addresses above) reveals the ways in which 'market-friendly' regulatory authorities have greased the wheels of corporate capital. 'When policy is left to be fought over by powerful commercial interests behind closed doors with no public awareness or participation – by what self-interested commercial parties call "experts" – one gets what one would expect', Robert W. McChesney remarks. That is, 'a media system that serves powerful corporate interests first and foremost' (McChesney 2004: 252).

The often subtle, seemingly 'common sensical' ways in which corporate interests influence news content can be rendered discernible for analysis with careful scrutiny. Important insights have been provided in thoughtful appraisals by self-reflexive journalists (for recent examples, see Adie 2002; Alterman 2003; Bell 2003; Brinkley 2003; Greenslade 2003; Hargreaves 2003; Kovach and Rosenstiel 2001; Lloyd 2004; Lule 2001; Newkirk 2000) and academic researchers alike. A key issue that these kinds of accounts consistently underscore is the commodification of news by owners intent on maximizing their profits. This process of commodification encourages journalists to internalize the values of media owners as being consistent with professionalism. In the case of Rupert Murdoch, for example, who is arguably the world's most famous media baron, news values are narrowly defined within the corporate culture of his empire. 'For Murdoch,' John Lloyd of the *Financial Times* argues, 'news is a business like any other: standards, balance and fairness are something the market can take care of' (Lloyd 2004: 118). His commitment to 'openly biased media' (Fox TV, the *Sun*, talk radio stations and so forth), Lloyd adds, is due to his conviction that it is what people want to purchase. A recent overview of the British newspaper market (one of several such markets around the world where Murdoch's holdings dominate) can be read in these terms:

Group Name and Executive Control	Market Share % and Circulation (Jan–June 04)
News International	34.6%
(Rupert Murdoch)	
Sun	3,365,844
Times	616,706
Sunday Times	1,347,665
News of the World	3,840,584
Daily Mail and General Trust	19.3%
(Lord Rothermere)	
Daily Mail	2,322,970
Mail on Sunday	2,269,271
Trinity Mirror	16.6%
(Victor Blank)	
Daily Mirror	1,883,274
Sunday Mirror	1,594,143
People	1,029,364
Northern and Shell	14.5%
(Richard Desmond)	
Daily Star	898,692
Daily Express	892,388
Sunday Express	889,973
Daily Star Sunday	515,200
Telegraph Group	7.2%
(Barclay brothers)[4]	
Daily Telegraph	878,030
Sunday Telegraph	672,554
Guardian Media Group	3.1%
(Scott Trust)	
Guardian	358,625
Observer	425,317
Pearson	3.0%
(Pearson board)	
Financial Times	414,377
Independent Newspapers	1.8%
(Tony O'Reilly)	
Independent	224,499
Independent on Sunday	174,573

Source: Market share based on national daily and Sunday figures from Audit Bureau of Circulations (www.accessabc.com), January to June 2004; Alden (2005: 15, 18).

In the *Sun*, Murdoch owns the most popular daily newspaper, and in the *News of the World*, a Sunday tabloid, the best-selling title overall. Neither title makes any pretence of being 'impartial' in its reporting. His share of the British newspaper market overall – 35.2 per cent according to the figures above – when coupled with his other interests in the country (especially Sky News) go some distance towards explaining why Prime Ministers listen so carefully to what he has to say. And, in turn, why any concerns they may raise about proprietorial ethics are likely to be met with indifference.

Financial figures such as these can provide only part of the picture, though. Particularly challenging to document is the lived materiality of news culture, such as the manner in which ownership dynamics give shape to a given news organization's journalistic ethos (see also Allan 2004). While some owners favour regular 'hands-on' interventions where key decisions are concerned, more typical are those owners who rely upon certain trusted subordinates to anticipate their preferences. A former reporter on the *Australian*, a Murdoch title, recalls: 'Journalists on Murdoch's papers aren't given the freedom to operate as journalists should operate.' This is less a matter of certain subjects being off limits, apparently, than a question of a certain stance having to be taken regarding how they are reported. 'Murdoch doesn't have to spell it out', he maintains. 'He doesn't send memos, to my knowledge, on the attitude his editors should take. The people who become Murdoch editors just know instinctively what is acceptable, what is not' (cited in Coleridge 1993: 489). What has been 'instinctively acceptable' for Fox News during the war in Iraq, for example, has been the stridently right-wing, pro-war stance informing its reporting and commentary. 'By the time US soldiers were headed across the desert to Baghdad,' David J. Sirota (2004) of *Salon* maintained, 'the "fair and balanced" network, owned by media mogul Rupert Murdoch, looked like a caricature of state-run television, parroting the White House's daily talking points, no matter how unsubstantiated.' For Jim Rutenberg (2003), writing in the *New York Times*, the 'Fox formula' proved that there were significant ratings to be gained in 'opinionated news with an America-first flair'. Fox, he pointed out, represents a new approach to television journalism – one that 'casts aside traditional notions of objectivity, holds contempt for dissent and eschews the skepticism of government at mainstream journalism's core'.

Andrew Neil (1996), a former editor of Murdoch's *Sunday Times* in London, recalls in his memoirs how the views of his proprietor set limits on editorial freedom in the newsroom. Reaffirming the point made about 'instincts' above, Neil writes that Murdoch 'picks as his editors people like me who are generally on the same wavelength as him: we started from a set of common assumptions about politics and society, even if we did not see eye to eye on every issue' (Neil 1996: 164). Evidently Neil felt that he was left to 'get on with it' in the main, although highlights several colourful exceptions to the rule. Tellingly, however, when describing Murdoch as a 'highly political animal', he remarks:

> Rupert expects his papers to stand broadly for what he believes: a combination of right-wing Republicanism from America mixed with undiluted Thatcherism from Britain and stirred with some anti-British

establishment sentiments as befits his colonial heritage [Murdoch was born near Melbourne, Australia]. The resulting pottage is a radical-right dose of free-market economics, the social agenda of the Christian Moral Majority and hardline conservative views on subjects like drugs, abortion, law and order, and defence.

(Neil 1996: 165)

In the case of another Murdoch title, the *New York Post*, journalist Danny Schechter (1999) observes that it 'becomes an unapologetic and blatant Republican campaign sheet at election time, with little pretense at nonpartisanship or even conventional journalism. The traditional separation of the editorial pages and the news pages all but disappears once Murdoch picks his candidate' (Schechter 1999: 378). On the few occasions when Murdoch has paused to characterize his political views, he has typically claimed that they are of little consequence. Rather disingenuously, he insists that all he does is ensure that his news organizations merely reflect what are already widespread, popular opinions. In any case, there can be little doubt that his shifting alignments with different political parties over the years demonstrates a strong pragmatic commitment to advancing his own corporate interests whichever way decisions happen to unfold at the ballot box.

Debates about the influence of corporate interests on journalism took an unusual turn during the controversy surrounding Michael Moore's film *Fahrenheit 9/11*. This time it was Disney at the centre of a fray sparked by its refusal to allow its Miramax Films subsidiary to release the film, evidently because of fears that its political content might antagonize the Bush administration during an election year. Eventually Miramax's founders, Harvey and Bob Weinstein, bought back the rights, and organized their own distribution arrangements. An astonishing hit with audiences worldwide, the film succeeds – at times poignantly so – in its efforts to cast light on a host of issues the mainstream news media have relegated to the shadows. In so doing, it must have made for uncomfortable viewing for many journalists themselves, who found their professional practice called into question. Likening his film to 'a work of journalism', Moore argued that it is 'the real journalism that the journalists should be doing', adding 'I present to you the facts.' Questioned about whether, as a documentary journalist, he had followed the rules of impartiality, he replied: 'Like bona-fide journalists do? Bona-fide journalists are not impartial. Bona-fide journalists in the U.S. supported this war, cheerleaded this war, got in bed with the administration, never asked the hard questions and completely failed the American people by not doing their job' (cited in the *Globe and Mail*, 18 June 2004). Journalists have typically presented the Bush administration to the public through a filter, in Moore's view, for the same reason Disney (through its vertical integration) had sought to silence his film – corporate control over the flow of information.

Fahrenheit 9/11, in blurring the boundaries of journalism with documentary, calls to mind the muckraking tradition of exposés. Its scrutiny of the public record produces an indictment of Bush's response to the September 11 tragedy, especially his decision to go to war in Iraq. Even before its release, the film ignited a political firestorm. Several conservative groups organized protests and boycotts so as to intimidate theatre owners into not screening the film, while others filed formal complaints with the Federal Election Commission on the grounds that it violated campaign rules. When these and related strategies failed, some critics promptly sought to have the film rated 'R' in the hope that it would be stigmatized. Unable to find inaccuracies in the film's factual statements, several of them attacked Moore personally, calling into question his patriotism. Meanwhile, certain voices from within media circles praised him for the public service his film performed, not least for journalism. 'Mr Moore's greatest strength', *New York Times* columnist Paul Krugman pointed out, 'is a real empathy with working-class Americans that most journalists lack' (*New York Times*, 2 July 2004). Neal Gabler of the *Los Angeles Times* credited the film-maker for challenging journalistic shibboleths. 'In noisily forswearing balance for genuine fairness,' he wrote, 'Moore has shamed an American press corps that, for fear of offending conservatives, refused to report what Moore was now reporting' (*Los Angeles Times*, 7 July 2004).

Whether the film – and the controversy it generated – will have any lasting effect on journalism remains to be seen. Interviewed by Katie Couric on the *Today* show, Moore himself described his film as 'a silent plea to all of you in the news media to do your job. We need you. You're our defense against this … And I just think a disservice was done to the American people' (cited in *Boston Globe*, 30 June 2004). Powerful words, passionately spoken. Journalism, Moore's comments seem to suggest, is too important to be left to the journalists. Whether journalists agree with him or not (and, it must be said, journalists are notoriously thin-skinned where criticism is concerned, a trait they share with academics), now is the time to demonstrate their capacity for introspection. For each news organization like the *New York Times* or the BBC (post-Hutton inquiry) prepared to be self-reflexive, to bravely acknowledge mistakes and to renew efforts to set them right, many more appear content to simply look the other way. Which explains, at least in part, why public criticism – if not outright cynicism – about the quality of the news reporting they provide is so widespread.

┃ The chapters

The discussion above begins to make apparent several pressing reasons why the contributors to *Journalism: Critical Issues* have been moved to participate in the debates which traverse these pages. Over the years it has been frequently remarked that journalism is at a crossroads – indeed so often that it risks sounding somewhat clichéd – yet there is every indication that its very forms, practices and institutions are being decisively transformed, with startling implications. Accordingly, the principal aim of this book is to help provide the basis for new dialogues to emerge regarding journalism today, as well as about where it may be heading tomorrow.

In each of its chapters, *Journalism: Critical Issues* poses a series of important questions afresh, questions deserving of much greater attention than they have typically received to date. Here it needs to be acknowledged, though, that this book makes no claim to be comprehensive in its scope – not in terms of the range of issues it raises, the multiplicity of journalisms in circulation, nor especially with respect to how journalism operates in different national contexts. What it lacks in breadth, however, it strives to make up for in depth. The contributors all seek to challenge conventional ways of thinking about the 'critical issues' at stake in their chapters. In so doing, it is their intention to further our understanding, but also to encourage future explorations with the potential to revitalize journalism studies. In adopting this approach, it is hoped that *Journalism: Critical Issues* will make for a lively, argumentative (in the best sense of the word) and engaging intervention.

▌Notes

1   For a discussion of Andrew Gilligan and the Hutton inquiry, please see Steven Barnett's chapter in this volume (Chapter 24). In brief, the inquiry was set up to investigate the chain of events which led to the Government weapons expert David Kelly committing suicide after having been named as the likely source of a BBC report by Gilligan. In the report Gilligan had maintained that an intelligence dossier on Iraq had been altered under pressure brought to bear by the Prime Minister's office. The inquiry report largely exonerated the government, sparking allegations of a 'whitewash' by critics. Reporter Jayson Blair resigned from the *New York Times* in May 2003, following allegations that he had committed repeated 'acts of journalistic fraud' (see Carey's (2003) essay for a perceptive assessment). In January 2004, foreign correspondent Jack Kelley (nominated five times for the Pulitzer Prize) resigned from *USA Today* after admitting to misleading editors over claims made in his reporting.

2   The Pew Center is an independent opinion research group, sponsored by The Pew Charitable Trusts (with assets of approximately $4.9 billion, it is one of the largest private philanthropies in the US). Its studies focus on attitudes toward the press, politics and public policy issues. Its Web site is: http://people-press.org/.

3   Bertelsmann is privately owned; figure refers to total assets declared by the company. Also note that Sony is excluded from the list because media interests are mostly music – www.sony.com.

4   At the time of writing, Conrad Black, the controlling shareholder of Hollinger International, is seeking to block the company's planned sale of the Telegraph Group to David and Frederick Barclay of Britain. The brothers, whose media assets include the *Scotsman* newspaper, purchased the group for an estimated £715 million in cash and debt, before taxes.

▌References

Adie, K. (2002) *The Kindness of Strangers*. London: Headline.

Alden, C. (ed.) (2005) *Media Directory 2005*. London: Guardian Books.

Allan, S. (2004) *News Culture*, Second Edition. Maidenhead and New York: Open University Press.

Alterman, E. (2003) *What Liberal Media?* New York: Basic Books.

Bell, M. (2003) *Through Gates of Fire*. London: Weidenfeld & Nicolson.

Brinkley, D. (2003) *Brinkley's Beat: People, Places, and Events That Shaped My Time*. New York: Knopf.

Carey, J. (2003) Mirror of the *Times*, *The Nation*, 16 June.

Coleridge, N. (1993) *Paper Tigers*. London: Heinemann.

Greenslade, R. (2003) *Press Gang*. London: Macmillan.

Hargreaves, I. (2003) *Journalism: Truth or Dare?* Oxford: Oxford University Press.

Hersh, S. M. (2004) Torture at Abu Ghraib, *New Yorker*, 10 May.

Kovach, B. and Rosenstiel, T. (2001) *The Elements of Journalism*. New York: Crown.

Lloyd, J. (2004) *What the Media are Doing to Our Politics*. London: Constable.

Lule, J. (2001) *Daily News, Eternal Stories*. New York: Guilford Press.

McChesney, R.W. (2004) *The Problem of the Media: US Communication Politics in the Twenty-first Century*. New York: Monthly Review Press.

Neil, A. (1996) *Full Disclosure*. London: Macmillan.

Newkirk, P. (2000) *Within the Veil: Black Journalists, White Media*. New York: New York University Press.

Okrent, D. (2004) Weapons of Mass Destruction? Or Mass Distraction? *New York Times*, 30 May.

Pew Research Center (2004) Bottom-Line Pressures Now Hurting Coverage, Say Journalists. Report of The Pew Research Center for The People and the Press, 23 May. http://people-press.org/.

Rutenberg, J. (2003) A Nation at War: The News Media, *New York Times*, 16 April.

Schechter, D. (1999) *The More You Watch, The Less You Know*. New York: Seven Stories Press.

Sirota, D. J. (2004) The Fox of War, Salon.com, 20 March.

PART I

Journalism's histories

1

Intimately intertwined in the most public way

Celebrity and journalism

P. David Marshall

- How does the profiling of celebrities transform news?
- What is the relationship between celebrity and the contemporary public sphere?
- How much of a newspaper is now devoted to journalism that focuses on celebrities?
- Can you see evidence of news coverage that has become similar to celebrity and entertainment coverage?
- How does the celebrity system fit into the spectrum of information production that moves from promotion, publicity and public relations into the discourses of journalism?

Although the celebrity and journalism have been twinned for most of the past 200 years, their intertwining has regularly betrayed the less noble side of journalistic practice. Both journalism and celebrity articulate a changing public sphere and a different constitution of engagement and significance by any nation's citizenry. That transformation of significance has been linked to the emergence of democratic polities and political debate; the transformation has also been aligned with the emergence of an elaborate entertainment industry and the panoply of information that fuels its cultural forms. This chapter investigates the way that journalism and celebrity intersect and how their alliance has produced very specific forms of presentation and writing practices that have become not only standard in the features section of newspapers but populate the organization of information throughout the news.

To begin this investigation, it must be understood that celebrity-inspired journalism has become so routinized in papers that its origins are no longer easily identifiable. For example, a 13 May 2004 *New York Times* article (Bumiller 2004) on Donald Rumsfeld, the Secretary of Defence in President Bush's administration was designed as a 'profile' of the man during a particularly vigorous scandal over abuse and atrocities committed by

Americans on their Iraqi prisoners. The headline 'Stolid Rumsfeld Soldiers on, But Weighs Ability to Serve' encapsulates the tone of the article: discerning the state of mind and psychological condition of a man under siege. Thus we learn the personal details of his daily life including that he 'spent last Sunday in the backyard of his elegant Washington home, poring over documents piled 10 inches high in his lap'. And that the visiting friend indicated 'that at least he was sitting outside – it was a beautiful day. That's a good thing if you are under a lot of pressure'. The article continues to provide personal background details about the man: that he had the president and his wife Laura Bush (along with Alan Greenspan) over to dinner at his home 'in the graceful, old-world Kalorama section of Washington' on the day the scandal broke and that 'everyone appeared relax in each other's company'; that 'despite Mr. Rumsfeld's ferocious exterior, he is a principled man' who with his wife regularly visited wounded soldiers on Sundays and stopped by three times a week to visit a high school friend, 'who was dying of brain cancer' even though at the time Rumsfeld was preoccupied with the war in Afghanistan. We also discover he is a relentless worker and finds 'stability in his normal workaholic routine'. The investigative element to the story was whether Rumsfeld would resign; but the kinds of information generated were classically derived from celebrity journalistic practice of finding out what the famous person is *really* like. Although the story is in the front section of the newspaper surrounded by other sobering articles about the occupation in Iraq, the Rumsfeld profile stylistically resembled what one would regularly find in the features section of the newspaper. In contemporary newswriting and presentation these delineations are no longer in play. To actually produce such an article, the reporter has to ensure access to the various sources. As a result, what sometimes emerges from celebrity journalism is a further convergence with the practices of public relations and promotion. In this particular instance, the author, Elisabeth Bumiller, had to build some sort of trust with friends of Rumsfeld to obtain the personal details and to gain these sources' consent to speak publicly about him. The building of trust ensured that the story would take on a more positive reading of Rumsfeld. The result: a story that crosses between a fluff personality profile and the underlying story of possible resignation.

Origins

Why this kind of reportage on the personality of the famous emerged in the nineteenth century along with the development of mass circulation newspapers is intriguing. The celebrity as a social category developed from a number of changes in the political and cultural landscape in the late eighteenth and early nineteenth centuries. First among them is a shift in participation in what has later been described as the public sphere. The concept of the celebrity articulates a distinct engagement by the famous individual with the public that is differentiated from the way royalty and significant leaders of the Church may have represented themselves. Celebrity is an acknowledgement of the public's power – indeed, the celebrity is in many ways the embodiment of the collective power of an invested audience in a particular person (Marshall 1997). Thus, the way to understand the emergence of the celebrity in the nineteenth century is its close affinity with democracy and the new forms of power it expressed. Images of heads of state may have been statically and ceremoniously replicated in coinage and other representations of power but with the expansion of democratic power a new kind of public identity developed that was dependent on the emerging power of the crowd and the masses. The celebrity embodied that contradiction of being individually elevated and thus relatively unique, but dependent on a new system of 'democratically inspired' value that was derived from popular audiences.

Journalism, although born from the origins of business reporting as much as political tracts and proclamations, has had a similar history in its association with the development of democracy. The expansion of newspapers and other print publications was partially dependent on a different organization of power. Combined with the expanded political enfranchisement and general literacy in the nineteenth century, the newspaper transformed into the key site for information and popular debate about political issues in countries such as the US, France and the UK. With the shift to a mass subscriber base for income and profits (through selling space to advertisers interested in reaching this wider audience), some newspapers in these countries at least symbolically came to represent the interests and desires of the populace. American newspaper magnates of the late nineteenth century such as Joseph Pulitzer and William Randolph Hearst built their empires on a brand of news story that acknowledged a wider proportion of the population and attempted to cater to what was believed to be their interests and desires. Typically called yellow journalism, reporters developed stories that were both sensational and closer to the everyday lives of this new urban readership. Profiles of celebrated individuals emerged alongside the development of what were perceived to be more salacious stories and muckraking to discover scandal. These profiles of famous people over the course of the nineteenth century began to change from carefully choreographed studies of public moments involving these people to revelations about their private lives and how that intersected with their public lives. As Charles Ponce de Leon's work has revealed, celebrity journalism changed, from the nineteenth to the twentieth century, from reporters piecing together stories from people who knew famous people to direct interviews with famous people in their private homes (Ponce de Leon 2002).

There were a number of reasons for the emergence and expansion of celebrity journalism from the nineteenth century into the twentieth century. First of all, the stories articulated a celebration of individuality that intersected with the ideologies of the self that had been advancing since the renaissance. Celebrities represented heightened examples of individual achievement and transformation and thereby challenged the rigidity of class-based societies by presenting the potential to transcend these categories.

The kind of individuality that celebrities embodied also intersected with the expansion of consumer capitalism enabling the populace to use consumption as a means of self-actualization and transformation. Consumer culture, through advertisements, department stores and the actual expanded range of products and services, presented a diverse array of possibilities for modern individuals to make themselves anew. Celebrities provided a refracted form of knowledge of the modern self that became another resource in the developing choices of consumer culture.

Celebrity journalism also worked to fulfil other rising apparent needs of contemporary culture. Emile Durkheim used the term 'anomie' to describe the isolating condition of urban social life that was ubiquitous (Durkheim 1964). In the mid-twentieth century David Reisman coined the term and title 'the lonely crowd' to express a similar sense of distance in mass society (Reisman 1950). The processes of industrialization, the migration of workforces to cities and internationally to new centres of manufacturing, and the general sense of disconnection and dislocation that had enveloped the architecture and organization of cities, helped create a sense of both anonymity and alienation. Profiles of celebrities provided a constellation of recognizable and familiar people who filled the gap and provided points of commonality for people to reconnect both with celebrities and with each other. Instead of a discourse that highlighted the distance and aura of the celebrity, celebrity journalism worked to make the famous more real and worked to provide a greater intimacy with their everyday lives. Celebrities, via these journalistic profiles, became better known for their ordinariness along with their extraordinariness as these stories worked to connect individually with the mass audience. Audiences in turn would have a degree of 'affective investment' (Marshall 1997) in particular celebrities because of the amount of personal background that was provided about them in newspapers and magazines.

As much as celebrity journalism appeared to be fulfilling a particular need in the cultural fabric of contemporary life, it was also clearly an instrument of the various political and cultural industries. Tom Mole's study of the emergence of literary celebrities is particularly revealing of some of the changed conditions that were connected to the mass production of cultural commodities. Mole's study found that as writing became less anonymous (anonymous attribution had been standard in the eighteenth century) publishers became more focused on differentiating their lists from others'. The most effective way to ensure the distinctiveness of a publisher's list was to invest in making the authors more visible and in many senses more real to the audience. Thus Byron was not only a literary figure; he was known for his personal life and became a widely known popular figure who had a clearly developed public persona. Mole also links this transformation to the need to connect to the newly distanced mass audience. The personal connection brought the material to life more by providing the massive reading public with the author's background (Mole 2004).

In the development of the mass circulation newspaper, owners and journalists alike were also developing techniques and discourses that pulled often disparate audiences together. In the US, the newspapers worked very hard at making stories that appealed across class and ethnic lines. Entertainment reporting over many decades gradually served as one of the principal sites for such a crossover. More popular arts were featured and reviewed by newspapers to appeal to the working class and their leisure interests; at the same time, this reportage on vaudeville and cinema worked to legitimize the 'artistic' merit of these newer cultural forms and thereby made them more acceptable as sources of stories for the middle class. Celebrity profiles of film actors and musical stars eventually were stories that transcended clear class differences quite acceptably by the 1920s and 1930s (Ponce de Leon 2002, 206–40).

In the wider dimensions of cultural activity, celebrity journalism functioned as a technique for simplifying the representational dimension of the public sphere. It helped focus attention on particular individuals above others and provided a constellation of the famous for the public's attention. In the US, this kind of construction was closely connected with the emergence of national markets and national politics. In the mid-nineteenth century P. T. Barnum, the ultimate huckster, tried to ensure that profiles of his individual stars, such as Jenny Lind, were in the local papers before his travelling show arrived in a particular community. He discovered that these background pieces added to the star quality and attracted the public to his events. Through this advanced publicity, national markets for entertainment were developed and buttressed by the press who also realized the value in creating celebrated individuals for the selling of their papers and magazines.

The subjective quality of celebrity journalism: its connection with press agentry and publicity

One of the most important reasons for studying celebrity journalism is that it often illustrates the particular dependencies journalistic practice has on its sources and what is considered news value. Celebrity status simplifies the determination of news value precisely because the level of fame of the person *a priori* establishes its newsworthiness. Whereas other news events may not produce the same effect of attracting readers, celebrity guarantees a certain high level of interest.

Parallel professions to journalism developed in the nineteenth century and flourished in the twentieth century to organize, contain and foster this interest in particular personalities. Press agentry was generally seen as the practice of ensuring the appearance of individuals and events in the newspaper in the most favourable light. P. T. Barnum's work in this area was seen to be seminal. Much like advertising, press agentry was involved in puffery and exaggeration of the significance of a particular event or personality for its greater impact on the public. Press agents were thus employed in the expanding entertainment industries both by individuals and corporations. A large element of their positions in Hollywood from the 1920s onwards in fact involved maintaining correspondence relationships with fans on behalf of the star. Public relations – as it was formulated in the early twentieth century – was established as a more legitimate profession in clear contra-distinction to the practices of the press agent. Working on behalf of corpor-ations and individuals, public relations specialists were expert at producing copy that resembled the manner that journalists would formulate for news-papers. The press release, as common for companies trying to control a potentially negative event as they were for entertainers and politicians trying to provide advance publicity about their respective tours, was the invention of public relations, which has been instrumental in shifting the balance of editorial content of newspapers throughout the twentieth century.

In certain areas of journalistic coverage, the work of press agentry, publicity and promotion became normalized into the structure of stories. Entertainment journalism, like other forms of journalism, has had to adapt to the cycle of news and events of its particular industry and 'beat'. Film releases, music releases, or the opening of a particular play or concert tour has demanded a certain close relationship with the press for mutual success. Publicity and promotion departments have been expert at controlling access to the stars for such releases. Thus, the press junket has become standard for the interview of movie stars in advance of the release of the film. With promotion predating the film, the junket might be in an on-location setting. As a film is released internationally, the stars may be part of the film's local premiere and the interviews are organized around such an event. Along with the critical review, most major films are twinned with this form of advance publicity where a feature interview of one of the stars appears in newspapers and on principal television networks. The elaborate press kit provides back-ground information for the journalists to complete their story. With more expensive productions, an 'electronic' press kit is provided: clips of the film are compiled along with an 'interview' with the star that can be used by local stations with the local interviewer asking the stock questions provided.

The development of the official and authentic story

The system of publicity is designed to provide an insider's role for the journalist. Through general cooperation between the entertainment industry and the journalist, it is tacitly agreed that having 'contact' with the star ensures a positive spin in the story. The system has produced what have now become standard structures and motifs for the celebrity profile or fea-ture interview in a large newspaper or mainstream magazine that can be summarized in series as follows:

A. The meeting of journalist and star in either domestic setting or café.
B. The description of the casual dress and demeanour of the star.
C. The discussion of their current work – which is essentially the anchor for why the story is newsworthy.

D. The revelation of something that is against the grain of what is generally perceived to be the star's persona – something that is anecdotal but is revealing of the star's true nature.

(Adapted from G. Baum, 1998)

This pattern has developed since the mid-1920s. It is a structure that is non-threatening, generally flattering and a celebration of the idiosyncratic self. Celebrity profiles possess, then, a combination of the reporter's obsequious-ness around the creativity and uniqueness of the individual and an effort to reveal something that is normally hidden, to uncover the 'true self' (Dyer 1979) of the celebrity.

The magazine industry has perhaps relied on the celebrity profile to a greater degree than newspapers. The magazine cover and the cover story function as the principal advertising mechanisms for magazine sales. Choosing a particular celebrity as the cover image, then, is as much a marketing strategy for the magazine as a news event. Thus, there have been moments where a particular celebrity has blanketed the covers of a wide range of magazines. At the time of the release of *Titanic* in 1997, it was difficult to find a magazine that did not have a cover image of Leonardo di Caprio: his image graced the covers of teen, news, gossip, entertainment and women's magazines. Being on the cover of many magazines was not a source of income for the star; rather it often meant some sort of editorial control of the content (Turner *et al.* 2000). Some of the most famous celebrity covers – for example, the naked and pregnant body-painted image of Demi Moore on the cover of *Vanity Fair* in 1991 – have been designed to help reposition a star's persona as much as to make a publicity flashpoint for the magazine.

Certain magazines have based their principal editorial content on celebrities. Andy Warhol's *Interview* was simply an oversized magazine devoted to fawning and often vacuous discussions with famous people. Historically, pictorial magazines such as *Life* and *Look* have organized their content periodically around profiles of celebrity figures. More recently, the American *People* magazine was built from the 'People' section of *Time* magazine and became a separate publication in 1974. It was designed to be a showcase for celebrities to give their side of any story. Exclusive interviews have been used by the Australian *People* franchise, *Who*, to not only sell magazines but also to ensure that the magazine's writers would have access to the private and domestic life of the celebrity (Turner *et al.* 2000: 132–5). The exclusive interview is also a way to ensure news values for the particular magazine; exclusive interviews are often the way in which a celebrity attempts to counteract bad press coverage around a scandal.

Exclusivity of a celebrity profile can become a bidding war as well as a source of some tension and rivalry among magazines and television networks in each national market. For instance, *OK!* magazine won exclusive rights to publish official photographs of the wedding of Michael Douglas and Catherine Zeta-Jones in 2000 for $1.6 million. Three days before the publication of the wedding by *OK!*, *Hello*, a competitor, had published some unauthorized paparazzi wedding photos. Douglas, Zeta-Jones and *OK!* sued successfully for damages and won a very modest legal fees settlement. Exclusive interviews of Michael Jackson or O. J. Simpson have been hotly contested in the American market among the major television networks and, when landed, they are often located in the flagship newsmagazine programmes for each network. Indeed, journalistic careers have been built through the journalist's capacity to allow famous personalities to speak on their programmes. In the US, Barbara Walters became a celebrity profiler and interviewer during and after a successful career as a television journalist and anchorwoman. David Frost and Clive James have built similar television careers as interviewers of the famed and infamous in the UK. Oprah Winfrey, in her occasional move from afternoon talk show host to prime time, became the interviewer of choice of Michael Jackson and Michael Jordan in the 1990s. In the United States, Katie Couric and Diane Sawyer have continued this tradition of providing a sympathetic platform for celebrities to address their massive audiences.

Scandal, celebrity and news reporting

Where official versions of stories have made journalistic practice veer closely to the role of publicists and public relations, reporting celebrity scandals places journalists in adversarial roles with regard to the entertainment publicity machines. The American-based *National Enquirer* had a reputation for its stories of aliens and other hard-to-believe accounts of human freaks along with photos of celebrities caught in clearly unsanctioned, private moments. Nonetheless, its relentless pursuit of the O. J. Simpson murder investigation netted some tangible evidence that linked Simpson to the murder of his ex-wife and her boyfriend. What was more remarkable was that other newspapers and magazines reported the findings of the *National Enquirer* and for a short period in the mid-1990s, the supermarket tabloid had achieved a new version of the journalistic high ground. Without the usual restrictions that have limited the muckraking of other established press institutions, the *National Enquirer* not only led with discovered facts in the O. J. Simpson case – it has also been the first to reveal Jesse Jackson's love child. Its greatest claims to fame are the series of celebrity images, whether it is an unflattering picture of Elizabeth Taylor or a clearly disturbed photo of Whitney Houston, that have populated its four decades of 'reporting'. There is no question that the fall of any celebrity is a major news story. Although this may be the primary content of tabloids, it has become an element of the most highbrow of newspapers. Treading the fine line between scandal and official story are the television programmes, which have spawned another layer of celebrity journalism. *Entertainment Tonight*, which began as a syndicated early evening nightly programme in the 1980s, has become the standard in the American television industry for reporting both gossip and officially sanctioned information about stars and their current projects. Variations of *Entertainment Tonight* have appeared in many countries throughout the world. Modelled on the evening newscast, it presents the entertainment news as standard news fare – with the added dimension of greater amounts of smiling by the news anchors.

Celebrity scandal has the potential to transform news values quite dramatically. Certainly the O. J. Simpson murder trial became front-page news beyond all proportion to what would be perceived as normal news values. The death of Diana, Princess of Wales, allegedly as a result of a car chase with paparazzis, generated an overwhelming amount of coverage in all media forms and dwarfed any other news event for weeks. Michael Jackson's arrest and trial connected with the alleged sexual assault of minors has similarly produced an inordinate amount of news coverage. From blanket coverage of Jackson's arrest to speculative reporting on his changing support and defence team, Jackson's latest scandal has maintained a media circus that allows some journalists to work full time on the story. When particular scandals with this kind of potency emerge they bleed from the entertainment sections of the newspapers towards the front pages. Celebrities have become focal points for the discussion of a wide range of issues and concerns. In a peculiarly contemporary way, celebrities, via journalistic reportage, have become the effective conduit for discourses about the personal: celebrities have become the discursive talking points for the political dimensions of a host of formerly private and personal concerns.

The all-encompassing celebrity system: journalist as celebrity

As much as journalists present the ideal profile of chronicler, which maintains a certain neutrality from their subjects, it is clear that journalism itself has become part of the celebrity system in its own power hierarchies. Throughout the latter half of the twentieth century, bylines have been increasingly used in newspapers and magazines (with perhaps *The Economist* one of the few exceptions in the English language). This practice has intensified the identification of the individual journalist and a celebration of particularly successful journalists. Similarly, from the emergence of television in the 1950s, there has been a cultivation of the broadcast news star. Walter Cronkite, anchor for more than two decades of the *CBS Evening News*, became a news star and remains an iconic figure of celebrity status in television journalism. Geraldo Rivera, an American talk-show host and confrontational journalist has become well known in the US more as a celebrity than for his journalistic expertise. In urban markets throughout the US, the local news anchor has developed lesser versions of the star quality of Cronkite. In print, journalists strive to move from the simple byline to columnist status. As a columnist, the journalist becomes more equal to the celebrated individuals that he or she may cover in politics, entertainment or sport.

This general transmogrification of journalist into celebrity has pushed certain individuals towards fabrication of their stories. It was discovered in 2004 that the *US Today's* star reporter, Jack Kelley, built part of his 20-year reputation on spectacular stories and images that were works of fiction built on coached informants who were not even present at the news events covered. Similarly, in 2003 the *New York Times* dealt with Jayson Blair's efforts at constructing fictional news stories in an effort to build his reputation. Perhaps one could link these developments to the new celebrity status of the Internet muckraker Matt Drudge and his *Drudge Report* as the related phenomenon of an industry that relies on celebrity status as much as politics and entertainment.

Conclusion

It is difficult to separate the histories of journalism and the emergence of the contemporary celebrity system. Journalism has been instrumental in proselytizing a new public sphere and celebrities have been a foundational means and method for the expansion of key elements of that new public sphere. In that convergence, journalism has expanded its 'coverage' of entertainment and sports by developing features on personalities. It has also used techniques developed in writing about entertainment stars for its coverage of the famed and notorious in politics and many other domains. The coverage of entertainment has expanded massively and has become a major component of information and news reporting in all media. With the celebrity reporting that has accompanied this expansion of coverage, there has been a naturalization and normalization of the close connection between the sources of information and journalistic practice; in other words, celebrity journalism is one of the key locations for the convergence of publicity, promotion and journalism in terms of the generated editorial content. Celebrity journalism has also been instrumental in the exploration of a different form of cultural politics that is an investigation of the self, the private and the intimate. Through celebrity profiles, the investigation of scandals in all their sordid details and the psychotherapeutic ramblings published in celebrity interviews, celebrity journalism is the location for the exploration of the 'politics of the personal' in our transformed and shifting public sphere.

References

Baum, G. (2004) A Celebrity Profile Formula. Online at http://www.aphrodigitaliac.com/mm/archive/celebprofile/, accessed, 8 March 2004.

Blakley, J. (compiler) (2004) Two or Three things I know about Celebrity Journalism. Seminar at USC Norman Lear Center, USC Annenberg School for Communication, 27 September 2002 online at http://learcenter.org/pdf/powers_notes.pdf, accessed 10 March 2004.

Bumiller, E. (2004) Stolid Rumsfeld Soldiers on, but Weighs Ability to Serve, *New York Times*, 13 May, p. A13.

Connell, I. (1992) Personalities in the popular media, in P. Dahlgren and C. Sparks (eds) *Journalism and Popular Culture*. London: Sage.

Durkheim, E. (1964) *The Division of Labor in Society*. Trans. George Simpson, New York: Free Press.

Dyer, R. (1979) *Stars*. London: BFI.

Keeps, D., Melcher, C., Virga, V. and Coz, S. (2002) *National Enquirer: Thirty Years of Unforgettable Images*. New York: Hyperion/Miramax.

Marshall, P. D. (1997) *Celebrity and Power: Fame in Contemporary Culture*. Minneapolis: University of Minnesota Press.

Mole, T. (2004) Romanticism and Celebrity. Paper presented at the Cultural Studies Association (US) Conference, Persona series, Northeastern University, Boston, 5–9 May.

Ponce de Leon, C. S. (2002) *Self-Exposure: Human Interest Journalism and the Emergence of Celebrity in America, 1890–1940*. Chapel Hill, NC: University of North Carolina Press.

Reisman, D. (1950) *The Lonely Crowd*. New Haven: Yale University Press.

Rojek, C. (2001) *Celebrity*. London: Reaktion.

Turner, G. (2004) *Understanding Celebrity*. London: Sage.

Turner, G., Bonner, F. and Marshall, P. D. (2000) *Fame Games: the Production of Celebrity in Australia*. Cambridge: Cambridge University Press.

12

Race, ideology and journalism

Black power and television news

Jane Rhodes

- Why was the civil rights struggle a popular subject for television news?
- How did television journalists frame this national crisis?
- Why did the emergence of Black Power politics pose a dilemma for the news media?
- How did Black Power activists use television to enhance their movement?
- What role did television news play in constructing national ideologies about the Black Panther Party?
- How do these representations from the 1960s continue to shape our understanding of race and protest today?

Ideologies of race are historically situated, regionally and nationally specific and constantly changing to reflect political, social, cultural and demographic shifts. In the US and much of the Western world, these ideologies are based on the assumption that there are biologically defined racial groups – that you can determine people's membership in a racial category by the way they look and behave. This concept – biological determinism – has remained a tenacious assumption even as scientists have increasingly disputed the idea that humans can be divided into pure, definable races. In the US, ideas about different racial categories can be traced to sixteenth-century European exploration of the New World and contact with indigenous peoples, and the emergence of the African slave trade. Numerous scholars, including Winthrop Jordan, Reginald Horsman and Alden Vaughan have traced the histories of these early encounters between Europeans and differently raced people and have noted the construction of a racial hierarchy that argued for the moral, intellectual and physical superiority of whites (Jordan 1977; Horsman 1981; Vaughan 1995). These ideals were circulated as part of the developing rationale for the plundering of North America and the extermination of hostile natives and for the enslavement for Africans. Over time, the US and its counterparts in the Americas developed an elaborate theoretical framework and public discourse that sought to reinforce the idea that non-whites were inferior, unable to govern themselves, unlikely to be assimilated into mainstream American society, and therefore a threat to national stability.

The press has played a central role in circulating ideologies about race in the US since the days of the nation's founding. African Americans and other minorities established their own independent presses in the nineteenth century to counter the distortions and racial mythologies perpetuated by white-owned media institutions. Until the early twentieth century, American newspapers and magazines were highly partisan and often openly racist, opposing the abolition of slavery, endorsing Indian removal, and serving as a catalyst for anti-immigrant and nativist sentiments. Readers who had limited first-hand contact with different racial groups relied on the stereotypes and distortions that were frequently disseminated in the news. There were often oppositional voices in the national press but their calls for an end to white supremacy and racial discrimination were generally muted by an industry that was fearful of alienating its primary audience. By the middle of the twentieth century, leaders in the field of journalism called for a serious transformation of the profession to take seriously the principles of objectivity, fairness and truth that governed other fields. In 1947, for example, the Committee on Freedom of the Press, also known as the Hutchins Commission, indirectly addressed the problem of racial coverage when it announced that press responsibility included 'projecting a representative picture of the constituent groups in society' (Leigh 1947: 20–7). This led to some improvements in news media coverage of underrepresented groups, but the press continued to underplay or ignore the severe national problems of racial inequality, rampant racial segregation and racial violence.

The arrival of the Southern-based civil rights movement in the late 1950s had a profound and lasting influence on these journalistic traditions. The following discussion highlights the influence of the struggle for civil rights on American journalism and the dilemma posed as black power activists became news subjects in the late 1960s. An important component here is the arrival of television as an emerging medium that transformed the news into a visual culture. The simultaneous ascendancy of television news with the rise of groups like the Black Panther Party meant that the struggle over racial ideologies in American society would be circulated in a medium more concerned with immediacy and visual and aural content than with complex ideas.

The Black Panther Party – as political entity and visual icon – first appeared in America's living rooms in the Spring of 1966, while Huey Newton and Bobby Seale were still planning their now-famous organization. Two national television networks broadcast feature stories about a Lowndes County, Alabama voter registration effort led by the Student Nonviolent Coordinating Committee (SNCC). The political organization established to lead this community's black majority was called the Black Panthers. Perhaps the most visible and telegenic figure in the forefront of this crusade was the young SNCC chairman Stokely Carmichael, who announced that the Alabama Black Panthers intended to exercise 'black power,' in their quest for the franchise (see also Van Deburg 1992).

ABC and CBS sent journalists to interview Black Panther workers in the town of Haynesville, Alabama, a place that had come to represent the intransigence of Jim Crow segregation (CBS Evening News, 10 March 1966; ABC News, 3 May 1966). It was in this town where four Ku Klux Klan members were acquitted by an all-white jury for the murder of civil rights worker Viola Liuzzo in 1965. A reporter for CBS Evening News stood in front of the Lowndes County courthouse, using the edifice as a metaphor for Southern racism. 'The hue of its fresh white paint is more than symbolic', he intoned. 'In it white officials collect taxes, regulate schools, choose jurymen, and handle the law in a county where they are outnumbered four to one by Negroes' (CBS Evening News, 10 March 1966). The CBS account presented the Black Panthers as an instance of noble black resistance to white supremacy. The enemy was embodied in the town's white sheriff, who drawled on camera: 'All the niggas as far as I'm concerned know I've been fair and straight with all of them.' The most powerful visual image came as the cameras lingered on the emblem of the snarling black cat, created because Alabama law required that political parties have a symbol for illiterate voters to identify. In these media constructions, the Black Panthers operated within the legitimate realm of electoral politics and through the discourse of equal rights. This news report ended with correspondent John Hart concluding that this story demonstrated the triumph of right over wrong: 'The potential power of Negroes here has changed the climate of county politics' (CBS Evening News, 10 March 1966; ABC News, 3 May 1966).

This was a familiar, even comfortable narrative for journalists who had covered boycotts, sit-ins, freedom riders and school desegregation in the deep South since the late 1950s. The prolonged, violence-filled effort to integrate Central High School in Little Rock, Arkansas in 1957, become the 'first on-site news extravaganza of the modern television era', according to one historian (Branch 1988: 223). Television news was essential for the visibility of and national mobilization around the civil rights movement. NBC news veteran Richard Valeriani, who covered many of these dramatic episodes, noted that 'television helped accelerate the progress of a movement whose time had come.' The visual evidence provided by broadcast journalism 'forced the print media to be more honest than it had ever been in covering these events', he argued (Williams 1987: 270). Movement organizers were keenly aware of the importance of television, and figures like Martin Luther King, Jr. courted national media recognition. When the National Guard, the US Attorney General, and eventually the President were drawn into these debates, civil rights – and its anointed leaders – were further legitimized as newsworthy subjects (see also Garrow 1986; and Payne 1995).

The press customarily framed stories about the civil rights movement within binary oppositions that reproduced the standard values of American journalism: good versus evil, justice versus lawlessness, and North versus South. News frames emerge from the selective process journalists use as they highlight and reinforce certain ideological positions (Entman 1993; Gitlin 1980). Previous events are crucial in defining and altering media frames; these early reports on the Black Panthers fit the existing frame of black protest against segregation and discrimination during a period rife with anti-war dissent, social upheaval and violent urban uprisings. At the heart of these stories were national discourses on race that were informed by African Americans' political and legislative quest for equal opportunity – white Americans might not yet be comfortable with integrated social relations, but few outside the South could publicly deny their constitutional rights. It was no coincidence that the movement gained greater visibility through broadcast venues as its participants became increasingly multicultural. The scenes of white protesters being arrested alongside blacks, the tragedy of slain white youth from the North, all contributed to the movement as news commodity. Civil rights found its resilience on television news through its clear explication of conflict – a favourite news value – and its ability to inspire moral outrage among white Northerners.

The logics of news coverage for civil rights would not be extended to the burgeoning black liberation movement, however. If CBS sensed the threat of black power in the reverberations of Lowndes County, such fears were not revealed in this liberal-minded, sympathetic report. But, the name and image of the Black Panthers would soon be dissociated from the battlefield of the black South to enter the sphere of Northern, urban racial discord. The meaning assigned to 'Black Panther', and the media representations that accompanied it, changed dramatically in the ensuing months. The Black Panthers would no longer be associated with the legitimate claims of the civil rights establishment.

This study evaluates the television news coverage of the early years of the Black Panther Party for Self Defense founded in 1966. Contrary to some commentary, which suggests the Panthers received widespread and indiscriminate coverage, this analysis found that the Panthers rarely appeared on television during the first two years of the California-based organization (see Pearson 1994: 338–9). Sources for this project include film from the CBS Television News Archives, the Vanderbilt University Television Archives and transcripts from ABC and NBC news. It should be noted that the latter two networks do not make their archived footage available for research; they only sell it for broadcast and entertainment purposes, thus limiting the scope of this inquiry. Nevertheless, during 1966 there were two network reports on the Lowndes County Black Panthers, and a half-dozen reports on the rise of black power in 1967. It wasn't until the summer of 1968 that the new Black Panthers became media subjects. Beginning in July of that year the networks produced more than 30 news stories that focused on the Panther's skirmishes with police, and the trial of Huey Newton.

The shift in media coverage and journalistic framing of the Black Panthers exemplifies the ideological function of news. The power of television news lies, in part, in its ability to construct a visual field that operates against or replaces literary representation. Numerous scholars have noted how television news does not provide a neutral replication of the 'real' so much as a socially/politically/culturally constructed version of events that have been produced by a close-knit community of gatekeepers. Borrowing from Baudrillard, Fiske explains that this state of hyperreality 'accounts for our loss of certainty in being able to distinguish clearly and hierarchically between reality and its representation, and in being able to distinguish clearly and hierarchically between the modes of its representation' (Fiske 1994: 62). Indeed, the domain created by visual media is itself a racial formation. Stuart Hall has explained that television news operates as a site for the struggle over race and power, where inferential racism is the foundation for all mediated discourses relating to racial difference (Hall 1980: 28–52).

In the US, the embeddedness of race in media representations is rooted in the dominant place of blackness in the white (or national) imaginary. The author Toni Morrison puts this most eloquently when she illustrates 'the self-evident ways that Americans choose to talk about themselves through and within a sometimes allegorical, sometimes metaphorical, but always choked representation of an Africanist presence' (Morrison 1992: 17). White American journalists, like their peers in other public institutions, have been shaped and motivated by this profound relationship to the other. To discuss the turmoil of the 1960s was to conjure up the spectre of blackness in all of its varied forms. Morrison defined these constructions of African Americans as 'a fabricated brew of darkness, otherness, alarm, and desire that is uniquely American' (Morrison 1992: 38). This racial imaginary in the hands of broadcast media formed the basis for the (mis)representations of black power in the 1960s. When confronted with a new, belligerent and defiant form of black expression, the national press was thrown into disarray. In the eyes of journalistic gatekeepers, groups like the Black Panthers failed to fit most traditional news values; indeed, they were the antithesis of the categories identified by Herbert Gans, such as responsible capitalism, democracy, small-town pastoralism and individualism (Gans 1979). Eventually, representations of the Black Panthers would dwell within the most common of these values – conflict and celebrity – as they embodied not only political discord in urban spaces, but conflicts between black and white, citizen or outsider, and black ideologies of accommodation or resistance.

As the Spring and Summer of 1966 passed, SNCC leaders Stokely Carmichael and H. Rap Brown gained rapid media visibility as they rallied young, radical civil rights workers behind cries of black resistance. This new and intensified media visibility was marked by a transformation of what it meant to be an advocate of black power. Television news accounts were confused and inconsistent in their framing as they searched for clearly definable leaders and symbols, and emphasized inflammatory rhetoric, while virtually ignoring the social and political circumstances that were the catalyst for these activists. A June 1966 rally in Greenwood, Mississippi was widely covered by the news media, which recorded Carmichael uttering his dissatisfaction with traditional civil rights tactics. 'We been saying freedom for six years and we ain't got nothin',' exclaimed Carmichael. 'What we gonna start saying now is Black Power!' As the crowd of SNCC workers shouted 'Black

Power!' before the national press, the era of black nationalism was ushered into the public sphere (Van Deburg 1992: 32) These activists – quickly labelled militants and radicals by the news media – challenged the nonviolent, legal rights strategy of their predecessors, while they issued defiant rhetoric in opposition to white authority.

Television news coverage of these activists was sporadic and brief – only one or two stories a month through mid-1967. Nevertheless, the media was clearly fascinated with their visual expressions of controlled rage and frustration. News reports quickly identified black power 'leaders', Carmichael, Brown and Floyd McKissick of the Congress on Racial Equality (CORE), and made them the centrepiece of each account. Thus, when Carmichael received a deferment from his draft board (13 March 1967), was jailed in Atlanta (23 June 1967), or visited France (6 December 1967), he made the network news (CBS Evening News transcripts). In the spring of that year, CORE's McKissick told the annual meeting of the American Society of Newspaper Editors that the press consistently ignored all but the most negative aspects of black life, and the story was broadcast on the CBS Evening News (CBS Evening News transcripts). But, few journalists were listening, as coverage of black power advocates continued its familiar pattern.

The Black Panthers of SNCC origin gradually moved north and spread their message of black power in numerous political venues. When they held a press conference in Chicago in January 1967 to announce support for embattled Congressman Adam Clayton Powell, the Black Panther insignia was once again in the foreground of the story's visual field, although nothing was actually said about the organization (CBS Evening News, 12 January 1967). The 'Black Panther' had simply become a signifier for black militance and resistance.

Within a year, Carmichael, SNCC and the Alabama Black Panthers were supplanted by Huey Newton and Bobby Seale's Black Panther Party for Self-Defense in the media's field of vision. These California activists were inspired by the Lowndes County Panthers, by Carmichael's rhetoric, and by the writing of revolutionary figures like Malcolm X, Mao Tse-Tung and Franz Fanon. They were equally influenced by the televisual models of 1960s dissent. Even the limited television coverage of earlier black radicals had a powerful impact on those poised to become activists. Former Minister of Culture Emory Douglas reminisced that his early days in the Black Panthers was 'like being in a movement you'd seen on TV and now you could participate and share in that movement; when you'd seen Malcolm on TV, when you had heard talk about Stokely Carmichael, Rap Brown . . . To become part of that brought a sense of pride' (Douglas interviewed for Hampton, *Eyes on the Prize II*, 1989: episode 3). For him, the processes of being and watching had become almost indistinguishable. Dominant audiences read these news stories as evidence of black resistance gone amok but Douglas decoded them as political and social expressions that answered his desire for action. The names of Huey Newton, Eldridge Cleaver and Bobby Seale would become familiar to national media audiences and the notion of what it was to be a Black Panther would be readily identifiable. Indeed, it could be argued that the representations of the Panthers disseminated by the local and network news media had a powerful role in shaping public discourse and public policy in relation to black nationalist movements of the 1960s.

The Black Panthers played to the press and the press actively responded. The new, more visible Black Panther Party distinguished itself as a media subject in its ability to produce distinctive, seductive symbols and rhetoric. Its supporters exploited their visual appeal and utility as commodity subjects through their garb, paramilitary display and deployment of inflammatory rhetoric such as the use of 'pig' to describe police and other authority figures. The mediated images of the Panthers naturalized fundamental themes of racist discourse, such as blacks' propensity for violent confrontation rather than resorting to reason. From their first appearances on TV the Panthers appeared as agitators who moved outside of conventional forms of protest – picketing and demonstrations – to march in uniformed formation, and conduct armed surveillance of the police. Television cameras captured the tense confrontations between Black Panthers and white authority figures, in which they used rhetoric like 'racist white power structure' and 'racist pigs' to establish their volatility and potential threat. Huey Newton explained that the use of 'pig' was a deliberate choice as the young Panthers fashioned themselves as new kinds of radicals. On the evening news, their routine use of 'Pig' aided in their framing as belligerents who displayed disrespect, if not outward hatred, towards symbols of authority. These were not protesters who were asking for their rights; these were armed and angry black figures who maintained they would take what was theirs 'by any means necessary'.

The Panthers anticipated the media's framing and used it to their advantage. Bobby Seale remembered that Newton predicted 'the papers are going to call us thugs and hoodlums'. But, according to Seale, black Americans would recognize the Panthers' potency within the context of these labels. Seale anticipated that blacks would be attracted to their mediated images: 'They've been calling us niggers, thugs and hoodlums for 400 years, that ain't gon' hurt me. I'm going to check out what these brothers is doing' (Seale quoted in Foner 1995: xxxi). In the Spring of 1967 television news took note of the new Black Panthers. The group staged their first choreographed public display at the California State Capital in Sacramento, expecting the event to heighten their media visibility. The Panthers leaped from the pages of the local press to the television screen when they marched to the State legislature, some brandishing loaded weapons, on 2 May 1967. The startled press corps, assembled for a day of routine reporting, let the tape roll for more than 30 minutes as they recorded Bobby Seale's statement opposing a pending arms control bill, and watched as police pursued them through the building and off the Capitol grounds. 'The Black Panther Party for Self-Defense believes that the time has come for Black people to arm themselves against this terror before it is too late', Seale announced (Executive Mandate No. 1 reprinted in The Black Panther Community News Service, 2 June 1967). The cameras recorded the Panthers being jostled by police, and later searched and arrested against a backdrop of shouting and disarray.

This story was initially broadcast in the Sacramento and San Francisco markets; the national coverage was relegated to wire-service briefs buried in the middle of daily newspapers. But the images remained, reproducing the popular images of the Panthers that would be used over and over again in national broadcast reports. Today, the recorded images of the local network affiliates function as an historical reproduction of the era: the black beret over a barely contained afro, scowling black faces partially hidden by dark glasses, black leather jackets, clenched fists, and guns confidently slung from their shoulders. The furore over the Sacramento protest was carried in the northern California press for several months, but it was considered a local story outside the interests of a national market, and it would be another year before network television news would pay close attention to the Panther phenomenon. This event revealed a contestation over forms of knowledge and visibility between the Black Panthers and the news media – a dialogic process in which the Panthers were remarkably effective in shaping their mediated image. The Panthers needed the media attention and some among its leadership desired the fame and notoriety. The press needed a steady diet of sensational, racially inflected news stories to maintain audience attention.

A study of the National Organization of Women described a dialogical relationship in which the news media was deemed a vital resource for the organization's mobilization, allowing feminist activists to analyse, and to some extent control, their own representations (Barker-Plummer 1995: 306–24). This model has some utility for understanding the relationship the Panthers sought to cultivate with the news media. The Black Panthers were clearly agents in their media constructions; many aspects of their actions, style, performance and language were all carefully created for the camera. However, NOW, the Students for a Democratic Society, and other white dissident groups did not have to contend with the rhetorics and deep-seated ideologies of race (see Gitlin 1980). White activists often benefited from strategic interactions with white journalists, some of whom could identify with and even support their agendas.

The news media attempted to have black journalists like Earl Caldwell of the *New York Times* and Gilbert Moore of *Life* magazine, cover the Black Panther Party, but black reporters were few and far between, and there were virtually no visible black journalists working in television. In 1968 the National Advisory Commission on Civil Disorders, also known as the Kerner Commission, noted that

> The journalistic profession has been shockingly backward in seeking out, hiring, training, and promoting Negroes. Fewer than 5 percent of the people employed by the news business in editorial jobs in the United States today are Negroes, and most of them work for Negro-owned organizations.
>
> (Kerner Commission 1968: 384–5)

Although some critics have maintained that white reporters were overly sympathetic towards the Black Panthers, the Kerner Commission understood that the potential for a positive two-way interaction between the press and the Panthers was limited: 'The lines of various news organizations to the militant blacks are, by admission of the newsmen themselves, almost nonexistent' (Kerner Commission 1968). While the media might have an appetite for stories on the Panthers, the opportunities for strategic negotiations over their representations would be limited and contested. Despite the substantial coverage they received, the Panthers would always complain bitterly about the 'racist pig press'. Huey Newton would see the press framing as part of a 'propaganda war against the Panthers':

> What never became clear to the public, largely because it was always de-emphasized in the media, was that the armed self-defense program of the Party was just one form of what Party leaders viewed as self-defense against oppression.
>
> (Newton 1996: 34)

Nevertheless, the Panthers, like most social movements of the era, were quite purposive in their use of the media. Television's ascent as the nation's main source of news and information meant that broadcast attention was an essential component of any group's mobilization and political strategy. The Panthers were incredibly savvy about their use of the media; they quickly learned how press attention would attract recruits, advance their campaigns and bring public scrutiny to issues like police brutality. Throughout this period, the entertainment value of news was being discovered by the television industry, which placed a premium on style and holding audience attention, rather than content or social responsibility. Techniques such as pacing, format, packaging similar stories together, the use of charismatic anchors, avoiding complex ideas, were pressed into service. The ideological bias projected by broadcast journalists, according to political scientist Edward J. Epstein, was whatever was in the interest or service of the network (Epstein 1975: 182–209). Thus, the Panthers satisfied television's growing need for sensationalism, continuing stories and compelling visual content. TV audiences were no longer content to watch clumsy charts and graphs, and the grainy background photos that had been broadcasting's staple. They needed and wanted pictures with action and indelible images.

The event that made the Black Panthers a national news story for the networks was the trial of Huey Newton for the murder of an Oakland police officer in the summer of 1968. Beginning in July, considerable time was allotted to stories about the Panthers on all three networks prompted by the organization's efforts to elicit support for Newton's case. Television news was attracted to the symbols and theatre that the Panthers supplied. A 'free Huey' campaign, to win public opinion to Newton's side, had been waged with pamphlets, flyers, posters, buttons and numerous fund-raising events in Oakland, San Francisco and other American cities, and even a film. As his trial began, dozens of Panthers would assemble outside the Alameida County Courthouse in Oakland, California, to stand at attention and hold banners aloft in a display of solidarity with their embattled leader. A story on ABC News captured the crowd of Panthers and white 'hippie' supporters listening to Bobby Seale condemn the Oakland Police Department as a 'terrorist organization' (ABC News, 18 July 1968). When Newton's jury began deliberation, the national networks returned to the story with extensive background pieces on the Panthers. Newton's guilty verdict attracted yet another round of stories that served as a catalyst for further coverage.

Why did these stories on a relatively routine court case attract such attention? These narratives neatly fit the Panthers into the news frame of law and order. Court cases are a familiar process for television audiences, and the criminal justice system could be seen as meting out fair retribution for the Panther's outrageous acts. Huey Newton, cast as martyr by his followers in the Panthers, could be framed as an anti-hero or a victim of the excesses of a police state. This flurry of television stories on the Panthers also occurred against the backdrop of the 1968 Democratic National Convention – a televised event that exemplified the perils of social protest and the extent of police violence. Prior to the convention, the Panthers held a news conference to announce that they would not demonstrate at the Convention (ABC News 28 July 1968). Nevertheless, they were a symbolic and actual presence; Bobby Seale would later be indicted as one of the 'Chicago 7', providing him his own starring role in a courtroom drama.

The Panthers' television presence was also elevated by the growing activism of chapters outside Northern California. What had once been deemed a local story now had national dimensions, particularly in New York City where the networks were headquartered. Right after the Democratic Convention, a group of 150 off-duty police officers attacked and assaulted a dozen Panthers at a Brooklyn courthouse. Instantly, all three networks jumped on this story. Media audiences began to see interviews with Panther members and leaders outside of the Oakland network. New York Mayor John Lindsay condemned the police actions, and several news features explored the discord between black community activists and white police. In the same month, errant police fired shots into the Oakland Panther headquarters, again focusing on what was now being called a 'war' between the Panthers and the police (ABC News, 5 September 1968; 9 October 1968; CBS Evening News, 4 September 1968). In all of the news accounts from this period, the police were constructed as an aggrieved group. In addition to the now familiar Panther stories, replete with the black cat emblem and the marching cadres, broadcasters produce long stories sympathizing with the difficulties of police work.

The television news coverage of the Black Panthers during this period exemplified the struggle to fit black power activists into existing systems of representation – neither the frames used to cover the civil rights movement nor those about white anti-war radicals could conveniently package this new movement that blended black nationalism, self-defence, leftist ideology and racialized, confrontational rhetoric. The visual and verbal images of the Black Panthers tapped into white American's primal fears of black male sexuality, black American violence and the potential of an all-out race war.

'The figure of the Black male out of control is a cultural nightmare for whites . . .' noted Fiske in his study of 1990s media events (Fiske 1994: xviii). These early stages of the Panthers' media visibility inform us about the ever-present racial discourses barely submerged in the national conscience.

These representations have remained remarkably resilient during the 30 years since the Panthers first entered the public consciousness. Visual and rhetorical representations of the Black Panther Party are deeply embedded in our collective and individual memories, regardless of whether we lived during their era, ever had direct contact with the organization, or directly sought them out. They have been commodified as symbols of black empowerment or black depravity. They have been reproduced as historical sources in modern news stories, documentaries and fictional film. This is a disturbing legacy for some who seek to redeem the 1960s from the criticism of the right. Recent literary attempts to reclaim the 1960s have tended to marginalize the Panther legacy, or condemn it. For example, political scientist Meta Mendel-Reyes, a nostalgic child of the 1960s, notes that 'To refer negatively to the sixties in political discourse is to call up memories of young people in revolt; disheveled, wild-eyed demonstrations; Black Panthers in leather jackets and berets, carrying rifles and shouting Black Power' (Mendel-Reyes 1995: 72).

Such responses to the spectre of black power reinforce Omi and Winant's observation that black nationalism in the 1960s dramatically disrupted the dominant political culture. 'White liberals reacted in horror when their ethnic prescriptions were put into practice by black militants,' they note (Omi and Winant 1994: 99–112). Some have argued that the media were a prime instrument for the undoing of 1960s activism (Gitlin 1980: 292). Others have cautioned against a purely hegemonic interpretation of the press. Hallin suggests that 'the hold of ideology over the journalist' doesn't guarantee that the media will consistently serve to legitimate the dominant institutions of capitalist society (Hallin 1994: 19–23). In his view, the contentious and ambivalent nature of US journalism keeps political authority at a distance. In the case of the Black Panthers, racial histories and the fear of social disruption mitigated against the potential for journalists to gain distance from the sites of power. Once the police, local and state governments and the FBI deemed the Panthers a problem to be eradicated, their fate in the media was sealed.

▌ References

Barker-Plummer, B. (1995) News as a Political Resource: Media Strategies and Political Identity in the U. S. Women's Movement, 1966–1975, *Critical Studies in Mass Communication*, 12: 306–24.

Branch, T. (1988) *Parting the Waters: America in the King Years, 1954–63*. New York: Simon & Schuster.

Entman, R. (1993) Framing: Toward Clarification of a Fractured Paradigm, *Journal of Communication*, 43(4): 51–8.

Epstein, E. J. (1975) *Between Fact and Fiction: The Problem of Journalism*. New York: Vintage Books.

Executive Mandate Number One (1967) *The Black Panther*, 2 June.

Fiske, J. (1994) *Media Matters: Everyday Culture and Political Change*. Minneapolis: University of Minnesota Press.

Foner, P. S. (1995) *The Black Panthers Speak*. New York: Da Capo Press.

Gans, H. (1979) *Deciding What's News*. New York: Pantheon.

Garrow, D. (1986). *Bearing the Cross: Martin Luther King, Jr. and the Southern Christian Leadership Conference*. New York: Random House.

Gitlin, T. (1980) *The Whole World is Watching: Mass Media in the Making and Unmaking of the New Left*. Berkeley: University of California Press.

Hall, S. (1980) The Whites of Their Eyes: Racist Ideologies and the Media, in George Bridges and Rosalind Brunt (eds) *Silver Linings: Some Strategies for the Eighties*. London: Lawrence & Wishart, pp. 28–52.

Hallin, D. (1994) *We Keep America on Top of the World*. New York: Routledge.

Hampton, H. (producer) (1989) *Eyes on the Prize*, Part II, episode 3.

Horsman, R. (1981) *Race and Manifest Destiny: The Origins of American Racial Anglo-Saxonism*. Cambridge: Harvard University Press.

Jordan, W. (1977) *White Over Black: American Attitudes toward the Negro, 1550–1812*. New York: Norton.

Kerner Commission (1968) *Report of the National Advisory Commission on Civil Disorders*. New York: E. P. Dutton, Inc.

Leigh, R. D. (ed.) (1947) *Commission on Freedom of the Press. A Free and Responsible Press, A General Report on Mass Communication: Newspapers, Radio, Motion Pictures, Magazines, and Books*. Chicago: University of Chicago Press.

Mendel-Reyes, M. (1995) *Reclaiming Democracy: The Sixties in Politics and Memory*. New York: Routledge.

Morrison, T. (1992) *Playing in the Dark: Whiteness and the Literary Imagination*. Cambridge, MA: Harvard University Press.

Newton, H. (1996) *War Against the Panthers: A Study of Repression in America*. New York: Harlem River Press.

Omi, M. and Winant, H. (1994) *Racial Formation in the United States: From the 1960s to the 1990s*, 2nd edn. New York: Routledge.

Payne, C. (1995) *I've Got the Light of Freedom: The Organizing Tradition and the Mississippi Freedom Struggle*. Berkeley: University of California Press.

Pearson, H. (1994) *The Shadow of the Panther: Huey Newton and the Price of Black Power in America*. New York: Addison-Wesley.

Van Deburg, W. (1992) *New Day in Babylon: The Black Power Movement and American Culture, 1965–1975*. Chicago: University of Chicago Press.

Vaughan, A. T. (1995) *The Roots of American Racism: Essays in the Colonial Experience*. New York: Oxford University Press.

Williams, J. (1987) *Eyes on the Prize: America's Civil Rights Years, 1954–1965*. New York: Viking.

13

The 'gender matters' debate in journalism
Lessons from the front

Linda Steiner

- Do men and women journalists work in significantly different ways – and if so, what are these differences?
- In what ways do sex and gender matter in journalism?
- What or whose interests are served by claiming that women cannot or do not produce the same kind of reporting as men?

Not merely in the eighteenth and nineteenth centuries, but also continuing well into the twentieth century, people heatedly debated the difference that sex makes. Usually the victorious orators managed to explain why a woman can't, in words of Henry Higgins, be more like a man. This claim was certainly applied to journalism. Male reporters, editors and publishers were quite certain that sex mattered a great deal in journalism. Notably, this meant that women could not succeed as journalists. Women could not handle the rough-and-tumble culture of the newsroom; moreover, the argument went, even trying to do so would damage women's health and ultimately 'unsex' them.

The only explicit exception was that women could write about women for women. Rhetorically, the logic was that women had special intuition regarding what women needed and wanted to know. Conversely, men lacked the vocabulary and sensitivity for describing fashion, child rearing, cooking, and interior décor. Some men came close to arguing that men would be 'unmanned' by writing for or about women. High status and professional prestige for men depended on segregating topics and audiences. It required men to monopolize reporting about public affairs, politics, and war; and confine women to women's topics and audiences.[1]

This chapter argues that an explanation of journalism practices grounded in 'sex' is not as antique as it might at first sound. For more than 30 years, both scholars and non-scholars have avoided explanations based on sex per se. Instead, they have referred to gender or the 'sex/gender system'. But 'gender' may have lost its rhetorical cachet, if not its explanatory usefulness. It's partly the decreasing importance of gender as a factor underlying the major issues in the newspaper industry, relative to economic and profit constraints, management expectations, as well as race, ethnicity, and even politics, including sexual politics. This chapter, therefore, will begin by returning, albeit very briefly, to the history of women in journalism. Yet the deployment of gender could use some overhaul, so this chapter will also critique current usage of the term.[2] Ultimately I will propose reintroducing references to sex and offer some evidence of how sex matters to journalism, with particular attention to war reporting. Women's reporting work is most controversial in sports and war, not coincidentally both arenas in which physicality and bodies are very much at issue.[3]

An overview of a century of women's journalism work

Henry Higgins's whine notwithstanding, the claim heard throughout the nineteenth century was that women cannot and should not be like men. The emotional and physical spheres of men and women were mutually exclusive. The same sociosexual division – between private and public, affective and instrumental, leisure and work – said to characterize other realms applied to news. At least in journalism, moreover, these spheres were hierarchical, not complementary. The division of expertise and labour by 'sex' was even more vigorously asserted as commercial commerce increased. Growing demand for news by larger numbers of readers and growing advertiser support generated an increasing number of newspapers. As salary increases made newspaper work more attractive as a job, however, men continued to oppose women's entry into newsrooms.

In the early and mid-twentieth century, this argument shifted slightly. Once women began trying to exploit new educational opportunities at the college and university level – including in journalism departments or programmes – editors and publishers correctly anticipated that women would start demanding newsroom jobs with greater vehemence. In response, editors and other male journalists argued that it was a waste of time to hire and intensively train women who would soon, or at least eventually, quit in order to marry and take care of their families. As is fairly well known, during the First and Second World Wars, many newsrooms were essentially forced to hire women. Women wrote, reported, and even edited across the sections of the newspaper, including sports. Each time, when the war was over, however, most women were ordered to make room for returning soldiers. The theory was that women would enjoy being at home full-time again. Just in case, some women had signed contracts agreeing to do so. Some women were moved to lower-status jobs; others were pushed out altogether.

Suggestions about sex differences were sometimes articulated indirectly, but more often, these were explicit. Journalism textbooks and career counselling books published in the early twentieth century referred to notions of sex differences in the course of warning women to expect hostility from men in the newsroom and to expect to write exclusively for the women's and society pages (Steiner 1992, 1997). Most of the early textbooks and career or vocational counselling literature about journalism was produced by men – usually active or former journalists. But women writing this literature also steered women towards low-rent, low-status districts of the newsroom.

As the references above suggest, women wrote about women for women. Newspapers needed to attract women readers, who were an important target for advertisers, and men essentially refused to write for (about) women. Because women's 'correspondence' was directed at women readers and women were encouraged to write in a non-journalistic, conversational style, they might not be recognized now as journalists. More to the point, many women accepted their derailment to the women's track as a condition of work. Often women needed the work; it was not merely a matter of 'pin money'. That is, some women developed different vocabularies/ethical principles – and often a gushier, more sentimental style – as the price of admission into professional journalism. Certainly women wrote about different topics. But the fact that some women developed quite different ways of doing work – or even that many women found satisfaction in their separate sphere and enjoyed the separate (courteous) treatment and deference from male colleagues – says more about how people respond to conditions of employment than about differences between men and women, and certainly about 'natural' differences.

Whether they accepted or resented the equivalence between the body of the female writer/subject/reader, all women – and more than a few men – noticed the newsroom's treatment of women 'as' women.[4] Even more importantly, as in many other spheres, normative ideals for and in journalism, including those articulated in prescriptive literature, could never wholly control actual behaviour. Some women managed to resist the ghettoizing of women, often by carving out an 'exceptionalist' space for themselves as different from women, as like men. Some women developed new ways of doing work, with different standards/vocabularies/ethical principles. A few women quietly went about their business, doing the same kind of work that men did. Meanwhile, it is worth pointing out, men did not necessarily act as sexist as their pronouncements might predict. A *New York Herald Tribune* editor declared that women reporters 'don't understand honor or fair play . . . as men understand it' (Walker 1934: 248). Yet, he often provided women, such as Ishbel Ross, with front-page opportunities.[5]

War reporters as the exceptional case

For over 100 years before the women's movement revolutionized understandings of womanhood, a few women, albeit not in great numbers, managed to achieve success as professional reporters. They wrote for general audiences about a variety of topics typically associated with men, including public affairs and political reporting. They even covered foreign and war news, which might seem the most obvious beat from which to bar women, given the danger of war and the association of men with fighting. For example, in 1846 Margaret Fuller, the *New York Tribune*'s literary critic and a well known intellectual and author (including of a pioneering treatise on women's rights), went to Italy to cover a revolution (ultimately unsuccessful) as well as attacks on Rome by France. On her way home, in 1850, Fuller, along with the young Italian aristocrat she had just married and their son, died in a shipwreck. Fuller's friends and family destroyed a substantial amount of her personal correspondence and papers, apparently in order to protect her honour (Von Mehren 1994). Nonetheless, Fuller remains celebrated as a foreign correspondent.

Jane McManus Storms is now less famous but she, too, was a romantic, powerful and thus controversial woman at the same time as Fuller, especially for her reports on battles between Mexican and American troops, as well as a civil war in Mexico. Storms had written for several newspapers, especially Moses Yale Beach's *New York Sun*. In 1846 Storms accompanied Beach on a secret peace mission to Mexico, in part to translate for Beach; but she also wrote up her own observations. Her wartime correspondence, published in the *Sun* and several other newspapers, won admiration, although at least one powerful senator complained of her 'masculine stomach for war and politics' (Reilly 1981: 21). After she returned to New York she became the editor of *La Verdad*, a Spanish-language paper that supported US annexation of Cuba.

Women served as war correspondents, albeit in small numbers, during the Russian Revolution, a war in 1897 between Greece and Turkey, and World War I, and in greater numbers in World War II. But they remained known as 'exceptions'. Some women acknowledged that they won wartime assignments by promising to provide a women's angle. Ruth Cowan, an Associated Press reporter, said she did not understand war tactics but she wanted to convey the Normandy beachhead to 'the women back home' (Wagner 1989: 38). More to the point, women understood that civilians, political leaders, soldiers and 'fellow' journalists regarded them 'as' embodied, as members of the female sex. The Prime Minister of Rumania repeatedly asked Second World War correspondents, 'When is Ann Stringer of the United Press coming back? She had the most beautiful legs in Rumania' (quoted in Wagner 1989: 7). The *Boston Globe* headlined a story by Iris Carpenter 'First Girl War Correspondent to Cross Rhine at Remagen'; an article about Carpenter herself was entitled 'Even More Attractive than Photo, Says Holt' (Wagner 1989: 28).

Women generally took this sexualization in their stride, even as they described themselves not as newspaperwomen but as newspapermen. Many boasted, most famously the *New York Herald Tribune*'s Berlin bureau chief Marguerite Higgins (1955), that men regarded them not as newspaper-women, but as newspapermen. Military officials seem to have been obsessed with the absence of bathrooms for women, leading Charlotte Ebener, to take but one example of many, to title her autobiography *No Facilities for Women* (1955). Women vigorously resisted military officials' attempts to use 'facilities' as an excuse for excluding women. US Army brass ordered Marguerite

Higgins out of Korea by claiming there were 'no facilities for ladies at the front'. Higgins circumvented the rule by appealing personally to her friend, General Douglas MacArthur; she later won a Pulitzer Prize for her combat accounts of the Korean War.

Women like Higgins were generally casual about men's attention to women's bodies, often regarding sexualization as inevitable. Recalling her 'Adventure' reporting in Europe and Asia, Irene Corbally Kuhn (1938: 73) remarked that, because of male reporters' war experiences, it was always 'sex o-clock' in the newsroom: Having lived with death, men now 'seized on life with a rapist's lust, and life meant women and women meant sex'. So Kuhn refused to criticize her *New York Daily News* editor's preoccupation with the human 'mid-section'. When the editor wanted her to lure a convicted draft-dodger back to France, Kuhn merely commented he 'had more confidence in my sex appeal than in the enterprise of any of his male journalists' (Kuhn 1938: 140).

The invention of gender

In the 1970s, academic feminists began to complain about the universal use of sex as an independent variable. They rejected as unproved and unlikely the claim that the physical body inevitably determined behaviour and thinking. They proposed 'gender' as a socially constructed conception to describe what otherwise had been assumed to be the biological or anatomical divide between the sexes. Gayle Rubin's now-classic (1975) article explained how 'raw biological sex' was transformed into a binary gender system, enforced and naturalized through language and a number of institutions and structures, including religion, education and, not coincidentally, the media. Moreover, the conceptual differentiation of gender and sex pointed to the possibility that sexual anatomy would eventually become irrelevant, thus no longer able to predetermine the abilities or potential of women and men, as a whole or as individuals. If men's domination was not biological but constructed, then male privilege could be resisted.[6]

The conception inspired massive research programmes across academic disciplines. While the initial focus was the social construction of womanhood and femininity, it eventually compelled scholars to problematize manhood and masculinity. Thus, what some critics of gender saw as a problem (by not naming women, gender sounds neutral and depoliticized) arguably led to one of its continuing strengths. Gender-inspired research called attention to how both masculinity and femininity are socially constructed in specific historical contexts. In journalism and mass communication, careful attention to gender led to understandings of, among other things, how journalists expected masculinity and femininity to regulate people's lives, applied gendered standards, and deployed gendered language. Feminist scholarship, with its attention to gender, inspired historical work to recover otherwise forgotten evidence of women's agency in journalism.

Researchers were far less successful in providing evidence that men and women 'essentially' acted differently as reporters or editors. At a minimum, evidence from reporters' autobiographies and memoirs, documentaries and interviews, as well as empirical data, can be interpreted in several ways. Women reporters tend to resent the claim that gender predicts news values, ethics, interviewing practices, writing styles.[7] On the other hand, some women not only see newsroom hiring and promotion practices as gendered (sexist) and conventional news values as masculine but they also interpret the evidence as supporting the claim that women, at least when hired in sufficient numbers to constitute a critical mass, act differently as journalists. The underlying logic is that because women's lives are different (more involved with home and family) they tend to see different topics and different people as newsworthy and important.

❙ Evidence from Vietnam

In 1898, women's reporting on the Spanish-American war was said to emphasize the effects of the war, such as the predicament of the wounded and refugees, whereas men focused on military technology and battle strategy. Echoing century-old debates about women's journalism and women's attitudes about war, the debate over whether women report war differently from men reemerged during the Vietnam War. A guerrilla-form war never officially declared, Vietnam was the first to be reported on television, virtually in 'real time'. The absence of front lines, loosened military restrictions, and the fact that reporters could book commercial airline flights to Vietnam without military officials' permission all helped to open up war reporting to women. Over the course of the war, 467 women reported from Vietnam (Rouvalis and Schackner 2000). This does not mean that men wanted women there. Liz Trotta, the first woman to report on Vietnam for US television in a sustained way, attributed male colleagues' hostility to them feeling threatened by competition from women (Trotta 1991: 98). More ominously, General William Westmoreland prohibited women reporters from staying overnight in the field after he recognized a young woman reporter whose family had lived in his neighbourhood; but women protested and the Defense Department rescinded the ban.

Recent recollections of nine women who covered Vietnam (Fawcett *et al.* 2002) demonstrate not only a range of experiences but also a range of responses to the question of gender. Some women said their visibility meant they were noticed at press conferences and had their questions answered first; some thought that soldiers liked talking to women, and helped them out. Other women said that men in the military refused to help them and the attention paid to them as women was unwanted. More to the point, some women described themselves as more attuned to the Vietnamese and the 'human side' of the war, while men reporters emphasized the American/ military position. A newspaper account of a reunion of these reporters described women trying to write about Vietnamese children and nurses – because war is not about 'bang-bang' but about destruction. According to Rouvalis and Schackner (2000) Tad Bartimus said she loved writing the Vietnam stories that men dismissed as 'sob-sister stuff'. Notably, Bartimus herself claims she covered what all Associated Press correspondents did: economics, refugees, maimed veterans, stalled peace talks. Likewise, Anne Morrissy Merick, a former sports reporter who implied that ABC-TV hired her to avoid sex discrimination suits (Fawcett *et al.* 2002: 92), suggests that she mainly produced 'feature stuff' because that was what she was assigned, while men loved to cover battles, partly because it guaranteed them a spot on the evening news.

Several women, in contrast, said they hated doing these sorts of stories. Some refused to do 'women's stories', either because the stereotype was demeaning or because these stories were more likely to be cut. Denby Fawcett quit her women's page job and followed her boyfriend to Vietnam as a freelancer; she got his combat work when he changed jobs. She insists, 'I made a point of covering exactly the same kinds of stories as my male colleagues, mainly because I never again wanted to be typecast as a women's page reporter' (Fawcett *et al.* 2002: 16). In fact, both men and women wrote 'human interest' stories and interpretative stories analysing what led to the war and effects of the war, as well as unsentimental accounts of battles and military strategy.[8]

More recently, women have again been described as covering war differently from men by focusing on the impact of war, including on citizens and non-military victims. For example, some say only women reporters were serious about exposing the systematic rape of Bosnian women as a weapon of war. Yet, one interpretation of this range of positions, from the Spanish-American War, to World War II to Vietnam, is that it says little about how men and women are naturally or socially conditioned to work. To the extent that women adopted a human-interest approach or a concern with 'collateral damage' whether in 1898 or 1998, this may reflect what editors assigned women to do or how men edited women's stories. It reflects what women promised to do to get a job and connived to do when sexist male/ military sources denied them access. Most importantly, these interpretative stories are the ones we recall and honour. Some reporters are more gifted, or courageous, than others. But women do not seem to have 'special qualities' in war reporting.

The argument against gender

The argument for reintroducing sex into the discussion rests on a few propositions, first that gender itself has been so distorted that it has lost its original value. Gender has become dichotomized even more strictly and completely than sex. Sex and gender have been conflated – automatically treated as the same. As Joan Scott (1999) has conceded, feminists could not prevent its corruption. Not all communication research puts the notion that 'genders' are absolutely, inevitably, universally, essentially opposites as crudely as John Gray PhD. This self-described 'expert' on gender differences, an author of more than a dozen books, purports to use 'gender' and 'gender insight' to explain how *Men are from Mars, Women are from Venus*, how they are 'opposite sexes'.[9] This is an extreme case of distortion. Still, more generally the meaning of gender, or at least its popular usage, has lost its critical edge. It now signals both ascribed and 'natural' differences between the sexes.

The problem extends to scholarly literature. A cursory examination of all issues of one major 'flagship' academic journal *Journalism and Mass Communication Quarterly*, published from 2000 to 2003, plus issues of several other media studies and journalism journals, showed that of those who took gender and/or sex as a variable seldom found that it mattered. Nonetheless, of those who addressed this, most used gender and sex interchangeably; a few used gender as a variable, defined as male or female.[10] This use of gender to refer to sex may be a verbal tic, reflecting widespread acceptance of the notion that both women and men are social beings. It may be a matter of political correctness, or an avoidance of a term like sex, with its physical-biological connotations. But this also suggests that the concept no longer destabilizes conventional discourse as it once did.

Another issue, with interesting corollaries in journalism and journalism history, is the continuing debate whether women essentially form a single group that is different from (or even opposite to) men, whether women have a unique sensibility (born in their distinct experience) or whether gender difference is at best an artefact, and potentially the means, of patriarchal power. A relevant example of this emerges in a chapter 'What difference do women journalists make?' by Kay Mills, a former reporter and journalism historian. Mills (1997), who uses the term 'female' and 'women' interchangeably but opens by noting the influence of 'gender', says women write and broadcast differently from men. Although their journalism training is the same, she says, women's 'different set of experiences' produces a special sensibility.

Mills' title might have been more meaningful stated in the past tense. Perhaps women's insistence on doing things differently (asking different questions, interviewing women, including low status women, covering women's experiences and topics of concern specifically to women, hiring women, rewarding women) has *over time* helped bring changes in definitions of news, newsroom culture and editorial policy such that male and female journalists now work in a changed environment in which gender is nearly irrelevant. That is, one can agree that once women have achieved a critical mass in the newsroom, and especially when they have cracked the glass ceiling and attained management positions, they succeeded in bringing to the fore new kinds of stories – stories that appealed to and were important to women audiences, that applied to women's lives. Nonetheless, the news we see – as consumers and as researchers – is not an unmediated product, but highly edited. Stories are published after many layers of mediation. Might a point in history arrive when critical mass renders reporters' gender irrelevant?

The importance of sex

None of the above is intended to deny that women's physical attractiveness and sexuality continue to be exploited, or that a double standard continues to be applied in the newsroom. Liesbet van Zoonen (1998: 44) comments that femininity has become 'an unmistakable ingredient of market-driven war journalism'. I would call it sexuality. That is, critiquing sex, instead of gender, more clearly identifies and names the problem. Although employment statistics themselves are reaching parity the issue is most obvious in television, for obvious reasons: attracting audiences is even more difficult than obtaining information. While male broadcast anchors and reporters are allowed to go fat and grey and even bald, older women are forced off the air, lest they alienate male viewers.

British women are apparently more concerned about this than Americans. At the BBC newsreading has long been a woman's job, since the newsreader has become decorative role, one performed for a voyeuristic male audience (Holland 1987). Anna Sebba (1994) speculated that the number of women covering the 1991 Gulf War conspicuously rose because of women's ability to offer visual appeal and pleasant relief from stories about violence. Foreign correspondent Kate Adie has criticized BBC management for preferring women with 'cute faces and cute bottoms' over those with journalistic experience (see Chambers *et al.* 2004). But US journalists also despair over the market/profit drive, requirements to personalize and focus on celebrities, and the turn to 'therapy' news. To be blunt, the problem is sex. Much of the pandering is done by women. It is women newscasters who smile flirtatiously, ask personal questions, hug rapists, and show cleavage. Women are manipulated to attract male and female audiences. But the fact that women are deployed in this mockery of news in name of gender difference represents not so much gender as exploitation of sex. Management hire market research organizations, issue memos and manuals, and announce at meetings very specific requirements in dress, degree of smiling and talk among reporters. Broadcast journalism, on a global scale, is especially marked by the crucial role of women's appearance in hiring and assignment decisions, even – or rather, especially – in the context of war journalism. Yet in print, too, management can order more human interest 'touches', and the insertion of personal address and personal information.

Female journalists, again, especially those covering war, have often said that they have faced differential/discriminatory treatment by sexist sources, but that this has no effect on them. They are quite sure that they are as disembodied as their male colleagues (which is to say, wholly) while at work, and as casual about after-hours sex. One can properly be suspicious of such claims that journalists are not like other humans. On the other hand, journalists do seem to work assiduously to deny their own experiences, including their embodied experiences. Whatever the distortions this attempt produces, perhaps journalists are among those relatively able to ignore gendered norms and expectations. In any case, what is clear is that print and especially broadcast journalists are increasingly pressured by market forces. They must compete for audience attention. They must help their corporate bosses satisfy advertisers and maximize profit. Increasingly, this translates into manipulating sex. Women have long been hired, fired and judged on the basis of appearance, although the standards of beauty change and critics are hard on women who are overly sexy. In the 1970s NBC's 'golden girl' Jessica Savitch (by her own admission) was promoted – beyond her ability – because of her beauty. In the 1980s Christine Craft was fired for being 'too ugly', despite the coaching ordered by her television station on jewellry, cosmetics and clothing. In 2002, to promote its top anchor Paula Zahn, CNN ran – until roundly criticized – an advertisement asking 'Where can you find a morning news anchor who's provocative, super-smart, oh yeah, and just a little bit sexy?'

Nor does critical mass solve the problem. Zoonen (1991) notes that in the Netherlands, where more women than men now do television reporting, this increase has brought an 'intimization' of television news. By this she means attention to human interest stories, a personal mode of address on part of newsreaders, and treatment of political issues as matters of personality. Zoonen bemoans a 'two-faced trap' confronting women: women can opt for full, equal integration in the public sphere, but then lose some highly esteemed private sphere values; or they can chose to maintain their private sphere values even in the public sphere, and remain different (Zoonen 1991: 228). But, while Zoonen's analysis is sophisticated, the sameness/difference dilemma is a historically specific product. At least in the media industry, it remains a production, not a choice.

Conclusion

At the risk of stating the obvious, these problems, and the ones with gender per se, are not the fault of feminism. 'Intimization' results not from intent to reformulate news along feminist principles but cynical attempts to serve corporate masters. Granted, feminist scholars and activists, in the abstract, reject codes of impersonality and objectivity as masculinist standards and they specifically support promoting women journalists. They do not advocate the importation of women's supposed skills in interpersonal communication and intimacy, or the hiring of sexually alluring women. Thus, women's numerical dominance in broadcasting rearticulates conventional femininity, not because of gendered assumptions (or misguided feminist principles) but because of marketing agendas.

Gender as a feminist concept honours the work and lives of women journalists. It may also encourage hiring women at the very upper reaches of management or other corners of the newsroom where parity has not yet been achieved. Yet, attention to gender, even as 'correctly' conceptualized, may divert critical attention away from more important problems in the newsroom, in content (the problem of sensationalism), journalists' attitude (including a self-fulfilling cynicism about the seriousness of the audience), and production processes and marketing. Feminist analysis is useful, understanding feminism as a liberatory, transformatory movement concerned with critiquing and dismantling interstructured constraints based on economic drives and oppressive assumptions about gender, class, race, sexual orientation and ethnicity. As such, what is required is feminist analysis of major problems, including sexualization of women.

Notes

1　This chapter is based on historical and contemporary evidence from the US. Nonetheless, the argument largely applies to the UK, although periodicization is very different (for example, UK women achieved newsroom success initially in even smaller numbers than the US and their numbers grew much later), and theoretical notions are also relevant.

2　Much of my own work addresses gender in the sense criticized here. Moreover, I admit from the outset that habits are difficult to break. Given the success of feminist theorizing in privileging social/cultural constructions over biology and anatomy, I refer to gender and not sex. I want to think of women and men as social categories, and while I sometimes use 'male' as an adjective, I avoid saying 'female journalists', which seems to overemphasize the body and sexuality of women, and prefer 'women journalists'.

3　Ironically, sports, and certainly locker rooms, remain male bastions, although women insist they can report on sports just like men.

4　Elizabeth Banks opened her *Autobiography of a Newspaper Girl* by describing how a publisher responded to her initial job application: 'Be anything, but don't be a newspaper girl' (Banks 1902: 6). Of the 100 or so autobiographies that I have read published since then by woman journalists, none failed to mention this issue.

5　The chasm between prescription and description went in the opposite direction in the 1970s: In the wake of the feminist movement, vocational literature and reporting textbooks quickly shifted from claiming sex was important to insisting that gender made no difference; but the real world of newsrooms took several decades to reflect this shift (Steiner 1992).

6　It is worth noting here, the potential for analogous distinctions between 'race' and 'ethnicity', or even better, the between 'homosexuality' as a term referring to sexual orientation and 'gay', referring to a constellation of cultural choices about politics and style.

7　Regardless of its scholarly merit, their view is thus consistent with journalists' general philosophy that they are objective professionals and therefore can transcend their bodies.

8　Contrary to stereotypes, both women and men were analogously divided on the 'rightness' of the war (see Elwood-Akers 1988).

9　The introduction to Gray's *Mars and Venus Diet and Exercise Solution* uses hormonal differences in brain chemistry as the basis of the claim, 'Gender insight also directly relates to our health, happiness, and weight management . . .'

10　Just as news stories themselves are edited (choices of wording and even in structure may be changed by editors), so book and journal editors may change words, or demand changes from authors.

References

Banks, E. (1902) *The Autobiography of a Newspaper Girl*. New York: Dodd, Mead.

Chambers, D., Steiner, L. and Fleming, C. (2004) *Women and Journalism*. New York and London: Routledge.

Ebener, C. (1955) *No Facilities for Women*. New York: Alfred Knopf.

Elwood-Akers, V. (1988) *Women War Correspondents in the Vietnam War 1961–1975*. Metuchen, NJ: Scarecrow Press.

Fawcett, D., Mariano, A. B., Webb, K. *et al.* (2002) *War Torn: Stories of War from the Women Reporters who Covered Vietnam*. New York: Random House.

Higgins, M. (1955) *News is a Singular Thing*. Garden City: Doubleday.

Holland, P. (1987) When a Woman Reads the News, in H. Baehr and G. Dyer (eds) *Boxed in: Women and Television*. London: Pandora, pp. 133–50.

Kuhn, I. (1938) *Assigned to Adventure*. Philadelphia: J.B. Lippincott.

Mills, K. (1997) What Difference do Women Journalists Make? In P. Norris (ed.) *Women, Media and Politics*. New York and Oxford: Oxford University Press.

Reilly, T. (1981) Jane McManus Storms: Letters from the Mexican War, 1846–1848, *Southwestern Historical Quarterly*, LXXXV: 22–44.

Rouvalis, C. and Schackner, B. (2000) Female Correspondents recall their historic role reporting from Vietnam. www.Post-Gazette.com/magazine/20000330namwomen2.asp (accessed 30 March 2003).

Rubin, G. (1975) The Traffic in Women: Notes on the Political Economy of Sex, in R. R. Reiter (ed.) *Towards an Anthropology of Women*. New York: Monthly Review Press.

Scott, J. W. (1999) *Gender and the Politics of History*. New York: Columbia University Press.

Sebba, A. (1994) *Battling for News: The Rise of the Woman Reporter*. London: Hodder & Stoughton.

Steiner, L. (1992) Conceptions of Gender in Newsreporting Textbooks, 1890–1990. *Journalism Monographs*, no. 135.

Steiner, L. (1997) Gender At Work: Early Accounts by Women Journalists, *Journalism History*, 23(1): 2–15.

Trotta, L. (1991) *Fighting for Air: In the Trenches with Television News*. New York: Simon & Schuster.

Von Mehren, J. (1994) *Minerva and the Muse: A Life of Margaret Fuller*. Amherst: University of Massachusetts Press.

Wagner, L. (1989) *Women War Correspondents of World War II*. New York: Greenwood.

Walker, S. (1934) *City Editor*. New York: Frederick A. Stokes.

Zoonen, L. van (1998) One of the Girls? The Changing Genre of Journalism, in C. Carter, G. Branston and S. Allan (eds) *News, Gender and Power*. London: Routledge.

Zoonen, L. van (1991) A Tyranny of Intimacy? Women, Femininity and Television News, in P. Dahlgren and C. Sparks (eds) *Communication and Citizenship: Journalism and the Public Sphere in the New Media Age*. London: Routledge.

| 4

Journalism ethics

Towards an Orwellian critique?

Richard Keeble

- Why is it important to highlight the political underpinnings of dominant media values?
- Why does the dominant ethical debate marginalize consideration of alternative, leftist media?
- How important is it to challenge radically both objectivity and subjectivity?
- What lessons can be drawn from George Orwell's attempts to confront journalistic ethical/political dilemmas and his commitment to authentic communication?

How do mainstream journalists discuss ethics?

When mainstream journalists and leading commentators discuss media ethics their views tend to fall within the following four main categories:

- The cynical, amoral approach according to which ethical issues have little relevance to journalists. The media, so the argument goes, are dominated by the profit motive (or ratings) and thus all talk of ethics is idealistic humbug. Linked to this view is the philosophical existentialist position (propounded by the nineteenth-century German, Max Stirner) which sees all human experience as immoral with all actions, however much they may be dressed up in the rhetoric of morality, as essentially egotistical (see Paterson 1971).

- The ethical relativist approach, which promotes *ad hoc* responses to ethical dilemmas. Formal codes of ethics – such as those promoted by the Press Complaints Commission, the National Union of Journalists and the new regulatory body, Ofcom – are rejected. As Bob Norris, former *Times* correspondent and associate director of PressWise, the media ethics body, comments on codes (Norris 2000: 325): 'They all have one thing in common: they are not worth the paper they are written on.' While he works according to his personal code of ethics, he stresses: 'Every story is different and every reporter is driven by a compulsion to get the story and get it first. To imagine that he or she is going to consult the union's code of ethics while struggling to meet a deadline is to live in cloud-cuckoo land.'

- The standard professional approach, which stresses journalists' commitment to agreed professional and trade union codes of ethics and editorial guidelines. Accordingly, ethical codes are seen as helping create a collective conscience for the profession. Linked to this approach is the notion that journalists have a social responsibility to serve the public interest. Thus while it is acknowledged that the profit motive and concern for ratings can influence journalists' conduct, it is stressed the market can operate benignly in the interests of everyone (Whale 1972). Professionalism also promotes the view that journalists' basic responsibilities are to be objective, neutral, detached, balanced, fair, accurate – and to distinguish clearly between fact and opinion. The media are seen as crucial to the promotion of democratic values reflecting society in all its complexity and with as many (legal) viewpoints as possible covered.

- The liberal professional approach which concentrates almost entirely on mainstream issues – criticizing the standard professional perspective from a range of standpoints. It may highlight the decline in the public service ethos (particularly in broadcasting) and the supposed emphasis throughout all the 'dumbed down' media on celebrities, randy royals, sporting heroes and reality television 'personalities' (Greenslade 2004; Thussu 2003). In his seminal work, Neil Postgate (1985) argued that entertainment had become the supra-ideology: the natural format for the representation of all experience. In a similar vein, more recent critics have expressed concerns over the increasing emphasis in the mainstream media on tabloidization, infotainment and journalistic subjectivity. 'Facts' and 'information' are giving way to 'feelings', with 'hard' news being replaced by endless 'soft', human interest, sensational stories, often based on unacceptable invasions of privacy (Mayes 2000). Reports about politics are giving way to endless lifestyle features with Parliament declining as a source of news (Franklin 2004: 188–93). The growing control over the global media industry by a small group of multinational companies (such as those run by Rupert Murdoch and the Italian Silvio Berlusconi) also draws criticisms (Hargreaves 2003).

The radical approach

The last two approaches tend to dominate mainstream ethical discussions. A fifth, more useful, political approach is virtually eliminated. It stresses journalism's function as one of social reproduction in the interests of dominant groups and classes – not of the whole society. And many of the central pillars of the professional perspectives (the free press, democracy, the public interest, objectivity, neutrality) are exposed as myths. Thus, it highlights critically:

- The objective/subjective duality
- The centrality of the individual (rather than the group or community) within dominant ethical discourse and the personal/political duality
- The free press problematic
- The democratic façade and the accompanying marginalization of the activities of the secret state
- The pluralism problematic
- The mainstream/alternative media problematic with issues relating to alternative media virtually eliminated from the debate.

Challenging the myth of the objective/subjective duality

Michael Schudson (1978), Gaye Tuchman (1972), Stuart Allan (1999: 7–26) and others have identified the centrality of the notion of 'objectivity' to the formation of journalistic professionalism during the second half of the nineteenth century and early twentieth century in the US and Britain. *The Elements of Journalism* by Bill Kovach and Tom Rosenstiel (2001), has recently been promoted by Alan Rusbridger, editor of the *Guardian*, as a model primer for journalists – rather as *Observer* editor David Astor promoted Orwell's 1946 Horizon essay, *Politics and the English Language* (see Orwell 2001: 397–410), as a sort of style book for his staff. Significantly a Thomas Gradgrindian devotion to facts dominates the *Elements*. Journalism's first obligation is to the truth, they say. All of the journalists interviewed for a survey by the Pew Research Centre for the People and the Press and the Committee of Concerned Journalists said 'getting the facts right' was journalists' major responsibility. Kovach and Rosenstiel speak alarmingly of 'an epistemological scepticism which has pervaded every aspect of our intellectual life – from art, literature, law, physics to even history', and of a 'new journalism of assertion which is overwhelming the old journalism of verification'.

Ian Hargreaves, formerly *Independent* and *New Statesman* editor, now of Ofcom, argues along with 2002 BBC Reith lecturer Onora O'Neill that the ethic of truthfulness and accuracy lies at the heart of journalism. But there is a certain hesitation as he adds: '. . . even if one accepts that neither quality is capable of incontestable definition'. Significantly, the National Union of Journalists' code of conduct (www.nuj.org.uk) stresses the importance of separating 'established fact' from 'comment and conjecture' and the Press Complaints Commission's code (www.pcc.org.uk) says newspapers, while free to be partisan, 'must distinguish between comment, conjecture and fact'.

Yet mainstream journalists' stubborn commitment to objectivity and the belief that 'fact' can be separated from 'comment' not only flies in the face of the postmodernist critique of the Enlightenment dualities – which prioritized the intellect over emotion, mind over body, head over heart, the objective over the subjective; by suggesting the pursuit of information can be value free, the ideology of objectivity also serves to marginalize the ethical and political dimensions within the dominant journalistic culture. As Brian McNair argues (1996: 33): 'News is never a mere recording or reporting of the world "out there" but a synthetic, value-laden account which carries within it dominant assumptions and ideas of the society within which it is produced.'

Significantly, some mainstream journalists become outspoken advocates of subjectivity as a way of challenging the myths of objectivity. For instance, James Cameron, the anti-nuclear peace campaigner who, during the Vietnam war, dared to portray the North Vietnamese as humans rather than communist monsters, commented: 'It never occurred to me, in such a situation, to be other than subjective. I have always tended to argue that objectivity was of less importance than the truth' (quoted in Keeble 2001a: 133). But the notion of 'subjective truth' needs to be radically challenged too. As Myra Macdonald (2003: 75) argues there can be both positives – such as Cameron's reporting – and negatives in subjectivity:

> Subjectivity can take very different forms, however, and some of these may aid knowledge formation. Self-reflexivity on the part of reporters and presenters enables better understanding of the discursive constitution of their account and dispels the myth of objectivity whereas a more egotistical presentation of the investigating self encourages an absorption in personality that is more akin to celebrity adulation.

She usefully suggests a discourse on tabloidization or infotainment built around constructed oppositions between information and entertainment confuses the issues:

> Because of its association with categories and forms of classification that are themselves ideologically weighted in favour of Enlightenment principles, it can blind us to problems with conventional methods of communicating information and to opportunities in some of the movements away from these. Personalisation, in particular, is worthy of closer inspection as a multi-dimensional rather than a singular process.
>
> (Macdonald 2003: 78)

Thus journalists' engagement with the issues they are confronting and their participation in the events they are recording can end up appearing self-indulgent. For instance, Donal MacIntyre's televised investigations tended to over-glamourize his role as the 'heroic, brave' celebrity sleuth and, in the process, marginalize the social issues under review (Keeble 2001). But handled sensitively and creatively (and with an awareness of the profound political and economic factors impacting on the formation of personality) journalistic reflexivity can give new meaning and authenticity to their reporting.

Accordingly, pieces as diverse as George Orwell's often idiosyncratic 'As I please' personal columns in *Tribune* (see Keeble 2001b) and Arundhati Roy's (2004) impassioned, informed polemics against US imperialism can be acknowledged as excellent 'subjective' journalism. The American writers of the New Journalism school (such as Tom Wolfe, Joan Didion, Truman Capote and Norman Mailer), beginning in the 1960s, daringly exploited journalists' subjectivity and fictional, narrative techniques (see Wolfe 1975). But this style of writing never caught on in Britain – probably because of journalists' over-commitment to the conventions of objectivity. In other words, a critical subjectivity could not only improve standards in media content: it could also extend the boundaries of journalistic genres.

❚ Challenging the myth of the personal/political duality

The dominant ethical debate also tends to focus on the responsibilities of the individual professional journalist abstracted from any broader political context. Karen Sanders (2003), for instance, highlights a range of day-to-day ethical dilemmas for reporters – such as over deception, reconstructions, the reporting of terrorism, racism and homophobia, invasions of privacy, whistleblowers and chequebook journalism. Yet her strategy for making 'good' journalism falls back on the individual: their need to be socially responsible, accurate, accountable to colleagues, sources, the public and to themselves. She quotes approvingly BBC journalist John Simpson: 'All you can do is make sure your conscience is as clear as a profession full of compromise and uncertainty will allow it to be.'

There are problems here. In the face of the enormous cultural, ideological and financial power of the dominant media and their hierarchically organized management structures, it is not surprising that isolated journalists (driven by their consciences) feel impotent to effect change. The professional ethic emerges out of the Western tradition of individualism (from the Protestant revolution, through the Enlightenment philosophers, John Locke and John Stuart Mill) – but the individual's conscience is, paradoxically, not protected by the UK codes. In March 2004, calls by the National Union of Journalists, the Commons select committee on culture, media and sport and the pressure group MediaWise to include a conscience clause in the Press Complaint's Commission's code of practice (providing a right to journalists rather than a responsibility) was significantly rejected.

Instead of the individual's conscience, the radical critique prioritizes the social, political and economic underpinnings of dominant media 'values' and routines (Hallin 1986: 10). The positioning of the media within dominant globalized, hyper-monopolized economic structures of exploitation and their close ties to global military-industrial complexes are identified as crucial determinants on standards (Keeble 1998; McChesney 2000). And the debate about journalistic ethics and objectivity becomes rooted in questions relating to politics, power and interest. Thus according to Des Freedman (2003), the actions of the millions of people globally who took to the streets on 15 February 2003 in protest against the Iraq invasion were 'more likely to create a space and a need for passionate, critical and contextualized reporting than a naïve belief in the power and professionalism of the traditional reporter'.

The free press problematic

The notion of the free press/media is a central feature of both the professional perspective and the dominant value system of Western capitalist societies. As John O'Neill comments (1992: 15):

> A free market brings with it a free press that supplies the diversity of opinion and access to information that a citizenry requires in order to act in a democratic, responsible manner. The free market, journalism and democracy form an interdependent trinity of institutions in an open society.

In a similar, quasi-religious vein, Charles Moore (1997), then editor of the *Daily Telegraph*, described the 1997 general election as 'the sacred moment in a democracy'. He continued: 'The people's choice is what validates the whole process. Newspapers must try to give their readers all the material they need to make that choice.'

Linked to the notion of the free press is the Renaissance/Enlightenment concept of the free individual – since without the freedom to choose, it could be argued, ethics becomes meaningless – as well as the notion of the press/media as the Fourth Estate. First propounded by the historian Thomas Babington Macaulay (1800–59), for whom the first three estates of the realm were the Lords temporal, Lords spiritual and the Commons, this concept highlights the watchdog function of the media in providing checks on abuses by both professionals and government. Accordingly, journalists assume the role of 'public guardians', protecting them against the failures of the authorities. This role is best reflected in the many campaigns local and national media run bringing authorities to account and exposing corruption.

Radical critics tend to highlight the economic roots of campaigning journalism, however, suggesting that journalists' claims to be operating freely as a noble Fourth Estate in the interests of the public, are mere rhetoric. As Colin Sparks (1999: 46) argues:

> Newspapers in Britain are first and foremost businesses. They do not
> exist to report news, to act as watchdogs for the public, to be a check on
> the doings of government, to defend ordinary citizens against the abuses
> of power, to unearth scandals or do any of the other fine and noble
> things that are sometimes claimed for the press. They exist to make
> money, just as any business does. To the extent that they discharge any
> of their public functions, they do so in order to succeed as businesses.

Significantly, the consistent anti-war, anti-racism and anti-sexism campaigns
of the alternative media are largely ignored by mainstream commentators
and academics.

The myth of democracy – and the secret state

Andrew Belsey (1998: 11) sums up the conventional view of media ethics.
For him, the 'reality of ethical journalism' is 'journalism based on the idea
of virtuous conduct, facilitating the democratic process and serving the public interest'. But for radical critics, even the notion of democracy, which
underpins the professional approach, is a myth serving to legitimize the rule
of the few over the many – both nationally and internationally. Daniel
Hellinger and Denis Judd (1991: 9–10) outline three main areas used by
elites for creating a sense of democratic legitimacy: the educational institutions, which assume the crucial task of inculcating in each new generation a
political ideology that legitimates the State, the mass media, which are 'pivotal for socializing mass publics into accepting sanctioned versions of political and economic reality', and finally the electoral processes, which are
elaborate, spectacular pageants experienced by most citizens vicariously
through television – providing 'ritualized opportunities for people to participate, as individuals and as members of a collective citizenry, in the
political process'.

Beyond this democratic façade lie massive institutional, military, financial
and cultural structures, which command the essential levers of power. In
particular, the professional perspective marginalizes the role of the secret
state in influencing the dominant news agenda – and mainstream journalists'
intimate links with it (Keeble 1997). In their analysis of the contemporary
secret state, Dorril and Ramsay (1991: x–xi) significantly give the media a
crucial role. The heart of the secret state they identify as the security services,
the Cabinet office and upper echelons of the Home and Commonwealth
Offices, the armed forces and Ministry of Defence, the nuclear power industry
and its satellite ministries together with a network of senior civil servants. As
'satellites' of the secret state, their list includes 'agents of influence in the
media, ranging from actual agents of the security services, conduits of
official leaks, to senior journalists merely lusting after official praise and,
perhaps, a knighthood at the end of their career'.

Identifying the precise extent of the links between hacks and spooks will always be difficult, but from the evidence available it appears enormous. Roy Greenslade, media specialist at the *Guardian*, has commented: 'Most tabloid newspapers – or even newspapers in general – are playthings of MI5' (see Milne 1994: 262), while Bloch and Fitzgerald (1983: 134–41) report the editor of 'one of Britain's most distinguished journals' as believing that more than half its foreign correspondents were on the MI6 payroll. In 1991, Richard Norton-Taylor revealed in the *Guardian* that 500 prominent Britons paid by the CIA and the now defunct Bank of Commerce and Credit International, included 90 journalists (Pilger 1998: 496). And Phillip Knightley, author of the seminal history of the intelligence services, has claimed they have a representative in every Fleet Street office (Keeble 2003).

During the row that erupted after the invasion of Iraq and the presumed suicide of arms inspector Dr David Kelly (and the ensuing Hutton inquiry) the spotlight fell on BBC Today reporter Andrew Gilligan and his source's claim that the Blair government (in collusion with the intelligence services) had 'sexed up' the September 2002 dossier justifying an invasion of Iraq. The Gilligan affair – and the later controversies over revelations by GCHQ worker Katherine Gun and former Cabinet minister Clare Short of intelligence service attempts to influence UN voting over a second resolution on the Iraq invasion – might appear to have reinforced the liberal notion of adversarial state-media relations. Yet, in fact, as Rogers (1997: 64) argues, 'this focus obscures the extent to which the media have actually supported and colluded with the secret state'. Significantly, the broader and more significant issues relating to mainstream journalists' links with the intelligence services were ignored by the inquiry and in the media coverage of the later controversies.

Similarly, the ethical dilemmas facing journalists when dealing with the intelligence services are hardly ever considered by mainstream theorists. According to *Guardian* journalist David Leigh (2000) reporters are routinely approached by intelligence agents. In a rare exploration of the issues, Leigh comments:

> I think the cause of honest journalism is best served by candour. We all ought to come clean about these approaches and devise some ethics to deal with them. In our vanity, we imagine we control these sources. But the truth is that they are very deliberately seeking to control us.

Most of the mainstream coverage of privacy invasion issues has focused on a stream of cases involving outraged celebrities – such as super-model Naomi Campbell, footballer Gary Flitcroft, television newsreader Anna Ford, Hollywood super-stars Catherine Zeta Jones and Michael Douglas, actress Amanda Holden and radio DJ Sara Cox – and the responses of the courts, various Commons committees, official inquiries and various regulatory bodies to these controversies (Mayes 2002). More serious threats to privacy come from the expanding secret state – with the moves by the security services and businesses to monitor and intercept e-mails and mobile phone conversations and the increasing presence of CCTVs in our everyday lives.

In particular, radical critics have highlighted the impact of the Regulation of Investigatory Powers Act (2000), which provides a statutory basis for the authorization and use by the security and intelligence agencies, law enforcement and other public authorities of covert surveillance, agents, informants and undercover officers (see www.privacyinternational.org).

The pluralism problematic

The professional perspective also stresses the notion of the mainstream media as functioning essentially to promote political and cultural pluralism. While it is acknowledged that the media operate according to the demands of a profit-oriented economy (with the BBC increasingly ratings led), it is still argued that the market can function benignly within the public interest – particularly when journalists exercise their social responsibilities (McQuail 1987: 116–17). Radical critics challenge these notions, highlighting the consensual values operating throughout the mainstream media with the range of opinions expressed being confined within clearly observable parameters. Thus, the collusion between propagandist dominant media and the national security state in the manufacture of consent to the status quo becomes a critical issue. Particular attention has focused on the media's coverage of a series of US/UK military adventures since the 1980s (the Falklands in 1982, Grenada 1983, Libya 1986, Panama 1989, Iraq in 1991, 1993, 1998 and 2003, Somalia in 1992–93, Kosovo/Serbia in 1999 and Afghanistan in 2001) and their role in largely legitimizing government actions and undermining dissent (Keeble 1997; Taylor 1998; Goff 1999; Hammond and Herman 2000; Miller 2004).

Mainstream theorists, such as Siebert, Peterson and Schramm (1963) in their seminal study, *Four Theories of the Press*, tend to see propaganda as a useful concept to apply to the media of totalitarian dictatorships and applicable to Western democracies only at exceptional periods of crisis or war. Edward Herman and Noam Chomsky, in contrast (1988: xi), present a propaganda model, which they see as applicable to the performance of Western media systems at all times with elites 'able to fix the premises of discourse, to decide what the general populace is allowed to see, hear and think about and to manage public opinion by regular propaganda campaigns'.

The alternative/mainstream dilemma

Most significantly, the mainstream ethical consensus succeeds in silencing virtually all consideration of the leftist alternative media – their ethical standards and contrasting histories (often of survival against the odds), work routines and organizational regimes (Harcup 2003). In effect, the definition of journalism operating within the dominant media (and academic) discourse is amazingly narrow. James Curran and Myung-Jin Park, in their seminal study, *De-Westernizing Media Studies* (2000: 3), refer to a 'minority tradition with a global orientation'. Typically the focus will be on London-based mainstream media with occasional references to controversies in the United States and elsewhere (but c.f. Sparks and Tulloch 2000). The diverse ethnic, trade union, religious, environmental, pacifist, revolutionary, anti-globalization, leftist, community, feminist media – many now Internet based and organized on cooperative lines – are largely ignored (c.f. Harcup 1994).

Atton (2003) warns against perpetuating another binary opposition – this time between alternative and mainstream media – as he illuminates the complex, often hybrid nature of the alternative media sector (from which racist and fascist publications are automatically excluded). Challenging conventional notions of objectivity, alternative media workers, according to Atton, link ethics and politics deliberately in their practices.

> Sceptical of what counts as balance in the mainstream media, they seek to set up their own counter-balance. Hence, the argument runs, the viewpoints already dominant in the mainstream media do not need repeating. What appears as bias and the absence of bias in the alternative media is to be considered not as a set of absolute truths: instead, it comprises a set of accounts told from different perspectives.
>
> (Atton 2003: 28)

These are important perspectives rarely considered in the mainstream media.

Conclusions: George Orwell to the rescue?

Ultimately I am suggesting we need to break away from the old Cartesian dualities: emotion and reason, objectivity and subjectivity, head and heart, thought and action, culture and nature – and seek new paradigms. And just as objectivity needs to be radically problematized – so too do our subjectivities.

But breaking away from these Cartesian certainties we enter shaky, unsettled territory. Can journalists operate among such uncertainties? George Orwell, I feel, offers a tentative solution. For him, the primary ethical/political decision made by the journalist was over the choice of outlet. Since he realized mainstream journalism was basically propaganda for wealthy newspaper proprietors, so he concentrated most of his writing (though not all) for small-scale, left-wing publications in Britain and the US. In this way he was engaging in the crucial political debate with the people who mattered to him. They were an authentic audience compared with what Stuart Allan (1999: 131) calls the 'implied reader or imagined community of readers of the mainstream media'. So some of the greatest journalism of the last century appeared in relatively obscure left wing journals – such as

Adelphi; *New English Weekly*; *Fortnightly Review*; *Tribune; Left News*; *Polemic*; *Progressive*; *Persuasion*.

In 1945, as the Nazi empire was crumbling, Orwell travelled to continental Europe as the *Observer*'s war correspondent. In all he despatched 14 articles (each roughly 1000 words long) to the *Observer* and five to the *Manchester Evening News* (Keeble 2001b). All the best elements of the journalistic style – immediacy, clarity, a sense of urgency, an ability to highlight the most interesting, a facility both to generalize effectively and to focus on the specific, relevant detail; an economy of language even within colourful, descriptive, eye-witness reportage; a political and moral stance; an openness to conflicting views – are evident in his reports (which have generally been either ignored or damned as dull). But, trapped within the Cartesian duality, he attempts both to admit subjectivity and yet acquire objectivity through assuming various voices – that of the newcomer, the eye-witness and the overhearer of conversations. Or he emerges as the confident essayist or secure in the first person. Orwell's voice emerges as one of vitality and power – but also one that is uncertain and troubled.

Yet through his radical engagement with both objectivity and subjectivity and his commitment to authentic communication, Orwell, in his writings, radicalized the content of journalism and its form. In his essays he virtually invented the discipline of cultural studies while in works such as *Down and Out in Paris and London*, *The Road to Wigan Pier* and *Homage to Catalonia* he mixed fiction, eyewitness reportage, biography, ethnographic study, political polemic and media content analysis. Orwell's voice in his 1945 articles significantly points to questions rather than answers. What is the authentic voice of the genre? What precisely is a journalist? What are the essential journalistic dilemmas? They remain crucial questions today.

References

Allan, S. (1999) *News Culture*. Buckingham: Open University Press.

Atton, C. (2003) Ethical Issues in Alternative Journalism, *Ethical Space: The International Journal of Communication Ethics*, 1(1): 26–31.

Belsey, A. (1998) Journalism and Ethics: Can they Co-exist? In M. Kiernan (ed.) *Media Ethics*, London: Routledge, pp. 1–14.

Bloch, J. and Fitzgerald, P. (1983) *British Intelligence and Covert Action*. London: Junction Books.

Curran, J. and Park, M.-J. (2000) *De-Westernizing Media Studies*. London: Routledge.

Dorril, S. and Ramsay, R. (1991) *Smear*. London: Fourth Estate.

Franklin, B. (2004) *Packaging Politics: Political Communications in Britain's Media Democracy*. London: Arnold.

Freedman, D. (2003) Witnessing whose truth? Available at http://www.opendemocracy.net/debates/article-8-92-1007.jsp. Accessed on 5 April 2004.

Goff, P. (ed.) (1999) *The Kosovo News and Propaganda War*. Vienna: International Press Institute.

Greenslade, R. (2004) Do these People have a Right to Privacy? *Guardian*, 26 January.

Hallin, D. (1986) *The 'Uncensored' War*. Oxford: Oxford University Press.

Hammond, P. and Herman, E. (eds) (2000) *Degraded Capability: The Media and the Kosovo Crisis*. London: Pluto Press.

Harcup, T. (1994) *A Northern Star: Leeds Other Paper and the Alternative Press 1974–1994*. London and Pontefract: Campaign for Press and Broadcasting Freedom.

Harcup, T. (2003) The Unspoken – Said: The Journalism of Alternative Media, *Journalism*, 4(3): 356–76.

Hargreaves, I. (2003) *Journalism: Truth or Dare?* Oxford: Oxford University Press.

Hellinger, D. and Judd, D. R. (1991) *The Democratic Façade*. Belmont, CA: Wadsworth.

Herman, E. and Chomsky, N. (1988) *Manufacturing Consent: The Political Economy of Mass Media*. New York: Pantheon Books. (Reissued 1994, London: Vintage Books.)

Keeble, R. (1997) *Secret State, Silent Press: New Militarism, the Gulf and the Modern Image of Warfare*. Luton: John Libbey.

Keeble, R. (1998) The Politics of Sleaze Reporting: A Critical Overview of the Ethical Debate in the British Press of the 1990s, *Recherches en Communication*, 9: 71–81.

Keeble, R. (2001a) *Ethics for Journalists*. London: Routledge.

Keeble, R. (2001b) Orwell as War Correspondent: a Reassessment, *Journalism Studies* 2(3): 393–406.

Keeble, R. (2003) Spooks are Represented on Every Newspaper, *Press Gazette*, 9 October.

Kovach, B. and Rosenstiel, T. (2001) *The Elements of Journalism*. London: Guardian Books.

Leigh, D. (2000) Britain's Security Services and Journalists: the Secret Story, *British Journalism Review*, 11(2): 21–6. Available online at www.bjr.org.uk/data/2000/no2_leigh.htm. Accessed on 27 March 2004.

McChesney, R. W. (2000) *Rich Media, Poor Democracy: Communication Politics in Dubious Times*. New York: The New Press.

McNair, B. (1996) *News and Journalism in the UK*. London: Routledge.

McQuail, D. (1987) *Mass Communication Theory: An Introduction*. London/Newbury Park: Sage.

Macdonald, M. (2003) *Exploring Media Discourse*. London: Arnold.

Mayes, T. (2000) Submerging in 'Therapy News', *British Journalism Review*, 11(4): 30–6.

Mayes, T. (2002) *Restraint or Revelation: Free Speech and Privacy in a Confessional Age*, London, spiked-online. Available online at http://www.spiked-online.com/articles/00000006DAC6.htm. Accessed on 27 March 2004.

Miller, D. (ed.) (2004) *Tell me Lies: Propaganda and Media Distortion in the Attack on Iraq*. London: Pluto.

Milne, S. (1994) *The Enemy Within: The Secret War Against the Miners*, London: Pan, p. 61.

Moore, C. (1997) The Right Way to Tell it, *Guardian*, 14 April.

Norris, B. (2000) Media Ethics at the Sharp End, in D. Berry (ed.) *Ethics and Media Culture: Practices and Representations*. Oxford: Focal Press.

O'Neill, J. (1992) Journalism in the Market Place, in A. Belsey and R. Chadwick (eds). *Ethical Issues in Journalism and the Media*. London: Routledge, pp. 15–22.

Orwell, G. (2001) *Orwell and Politics*, P. Davison (ed.). London: Penguin Books.

Paterson, R. W. K. (1971) *The Nihilistic Egoist: Max Stirner*. Oxford: Oxford University Press.

Pilger, J. (1998) *Hidden Agendas*. London: Vintage.

Postgate, N. (1985) *Amusing Ourselves to Death*. London: William Heinemann.

Rogers, A. (1997) *Secrecy and Power in the British State: A History of the Official Secrets Act*. London: Pluto.

Roy, A. (2004) *The Ordinary Person's Guide to Empire*. London: Flamingo.

Sanders, K. (2003) *Ethics and Journalism*. London: Sage.

Seibert, F., Peterson, T. and Schramm, W. (1963) *Four Theories of the Press*. Urbana: University of Illinois Press.

Schudson, M. (1978) *Discovering the News: A Social History of American Newspapers*. New York: Basic Books.

Sparks, C. (1999) The Press, in J. Stokes and A. Reading (eds) *The Media in Britain: Current Debates and Developments*. Basingstoke: Macmillan, pp. 41–60.

Sparks, C. and Tulloch, J. (2000) *Tabloid Tales*. London, Boulder, New York: Rowman & Littlefield.

Taylor, J. (1998) *Body Horror: Photojournalism, Catastrophe and War*. Manchester: Manchester University Press.

Tuchman, G. (1972) Objectivity as Strategic Ritual: An Examination of Newsmen's Notions of Objectivity, *American Journal of Sociology*, 77(4): 660–79.

Thussu, D. K. (2003) Live TV and Bloodless Deaths: War, Infotainment and 24/7 News, in D. K. Thussu and D. Freeman (eds) *War and the Media*. London: Sage, pp. 117–32.

Whale, J. (1972) *Journalism and Government*. London: Macmillan.

Wolfe, T. (1975) *The New Journalism*. London: Picador.

5

News on the Web

The emerging forms and practices of online journalism

Stuart Allan

- What can a historical perspective tell us about online journalism today?
- Which reportorial innovations helped to attract public attention to news on the Web in the early days?
- To what extent have the forms and practices of online journalism become conventionalized?
- What factors are shaping the gradual consolidation of these conventions?

For reasons that will be made apparent, I wish to begin this chapter about online journalism by noting the recent passing of veteran broadcast journalist and news anchor, David Brinkley. Brinkley's television career began in 1951 as a correspondent with the *Camel News Caravan*, where he played a key role in introducing television news to US audiences. In October 1956, the *Caravan* was replaced by *The Huntley-Brinkley Report*, which featured co-anchors Brinkley in Washington, DC and Chet Huntley in New York City. As the NBC network's flagship television newscast, it was widely credited for developing a number of innovative features over the years. Following Brinkley's retirement in 1970, the programme was renamed *NBC Nightly News*.

On the occasion of Brinkley's death on 11 June 2003, Tom Brokaw, current anchor of *NBC Nightly News*, recalled: 'David Brinkley was an icon of modern broadcast journalism, a brilliant writer who could say in a few words what the country needed to hear during times of crisis, tragedy and triumph' (cited in Haberman 2003). Evidently years earlier, when asked in an interview what he thought his legacy to television news would be, Brinkley had remarked:

> [E]very news program on the air looks essentially as we started it (with *The Huntley-Brinkley Report*). We more or less set the form for broadcasting news on television which is still used. No one has been able to think of a better way to do it.
>
> (cited in Waite 2003)

In an essay adapted from his memoirs, however, Brinkley's (2003) views on the current state of television news could hardly have been more critical. He wrote:

> TV anchors and reporters serve the useful function of delivering the goods, attractively wrapped in the hope of attracting some millions of people to tune in. In recent decades, I fear, the wrapping has sometimes become too attractive and much television news, in response to economic pressures, competition and perhaps a basic lack of commitment to the integrity and value of the enterprise, has become so trivial and devoid of content as to be little different from entertainment programming. But even at its best, television news is driven less by the ideology of those who deliver it than by the pressures of the medium itself. And as a result, individual journalists, from the anchors to the local news beat reporters, are all constrained in their power by the skepticism of a public that from the beginning saw in television something closer to the tradition of entertainment (movies, theater and the like) than to the tradition of the press.

> (Brinkley 2003)

These words, written by someone who played such a significant part in helping to consolidate the conventions of television journalism, deserve careful attention. Not only do they constitute a warning about the future direction of television news, but Brinkley also makes the crucial point that it is 'the pressures of the medium itself' that are necessarily shaping its ongoing configuration. That is to say, the basic tensions engendered 'from the beginning' between the 'tradition of entertainment' and the 'tradition of the press' continue to inform its development, for better and – clearly in his view – for worse.

My rationale for discussing Brinkley's argument is probably becoming clear by now. It is my contention that we are currently witnessing a similar process of consolidation where the forms and practices of online journalism are concerned. The types of issues he touched upon regarding the early days of television news resound in current debates about how best to realize the extraordinary potential of online news sites, not least with respect to – using his phrase – their 'useful function of delivering the goods' for diverse publics around the globe. As this chapter will show, of course, news sites are hardly immune from the types of economic pressures, competition from rival news organizations, and concerns about reportorial commitment and integrity that his views highlight in relation to television news. Arguably more challenging to discern, however, are the 'pressures of the medium itself' associated with online journalism, namely because of its still relatively inchoate status. And yet, to the extent that these pressures are tacitly characterized as taken-for-granted features of the medium, they become all the more difficult to change.

Breaking news online

Over the course of this chapter's discussion, certain formative instances in the early development of online journalism will be identified and assessed. In adopting a historical perspective, I wish to emphasize from the outset that each of them needs to be seen as being indicative of a complex – and always contradictory – array of imperatives. To the extent that it is possible to map the contours of these imperatives, especially in terms of the dynamics which imbue their logics, it is likely that they will be more apparent in retrospect than they were at the time. That said, however, from the vantage point of today, it is difficult to appreciate the socially contingent, frequently contested nature of their lived negotiation. Any sense of inevitability where these formative processes are concerned, then, must be resisted at all costs.

Bearing this in mind, a consideration of the online reporting of the Oklahoma City bombing of 19 April 1995 is an appropriate point of departure. Thrown into sharp relief on that tragic day was the potential Internet news sites possessed for providing breaking news at a time when the World Wide Web was in its infancy. It was 9.02 am on the Wednesday morning when a rented truck, packed with some 4,800 lb. of explosives, detonated in front of the Alfred P. Murrah Building, a nine-storey concrete office block housing a number of federal government agencies. The resultant blast, it was claimed, could be felt over 15 miles away. Described by authorities at the time as the worst terrorist attack ever to take place on US soil, the bombing reportedly killed 168 people, including 19 children who attended a day-care centre on the second floor, and wounded more than 500 more. Approximately 90 minutes after the explosion, Timothy McVeigh was stopped by the police for driving without a licence plate near the town of Billings. Found to be carrying a concealed weapon, he was promptly arrested. Two days later, as he was about to be released, McVeigh was identified as a bombing suspect. Also that day, Terry Nichols, a friend of McVeigh, surrendered in Herington, Kansas. He and his brother, James Nichols, were held as material witnesses. Like McVeigh, Terry Nichols would be eventually indicted on 11 counts for the bombing. Both men pleaded not guilty at separate arraignments in Oklahoma City's federal courthouse in August of that year.

In 1995, a time when news Web sites were typically little more than repositories of reports previously published elsewhere, the role of the Internet in creating spaces for information to circulate that fateful day in April has since been hailed as a landmark moment in online history. Worthy of particular attention at the time was the immediacy of the news coverage, as well as its volume and breadth. Minutes after the bombing, journalists and their editors at online news services were rushing to post whatever information they could about the tragedy. 'Within an hour of the blast', stated Beth Copeland, deputy managing editor at *Newsday Direct*, 'we had a locator map of Oklahoma City, the latest AP [Associated Press] story, [and] a graphic talking about various types of bombs used in terrorist attacks' (cited in Agrawal 1995). Elsewhere on the Web, eyewitnesses posted their descriptions of the excavation scene, often with heart-rending details. Others transcribed news reports, especially with regard to the disaster relief work underway. Listings of survivors, and the hospitals treating them (complete with telephone contact details) similarly began to appear. For people anxious to contact relatives but unable to get through on long-distance telephone lines, some Oklahoma City residents offered to make local calls for them. Discussion forums called newsgroups appeared, where people gave expression to their rage, others to their grief, while still others offered emergency aid for victims. Such was also the case with online chat rooms, where several Internet service providers (ISPs) opened multiple rooms dedicated to sharing views about the bombing. CompuServe's Daphne Kent described the chat rooms she visited as the most emotional she had seen, apparently due to the fact children had been killed and 'it could have happened anywhere' (cited in Haring 1995).

As quickly as it could manage, the *Oklahoma City Daily* began to post related stories, as did local television station KFOR, 'where people could query station staff about events and inquire about the station's progress in getting word out to the rest of the broadcast media' (Oakes 1995). Internet service providers such as America Online, created repositories devoted to the bombing, making available news feeds from the wire services. Prodigy and AT&T Interchange also offered their members news coverage of ongoing developments (as did CompuServe, although not on the first day). Evidently within 3 hours of the explosion, Newsday Direct users were able to ask questions of an expert, author and retired Navy Seal Richard Marcinko, on the service's bulletin boards (Agrawal 1995). For many of the newspapers with an online presence, such as the *New York Times* with its @times site or the *Chicago Tribune*'s Chicago Online, it would be near the end of the day before a pertinent story was posted. Few offered much by way of provision for unfolding news events beyond copy taken from the wire services, preferring instead to post the daily's news items once they had been published. News photographs were particularly rare. The site associated with the *San Jose Mercury News*, along with that operated by *Time* magazine, were among the very few able to post photographs. ABC News made a video clip available to users of its service on America Online, although it apparently took 11 minutes to download what was a grainy, postage-stamp size 15 s clip, even with the fastest modem connection available (Agrawal 1995; Hanson 1997). Beginning the next day the amount of online coverage improved, with some news sites also allowing users to access archived stories on terrorism, militia groups and related topics.

Confusion reigned over who was responsible for the bombing. Many mainstream news organizations, such as CNN, repeated unfounded rumours that 'three men of Middle Eastern extraction' were the prime suspects. Other experts called upon to conjecture, pointed out that 19 April was the second anniversary of the disastrous assault by Federal agents on the Branch Davidian compound near Waco, Texas, which ended in the death of 80 people (the agency blamed for the ill-fated operation had offices in the destroyed

Oklahoma City building). In the ensuing whirl of speculation, where claim and counter-claim clashed, people were turning to the Internet for breaking developments in numbers never seen before. There too, however, much heat was being generated, with little light. The Internet's capacity to place an astonishing amount of information at the user's fingertips was not without its pitfalls. Talk of conspiracies concerning the bombing resounded across the Web, especially in the case of sites used by members of right-wing militias, pro-gun groups, neo-Nazis, survivalists and similar conspiratorially inclined organizations. 'To those who've followed the coverage of the Oklahoma City bombing,' observed Todd Copilevitz (1995), 'it might seem like the tools of terrorism are teeming across the Net.' Many analysts and politicians were incensed that technical instructions regarding how to make a copy of the bomb used to destroy the office building, which reportedly used a combination of ammonium nitrate fertilizer and racing fuel, were all too readily available. Was the Internet responsible, some wanted to know, for inciting the violence of extremists? 'Fast-spreading computer technology' was being recurrently blamed for allowing disaffected individuals and groups to communicate with one another, and thereby spread their messages of hate. 'In the past, someone who held those views was in isolation, was disenfranchised', argued one commentator in a *Washington Post* article. 'With this technology,' he added, 'they can gather. They couldn't even find each other before' (cited in Schwartz 1995).

In the aftermath of the national crisis engendered by the Oklahoma City bombing, advocates of the Internet insisted that it had proved itself to be an indispensable news and information resource. Critics, in sharp contrast, were sceptical about the value of news sites, arguing that they were slow to react, and in the main offered news that was otherwise available in evening newspapers or on television. Others pointed to technical glitches, observing that several of the major news sites had ground to a halt because they were overwhelmed with demand in the early hours, when they would have been especially valuable (Andrews 1995). For Rosenberg (1995), writing in the *San Francisco Examiner*, all of the 'post-Oklahoma traffic between the on-line world and the news media represents a coming of age for relations between the two realms.' Cyberspace, he argued, was fast becoming a 'real place', one which acted as a 'kind of transnational meeting ground where people talk, rumors spread and news happens, and where reporters need to know the customs and pitfalls, or risk massive goofs'. In his view, the Oklahoma story created a type of 'feedback loop' between the news media and the online community, which possessed the potential to be either informative or treacherous depending on the amount of care used by reporters.

Nevertheless, analyses of Internet traffic in the first two weeks after the bombing discerned dramatic increases in the 'hits' registered by online news sites. 'Broadcast is no longer the only medium for breaking news,' stated Bruce Siceloff, editor at NandOnet, the online service of the *News and Observer* in Raleigh, North Carolina. 'We didn't have to stop a press to replate,' he added.

There were no deadlines. No readers who lost out because they got an early edition . . . Like CNN and radio, we can and did break and update and expand the story on a minute's notice – numerous times in a single hour.

(cited in Agrawal 1995)

According to Siceloff's figures, the weekly count of hits for the NandOnet site grew by about 300,000 a week for the first two weeks, reaching 2.37 million hits for the week that ended 30 April. Of particular interest to users, he argued, was the wealth of information from primary sources available online (such as the University of Oklahoma's student newspaper, the White House, relief agencies, pro- and anti-militia groups, and so forth), its instant availability, and also the opportunity to interact (Agrawal 1995; Kenworthy 1997; Weise 1997).

Of fact and fakery

Discussions about the potential of the Internet as a news source assumed a far greater salience in journalism's inner circles in the months following the Oklahoma City bombing. For those in the newspaper industry it was becoming increasingly obvious that they would not be able to compete with their electronic rival where breaking news was concerned. This was particularly so at a time of crisis, when people's need for information to provide context to rapidly unfolding events was of paramount importance. As Chris Oakes (1995) wrote at the time of the bombing, information is the lifeblood of the Internet.

Information in the form of raw news, opinion, condolence and all else that spews from connected humans when their world goes haywire. Perhaps more than any Web use, this Internet response to a national tragedy presages what the future of online will be (Oakes 1995).

The reliability of the information available online increasingly became a matter of dispute in the months to come, however, particularly with respect to the circumstances surrounding the crash of TWA flight 800. On 17 July 1996, the Boeing 747 airliner, *en route* from New York to Paris, plunged into the Atlantic Ocean off eastern Long Island. All 230 people onboard were killed. Beginning with the breaking news reports, speculation was rife as to who or what might have been responsible for the explosion, which took place about 20 minutes into the flight. A number of eyewitnesses offered their perspectives in these reports, several of whom were convinced that they had seen some type of object or streak of light closing in at high speed on the airliner. Several 'terrorism experts', called upon for their views, were quick to blame Arabs and Muslims for the explosion (echoes of Oklahoma City), contending that a bomb was surely involved (Husseini 1997). Others insisted that its cause would probably prove to be due to some sort of mechanical failure or design flaw in the airliner, among other technical possibilities. In the ensuing rush to judgement, a number of mainstream journalists recurrently relied on anonymous sources, some of the more far-fetched of which were attributed to the Internet. At the same time, however, the Internet was being recognized as an important resource for official inquiries into the crash. In the case of the Federal Bureau of Investigation (FBI), for example, its New York homepage address was regularly mentioned at press conferences, together with an appeal for help to determine the cause (both an e-mail address and a toll-free telephone number were provided). The homepage reportedly received more than 1,500 pieces of information in the days immediately following the crash, some of which was described as being 'extremely valuable' by a spokesperson (Chester and Shotnicki 1996).

In the days that followed, as speculation about the reason for the crash became evermore intense, something resembling a consensus had begun to emerge across several online newsgroups. The preferred theory was that the TWA 800 had been accidentally shot down by a US navy cruiser engaged in exercises off the coast of Long Island, a tragic case of so-called 'friendly fire'. According to *Sunday Times* reporter James Adams (1996), the theory first appeared in the alt.conspiracy.com newsgroup, from where it copied and circulated to other newsgroups, such as activism.militia, survivalism.com and impeach.clinton.com. It was further amplified, in turn, by local television news stations, to the point where it began to surface in mainstream news reports around the world. 'Within a week of the crash', Adams wrote, 'the friendly fire story was the hot topic of Washington dinner parties and had already been investigated and dismissed by the Pentagon.' The Pentagon's refusal to affirm the theory engendered, not surprisingly, allegations of a government cover-up. One popular explanation for the alleged cover-up 'making the rounds on the Internet', Dennis Duggan (1996) reported in *Newsday*, was that 'the plane was targeted because two Arkansas state troopers who were once part of Bill Clinton's security detail were on their way to Paris to tell all about Clinton's extra-curricular affairs to *Le Monde*.' This story, he maintained, was printed in the *Miami Herald*.

For those following the conspiracy claims being made, events took an unexpected turn in November of the same year. Speaking at an aviation conference in Cannes, Pierre Salinger, a former ABC News correspondent (and one-time press secretary to President John F. Kennedy), made a startling announcement. To the astonishment of his audience, he claimed that he was in possession of evidence proving that the TWA 800 had been shot down by US forces. His allegation, based on a report that he insisted had been obtained from a French intelligence agent, created a media sensation. Days later, however, Salinger was made to acknowledge what certain Internet commentators were pointing out, namely that the report with its apparently authoritative details had been in circulation on the Web for several weeks. Crash investigators at the FBI, as well as the National Transportation Safety Board, were scathing in their criticism, with one official from the latter describing the retired Salinger as a 'once-respected journalist' (cited in Harris 1996). Much of the mainstream media criticism went beyond Salinger, however, focusing instead on the Internet as a platform for delivering spurious information. Newspaper critics were particularly harsh, some contending that facts rarely get in the way of a good conspiracy on the Internet.

Television journalists, typically much less troubled by the rise of the Internet than their counterparts in the press, were strongly critical as well. 'Forgery, fakery, falsehoods – they're everywhere on the Internet,' declared Leslie Stahl of CBS's popular news programme, *60 Minutes*, in a story that addressed the alleged 'cover-up' concerning the TWA 800. 'And rumors are so rampant', she added, 'that cyberspace is becoming a dangerous place . . .' (transcript, *60 Minutes*, 2 March 1997). Less than a fortnight after the programme was broadcast, Salinger reiterated his allegations at a Paris news conference, this time releasing a 69-page document and radar images to support his contention. Assistant FBI Director, James Kallstrom, promptly derided the charges. 'It's the big lie,' he stated. 'There's no facts. It's based on Internet gossip, hearsay, things that can't be substantiated, [and] faulty analysis' (cited in Rashbaum 1997). Shortly afterwards, Maggie Canon, *ComputerLife*'s editor-in-chief, stated that she was one of several journalists who had received – and had decided to ignore – the same 'official military document' that Salinger interpreted as confirmation of his missile theory. 'The nature of the Internet leads people to more readily believe rumors too,' she commented. 'The Internet is often viewed by its users as an unfiltered, primary source of information and not to be distrusted like the traditional news media. There is almost an immediate acceptance of information on the Internet.' Still, she added, in actuality 'there are far more lies, rumors and hoaxes transmitted on the Internet than anywhere else' (cited in *PR Newswire*, 18 March 1997). Nevertheless, the value of the Internet was underscored by Ford Fessenden, a *Newsday* (Long Island) journalist, who won the Pulitzer Prize for his reporting of the crash. The newspaper's coverage, he observed, 'owes a deep debt to the technology of computer assisted reporting'. Describing his methods, he explained that 'hourly consultation of the Internet and daily querying of safety databases became routine . . . Computer-assisted reporting has the ability to transform public understanding of aviation safety' (cited in Campbell 1997). Reporters like Fessenden, although still very much in the minority, were making inroads in the struggle to change perceptions of this medium and its potential.

Immediacy, depth, interactivity

Notions such as 'new media', and with it 'computer-assisted reporting', were slowly becoming a part of the journalistic lexicon. For every journalist heralding the promise of new technological possibilities, though, there were likely to be several more calling for restraint to be exercised. Speaking on a CNN broadcast in December 1996, *Washington Post* media reporter Howard Kurtz had argued:

. . . the thing we shouldn't lose sight of here is that, for a lot of people this is still a toy. They surf around, they check out what's there. Nobody has made money on it yet. But the reason that all these big news organizations, including mine, are investing in going onto the net, is because of the feeling that in three or four or five years when you can get video and when it really becomes faster and more reliable, that this will be a more [serious] news player.

(Transcript, CNN 'Reliable Sources', 1 December, 1996)

By March of 1997 the situation was improving, but not nearly fast enough in the eyes of some advocates of online journalism. Jon Katz (1997a), in his *Wired News* opinion column that month, remarked that more than '700 newspapers have dumped their static, stale content online, to little effect. With a handful of exceptions – the *San Jose Mercury News*; *The Wall Street Journal* – papers' use of the Web as a news medium has been dull, expensive and counterproductive.' Old media, he argued, must embrace the changes created by new media, especially where the latter enable journalists to break the news first. 'Newspapers,' he wrote, 'have clung beyond all reason to a pretense that that they are still in the breaking news business they dominated for so long, even though most breaking stories are seen live on TV or mentioned online hours, sometimes days, before they appear on newspaper front pages.' To reverse their decline, one commentator after the next was contending, newspapers would have to recognize the speed-driven imperatives of the Internet. Merrill Brown, Editor in Chief of the all-news network MSNBC (set up the year before), echoed this point, arguing that a key objective of Microsoft and NBC's joint venture was 'to break stories with frequency on the Internet' (cited in Parenthoen 1997).

Later that same month, a shocking incident took place that further pinpointed certain unique qualities that online journalism could contribute to the coverage of breaking news. The Heaven's Gate mass suicide, as it was promptly dubbed at the time, transpired over several days in an affluent neighbourhood in Rancho Sante Fe, near San Diego, California. The police arrived on the scene on 26 March, having been contacted by a fallen member of the Heaven's Gate cult who had received a videotape from its members. The cult's leader, along with 38 members, had taken their own lives by consuming applesauce pudding laced with phenobarbital, followed by vodka. Evidently it was their fervent belief that the passing of the Hale-Bopp Comet was to be interpreted as a sign indicating that they were to leave behind their earthly bodies ('containers') and board a spacecraft travelling in the comet's wake. News of the suicide created an instant media sensation. Among the online news sites, *The Washington Post*'s helped lead the way. 'When this story broke at 8:00,' recalled Jason Seiken, editor of washingtonpost.com at the time, 'we put it up immediately. Any time there was any sort of update, that went up immediately' (transcript, National Public Radio, 3 April 1997).

This immediacy, in Seiken's view, was one of three important advantages the site had over its press and television rivals. The second advantage was the capacity for greater depth in online reporting. 'There's really no limit on what you can put on a web site,' he argued. 'So, whereas when publishing *the Washington Post*, we have to be very cognizant of how many pages we put out, when we're publishing washingtonpost.com, well, we currently have more than 40,000 pages.' In the case of the Heaven's Gate story, when it became apparent that the cult's own site was being overwhelmed with online traffic, Seiken made its contents (including a book they had written and transcripts of their videos) available for washingtonpost.com users from a copy derived from an America Online cache. This strategy allowed users to see for themselves what the cult members believed in their own words, as opposed to having to rely on a journalist's interpretative summary. Seiken also arranged to have a timeline created. Interspersed throughout the descriptions of the different periods in the cult's history were links to members' primary source documents. Previous articles by *Washington Post* journalists were also made available so as to help contextualize events. A third advantage identified by Seiken was the capacity of online media for interactivity. 'We were able to find one of the world's foremost UFO experts and actually put him online and have him answer questions from our readers', he commented. This strategy, commonplace today, was novel at the time. When asked whether he could anticipate a future where online news would be better placed to cover breaking news than traditional news organizations, he replied: 'As the Web becomes really interwoven into the fabric of more and more people's lives, it's just common sense that that's going to happen.'

Public interest in the Heaven's Gate suicides was so intense that media attention did not subside for quite some time. Weighing into the ensuing discussions about the significance of the events were those who felt they needed to be understood, at least in part, in relation to the growing influence of the Internet on public life. Much had been made in news reports about the fact that the group was supported in the main by money earned by members who were professional Web page designers. Once again, Katz (1997b) was quick to offer pertinent insights:

> Wherever these people really went when they died, they left us with the first Web tragedy. For the first time, the dead are very definitely us, not them. Their lives, work, beliefs, and passing are woven into the machinery of the digital culture, already part of our archives and history. This wasn't some remote cult hidden away in some faraway jungle, to kill and die in private. Their messages, fingerprints, voices, and handiwork are ineluctably available on the World Wide Web, easily and instantly accessible, a couple of clicks away on any browser. Web sites from Pathfinder to Yahoo! to Wired News threw up links, dug out postings, reproduced Web sites and pages within minutes; a medium within a medium, covering the destruction of part of itself.
>
> (Katz 1997b)

Adopting sharply contrasting positions, however, were other commentators already predisposed to regard the Internet as posing an inherent danger to society. Many sought to characterize the Heaven's Gate members' involvement with the Internet as evidence to support their criticisms. The Web, they argued, was a recruiting ground for cultists. Young people, in particular, were at risk of being 'brainwashed' in their view, hence their demands for controls to be imposed over the type of information allowed to circulate on the Web. Much of this criticism echoed emergent campaigns against the availability of pornography online, a growing threat to morality in the eyes of some.

Above dispute, however, was the role online news sites had played in making available resources to help contextualize the news story, thereby bringing to light dimensions otherwise not being addressed by their print and television rivals. Still, searching questions continued to be raised about the credibility of the new medium in journalistic terms. Would the primary role for online news sites be an ancillary one, that is, mainly to provide background information to supplement the reporting undertaken by these rival media? Or, alternatively, would these sites contribute to the elaboration of a different type of journalism altogether?

Confirming authenticity

Ongoing debates about these and related questions, not least regarding the relative quality of the information circulating on the Web, took an unexpected twist in the aftermath of the shocking news that Diana, the Princess of Wales, had been killed in a car crash in Paris. She died along with her lover, Dodi Al Fayed, and their chauffer (a fourth person in the car, a bodyguard, was seriously injured). The story broke in the early hours of 31 August 1997 with online journalists scrambling to post whatever information they could gather. Matt Drudge of the online *Drudge Report* would later claim to have been the first to break the news to US audiences (transcript, National Press Club Luncheon, 2 June 1998). In any case, the BBC's online news site, as well as that of the *New York Times*, ABCNews.com, CNN.com and Yahoo!'s Current Events, amongst others, rapidly posted stories after television reports announced the initial details. Even before Diana's death had been officially announced at a news conference at Paris's Hopital de la Pitie-Salpetriere, online news coverage encompassed the globe.

Just as television news has long been considered to have had its legitimacy confirmed by the coverage of US President John F. Kennedy's assassination and funeral, some felt that a parallel of sorts could be drawn with the online reporting of Princess Diana's demise. For those looking for updates on breaking developments, as well as for background information, yet impatient with the repetitive cycles of television news, once again the Web came into its own (CNN.com apparently attracted some 4.3 million page views on Sunday, an extraordinary figure for the time: see Macavinta 1997). Some news sites made available links to audio and video files, as well as to related Web sites, such as those of the charities with which she was involved.

Timelines were widely used, as were story archives and bulletin boards. 'Perhaps the key benefit of the Net as a news-delivery mechanism', observed Bruce Simpson (1997), 'is the way that users can do their own research and scan huge amounts of information [in] such a short space of time – while users of other media are "spoon-fed" whatever the news-editors feel appropriate.' This capacity to enable users to pursue their own paths of enquiry was underscored by the extent to which other media focused, almost exclusively for hours on end in the case of some television networks, on the officially sanctioned details of the Diana story. Much of the television reporting adopted a reverent, even deferential tone, with newsreaders serving as the 'mourners in chief', as they were described by the *New York Times* television critic.

In contrast, certain voices on the Web were posing awkward questions, and in so doing raising difficult issues. 'I welcome the opportunity to be franker and quicker in this medium,' Andrew Ross, managing editor of *Salon*, remarked. 'The traditional media felt the need to be more stately and official and to parrot conventional wisdom' (cited in Macavinta 1997). Elsewhere on the Web, users went online to express their viewpoints in a collective response widely described, as noted in the *Sunday Times* a week later, as an 'unprecedented electronic outpouring of grief'. Heartfelt memorial pages appeared, allowing mourners to pay their respects, share their memories, and offer condolences. Similar sentiments were expressed across hundreds of chat rooms and discussion forums. At the same time, debates raged over topics such as the possible implications for the monarchy's future status, whether a boycott of the tabloid press should be organized, and the conduct of the paparazzi in the events surrounding the high-speed crash. In the case of *Newsweek Interactive*'s 'My Turn Online,' for example, one day's topic was: 'Princess Di vs. the Press. Princess Diana's car crash apparently happened as she was trying to elude news photographers. Did the press kill her? Did we, its readers?' (cited in Peterson 1997). Meanwhile proponents of contending conspiracy theories posed their 'unanswered questions' on different newsgroups (for example, alt.conspiracy.princess-diana), seeing in the crash sufficient grounds to suspect foul play.

Interestingly, from the very outset of the online coverage, various commentators were predicting that photographs of the accident scene would find their way on to the Web. The Paris police had moved quickly to try to confiscate the film shot by the paparazzi (one of whom was reportedly beaten by angry witnesses at the scene), and a number of newspapers made it clear to their readers that they would refuse to pay for images depicting the accident's victims. Still, there seemed to be little doubt that a story of this magnitude would generate photographs online before too long. 'The 'Net always contains the most scandalous, dubious and exploitative information you might possibly want or stumble into', commented 'Web expert' J. C. Herz at the time. 'There's no mechanism for suppression of information on the Internet, and while that's part of the beauty of the medium, [it is] also the downside' (cited in McNamara 1997). Less than a week after these remarks were made, a photograph ostensibly depicting Diana in the crashed Mercedes surfaced on the Web. Specifically, the image appeared on a site providing 'an archive of disturbing illustration' operated by an anti-censorship group called Rotten Dot Com. Based in California, the group claimed to have received it via an e-mail from an undisclosed source (no credit line for the photograph was provided). While the image shows the aftermath of a very serious car accident, it was unclear whether the blood-ied, blonde-haired woman trapped in the twisted steel was actually Diana. The group's own stance was ambiguous at first, neither confirming nor deny-ing the photograph's authenticity. The image was posted, the homepage stated, 'for political reasons, to make people think, and to make them upset.' If indeed this was the group's intention, it succeeded. The number of visitors to the site – many of whom responded with e-mails expressing their outrage – was such that the available bandwidth was insufficient, forcing the group to remove the image so as to allow the site to continue to operate.

'Group posts picture purporting to show dying princess' was the Agence France-Presse headline for the wire service story that broke the news. The Italian news agency ANSA, along with several newspapers, including the Paris daily *France-Soir*, also put the unverified photograph into public circu-lation. Various news sites promptly linked to the Rotten.com site, although in at least one instance the pertinent ISP proceeded to delete the image in response to what was fast-becoming an ethical controversy over the relative appropriateness of its use (Pelline 1997). Within 24 hours, French author-ities were being quoted in news reports as stating that the photograph was indeed a fake. Certain inconsistencies were identified, including the fact that the rescue workers depicted were not wearing French emergency service uniforms, nor were the emergency telephone numbers on their equipment the correct ones for France (999 being the British emergency code). A number of embarrassed newspaper journalists, not surprisingly, placed the blame for the hoax directly on the Internet. The editor in chief of *France-Soir*, Claude Lambert, told the *New York Times*:

> Not very adroitly, perhaps, we did it to put a spotlight on the excesses of the Internet . . . There were heated arguments about the decision in the office on Friday, and not everybody on the staff agrees we executed it properly. Maybe the headline should have said 'Diana, the Phony Internet Photo,' but we still would have gone ahead and published it.
>
> (cited in Harmon 1997)

If the incident was a test of the Internet's credibility as a news source, as some said, then in the eyes of many it had failed. Examples of photographic hoaxes abound in journalism's history, but the capacity of Internet users to disseminate misleading material so far and so quickly, deeply troubled some critics. For newspaper reporter Amy Harmon (1997), the controversy sur-rounding the Diana photograph 'underscores the public's apparent eager-ness to give the Internet's indiscriminate electronic press the benefit of the doubt. Or at least its tolerance for the often sensational appeal of material it carries.' In other words, one might be tempted to reply, much like the public response to the mainstream news media.

Conclusion

In bringing this chapter to a close, I would like to call for further historical work to be conducted into the early days of online journalism. So many of the issues briefly touched on above warrant close, thoughtful scrutiny and analysis. While I readily acknowledge that there currently exists a multiplicity of distinctive strategies for presenting news online – strategies that can vary markedly from one news site to the next – it is my sense that these sites are beginning to share more similarities than differences. This is so, in my view, not only in their appearance but also, more troublingly, in their preferred definitions of what counts as news and how best to report it.

One of the reasons the late David Brinkley's (2003) words, quoted at length at the outset of this discussion, resonate so powerfully for me is that I believe online journalism is slowly becoming more closely aligned with the 'attractive wrapping' of television news. This when I am convinced that it needs to reaffirm a stronger commitment to the reportorial ethos of the investigative press. As I have sought to show, however, to better understand the imperatives informing this contested, always uneven development, a historical perspective is invaluable. After all, these imperatives, to varying degrees, continue to constrain our ability to envisage new ways of improving the quality of online journalism for tomorrow.

References

Adams, J. (1996) A World Wide Web of Conspiracy, *Sunday Times*, 22 September.

Agrawal, R. (1995) Getting the Word Out, *The Quill*, 83(6): 32.

Andrews, P. (1995) Net Falters in Coverage of Bomb Aftermath, *The Seattle Times*, 30 April.

Brinkley, D. (2003) On Being an Anchorman, *New York Times*, 14 June.

Campbell, D. (1997) Untapped Sources, *Guardian*, 10 July.

Chester, R. and Shotnicki, T. (1996) Top US Crime-Busters Enter Cyberspace to Net Terrorists, *Courier Mail*, 6 August.

Copilevitz, T. (1995) Internet is Hardly a Hotbed of Terrorism, *The Dallas Morning News*, 7 May.

Duggan, D. (1996) Oh What a Tangled Net the Plot Nuts can Weave, *Newsday*, 24 November.

Haberman, L. (2003) David Brinkley Dies, *E! Online News*, 12 June.

Hanson, C. (1997) The Dark Side of Online Scoops, *Columbia Journalism Review*, May/June.

Haring, B. (1995) Oklahoma Bombing Echoes through Cyberspace, *USA Today*, 21 April.

Harmon, A. (1997) Phony Diana Photo Reignites Debate on Internet Postings, *New York Times*, 22 September.

Harris, M. (1996) Truth a Casualty Once Again? *Toronto Sun*, 12 November.

Husseini, S. (1997) Media Bombed on TWA Crash, *Chicago Tribune*, 2 January.

Katz, J. (1997a) Scoop Story, *Wired News*, 4 March.

Katz, J. (1997b) Deaths in the Family, *Hotwired*, 31 March.

Kenworthy, T. (1997) Report of Admission Throws Oklahoma Bomb Case into Turmoil, *Washington Post*, 1 March.

Macavinta, C. (1997) Net Mourns Di, Debates Media Role, *CNET News.com*, 2 September.

McNamara, P. (1997) A Crying Shame; Princess Di's Death Brings Out the Worst of the Web, *Network World*, 8 September.

Oakes, C. (1995) Shock Waves: Communication about Oklahoma City Bombing on the Internet, *Los Angeles Magazine*, 40(6): 112.

Parenthoen, I. (1997) Electronic Journalism Speeds onto the Internet, *Agence France-Presse*, 5 March.

Pelline, J. (1997) Alleged Diana Photo Appears Online, *CNET News.com*, 18 September.

Peterson, C. (1997) Newsy Web Pays Homage, *Modesto Bee*, 9 September.

Rashbaum, W. K. (1997) 'Salinger – I have more TWA Evidence,' *Daily News*, 14 March.

Rosenberg, S. (1995) Digital Culture, *The San Francisco Examiner*, 30 April.

Schwartz, J. (1995) Advocates of Internet Fear Drive to Restrict Extremists' Access, *Washington Post*, 28 April.

Simpson, B. (1997) Media frenzy over Diana's death spreads to Web, *Aardvark News*, 1 September.

Waite, C. H. (2003) David Brinkley, *The Museum of Broadcast Communications*, www.museum.tv/archives.

Weise, E. (1997) Newspaper scoops self to get the word out on bombing story, Associated Press, 1 March.

PART II

Journalism and democracy

16

Is there a democratic deficit in US and UK journalism?

Robert A. Hackett

- Does journalism in the US and UK adequately serve the needs of a democratic political communication system?
- What do different political perspectives have to say on this question?
- If there is a democratic deficit, what can we do about it?

By framing and directing attention to public issues, journalism has a key role in contemporary political life, one commonly described as vital to informed citizenship and accountable government. Many critics, however, argue that even in established liberal democracies like Britain and the US, journalism is falling short of expectations of how it should function as an agent of democratic rule.

Whether journalism has such a 'democratic deficit', and why, is this chapter's topic. Positions on these questions vary, for two reasons. First, the evidence on media performance is not always clear cut. The influences on news selection, the patterns of news content, and their impact on political life, are questions much debated among journalists, politicians, media scholars and publics.

More fundamentally, though, how we evaluate the media's democratic performance depends greatly on what 'grading' criteria we use. This chapter sketches contending perspectives on what democracy entails, and what the roles of journalism in contributing to democratic governance ought to be. Competing conceptions of democracy are not simply matters for 'policy wonks'. They are 'weapons' in fundamental political divisions over social and economic policy, and alternative futures are ultimately at stake. For instance, the business sector and some of the affluent middle class favour 'free market' policies of privatization, market reregulation (often called deregulation), trade liberalization and the dismantling of the 'welfare state'. Trade unions, progressive social movements and other groups, by contrast, advocate a positive role for the public sector in protecting the environment, labour standards, public services and some measure of social equality. Academics, political parties, policy institutes and interest groups involved in these debates draw upon and develop quite different paradigms of democracy, which in turn imply different normative expectations of journalism. We now turn to these contending perspectives.

The conservative critique: market liberals and elitist democrats

Since the 1980s, the 'free market' vision of democracy has gained political and cultural hegemony. Known variously as market liberalism, neoliberalism or neoconservatism, this ideology holds that 'that government is best which governs least' – with the exception that the State's military, police, and prisons are seen as necessary to preserve the social order. Democracy is seen not as a end in itself but as normally the best institutional arrangement to maintain political stability and a liberal political culture characterized by individual rights and choice, particularly economic rights of ownership, contract and exchange.

It often adopts a populist and anti-elitist stance, but this 'free market' vision actually fits well with an elitist version of democracy, classically articulated by Joseph Schumpeter (1976; cited in Baker 2002). His theory of 'competitive elitism' (Held 1987, 164–85) meshes with market liberalism's emphasis on private consumption rather than public virtue. Given the complexity of modern political issues, the vulnerability of the masses to irrational and emotional appeals, and the risk of overloading the political system with competing demands, Schumpeter argued, ongoing public participation is neither necessary nor even desirable. Policy-making elites should be fairly autonomous from the mass public; they can be held sufficiently accountable through periodic elections, the entrenchment of individual political rights (assembly, expression), and a free press. In this view, democracy is a procedure for selecting leaders, with citizen participation confined mainly to voting every few years – essentially, the role of consumers in a political marketplace.

Journalism in this model would have several roles. By exposing corruption and the abuse of power, the press should act as a watchdog on government, which is considered the main threat to individual freedom. The press 'need not provide for nor promote people's intelligent political involvement or reflection', since 'meaningful understanding of social forces and structural problems is beyond the populace's capacity' (Baker 2002: 133); nor need it raise fundamental questions about State policy or the social order. But journalism, particularly the 'quality' press, can usefully report intra-elite debates and circulate 'objective' information helpful to elites themselves. This 'elitist' mandate for journalism was articulated as early as the 1920s by the legendary American political columnist Walter Lippmann (1963).

If free market conservatives see a democratic deficit in contemporary journalism, they usually focus on one of two perceived problems. One is the influence of the State, whether through informal attempts by governing politicians to manipulate journalists, or through formal laws and regulations, such as restrictions on media concentration, or 'public service' content requirements in broadcasting. Public service broadcasters that receive licence fees or taxes, like the BBC, come under particular fire from market liberals, for allegedly being too vulnerable to pressure from the governments that fund them, eroding its 'watchdog' function. Market liberals regard commercial, privately owned media as more democratic, shaped as they allegedly are by reader, viewer and listener preferences. A commercial media system, it is argued, gives audiences what they want: the consumer is 'sovereign'.

Conservatives, especially in America, see a second problem with news media – a pervasive hostility towards mainstream or middle American authority figures or values, due mainly to the 'left-liberal' political biases of journalists. Some commentators portray journalists as part of a 'new class' of bureaucrats and intellectuals with a value system at odds with the achievement orientation of business and with a vested interest in expanding State regulation (see, for example, Lichter, Rothman and Lichter 1986; Hackett and Zhao 1998: 258). In the US, where conservatives continue to expound the left-liberal bias thesis on radio talk shows and in best-selling books (for example, Goldberg 2001) it has become almost conventional wisdom (although it is less so in the UK). A more recent version of the conservative critique sees journalists as holding 'postmaterialist' values, like feminism or environmentalism, more than the general population (Miljan and Cooper 2003: 56–9).

Social conservatives (as distinct from market liberals) are angered by journalism's perceived violations of morality or social order – too much sex, violence, sensationalism and invasion of privacy. These concerns are politically important but because they span the political spectrum and are not easily related to models of democracy I shall not pursue them here.

Conservatives (market liberals) fear that left-liberal and State-regulated journalism could threaten public support for business, and for the economic and military policies that (in their view) underpin freedom and prosperity. What solutions flow from their analysis? Deregulate private media and defund public service broadcasters. Hire more conservative journalists, and/or subject journalists to more editorial/owner supervision.

Both of these market liberal critiques rest on very debatable assumptions. As an explanation of news output, the left-liberal thesis is dangerously partial and misleading. Its persistence is accounted for not by genuine merit, but by a generation-long corporate and right-wing 'ideological mobilization' to undo the impact of the 1960s protest movements, to restore the unchallenged legitimacy of corporate capitalism, and to reverse the progressive aspects of the welfare state (Dreier 1982; Hackett and Zhao 1998: 138). The thesis focuses on journalists as individuals, and downplays their institutionalized routines and pressures (especially from business and the State) that in the view of most media sociologists largely determine the shape of news (Shoemaker and Reese 1996). Conservative critics offer relatively little evidence that journalists' presumably liberal attitudes systematically influence actual news content. Conservatives exaggerate the extent and radicalism of media attacks on authority, ignoring their selective focus on government rather than private-sector institutions, and on transgressions that confirm rather than contradict neoliberal assumptions. Government red tape or taxes ill spent are usually more newsworthy than business corruption or exploitation (Hackett and Zhao 1998: 138–41).

The second market liberal critique, that media regulation contradicts the democratic principle of consumer sovereignty, assumes first, that media audiences are primarily consumers rather than citizens. From a democratic standpoint, the two concepts are radically different. 'Citizen' implies active participation in civic affairs; 'consumer' implies the more private and passive role of material consumption. Citizens in a democratic state are in principle equal; consumers in a market economy are unequal, because their ability to consume commodities depends upon their purchasing power.

Second, the 'consumer sovereignty' argument does not work even on its own terms. It conveys an image of unified and determined consumers barking orders to compliant media corporations, who then produce the programming that consumers want (Curran 2000: 129–33; Hackett and Zhao 1998: 185–8). In reality though, many structural factors, discussed below, refract or undermine the expression of consumer preferences in commercial media content. And even if media could be made as responsive as possible to consumer preferences, they would not necessarily produce the kind of public forum and quality news that are a precondition of informed citizenship. People express their values not only through consumer purchases, but also through their votes and their taxes; and some valued public goods, like public health and citizen-oriented journalism, cannot easily be supplied through market mechanisms. This limitation is relevant though, only if the goal is participatory rather than elitist democracy.

❚ 'Public sphere' liberalism

The elitist model of democracy has been criticized on many grounds. Its negative view of citizens' participation is unduly pessimistic; in referenda and elections on fundamental issues (like EU membership, or Canada-US free trade in 1988) citizens have shown a remarkable capacity for learning and civic engagement. Conversely, scandals such as the apparent manipulation of security intelligence by the Bush and Blair governments before the 2003 Iraq war, suggest that the elitist model overestimates the competence and accountability of policy makers, in the absence of ongoing public participation.

Similarly, the related market liberal approach to democracy overlooks the excessive power of concentrated wealth in policy-making processes. It dismisses the threat to political equality and even meaningful individual freedom posed by the growing gap between rich and poor. And it ignores the erosion, by a culture of acquisitive individualism, of the sense of community underpinning democratic governance.

Such considerations have strengthened an alternative vision that accepts the elitist democrats' support for individual rights and an independent 'watchdog' press, but places a much higher value on popular participation through established political channels. Participation can be valued as a means to both produce more just and legitimate policies, and to develop the democratic capacities of citizens.

Liberal participatory democrats prioritize the role of media in facilitating or even constituting a public sphere – 'that realm of social life where the exchange of information and views on questions of common concern can take place so that public opinion can be formed' (Dahlgren 1995: 7). As theorized by Jürgen Habermas, the public sphere is not necessarily a physical setting, but a conceptual space within various venues and groups, one characterized ideally by discussion free of domination, equality of participation, and rationality in the sense of an appeal to general principles rather than sheer self-interest. In a participatory democracy, government policy would reflect the decisions of a civil society collectively debating and determining its future. The media would provide an arena of public debate, and reconstitute private citizens as a public body in the form of public opinion (Curran 1996: 82–3).

In a participatory democracy, what specific roles or tasks are expected of public sphere-building journalism? Baker (2002: 129–53) advocates two offsetting types of news media: first, a segmented system that provides each significant cultural and political group with a forum to articulate and develop its interests; and second, journalism organizations that can facilitate the search for society-wide political consensus by being universally accessible, inclusive (civil, objective, balanced and comprehensive), and thoughtfully discursive, not simply factual.

Norris (2000: 25–35) proposes a checklist of 'public sphere' tasks for journalism. If news media are to provide a civic forum that helps sustain pluralistic political competition, do they provide extensive coverage of politics, including a platform for a wide plurality of political actors? Do media provide 'horizontal' communication between political actors, as well as 'vertical' communication between government and governed? Are there multiple sources of regular political news from different outlets, underpinning effective government communication, multiple venues for public debate, and reduced costs to citizens for becoming politically informed? Is there equal or proportionate coverage of different parties? Finally, as an agent in mobilizing public participation, does journalism stimulate general interest, public learning and civic engagement vis-à-vis the political process?

Not only public sphere liberals, but many journalists themselves, would answer 'no' to many of these questions, especially in the US (for example, Fallows 1996). The view that media are failing their democratic responsibilities – a 'media malaise' thesis – has become almost an orthodoxy. As Norris (2000: 4–12) summarizes it, the thesis blames journalism for many perceived negative trends since the 1970s. Political participation and civic engagement, indicated by voter turnout rates, are on the decline. Citizens have become more cynical about politics and less trusting in government; conversely, political leaders have lost credibility, and official political agendas are less connected to the concerns of ordinary people. Public political discourse has become 'dumbed down', and public learning about politics has eroded, as scandal-mongering and personality-oriented fluff replaces substantive news about political issues. Single-issue interest groups have displaced political parties as mediating forces, undermining societal-wide civic, and civil, dialogue.

What lies behind this putative malaise of democracy? Malaise theorists find some of the causes in the political environment – the fragmentation of social consensus associated with environmental, economic and other divisive new issues; voters' weakening allegiance to political parties; the professionalization, 'marketization' and image-orientation of political campaigns (Blumler and Gurevitch 1995: 206). But fingers are also pointed at journalism's own practices, and to a lesser extent, its structures. Economic pressures are producing a downmarket shift in political journalism towards tabloidization and infotainment, as has the emergence in the 1970s of network television as the dominant news medium in the US, followed in the 1980s by deregulation of private broadcasting in the US, and governmental attacks on the independence and resources of public service broadcasting in the UK. The fragmentation of media audiences as channels proliferate has undermined the cohesion of the public sphere, and facilitated a politics of division. Journalists' struggle for autonomy from politicians' 'spin doctors' has led them to adopt a semi-adversarial stance towards government (and here there is some overlap with the market liberals' critique), and to focus on the strategies of politicians, rather than the substance of policies.

The perceived 'crisis of public communication' (Blumler and Gurevitch 1995) has led to modest efforts at reforming journalism practices, if not structures. One example is the public journalism movement in the US, involving experiments by newspapers to facilitate community discussion of public issues, rather than simply to report on official sources (Baker 2002: 158–63). In recent years, though, some public sphere liberals have launched a three-pronged counter-attack to these 'narratives of decline' (McNair 2000: 197).

First, they suggest, the pessimistic reading of news media's changing structure and political impact is one-sided or lacks supporting evidence. Market forces do not lead only to downmarket sleaze and the decline of traditional political news in newspapers, argues McNair (2000: 202, 208); they can also create incentives to invest in quality journalism, and they have helped expand the styles and formats of political information in broadcasting and the Internet. And far from engendering cynicism, ignorance and disengagement, Norris (2000: 318) finds that 'exposure' to news media, and trust/participation in the political system, are mutually reinforcing, thus constituting a 'virtuous circle'.

A second 'optimistic' line of reasoning acknowledges some of the trends identified by the pessimists, but re-evaluates them as harmless or even beneficial to democracy. Tabloid journalism is not a straightforward deterioration of quality, but has in certain senses popularized political culture, democratized news agendas, and even constituted 'sites of popular opposition to the dominant order' – by highlighting the abuses of privilege or the once-closeted foibles of the powerful, for example (Sparks 2000; McNair 2000; Connell 1992). Politics-as-game journalism is a reasonable adaptation to manipulation by political spin doctors, and lends more transparency to the political process; and given their insider knowledge, the media pundits who are elbowing out politicians and traditional journalists may deserve their celebrity status (McNair 2000). Such optimistic re-evalution is reinforced by suggestions to moderate our expectations of journalism; thus Norris (2002: 208, 211, 227) argues that voters do not need broad civics knowledge, just sufficient context-specific information to enable them to assess the consequences of their political choices.

Finally, while the 'optimists' deny a general crisis of democracy in the US or UK, they do concede that there are significant challenges, such as low voter turnout or big money's influence in American elections. But they argue that journalism should not be blamed for flaws rooted elsewhere in power relations and social structure (Norris 2000: 319) – a consideration which leads to a third tradition of media critique.

Radical democracy and the political economy critique

The public sphere liberals' critique is vulnerable to refutation partly because it is a limited one; it seeks to reform the practices of journalism but does not raise fundamental questions about the market-oriented corporate structures of news media, and still less the social and political order. By contrast, radical democrats offer a more robust set of benchmarks for evaluating media performance. If market liberals emphasize individual liberties and restrictions on government power, and public sphere liberals highlight public deliberation about policy, radical democrats add a third dimension – a thoroughgoing view of democracy as not just a set of procedural rules, but a societal environment which nourishes developmental power – everyone's equal right to 'the full development and use' of their capabilities (Macpherson 1977: 114; Downing *et al.* 2001: 43–4).

Such a standpoint transcends public sphere liberalism in several respects. First, radical democrats seek not just to reinvigorate the existing system of representative democracy, but to move beyond it towards direct citizen participation in decision-making in the neighbourhood, workplace, and family and gender relations – the lifeworld.

Second, they prioritize equality as a core principle of democracy, one increasingly undermined by neoliberal governments in the US, UK and Canada since the 1980s. Citizens should have not only equal legal and political rights, but also approximate equality in wealth and power.

Third, radical democrats regard power relations as antagonistic in societies with structured inequalities; even in prosperous capitalist democracies, political and economic elites may have interests which conflict with those of the rest of the population.

Fourth, drawing from the tradition of critical political economy, radical democrats analyse power holistically. A democratic public sphere cannot be insulated from power hierarchies embedded in State, economy, gender and race; so long as they exist, they will tend to undermine equality of voice in the public sphere.

Finally, given these and other assumptions, radical democrats are often quite critical of unregulated corporate capitalism and its impact on politics, society and the environment.

Given this view of democracy, what political roles are expected of news media? Radical democrats endorse the watchdog and public sphere functions celebrated in the other models respectively, but add such criteria as these:

- Enabling horizontal communication between subordinate groups, including social movements as agents of democratic renewal (Angus 2001). By giving public voice to civil society, media can facilitate needed social change, power diffusion and popular mobilization against social injustices.

- Expanding the scope of public awareness and political choice by reporting events and voices which are socially important but outside, or even opposed to, the agendas of elites. Such issues include environmental sustainability and other extra-market values integral to a just and humane society.

- Counter-acting power inequalities found in other spheres of the social order. As McChesney (1999: 288) has put it, 'unless communication and information are biased toward equality, they tend to enhance social inequality'.

Given these criteria, radical democrats find much to criticize. Whereas public sphere liberals worry about public mistrust of government, radical democrats like Herman and Chomsky (1988) worry that media are altogether too successful in 'manufacturing consent' for unjust State and corporate policies, while marginalizing dissenters and ordinary citizens from political debate. Many aspects of the structure of news media industries contradict democratic equality and informed participatory citizenship. The links between media owners and the rest of the business elite (through social interaction and intercorporate directorships), the disproportionate political power of corporate-financed advocacy groups both as sources for journalists and as pressures on newsroom managers, and the political biases and interests of major media owners like Rupert Murdoch, are all factors that skew journalism towards the political right. High entry costs and oligopoly (the small number of competitors) in most media markets; the growing regional and national concentration of ownership in newspaper and broadcasting industries; the technological and ownership convergence between these once separate industries; the rationalization of news gathering resources within newspaper chains; the brand-name recognition, economies of scale, access to distribution networks, and the cross-promotional strategies of large media corporations – all potentially threaten meaningful diversity of perspective in the journalism of dominant media (Hackett 2001).

News organizations increasingly belong to transnational conglomerates, companies with a range of holdings in different media and industries. Shareholders and large merger-fuelled debt loads often drive conglomerates to maximize short-term profits. The consequences for journalism, which typically comprises only a fraction of conglomerate revenues, can be severe. The economic incentive is not to nurture 'serious' journalism, but to provide a diet of infotainment as the cheapest, safest way to grab audiences. Conflicts of interest bedevil news judgement, as journalists may feel pressured to promote or suppress stories about the conglomerate's empire. Alternative views and products are pushed to the margins, as conglomerates recycle the same expensively produced brand-name fare through various formats and channels. Newsroom culture shifts from an ethos of public service, as journalists are asked to become corporate team players. The controversial promotion by the *Los Angeles Times* of the Staples Center, a sports complex in which its parent company had a financial stake, is an example of several of these dangers.

In theory, government legislation (such as anti-trust law and broadcasting statutes), along with regulatory agencies like the US Federal Communications, are supposed to protect the public interest, especially with respect to broadcasting. In practice, critics argue, the relationship between the State and big media corporations is symbiotic, indeed almost corrupt (McChesney 1999); crudely put, politicians want favourable publicity and media companies want regulatory and legislative favours.

The potentially anti-democratic implications of advertising for journalism deserve special consideration because economically, the commercial media's bread is buttered not by audiences primarily, but by advertisers who pay for access to audiences of the right kind. Baker (1994: 69–70) identifies four predictable consequences for journalism. First, advertising discourages 'media accounts of inadequacies or dangers of advertisers' products, exposés of wrongdoing by advertisers, and serious critiques of those aspects of the social world on which advertisers depend'. Second, advertising encourages political blandness over partisan positions on controversial issues, because advertisers seek to reach maximum audiences and avoid offending potential purchasers. Third, in order to promote a buying mood, advertising favours 'lighter material' over critical thought or attention to social problems – or values like environmentalism, which contradict the ethos of consumerism. Finally, because advertisers particularly want to reach people able and willing to buy their products, the media tend 'to adopt the perspectives and to serve the informational and entertainment needs of the comparatively affluent'.

This last point has particular implications for democratic equality. Affluent consumers have disproportionate influence regarding what kinds of media outlets and content will flourish economically, and which ones will die (Hackett 2001). Such inegalitarian biases are not likely to be corrected through market forces. If the critical political economists are right, the market is more the problem than the solution. Nor can we count on the much-touted Internet to provide a more egalitarian communication network. For all its democratic and interactive potential, the Internet, under current policy directions in the US and UK, is becoming colonized by the same commercial logic and corporate giants (joined by telecommunications and computer conglomerates as well) that dominate the traditional information media (McChesney 1999, Chapter 3; Hackett and Zhao 1998: 190–200).

If the proof is in the eating of the pudding, what are the implications of these structural features for news content? One useful approach to this question considers what is not in the news. Each year in the US, Project Censored lists important and seemingly newsworthy stories that are virtually ignored by the corporate media. Its top stories for 2003 included the hidden agendas behind the US government's attack on Iraq, the threat to civil liberties from homeland security measures, a Pentagon plan to actually provoke terrorist actions in order to enable a counterattack, the Bush administration's largely covert campaign to undermine labour unions and worker protections, and increasing monopoly control over the Internet (Phillips and Project Censored 2004). Such stories bespeak a lack of investigative journalism in US media, and a failure of the 'watchdog' function vis-à-vis corporate and State power. Conversely, at least in the crucial period leading up to the March 2003 invasion of Iraq, US corporate media, particularly the television networks spearheaded by Rupert Murdoch's Fox Network, arguably beat the drums for war. For instance, they amplified the Bush administration's (highly dubious) claims about Saddam Hussein's weapons of mass destruction, and highlighted Saddam's atrocities against Kurds in the 1980s, while virtually ignoring US (and British) support for his regime at that time (Rampton and Stauber 2003).

A related project found similar blind spots in Canada's press during the 1990s, including poverty and inequality, Canada's involvement in global militarism, religion and traditional social values, the power of the public relations industry, most news about labour apart from disruptive strikes, the vested interests of media companies themselves, and white-collar and corporate crime (Hackett and Gruneau *et al.* 2000, Chapters 6 and 7).

▎Towards media democracy?

The analysis above indicates a democratic deficit in Anglo-American journalism, vis-à-vis both equality and the watchdog function. To be sure, the deficit is arguably greater in American mass media, dominated by corporate-owned monopoly metropolitan dailies, and by commercial broadcasters who have largely abandoned the public service ethos; the UK still has a strong public service broadcasting tradition and a certain (though conservative-weighted) diversity in its national press. The public sphere and radical democratic critiques suggest though, that both countries need to nurture a more effectively democratic media system. 'Fixing' the democratic deficit requires addressing not just journalistic practices and ethics but also the institutional structures within which journalism is practised.

What should be the object of such media reform? No single type of news organization or journalism can serve all democratic purposes. The news system needs to be structurally pluralistic, with different types and sectors of media offsetting each other's limitations. Curran (2000) suggests a five-sector media system anchored on public service media, which can comprise a public sphere and offset the structural biases of advertising; but it also includes commercial media, which are relatively effective at providing audience-pleasing entertainment, and community/advocacy media, which enable civic groups to speak for themselves.

Such pluralism requires regulatory and legislative initiatives, such as subsidies and media ownership ceilings because, left to themselves, commercial pressures will generally deepen rather than reduce the undemocratic aspects discussed in this chapter. But fearful of antagonizing media corporations and often politically 'in bed' with them, governments are unlikely to enact democratic media reform without strong pressure from an organized coalition within civil society. As they have the most robust critique of media, radical democrats are likely to be in the forefront of a reform coalition. They also have the most uphill battle, because their challenge is not only to specific journalistic practices, but to corporate power and market logic more broadly.

Nevertheless, there may be openings to move towards their vision, including alliances with groups within the other two traditions. Most obviously, radical democrats and public-sphere liberals share an interest in defending public service broadcasting. And while they will often be on opposing sides, 'honest' market liberals have reason to work with progressives on issues of competition, consumer choice and the press's watchdog role, given the realities of corporate media domination. This possibility is not just hypothetical. In 2003, right-wing groups joined with progressives in an unprecedented upsurge of media activism against the regulatory raising of American media concentration limits. Groups like Free Press in the US and the Campaign for Press and Broadcasting Freedom in Britain may be in the forefront of renewed struggles for a democratic public sphere in the twenty-first century.

References

Angus, I. (2001) *Emergent Publics: An Essay on Social Movements and Democracy*. Winnipeg, Arbeiter Ring.

Baker, E. C. (1994) *Advertising and a Democratic Press*. Princeton, NJ: Princeton University Press.

Baker, E. C. (2002) *Media, Markets and Democracy*. Cambridge: Cambridge University Press.

Blumler, J. G. and Gurevitch, M. (1995) *The Crisis of Public Communication*. London: Routledge.

Connell, I. (1992) Personalities in the Popular Media, in P. Dahlgren and C. Sparks (eds) *Journalism and Popular Culture*. London: Sage, pp. 64–83.

Curran, J. (1996) Mass Media and Democracy Revisited, in J. Curran and M. Gurevitch (eds) *Mass Media and Society*, 3rd edition. London: Arnold, pp. 81–119.

Curran, J. (2000) Rethinking Media and Democracy, in J. Curran and M. Gurevitch (eds) *Mass Media and Society*, 3rd edition. London: Arnold, pp. 120–55.

Dreier, P. (1982) Capitalists vs the Media: An Analysis of an Ideological Mobilization among Business Leaders, *Media, Culture and Society*, 4: 111–32.

Dahlgren, P. (1995) *Television and the Public Sphere: Citizenship, Democracy and the Media*. London: Sage.

Downing, J. D. H. with T. V. Ford, G. Gil and L. Stein (2001) *Radical Media: Rebellious Communication and Social Movements*. Thousand Oaks: Sage.

Fallows, J. (1996) *Breaking the News: How the Media Undermine American Democracy*. New York: Pantheon.

Goldberg, B. (2001) *Bias*. Washington, DC: Regnery.

Hackett, R. A. (2001) News Media and Civic Equality: Watch Dogs, Mad Dogs, or Lap Dogs? In Edward Broadbent (ed.), *Democratic Equality: What Went Wrong?* University of Toronto Press, pp. 197–212.

Hackett, R. A. and Gruneau, R., with D. Gutstein, T. A. Gibson and NewsWatch Canada (2000) *The Missing News: Filters and Blind Spots in Canada's Press*. Toronto and Ottawa: Garamond/Centre for Policy Alternatives.

Hackett, R. A. and Zhao, Y. (1998) *Sustaining Democracy? Journalism and the Politics of Objectivity*. Toronto: Garamond.

Held, D. (1987) *Models of Democracy*. Stanford, CA: Stanford University Press.

Herman, E. and Chomsky, N. (1988) *Manufacturing Consent: The Political Economy of the Mass Media*. New York: Pantheon.

Lichter, R. S., Lichter, L. S. and Rothman, S. (1986) *The Media Elite: America's New Powerbrokers*. New York: Hastings House.

Lippman, W. (1963) *The Essential Lippmann: A Political Philosophy for Liberal Democracy*. C. Rossiter and J. Lare (eds) New York: Random House.

Macpherson, C. B. (1977) *The Life and Times of Liberal Democracy*. Oxford: Oxford University Press.

McChesney, R. W. (1999) *Rich Media, Poor Democracy: Communication Politics in Dubious Times*. Urbana and Chicago: University of Illinois Press.

McNair, B. (2000) Journalism and Democracy: A Millennial Audit, *Journalism Studies*, 1(2): 197–211.

Miljan, L. and Cooper, B. (2003) *Hidden Agendas: How Journalists Influence the News*. Vancouver and Toronto: UBC Press.

Norris, P. (2000) *A Virtuous Circle: Political Communications in Postindustrial Societies*. Cambridge: Cambridge University Press.

Phillips, P. and Project Censored (2004) *Censored 2004: The Top 25 Censored Stories*. New York: Seven Stories Press.

Rampton, S. and Stauber, J. (2003) *Weapons of Mass Deception: The Uses of Propaganda in Bush's War on Iraq*. New York: Jeremy P. Tarcher/Penguin.

Schumpeter, J. (1976) *Capitalism, Socialism and Democracy*. New York: Harper & Row.

Shoemaker, P. and Reese, S. (1996) *Mediating the Message: Theories of Influences on Mass Media Content*. 2nd edition. White Plains, NY: Longman.

Sparks, C. (2000) Introduction: The Panic over Tabloid News, in C. Sparks and J. Tulloch (eds) *Tabloid Tales: Global Debates over Media Standards*. Lanham: Rowman & Littlefield, pp. 1–40.

7

Active citizen or couch potato? Journalism and public opinion

Justin Lewis and Karin Wahl-Jorgensen

- What is public opinion, and what is its role in a democratic society?
- What are public opinion polls and what are some problems for journalists in using them?
- How is public opinion represented in the news media?
- What are the consequences of how journalism represents public opinion?

Democratic governments gain legitimacy to the extent that they reflect the will of the people. To demonstrate that they have support for their policies and decisions they must seek the consent of the governed (Splichal 1999: 272), generally through periodic elections. Despite the claims of victorious parties or candidates, elections are fairly weak and intermittent forms of citizen approbation. Simply voting once every few years suggests a limited interaction between the governors and the governed, allowing citizens no opportunity to express their opinions beyond selecting politicians to represent their interests. Many democratic theorists, such as McNair (2000) stress the importance of a more active and engaged citizenry: 'the public in a democracy should have opportunities not just to read about, or to watch and listen to the development of political debates as spectators, but to participate directly in them' (McNair 2000: 105).

Even if democratic societies tend to fall well short of this kind of democratic ideal, it is fair to say that public opinion does play several roles in democracies. First, it is used by policy makers to determine whether their decisions are met with approval. Showing what members of the public believe about issues, whether they have to do with government decisions to wage wars, increase pension benefits, or raise taxes, provides both a corrective to politicians and an opportunity for citizen participation. Perhaps more importantly, the expression of public opinion is a central form of political participation as well as a sounding board for citizens, allowing them to weigh their own thoughts and opinions against those expressed by others (see, for example, McLeod, Pan and Rucinski 1995: 56).

The notion of public opinion – especially *a* public opinion, or 'a public mind' – does tend to homogenize people into a collective mass (thereby suppressing differences and contradictions). So we might paraphrase Raymond Williams to say that there are no publics, there are only ways of seeing people as publics (Williams 1963). Yet public opinion also gives individuals a *social* identity, stressing as it does the importance of *collective* rather than individual expression.

The problem of how to express public opinion – and thus facilitate citizen participation in politics and communicate consent or dissent for decisions made by government – is a complex one. Any attempt at capturing public opinion immediately runs into a multitude of problems in defining what it really is, and how we should measure it (Noelle-Neumann 1995: 36–7; Price 1994). So, for instance, should we understand public opinion as the sum aggregate of all individual opinions? Or should public opinion be found in consensus on the basis of debate? Can we see any one individual's opinion as being representative of a larger public opinion? Can there be more than one public opinion? There is no 'right' answer to these questions: we simply need to understand that there is no absolute or authentic public opinion against which representations (whether by polls, the media or by politicians) can be measured. Indeed, we are obliged to define public opinion in limited ways in order to be able to measure it. A poll, for example, tells us how people respond 'on the record' to questions put to them by a stranger – it relates to public opinion, but it does not capture it once and for all.

Ancient Greek philosophers suggested that democracies could only be viable in societies with populations smaller than 10,000 – any population larger than that would be ungovernable because it would be impossible for all citizens to participate in discussion of politics and thus to form a viable public opinion (Peters 1999). While the Ancient Greeks relied on the direct participation of all citizens in political discussion, such intensive involvement is not possible in contemporary societies. Instead we live in mass societies where most citizens have little direct involvement in politics and where politicians can only meet a fraction of the people they represent. Mass media – and especially the news media – have thus become the main channel for communication between citizens and politicians. As a result journalism has become central to the successful functioning of democratic societies, as journalists create space for a dialogue between politicians and the public. In so doing, a key part of a journalist's job is to define and represent public opinion.

Ever since their emergence, newspapers have been important social institutions precisely because they have provided a forum for citizens (albeit sometimes a fairly limited group of people) to discuss the issues that concerned them, and thereby articulate a public (rather than an individual) opinion and hold government accountable for its actions (see, for example, Habermas 1989: 42). Because it has always been imperative for journalists to understand and report on public opinion, journalists draw on a range of methods to gain access to the elusive 'will of the people'. Key among these is the use of public opinion polls.

Journalism and the use of polls

There is, among both journalists and politicians, a degree of ambivalence about opinion polls. On the one hand, polls are seen as relatively scientific and objective forms of citizen representation, and pollsters like Gallup and MORI are regarded as having both independence and expertise. Yet few journalists devote much time to examining what polling data suggest about the nature of public opinion and there is a well-rehearsed cynicism about both the accuracy of polls and their importance in the political process. Indeed, the 'poll-driven politician' (in as much as such a creature exists) is often regarded not as someone acting in a democratic spirit, but as a weak, pandering figure, generally lacking in principle.

In some ways, this ambivalence reflects the academic literature on polls, where a stress on methodological precision by academic pollsters is countered by a series of critiques about the use and meaning of polling data. So, for example, polls have been seen as a substitute for public opinion rather than a representation of it (Blumer 1948), as creating the illusion that the public hold clear and firm views when they often do not (Bourdieu 1979), and as providing a great deal of power to the pollster – who scripts the entire interview – and very little to the citizen, who can only offer consent or refusal to a prescribed agenda (Salmon and Glasser 1995). In short, these academic critiques have tended to focus on the way in which polls use the precise language of science and statistics to conceal the socially constructed nature of the enterprise.

It would, however, be misleading to see journalistic scepticism as grounded in this kind of sociological critique. Journalists tend to cling onto the scientific aspects of polls, and hold them to account on this basis. So, for example, rather than question the limited nature of 'horserace' polls, which measure the popularity of candidates and parties (notably during election campaigns), pollsters are used or taken to task for their ability or failure to predict the outcome of elections (Lewis 2001).

Certainly, the news media's use and commissioning of polls has become a routine part of political coverage – especially during elections. Between 1976 and 1988, one study found that the commissioning of polls by major US media organizations rose from an annual average of four to 32 (Ladd and Benson 1992), whereas another found that one-third of the cover stories in *Time*, *Newsweek* and *US News and World Report* involved the use of polls or surveys (Asher 1998). Indeed, in most developed countries it has become commonplace for newspapers and broadcasters to publish their own poll findings (Brule and Giacometti 1990).

Like many professionals with a claim to expertise, academics are often mindful of what they perceive as a journalistic lack of understanding of the nature and limits of surveys research, and there are many examples of journalists misinterpreting polling data (Asher 1998), or using data to make unwarranted claims (Krosnick 1989). Brady and Orren see this as an inherent function of the journalistic emphasis on speed and storylines (Brady and Orren 1992). For them, this contrasts with the surveys researcher's emphasis on precision and method. What is more striking, perhaps, is that for journalists the main function of a poll is *not* its ability to provide information or insight into public opinion but its news value.

This, in turn, means that the news reporting of polls is bound up with a series of news conventions. Perhaps the most pervasive of these is the 'top-down' nature of political news coverage (Tuchman 1978; Gans 1980; Glasgow Media Group 1982; Paletz and Entman 1981; Edelman 1988, 1995; Zaller 1992; Croteau 1998). In their analysis of the relationship between media and public opinion, Behr and Iyengar found that although the public often responded to media agendas, the media rarely responded to the public's stated political concerns or priorities (Behr and Iyengar 1985). For most journalists, covering politics means covering politicians. This means that an issue that is a matter of controversy and debate between the main political parties is newsworthy, even if it is a matter of little concern to most citizens. Conversely, an issue of concern to citizens is often ignored if it has no resonance with mainstream party politics.

Public opinion thus plays a minimal role in driving the news agenda. The agenda is set by politicians and other elites. As such, politics on the news is usually about what politicians do, and not necessarily about what people want them to do. For instance, in the British 2001 general election, the issue on which public opinion was most often cited was that of the country's future in the European Union, and the stand on the common currency (Brookes, Lewis and Wahl-Jorgensen 2004). Issue polls conducted at the same time showed that most people ranked Europe as a relatively unimportant topic. However, the Conservative Party had made the question of Europe the cornerstone of its election campaign, while sections of the British press were strongly anti-Europe, making public opinion on this issue 'relevant' to the political debate.

Another news convention that circumscribes the use of polls is the notion of 'balance' in political coverage. For news organizations bound by legislation (such as the requirement for British news broadcasters to be politically impartial) or by custom to adopt a neutral tone, polling data that suggests clear majority support for a particular view can be awkward. To report the main parties' different positions on an issue and then suggest that one of these parties has majority public support may risk appearing to be partisan. So, for example, if one party wants to spend more money on education and another does not, a journalist may feel that pointing out that the former has clear majority public support would compromise the appearance of impartiality. As a consequence, journalists tend not to report policy or issue based polling data in which the public state a clear majority – and ideologically inflected – preference.

While the same could be said of 'horserace' polls – especially if those polls show a party or candidate with a clear lead – such polls have, nonetheless, become a routine feature of political news coverage, punctuating election campaigns (although concerns about the effect of publicizing such polls has led some countries, such as France, to prohibit their publication in the period immediately before an election). The function of these polls has little to do with a desire to represent what people think – horserace polls are, after all, extremely ambiguous, and cannot be assumed to indicate a clear set of policy preferences. Rather, horserace polls become a way of *structuring the narrative* of election coverage. They provide a commentary on the campaign itself – who's ahead, who's catching up, who's behind and so forth – rather than on the political desires of the electorate.

In sum, we can say that while opinion polls now play a routine part in the coverage of politics, their use is shaped or constrained by news values and news conventions that make some polls 'relevant' to news stories and others not. The picture we receive of public opinion is therefore incomplete. Ironically, it may therefore be difficult for members of the public to know what the polling data say on a variety of issues, or to have a clear sense of the detail or context of public opinion.

Representations of public opinion

Journalists, however, do not just rely on polls to indicate what citizens think, but use a number of devices to represent public opinion. Indeed, news reports on television and in the press often draw on the voices and perspectives of citizens. Our study of more than 5,600 television news stories in the US and UK showed that during an average week, between 30 per cent and 40 per cent of all news stories include some reference to citizens or publics – even if these are often vague or imprecise (Lewis, Wahl-Jorgensen and Inthorn 2004). For many types of news story it is an integral part of reporting practice to include or refer to the reactions of 'regular' people, whether the issue is taxes on fuel, the quality of education, or the behaviour of sports stars.

However, while our study demonstrated that the viewpoints of citizens are often represented on the news, the great majority of references to citizen or public opinion *do not* involve polls or surveys of any kind. Instead, the most common representation of public opinion comes in the form of inferences – that is to say, statements that infer something about public opinion in general, without reference to polling data or other systematic evidence. Such inferences accounted for more than 40 per cent of all representations of public opinion in both the US and the UK. A typical instance of this kind of reference to public opinion is a reporter's commentary in a BBC story about illegal immigration:

> (the decision not to take train driver to court is) . . . not going to play particularly well with many people in the South-East constituency who

already feel illegal immigrants are getting in too easily . . . and not well with lorry drivers either . . .

(BBC 6 pm News, 4 February 2002)

Such stories are based on the reporter's own impression of public opinion, which may or may not be accurate. There is an assumption here that a general public opinion is transparently available to journalists, who claim to have a special ability and authority to communicate the will of the people. Thus the people heard speaking *about* public opinion on television news most frequently are journalists – who are the source of 83 per cent of references to public opinion overall.

Citizens do routinely appear on the news through the 'vox pop', or brief interviews with 'people in the street'. This is a fairly common device, and, after inferences, is the second-most common way of representing the citizenry. Around 40 per cent of references to or representations of citizens are vox pops. Such references provide an impression of public opinion, but they are rarely used in the context of survey data that might suggest how common the views expressed by individuals interviewed really are. Indeed, the BBC's guidelines specifically state that 'vox pops' are not indicative of the weight of public opinion – yet this caveat is rarely given in a news report, allowing 'vox pops' to create an impression about the state of public opinion (Brookes, Lewis and Wahl-Jorgensen 2004). In the following example, a vox pop is used to convey an impression of public frustration with the weather:

'The wild winter storm leaves a blanket of snow and ice unusually deep in the South. From the Gulf Coast of Alabama up to the Carolinas and Virginia, eight inches so far in Raleigh, 10 in Richmond.'
Unidentified woman: 'Richmond and the snow drives me bonkers.'

(NBC Nightly News, 3 January 2002)

This example highlights how casual representations of public opinion are often slotted into news narratives to fit the news agenda.

By contrast, opinion polls – which, for all their limitations, are the only form of systematic evidence available – account for only 2 per cent of all references to public opinion in both the US and British broadcast news (Lewis, Wahl-Jorgensen and Inthorn 2004). While this figure goes up during election campaigns (Brookes, Lewis and Wahl-Jorgensen 2004), it is striking how little the voluminous body of polling data available to journalists is actually used.

Moreover, what is troubling about journalists' reliance on unsystematic evidence, such as their own guesses about the 'public mood' or their interviews with people encountered in the street, is that there is little reason to believe such representations are accurate. Susan Herbst, an American political scientist who has done extensive work on how actors in the political process view public opinion, suggests that although 'public opinion is highly valued . . . it is badly conceptualized, poorly measured by important political actors, and sometimes ignored entirely' (Herbst 1998: 2). Thus while journalists have a certain respect for the 'scientific' independence of polling data, they are more likely to revert to their own highly subjective impressions. As she explains it, we 'conceptualise "public opinion" – the embodiment of our fellow citizens' concerns and ideologies – as it intersects with our own lives and goals' (Herbst 1998: 150). That is to say, even for those who are most dependent on knowledge of public opinion, such as journalists and politicians, their understanding of it is often not derived from scientific methods. Instead, it is filtered through the lens of the individual's own interests, perceptions and environments.

Journalists do use a range of strategies to gain information about public opinion, though they ultimately do not guarantee precise or representative information. In fact, most studies show that journalists have little direct interaction with citizens. Instead, they rely on their own ideas about readers and viewers. In a classic study of newsroom culture at news magazines and television news programs in the US, Herbert Gans (1980: 230) found that editors tended to routinely reject feedback from their audiences. It didn't matter whether this feedback came in the form of polls, market surveys, letters or phone calls – journalists mistrusted both statistics and the views represented in these forms of feedback. In their search for audience opinion, they were much more likely to rely on 'known' groups such as family members, friends, or people in their local communities.

Similarly, Sumpter's (2000) ethnographic study of staff at a Texas daily newspaper suggested that journalists, when trying to imagine audience reactions and opinions, construct 'imaginary, local readers' who nevertheless 'often resembled the interests and demographics of the people in the newsroom' (Sumpter 2000: 338). More alarmingly, perhaps, Wahl-Jorgensen's (2002) work on how journalists discuss the people who write letters to the editor indicates that the culture of the newsroom is all too often steeped in disdain for the public, as journalists routinely make fun of members of the public. Those motivated to express themselves by writing letters are not seen as the actors on whom a democratic public sphere depends, but as irrational and atypical.

This indicates that journalists' inferences about public opinion cannot be taken at face value but should be understood as culturally constructed ideas, built on what is often flimsy evidence. These impressions *may* accord with more systematic forms of evidence, but they may also run counter to what surveys suggest that citizens really think. King and Schudson (1995) demonstrated that journalists consistently lauded President Reagan for his popular touch, despite the fact that polls suggested he was, in his first two years, one of the least popular presidents in the post-war period. They conclude that

> the evidence indicates that Ronald Reagan came to be described as a Great Communicator in the press not because of special skills in communicating directly to the American people but because of significant skill in communicating with key elites, including the media itself.
>
> (King and Schudson 1995: 148–9)

In other words, the conventional wisdom built up among journalists about public attitudes may have little to do with majority opinion.

Furthermore, when citizens are allowed a voice in the public debate on the news, it is often restricted to discussion of apolitical issues, or emotional and self-interested responses to political events unfolding around them. During coverage of the 'war on terrorism', for example, citizens appeared in news stories discussing various fears or concerns: of flying, of receiving an anthrax letter, or of spending time in tall buildings. However, they were rarely given a chance to respond politically, or in a way that went beyond their own personal experience or concerns (Lewis, Wahl-Jorgensen and Inthorn 2004).

When people are shown expressing political views, it is most likely to involve giving – or failing to give – support for the policies or actions of political leaders. When we are given a political voice, in other words, we tend to be shown following rather than leading. Around 11 per cent of references to citizens or public opinion come in this form, and include things such as horserace polls, approval ratings, and support for a politician's style or handling of an issue. Only around 5 per cent of references to public opinion involve citizens directing suggestions about what should be done in the world to government, the corporate world or to their fellow citizens. Overall, then, citizens in the news are largely excluded from active participation in public deliberation.

The present and future role of citizens in the news

In this chapter we have tried to shed light on the relationship between public opinion and journalism. While the citizens of ancient Greece could gather together and engage directly with their political representatives, the news media have become the modern day forum for that engagement. It is therefore the task of journalism to speak on behalf of or represent public opinion. Yet in doing so journalists are faced with demands which have more to do with deep-rooted newsroom practices than with the needs of a democratic society.

Journalists have traditionally relied on various sources to understand and report on public opinion. Although it has its problems, public opinion polling is the most systematic and empirically grounded form of data that journalists have available to them. But while polls are now a routine part of news reporting, they are only used in limited ways, constrained by their news value and relevance to elite-driven political debate. Indeed, journalists tend to prefer a range of more impressionistic strategies for representing public opinion. As a result of this, their understanding of public opinion rarely relies on any systematic data. Instead, they tend to use anecdotal evidence, often based on conversations with people similar to them, to convey impressions about public opinion that may tell us more about the journalist's world view than what citizens actually think.

Moreover, the media coverage of public opinion tends to portray citizens as passive observers of the world. They have fears, impressions and desires, but they don't have much of a say about what should be done about health care, education, the environment, crime, economic policy, taxes, war and peace, and any other issue in the public sphere. They are not, in this sense, given space to express any public opinion about politics. Citizens, although appearing often in the news, are largely shown as apolitical creatures who are allowed to have opinions only on issues that affect them personally, whether sports, fashion, shopping, royals or the quality of public transportation. The news agenda is set by politicians and other elites, and citizens can, at best, react to the already-existing agenda, but cannot easily contribute their own ideas.

Journalists' reporting of public opinion works in the service of democracy when it engages citizens to express substantive political opinions, and it is at its worst when it portrays citizens as apathetic and apolitical. All too often, what journalism gives us is thus a series of vague, democratic gestures rather than a dialogue between the people and their political representatives. In this formulation, public opinion is an overwhelmingly reactive, rather than a creative, force.

There are, however, some signs of the emergence of a new kind of participatory journalism, with e-mails and text messages punctuating certain forms of news programming – especially on public radio channels like the BBC's Radio 5 Live. So, for example, when Iraqis were shown pulling down a statue of Saddam Hussein during the Iraq war – as victorious US troops entered Baghdad – the incident received rather uncritical coverage from most broadcasters, who implied that the small celebratory group of Iraqis involved were representative of Iraqi public opinion (Lewis and Brookes 2004). One of the few moments of dissent came from Radio 5 listeners, who suggested that the focus on the events in Paradise Square was propagandist. Although the show's presenters suggested this concern was misplaced – again, relying more on conventional wisdom than hard evidence – citizens with clear and relevant political views were at least given space to express themselves and thereby broaden the perspectives available to the listener:

> Quick couple of e-mails . . . another cynic, Richard, suggests in a city of six million, what looks like a couple of hundred young men shouting to me doesn't seem . . . 'don't exaggerate and push the Blair propaganda', that from Richard. So some people not overwhelmed by what we've seen. I would say that the scenes in that centre were undoubtedly very televisual, but from what we've heard there are a lot of people in exactly that mood, in the mood to celebrate the arrival of the American troops, it's not just a few hundred we see pictured.
>
> (Peter Allen, Radio 5 Live, 9 April 2003)

Exactly how this form of news coverage develops remains to be seen. There is no doubt that public service broadcasters like the BBC are concerned by the decline in citizen engagement with representative politics – especially among young people – and that the conventional representations of public opinion do little to encourage a more engaged citizenry. The time is right for more imaginative and inclusive forms of journalism, in which citizens are seen playing a more deliberative role in their democracy – as so many of them actually do – rather than simply being spectators of a show being played out in Westminster or Washington. This means more than simply creating spaces – whether online or in talk radio – where citizens can go if they wish. It means taking public opinion seriously, and thereby rethinking basic journalistic conventions about covering politics from the top down.

| References

Asher, H. (1998) *Polling and the Public*. Washington: Congressional Quarterly Press.

Behr, R. and Iyengar, S. (1985) Television News, Real World Cues, and Changes in the Public Agenda, *Public Opinion Quarterly*, 46: 38–57.

Blumer, H. (1948) Public Opinion and Public Opinion Polling, *American Sociological Review* 13: 542–7.

Bourdieu, P. (1979) Public Opinion Does Not Exist, in A. Mattelart and S. Siegelaub (eds) *Communication and Class Struggle*. New York: International General.

Brady, H. E. and Orren, G. R. (1992) Polling Pitfalls: Sources of Error in Public Opinion Surveys, in T. E. Mann and G. R. Orren (eds) *Media Polls in American Politics*. Washington, DC: Brookings Institution.

Brookes, R., Lewis, J. and Wahl-Jorgensen, K. (2004) The Media Representation of Public Opinion: British Television News Coverage of the 2001 General Election, *Media, Culture and Society* 26(1), 63–80.

Brule, M. and Giacometti, P. (1990) Opinion Polling in France at the End of the 80s, *Public Perspective*, March–April.

Croteau, D. (1998) *Examining the Liberal Media Claim*. Virginia Commonwealth University, Department of Sociology and Anthropology.

Edelman, M. (1988) *Constructing the Political Spectacle*. Chicago: University of Chicago Press.

Edelman, M. (1995) The Influence of Rationality Claims on Public Opinion and Policy, in C. Salmon and T. Glasser (eds) *Public Opinion and the Communication of Consent*. New York: Guilford Press.

Gallup, G. (1966) Polls and the Political Process – Past, Present and Future, *Public Opinion Quarterly*, 29, 544–9.

Gans, H. J. (1980) *Deciding What's News*. London: Constable.

Glasgow Media Group (1982) *Really Bad News*. London: Writers and Readers.

Habermas, J. (1989) *The Structural Transformation of the Public Sphere*. Cambridge, MA: MIT Press.

Herbst, S. (1998) *Reading Public Opinion: How Political Actors View the Democratic Process*. Chicago: University of Chicago Press.

King, E. and Schudson, M. (1995) The Press and the Illusion of Public Opinion, in C. Salmon, and T. Glasser, (eds) *Public Opinion and the Communication of Consent*. New York: Guilford Press, pp. 132–55.

Krosnik, J. (1989) Question Wording and Reports of Survey Results: The Case of Louis Harris and Associates and Aetna Life and Casualty, *Public Opinion Quarterly*. 53(Spring): 107–13.

Ladd, E. C. and Benson, J. (1992) The Growth of News Polls in American Politics, in T. E. Mann and G. R. Orren (eds), *Media Polls in American Politics*. Washington, DC: Brookings Institution.

Lewis, J. (2001) *Constructing Public Opinion*. New York: Columbia University Press.

Lewis, J. and Brookes, R. (2004) How British Television News Represented the Case for the War In Iraq, in S. Allan and B. Zelizer (eds) *Reporting War*. London: Routledge.

Lewis, J., Wahl-Jorgensen, K. and Inthorn, S. (2004) Images of Citizenship on Television News: Constructing a Passive Public, *Journalism Studies* 4(2).

McLeod, J., Pan, Z. and Rucinski, D. (1995) Levels of Analysis in Public Opinion Research, in C. Salmon and T. Glasser (eds) *Public Opinion and the Communication of Consent*. New York: Guilford Press, pp. 55–88.

McNair, B. (2000) *Journalism and Democracy: an Evaluation of the Political Public Sphere*. London: Routledge.

Noelle-Neumann, E. (1995) 'Public Opinion and Rationality', in C. Salmon and T. Glasser (eds) *Public Opinion and the Communication of Consent*. New York: Guilford Press, pp. 33–54.

Paletz, D. and Entman, R. (1981) *Media Power Politics*. New York: Free Press.

Price, V. (1994) *Public Opinion*. Thousand Oak, CA: Sage.

Peters, J. D. (1999) Public Journalism and Democratic Theory: Four Challenges, in T. Glasser (ed.) *The Idea of Public Journalism*. New York: Guilford, pp. 99–117.

Salmon, C. and Glasser, T. (1995) The Politics of Polling and the Limits of Consent, in C. Salmon and T. Glasser (eds) *Public Opinion and the Communication of Consent*. New York: Guilford Press.

Splichal, S. (1999) *Public Opinion: Developments and Controversies in the Twentieth Century*. Lanham, MD: Rowman & Littlefield.

Sumpter, R. S. (2000) Daily Newspaper Editors' Audience Construction Routines: a Case Study, *Critical Studies in Media Communication*, 17(3), 334–6.

Tuchman, G. (1978) *Making News*. New York: Free Press.

Wahl-Jorgensen, K. (2002) 'The Construction of the Public in Letters to the Editor: Deliberative Democracy and the Idiom of Insanity', *Journalism*, 3(2), 183–204.

Williams, R. (1963) *Culture and Society*. New York, Columbia University.

Zaller, J. R. (1992) *The Nature and Origins of Mass Opinion*. Cambridge: Cambridge University Press.

18

In defence of 'thick' journalism; or how television journalism can be good for us

Simon Cottle

- A 'thought experiment': how should journalism intervene in the life of societies to deepen democracy?
- Critical media theorists have much to say about how media reproduce the voices of the powerful and reinforce dominant social structures, but relatively little about how the representations of journalism can or should contribute to a civil and democratic society. Do we now need to develop a sharper sense of 'the possible' as well as 'the problematic' in our evaluation of media performance and potential?
- Is it conceivable that some forms of contemporary journalism already provide modes of representation that uphold and strengthen democracy?
- If so, what exactly are some of these 'democratizing' forms of journalism and what do they contribute that is worth recognizing, defending and extending?

The anthropologist Clifford Geertz famously used the phrase 'thick description' to describe how the pursuit of cultural meanings by ethnographers can help us to interpret and understand the meaningful worlds of others (Geertz 1973: 10). The professional practices and public representations of journalism are no less 'suspended in webs of significance' (as well as structures of power) and, in its more in-depth reportage, journalism also embarks on 'an elaborate venture in thick description' (Geertz 1973: 6). The term 'thick journalism', then, is coined here to refer broadly to reportage, and television journalism particularly, which seeks to go beyond 'thin' news reports, headlines and news values, to reveal something of the deep structures, contending perspectives and lived experiences that often underpin if not propel news stories forward and which grant them meaning – both for the participants and protagonists involved as well as potentially for us, the audience, witnessing them at home.[1] Television can be a powerful medium for improving public understanding of the views and values that clash and clamour within news stories. 'Thick journalism' typically provides in-depth 'ways of knowing'. It does so by various practices and techniques: observation and first-hand testimony; investigation, documentation and exposé; presentation of conflicting interests and identities; and specific programme formats and technologies that serve to disseminate and/or deliberate powerful images and contested issues.[2] 'Thick journalism', it needs to be said, is not the preserve of any particular television genre, whether news, current affairs or documentary. The distinctions between these genres have, in any case, become increasingly blurred in recent years. Nor is 'thick journalism' exclusively preoccupied with 'capital P' politics or 'capital A' affairs of state. Today's mediatized public and private spheres, as we shall hear below, often interpenetrate and condition each other.

Unfortunately the complexities of today's television journalism are rarely acknowledged (Cottle and Rai 2006). Researchers are quick to point out that today's media 'marketplace' is increasingly competitive, deregulated and consumer-oriented, and that these trends have eroded the quality of television news and both the quantity and quality of current affairs and documentary programmes. The rise of 'reality TV', populist news agendas, infotainment-based and personality-led current affairs magazines – with documentary strands decommissioned or banished to grave-yard slots – has been well documented in the UK (Cottle 1993; Bromley 2001; O'Malley 2001; Tumber 2001), the US (PEJ 1998; Nahra 2001) and Australia (Turner 2001; Cottle and Rai 2006).[3]

These developments are all too real, but some forms of television journalism do manage to contribute something of value to the democratic life-blood of society. Television journalism, notwithstanding the encroaching forces of commerce and consumerism, occasionally manages to produce 'exceptional' programmes – 'exceptional' because they subvert current programming trends and also because they are of outstanding quality. These exceptional forms of journalism provide an important contribution to that inter-discursive, mediatized social space that constitutes, to some imperfect degree, a 'public sphere' of common intercourse and shared public understanding. They are, therefore, worthy of serious thought and analysis.

This chapter sets out to demonstrate how these exceptional forms of television journalism provide rich, sometimes compelling, resources for engaging audiences as citizens and 'members of the public'. It does so by focusing on ten examples of how television has engaged with the politics and dehumanizing depictions of the 'other'. Ten arguments, if you will, in defence of television's performance of 'thick journalism', and ten reasons why this type of practice demands to be taken seriously and nurtured in the future.

| Behind the headlines, beyond news agendas

Television journalism occasionally manages to produce programmes that go behind headlines and beyond news agendas and get to places, both geographic and social, that otherwise would not find public exposure. It does so despite news organizations' cutbacks on foreign correspondents and foreign news bureaus. Consider, for example, the following programme extract.

FOUR CORNERS: ABOUT WOOMERA

Protestors on roof of building wave banner 'We refugees have request – from Australian people for help'

Debbie Whitmont, Reporter: These pictures were filmed by guards at Woomera Detention Centre in February last year. They show scenes children, adults and staff witnessed, sometimes daily, in an Australian detention centre. For Woomera this isn't an unusual day. There are demonstrations in three of the compounds and, here, a 19-year-old Afghan man has climbed into the razor wire . . . Those who starved or harmed themselves in Woomera weren't a small minority. And, ultimately, most were found to be genuine refugees and given temporary visas . . . One man sees the camera as a chance to speak to people he's never met – ordinary Australians, outside Woomera . . . He tries to explain that the detainees have nothing left to use but their bodies to plead their desperation.

Man: We are crying, we are screaming. And we are all, 'What to do?' We have nothing. This is what you want? This is Australia say to us? Please help us and listen as we are suffering inside. We don't want to make any rampage. We don't want any things to this (sobs). We all came from bad condition. We want help.

ABC, *Four Corners*, About Woomera, 19 May 2003

This programme about refugees and asylum seekers incarcerated in Australia's notorious detention centre, 'Woomera', in the South Australian desert proved to be a powerful indictment of the Australian government's anti-asylum seeker policy, and helped to place in the public domain arguments and accounts that had not been aired previously. The programme tried to go behind news headlines about 'riots' in detention centres to reveal something of the motivations and injustices animating these desperate attempts for public recognition and action. As in this case, in-depth journalism can itself prompt headlines responding to the revelations and dramatic scenes. Such programmes sometimes send powerful ripples across society (or segments of it) and may even contribute to a growing wave of public disquiet, protest and change.

Investigation and exposé

The investigative and exposé role of journalism is traditionally identified with its Fourth Estate function within liberal democratic theory as well as the profession's idealized view of itself (De Burgh 2000). Although not enacted as often as journalists are apt to suggest, this role is evident in current television journalism. As well as revealing actions and events hitherto hidden from public view, such programmes can also contribute to what John Thompson has termed 'the transformation of visibility' (Thompson 1995) – where the operations of power and the powerful have become, courtesy of the media spotlight, increasingly subject to public surveillance and critical scrutiny.

DATELNE: INSIDE NAURU – PACIFIC DESPAIR

Journalists are not welcome in Nauru. Neither are lawyers, human rights advocates, or even concerned citizens. This isolated Pacific nation plays host to two detention centres the Australian and Nauruan governments would rather you didn't see. 18 months ago, asylum seekers on board the 'Tampa' were intercepted en route to Australia. They were diverted to Nauru and John Howard's so-called 'Pacific solution' was born. It's a plan to detain and process asylum seekers outside of Australia. Out of sight and away from access to Australian courts and appeals. I'm in Nauru as a transit passenger on the way to Fiji. I have three days. I've come to investigate rumours that have reached Australia – rumours of a major crisis at the smaller of the two detention centres . . .

SBS, *Dateline*: Inside Nauru – Pacific Despair, 29 January 2003

This programme captures on film the Australian government's attempts to conceal from public view the conditions and squalor found within this detention centre, which is situated off-shore on the remote pacific island of Nauru. *Inside Nauru* was broadcast in the mainstream Australian media, much to the dismay, no doubt, of the Government agencies responsible. Its insights into the human consequences of the government's policies towards asylum seekers and refugees generated considerable public debate.

| Circulating public rhetoric, reason and debate

Some forms of television journalism also act as a public interlocutor, demanding answers from policy makers and authorities: in so doing, they help to produce rhetoric and explanation that are essential for 'deliberative democracy' (Dryzek 2000; Benhabib 2002). Consider, for example, the following exchange between a news presenter and the Australian Minister for Immigration, at that time responsible for the Australian government's controversial policy on refugees and asylum seekers.

LATELINE: CHILD DETAINEES

Tony Jones, reporter: Immigration Minister Philip Ruddock has defended the detention of children, saying there is no other realistic way of dealing with asylum seekers. Mr Ruddock claims the separation of children from their parents would cause more psychological harm than keeping them in detention.

Tony Jones: How are you going to rebuff this almost united body of medical opinion? Why are you right and all these doctors and psychiatrists are wrong?

Philip Ruddock: Well, I don't think I've ever asserted that, Tony. What I assert is that in detention of unauthorized arrivals as a matter of public policy there is no other realistic way to be able to deal with people who come, whether with families or otherwise, who come without any authority than to properly detain them, process them, and have them available for removal if they have no lawful basis to be here . . .

ABC, *Lateline*, 19 March 2002

Here we see how the news presenter's questioning prompts the interviewee to produce reasons and rhetoric, claims and counter claims, as he tries to present a reasoned and reasonable defence to the criticism put to him. As he does, so we, the audience, are provided with resources – propositional, argumentative, rhetorical and performative – with which to evaluate both the issue in contention as well as the credibility of the interviewee.

Mediatized 'liveness' and social charge

Live talk, in contrast to pre-scripted and edited talk, has the capacity to generate revealing, sometimes dramatic, exchanges and impromptu remarks. A live televised interview, for example, has an integral wholeness and dynamic that can generate tension and prompt verbal virtuosity as the protagonists engage each other, get to the heart of the issue and/or produce apparent evasions (Cottle 2002, 2003). Consider, for example, the continuation of the same live news interview discussed in the previous section.

LATELINE: CHILD DETAINEES

Tony Jones, reporter: Can I come back to the question of their mental health, Minister, because that is the question that is at stake here. Can you name one?

Philip Ruddock: It is not the only question, Tony.

Tony Jones: It is the question we're discussing tonight.

Philip Ruddock: No that's the question you want me to, no, Tony, that's the question you want me to deal with.

Tony Jones: With respect, Minister, that is the question we asked you to come on and deal with. Can you name one medical body that supports your argument that children and their families should remain in detention at risk to their psychological state.

Philip Ruddock: I haven't seen arguments from organizations that believe that it is preferable to have no effective control of our borders in order not to face some difficulties in the management of that process. I haven't seen that argument. That's not what they're arguing. What I am saying to professional bodies and others – if you are of the view that the risk to the child is so great that the child ought to be removed from that environment and be separated from their parents, and that it is in their best interests, I will take that advice, but that's not the advice I received.

Tony Jones: This is the advice we're getting from the people we're talking to. This is the advice the medical bodies, including all the medical committees, appear to be getting. Let me cite to you what we've just heard Dr Raman say, the senior paediatrician from Sydney's Western Area Health Services: 'Young babies are not developing properly, they're not talking, they're not engaging, there's a lack of curiosity.' Another paediatrician writes to the Royal College of Physicians that 'Children at Woomera are living in a chronically deprived environment that's affecting their psychological development'. Does that worry you?

Phillip Ruddock: Of course it worries me. It ought to worry their parents. It ought to worry people who bring children to Australia without lawful authority.

Tony Jones: Minister, they are here in Australia now and with respect, you are their guardian, their legal guardian. Those children . . .

Philip Ruddock: No Tony, I am only the guardian for those children who come unaccompanied . . .

ABC, *Lateline*, 19 March 2002

As we can see, there is often an unpredictable quality and dramatic potential within live televised encounters, and these contain risks as well as opportunities in the public elaboration of contending points of view. Here the news interviewer doggedly pursues a line of questioning – an agenda – as the interviewee, equally determinedly, seeks to agenda-shift to safer, less politically damaging ground. Throughout these verbal twists and turns the audience is positioned, perhaps compelled, to consider where the moral responsibility (or culpability) should be placed for the plight of children and their families in detention centres.

| Public performance, emotion and affect

If engaged views and voices are the raw material for processes of deliberative democracy, as illustrated above, so too are the emotions and feelings that often lie beneath deeply held convictions and interests. Televised encounters often reveal something of the private hurt and anguish connected with public postures and policies. Histories and 'her-stories' communicated not in the televisual 'agora' of so-called rational debate, but within the filmed domestic milieu of the family, can also show how today's public and private worlds often collide. Here, the daughter of (then) Immigration Minister demonstrates the private dilemma posed by her relationship with her father and his public commitment to policies that she strongly disagrees with. As in previous examples, this programme generated many headlines after it was aired.

AUSTRALIAN STORY: THE GATEKEEPER

Kirsty Ruddock: I suppose what upsets me is that he can't take a more compassionate approach to some of the issues. I understand that there's difficult economics behind some of the issues, that obviously they're worried about some of the implications of sort of opening the floodgates and things like that, but that doesn't give you an excuse to not treat people with compassion and as human beings.

Philip Ruddock: I, I mean, I have compassion for everyone, but I can't help everyone . . .

Kursty Ruddock: I don't think he is going to give any kind of amnesty to the current people that are in asylum, but I'd like to see him do it. Obviously, you know, I love my dad, but sometimes you do feel a bit let down that you can't change his view on things and that you're not getting through to him as well, and that somehow it's my fault what he's doing is wrong. I have decided to live overseas for a period of time as a volunteer . . .

ABC, *Australian Story*: The Gatekeeper, 16 September 2002

The private world of family relationships, emotions and feelings, then, need not be seen as trivial or outside the 'serious stuff' of politics. Some programmes, such as the popular *Australian Story* series, which focuses on individuals and personal lives, can be vehicles for showing the human consequences of policies, events and decisions enacted in the public domain.

Voice to the voiceless, identity to image

Television journalism delegates who is seen, who is permitted to speak, and what 'views' are heard. News agendas and news representations can also affect how groups and individuals are portrayed: individuals and groups can be presented as deviant, outsiders and 'others', rendered 'speechless', or stripped of their identity in stereotypical or spectacular news visualization. 'Thick journalism', however, has the potential to redress such imbalances and injustices. It can extend access to otherwise unseen groups, concede degrees of editorial independence and control to these groups, and adopt differing narrative strategies and authorial positions. These can range from the impartial and detached to the committed and engaged, and from the mimetic to the ironic and parodic. Today, the 'politics of recognition' (Taylor 1995) as much as the 'politics of redistribution', demands to be played out in television news, current affairs and documentaries. Here a reporter helps to put human faces to 'terrorism suspects' who have been publicly silenced and 'disappeared' in America's 'war on terrorism'.

PANORAMA: INSIDE GUANTANAMO
Vivian White reporter: The call to prayer at Guantanamo Bay. Over 600 men are being held here by the USA as part of its war against terror. We've been to investigate Guantanamo justice . . .

White: While Alif Khan was inside Guantanamo, branded as an Al-Qaeda suspect, his business rivals grabbed his assets, including these shops, from him. Since his release he's fought to get his property back . . .

Alif Khan:. . . . I am not Taliban, not a terrorist, not Al-Qaeda. People handed me over because someone wanted to gain influence – dollars or because of a personal dispute.

White: But Alif Khan was transported from Afghanistan to Guantanamo. This is his testimony.

Khan: They put cuffs and tape on my hands, taped my eyes and taped my ears. They gagged me. They put chains on my legs and chains around my belly. They injected me. I was unconscious. I don't know how they transported me. When I arrived in Cuba and they took me off the plane they gave another injection and I came back to consciousness. I did not know how long I was flying for. It might have been one or two days. They put me onto a bed on wheels. I could sense what was going on. They tied me up. They took me off the plane into a vehicle. We go to a big prison and there were cages there. They built it like a zoo.

BBC1, *Panorama*: Inside Guantanamo, 5 October 2003

This BBC *Panorama* programme, which was broadcast in other countries as well as the UK, was the first serious attempt to give a human face and identity to the hitherto invisible 'terrorism suspects' transported by the US military to Cuba and incarcerated without trial at Guantanamo Bay. The programme provided the first insights into the suffering of countless 'suspects' caught up in the 'war on terror': by allowing their voices and testimonies to be heard, the programme revealed something of their sense of injustice and denied humanity.

Challenging society's meta-narratives

Some television programmes go further in their public revelations of power and challenge accepted social beliefs and views promulgated elsewhere in the media. Here a programme constructs its narrative by accessing opposing views – but there is no doubting where its sympathies lie or what its final judgement is.

PIPER FILMS: 'SEEKING ASYLUM'

Malcolm Frazer, Former Prime Minister: People have been demonized. In international terms they're not illegal they're asylum seekers seeking refuge. We're told they're queue jumpers, but there's been no queue to jump.

Sharif (subtitled): In Woomera is very bad condition. There is no difference between Woomera Detention and Cuba jail.

Hon. Malcolm Frazer: I'm going to stop using the word 'Detention Centres' because they are in fact prisons.

Hon. Philip Ruddock, Minister for Immigration and Multicultural Affairs: As far as we're concerned detention has to be humane, we're not about punishing people. It's not intended to be punitive.

Nassem: It's not so difficult to process people, but unfortunately many people remain for two years, three years without any reason.

Arif: If they are staying detention centre for long time, really, they become crazy.

Sharif: I was in Woomera, there I saw many childrens, they had no futures. Don't destroy the future of the children.

Hon. Philip Ruddock: Governments agree that you have to be able to manage borders. Governments agree that sovereignty is important.

Hon. Malcolm Frazer: Australia was never under threat. Can anyone really believe that four or five or even six thousand refugees offer a threat to the sovereignty of Australia?

Arif: My father was a judge in Afghanistan. He was killed by Taliban. Now how can I prove to Government of Australia I lost my father? How can I prove, I don't have any picture? Can you feel my situation or not?

Super Title: 'Everyone has the right to seek and enjoy in other countries asylum from persecution.' Article 14.1 United Nations Declaration of Human Rights.

SBS and Piper Films (Producer/Director Mike Piper), *Seeking Asylum*,
August 2002

As we can see, this particular programme drives the viewer towards a particular destination and, as it does so, challenges widely held ideas about the 'threat' posed by refugees to Australian sovereignty and security. No less than a former prime minister is accessed to challenge the current government, and the programme also makes effective use of refugee testimonies and scenes appearing to contradict the words of the immigration minister, Phillip Ruddock. The programme concludes by presenting Article 14.1 of the United Nations Declaration of Human Rights. Such programmes, then, are capable of articulating a strong point of view, challenging assumptions and prompting public deliberation and debate.

Recognition, difference and cultural settlement

Memories of past violence, trauma and injustice inform the struggles of the present and create demands for wider acknowledgement of both historical and ongoing pain. The community increasingly recognizes that symbolic gestures acknowledging the hurt caused by past deeds are necessary for 'reconciliation' between groups that have clashed in the past, and for them to live together successfully in the present. Although John Howard's Australian Government has felt unable to say 'sorry' to the Aboriginal communities of Australia for white settler genocide and the stealing of land, television journalism has sought on occasion to play a more progressive part in the process of reconciliation.

AUSTRALIAN STORY: BRIDGE OVER MYALL CREEK
On 10 June, 1838 a gang of stockmen led by a squatter rode into Myall Creek Station and brutally murdered about 28 unarmed women, children and old men.

Sue Blacklock: We haven't forgotten them, but we know that they are still here. They're still in our memories, they're in our hearts. They will always be remembered. And it's just a very emotional time for us. And we just want to remember them so they will be at peace.

Beulah: It's a very satisfying experience. We've committed ourselves to follow this right through and to remember our history – the history of the Aboriginals and our history, because it is our history as well. So it is very humbling and it's a privilege . . .

Rev. Brown: We had planned a beautiful memorial, and it remains a beautiful memorial. But to actually have descendents of those who carried out the murder and descendents of those who were killed come together in an act of personal reconciliation as part of the process of . . . of . . . dedicating this memorial was just marvelous. It was something we couldn't have planned, but it was a great gift to us. And a great gift, I think, to the people of Australia.

Des: I was there to say how sorry I was on behalf of all my family, and of all those who would wish me to say I was sorry, how sorry we were. When we said the words and said the prayers, the feeling I had was that I had done something in my life that was really meaningful to those people. The whole day was one where, you know, I really felt . . . it was probably the best thing I'd done . . . There are still many people who don't want to know about it, but as this happens in various places around Australia I think it'll just expand from there.

ABC, *Australian Story*: Bridge Over Myall Creek, 26 July 2001

This programme, as we can see, gives expression to the efforts of local communities to acknowledge past injustices by sharing family knowledge and collective memories of the murderous acts committed by white Australians against Aboriginal people. By representing these events in the public arena, the programme performatively extends their reach to wider Australia and perhaps contributes symbolically at least, to the reconciliation process.

Media reflexivity

Today's media occasionally monitors and comments on its own performance and practices. Sometimes this is institutionalized in programmes designed to do just this, such as *Media Watch* in Australia or *Right to Reply* in Britain, or sometimes it takes place in and through existing programmes. Given that today's politicians and other power brokers make extensive use of the media in their battle for hearts and minds (and votes), such media reflexivity is vital for deconstructing 'spin' and understanding symbolic and rhetorical forms of power – as well as for analysing the media's seeming complicity with powerful interests. Here a war photographer reflects on his own practice, and in so doing gives voice to his informing humanism and hopes for a more critically engaged media and public.

CHRISTIAN FREI: WAR PHOTOGRAPHER:

Why photograph war? Is it possible to put an end to a form of human behaviour which has existed throughout history by means of photography? The proportions of that notion seem ridiculously out of balance. Yet that very idea has motivated me. For me the strength of photography lies in its ability to evoke a sense of humanity. If war is an attempt to negate humanity, then photography can be perceived as the opposite of war; and if it is used well it can be a powerful ingredient in the antidote to war. In a way, if an individual assumes the risk of placing himself (sic) in the middle of a war in order to communicate what is happening, he's trying to negotiate for peace. Perhaps that's why that those who are in charge of perpetuating a war do not like to have photographers around . . . But everyone can't be there; so that's why photographers go there. To create pictures powerful enough to overcome the deluding effects of the mass media and to shake them out of their indifference. To protest and by the strength of that protest to make others protest.

The worst thing as a photographer is the thought that I'm benefiting from someone else's tragedy. This idea haunts me; it is something I have to reckon with everyday because I know if I ever let personal ambition overtake genuine compassion then I will have sold my soul. The only way I can justify my role is to have respect for the other person's predicament. The extent to which I do that is the extent to which I become accepted by the Other. And to that extent I can accept myself.

ABC, *War Photographer*, Christen Frei, 15 February 2004

Reflexive programmes such as these, though rare, nonetheless encourage critique of routine media reporting and reveal something of the dilemmas and ethical difficulties behind the production of news, current affairs and documentary programmes. They invite a more reflexive stance in relation to the programmes that fill our TV screens and artifices that go into their production.

▌Bearing witness in a globalizing world

Our increasingly globalizing and interconnected – yet unequal – world impels us to be informed of, and responsive to, human needs and the plight of others. Bonds of commitment and solidarity are needed if we are to overcome ethnic, nationalist and other fragmenting forces and confront the moral challenges posed by global change. Television journalism, notwithstanding its capacity to trivialize and render into spectacle images of human suffering (Tester 1994, 2001), also has the potential to prod consciences and deepen public understanding of the dynamics of global poverty and social injustices. It can also help dismantle historically anachronistic images of the 'other' (Ignatieff 1998). BBC reporter Michal Buerk, for example, returned to Ethiopia 20 years after helping to bring to public notice the devastating 'biblical' famine, which had then galvanized public sympathies and charitable donations.

BBC ETHIOPIA: A JOURNEY WITH MICHAEL BUERK

Michael Buerk, reporter: This is a story of a forgotten people in a lost land. The story of how hundreds of thousands died of starvation on a planet choked with food. Of tyranny and neglect. Yet it's also a story of how three million Iron Age families were saved by the power of television, by our shame that made us feel their pain in a way that has never happened before and has never happened since. It's a story of betrayal . . .

BBC2, *Ethiopia: A Journey with Michael Buerk*, 11 January 2004

The programme was broadcast in a number of different countries. Deploying the techniques of personalization – a narrative of personal testimony – as well as online discussion following the broadcast, the reporter manages to contextualize and analyse the continuing desperate situation in Ethiopia. This was more than Third World as 'victim', as 'emotional sump', as 'other'. It is simply deficient and morally vacuous to assume that such programmes have no part to play in the changing consciousness and politics of understanding that condition our responses and ability to interact with today's globalizing world. As argued below, television's capacity to 'bear witness' (Sontag, 2003) has to be protected at all costs and journalists must be further enabled to provide the 'thick descriptions' necessary for engaged understanding and moral citizenship.

❙ Conclusion

This chapter has set out ten examples of how existing television journalism provides invaluable resources for deepening understanding of public events and shaping responses to them. Though exceptional within contemporary television programming, these examples of 'thick journalism' nonetheless exist and occasionally make an impact beyond their marginalized status within television schedules. I have presented just a few illustrations of how these forms of journalism can and do make a difference. Each example has served to demonstrate how the media can challenge prevailing ideas and images of the 'other'. On their own, or even collectively, they are unlikely to have transformed dominant political agendas or widened cultural horizons. However, they have disseminated important and necessary flows of information, images and ideas into the currents of change.

What I have called 'thick journalism' contributes to wider processes of social reflexivity whether conceived in terms of 'democratic deepening' and the 'democratization of democracy' (Giddens 1994), the public articulation of 'sub-politics' (Beck 1997), or the representation of identities and inequalities, both old and new, that characterize today's globalizing 'network society' (Castells 1997). 'Thick journalism' finds its normative mandate within the discourses of civil society and the contention that surrounds ideas of the 'social good' (Habermas 1996), as well as, increasingly, the circulation of global risks or 'social bads' (Beck 1992). For the most part, the inequalities and injustices of the world ontologically precede their representation within the media and so long as these produce collective forms of opposition so there will be calls for their wider recognition within mainstream media. However, the forces of commercialism and consumerism present powerful constraints to the production of 'thick journalism': the extent to which these programmes can continue to find a foothold within the schedules of television broadcasting is of critical concern. If journalists are to get 'behind the headlines' and 'beyond news agendas', to pursue 'investigation and expose', they require integrity, independence, resources and organizational support – and programme slots in which to elaborate their analyses. Similarly, 'circulating public rhetoric, reason and debate' demands access to suitable television formats and to the powerful as well as the dispossessed within the fields of contestation. More creative use of 'live media' requires journalism and journalists to overcome their professional 'agoraphobia' towards 'wide-open' mediatized spaces (Cottle 2002) and to permit dialogue and debate without always keeping to predetermined scripts and self-defined agendas. Displaying 'public performance, emotion and affect' further demands that journalists do not always prefer and defer to rationalist models of argument and debate, while nonetheless resisting the temptation to simply evoke and display private stories, emotions and feelings for sentimental effect. If journalists are to give 'voice to the voiceless' and 'identity to image' they have to make concerted efforts to identify, access and support those who are marginal or disenfranchised within society and seek a deeper understanding of their lives. 'Challenging society's meta-narratives', calls for journalists to challenge conventional thinking and move beyond national parameters and normative paradigms. Well-informed cultural sensibilities are also needed when reporting and representing the difficult processes of 'recognition, difference and cultural settlement'. 'Media reflexivity' challenges the normally unspoken epistemology of television journalism with its claims to be able to 'know', 'report' and 'represent' but, by so doing, opens up the need for ethical vigilance and a deeper appreciation of the 'politics of representation'. Finally, 'bearing witness in a globalizing world' requires that journalists have the organizational capacity and moral commitment to report on those whose fate and life chances are placed at risk by globalization.

What I have termed 'thick journalism' then, confronts formidable obstacles to its current enactment, much less further development. These democratizing forms of media are nonetheless worth struggling for. They are part of wider processes of social reflexivity and they can serve to deepen democratic processes and help create a fairer and more civil society. As demonstrated by the examples I have used in this chapter, this kind of journalism is often compelling to watch. By intervening into the life of societies and the dynamics of change, 'thick journalism' can be good for us – and sometimes not bad for 'others' too.

Notes

1   This question is currently being researched by the author and Mugdha Rai in a major study of television journalism forms in Australia, the UK, the US, India, South Africa and Singapore funded by the Australian Research Council titled *Television Journalism and Deliberative Democracy: A Comparative International Study of Communicative Architecture and Democratic Deepening* (DP0449505).

2   Some types of journalism, whether 'peace journalism' (McGoldrick and Lynch 2000; Galtung 2004), 'development journalism' (Thussu 1996) or 'civic/ public journalism' (Glasser 1999) have sought to be more prescriptive than this general mapping of television's 'thick journalism' presented here. First-hand and experiential reportage also has a history, of course, that precedes news organizations (Carey 1998).

3   Exceptionally, however, see Corner (1995) on television forms, Holland (2001) on changing current affairs TV, and Nichols (1991) on documentary modes.

References

Beck, U. (1992) *Risk Society*. London: Sage.

Beck, U. (1997) *The Reinvention of Politics*. Cambridge: Polity Press.

Benhabib, S. (2002) *The Claims of Culture*. New Jersey: Princeton University Press.

Bromley, M. (ed.) (2001) *No News is Bad News*. Harlow: Pearson Education.

Carey, P. (1998) *The Faber Book of Reportage*. London: Faber & Faber.

Castells, M. (1997) *The Information Age* (three volumes) Cambridge: Blackwell.

Corner, J. (1995) *Television Form and Public Address*. London: Edward Arnold.

Cottle, S. (1993) *TV News, Urban Conflict and the Inner City*. Leicester: Leicester University Press.

Cottle, S. (2001) Television news and citizenship: Packaging the public sphere, in M. Bromely (ed.) *No News is Bad News*. Harlow: Pearson Education.

Cottle, S. (2002) Television agora and agoraphobia post September 11, in Barbie Zelizer and Stuart Allan (eds) *Journalism After September 11*. London: Routledge.

Cottle, S. (2003) Television and deliberative democracy: Mediating communicative action, in S. Cottle (ed.) *News, Public Relations and Power*. London: Sage.

Cottle, S. and Rai, M. (2006) Between Display and Deliberation: Analyzing Television's Communicative Architecture, *Media, Culture and Society*, 28(1).

De Burgh, H. (ed.) (2000) *Investigative Journalism*. London: Routledge.

Dryzek, J. (2000) *Deliberative Democracy and Beyond*. Oxford: Oxford University Press.

Galtung, J. (2004) Media: Peace Journalism, https://www.nicr.ca/programs/PeaceJournalism.htm.

Geertz, C. (1973) *The Interpretation of Cultures*. New York: Basic Books.

Giddens, A. (1994) *Beyond Left and Right*. Cambridge: Polity Press.

Glasser, T. (ed.) (1999) *The Idea of Public Journalism*. New York: Guildford Press.

Habermas, J. (1996) *Beyond Facts and Norms*. Cambridge: Polity.

Holand, P. (2001) Authority and authenticity: redefining television current affairs, in M. Bromely (ed.) *No News is Bad News*. Harlow: Pearson Education.

Ignatieff, M. (1998) *The Warriors Honour: Ethnic War and the Modern Conscience*. London: Chatto & Windus.

McGoldrick, A. and Lynch, J. (2000) Peace Journalism: How to Do It, http://www.transcend.org/pjmanual.htm.

Nahra, C. (2001) British and American television documentaries, in M. Bromely (ed.) *No News is Bad News*. Harlow: Pearson Education.

Nicols, B. (1991) *Representing Reality: Issues and Concepts in Documentary*. Bloomington: Indiana University Press.

O'Malley, T. (2001) 'The decline of public service broadcasting in the UK 1979–2000' in M. Bromely (ed.) *No News is Bad News*. Harlow: Pearson Education.

Project for Excellence in Journalism (1998) *Changing Definitions of News*, Washington DC, www.journalism.org.

Sontag, S. (2003) *Regarding the Pain of Others*. New York: Farrar, Straus & Giroux.

Taylor, C. (1995) *Multiculturalism and the Politics of Recognition*. Princeton: Princeton University Press.

Thussu, D. (1996) Development News, Module 7, Unit 38b, MA Distance Learning. Leicester: Leicester University.

Tester, K. (1994) *Media, Culture and Morality*. London: Routledge.

Tester, K. (2001) *Compassion, Morality and the Media*. Buckingham: Open University Press.

Thompson, J. (1995) *The Media and Modernity*. Cambridge: Polity.

Tumber, H. (2001) 10pm and All That: The Battle over TV News, in M. Bromely (ed.) *No News is Bad News*. Harlow: Pearson Education.

Turner, G. (2001) Sold out: Recent shifts in television news and current affairs in Australia, in M. Bromely (ed.) *No News is Bad News*. Harlow: Pearson Education.

9

Fourth estate or fan club? Sports journalism engages the popular

David Rowe

- To whom are journalists primarily responsible – their employers or their public?
- Should sports journalists be representative of, or distinguishable from, their audiences?
- How dependent should journalists be on particular sources?
- Should journalists always be committed to critical coverage of their 'round', even if this means that key sources will no longer speak to them?
- Is it acceptable for some journalists in popular fields, such as the sports round, to leave 'hard', investigative and critical journalism to others on the more 'serious' journalistic rounds like politics, law and business?

Introduction: questions of the popular

Since the inception of journalism as a key mode of communication in modernity (Hartley 1996), journalists have been confronted by several difficult questions of practice. These have concerned issues of commercial influence and critical independence that are relevant to all journalists, especially those who cover the burgeoning areas of popular culture, celebrity and entertainment (Turner *et al.* 2000). Newspapers have always covered areas of 'light entertainment' as well as 'hard news', but today, under pressure from many other news and entertainment sources, there is a detectable shift in the balance of newspaper content towards lighter, more 'user-friendly' topics (Bennett 2003).

Sport, as an important subject for journalism, is perfectly positioned to discharge both a news role based on immediacy and an entertainment function founded on celebrity (Turner 2004), while also offering many rich opportunities for the exploration of the role of popular culture in contemporary society. Striking an appropriate balance between information, entertainment and critique is, therefore, a significant dilemma for sports journalism. For example, in their professional practice sports journalists are expected both to cover sport 'objectively' as a news item but also often to celebrate (or, perhaps, denigrate) particular sportspeople and teams as partisan sports supporters. Such tensions do not apply to sports journalists alone, nor only to print journalists (the primary focus here), but they are especially intense on the sports round (Lindsey 2001).

By addressing the key questions raised above in relation to journalistic coverage of popular cultural forms such as sport, and interrogating some sports journalists' own reflections on their activities, this chapter seeks to illuminate critical issues applying to popular journalism. Before developing the case study analysis of sports journalism, though, it is necessary briefly to trace wider developments in the structure and practice of journalism.

| Popularize or perish?

Newspaper journalism is currently confronted by a series of difficult challenges that, represented most dramatically, concern not merely how newspapers can prosper, but whether they can survive. The problems of contemporary newspapers have been well documented, and include increasing competition from more immediate electronic media, especially television and the Internet; greater time pressures on the population that squeeze out time for reading about, and reflection on, the significant events of the day; and an inter-generational decline in the habit of purchasing and reading daily newspapers, with younger women, in particular, proving to be a difficult readership to reach and retain (Greenslade 2003). The falling circulation and sales of newspapers has produced a range of strategic responses, from changes in newspaper size and style towards the more easily handled and digested tabloid format (indeed, in 2003 the British broadsheets the *Independent* and *The Times* began publishing simultaneously in both formats, with both going exclusively tabloid in 2004), to the supplementation of print by online text under established newspaper mastheads such as the *Guardian* and the *New York Times*.

Broadsheet newspapers, customarily described as 'quality' and 'serious' journals of record, are now constantly revamped to make themselves brighter, livelier, less 'stuffily' formal in style, and more populist in their approach to news values. They have adopted practices conventionally associated with their tabloid competitors in their use of photographs, headlines, and text to tell news stories more directly, succinctly and with greater 'brio' (Dahlgren and Sparks 1992). Newspapers have, historically, always experienced a tension between news and entertainment values (Allan 1999), but a contemporary trend can be discerned that has broadened the content and reshaped the news priorities of most newspapers. Many critics of this trend have represented it as a regrettable move towards a soft, consumerist 'lifestyle journalism' among the broadsheets or, worse, as evidence of a wholesale 'tabloidization' of newspapers irrespective of their size, format and editorial ethos (Franklin 1997). Others, in contrast, have interpreted the change as a positive challenge to elite, patriarchal journalistic norms (Lumby 1999).

These viewpoints have been intensely debated, but there is common agreement, as well as some empirical evidence, that, for good or ill, journalistic coverage of popular culture is now more prominent in newspapers (Sparks and Tulloch 2000). One topic that has seen a vast expansion, both in its own dedicated section and throughout the newspaper, is sport. Indeed, sport has become omnipresent in newspapers, from banner front-page headlines to the more sober analysis of the business pages, and what precisely constitutes sports journalism itself is now uncertain. Newspapers and the wider media have become so intimately involved in sport – and *vice versa* – as to suggest a convergence of these formally (and formerly) separate institutions (Rowe 2004). Sports journalism, as a result, seems to oscillate between a rather sycophantic cultivation of key sports sources (such as clubs and players) and a sometimes shrill demonization of those same organizations and individuals through sports scandals and exposés.

This chapter seeks to analyse some ways in which contemporary newspaper (and some broadcast) journalists and editors engage with sport, especially under conditions where they are confronted regularly by a stark choice: to celebrate or criticize. Such questions go to the heart of the claims of journalism to be a profession in which trained personnel work diligently in the service of an approved set of prescribed higher values – in short, the 'Fourth Estate' role of the news media as a critical check on the use and abuse of power (Curran and Seaton 2003). While, as noted above, these issues apply to every round from politics and business to travel and entertainment, the specific socio-cultural dynamics of the sports round make it an especially informative test case for analysing the conditions of contemporary journalistic practice.

Doing sport journalism

Professional sport involves a form of elite physical culture that is essentially arbitrary and useless, but in which large sections of the world's population invest much passion and energy as spectators (Tomlinson 1999). Sportspeople, therefore, can be regarded as mobile canvases onto which fans project their aspirations, fantasies and identities. Thus, journalists covering sport deal with individuals who are extraordinarily good at performing some tasks on the field of play but who may be unremarkable in other respects (Andrews and Jackson 2001; Whannel 2001). Sports journalists report the on-field exploits of sportspeople in great detail, but at the same time are required to 'flesh out' athletes as human subjects, both by drawing connections between their sports practice and their off-field character and behaviour, and also by covering sportspeople's 'extra-curricular' activities as rich, high-profile entertainment celebrities in the contemporary media. Several difficulties might present themselves when attempting this task. What if, for example, the sports star is an uninspiringly dull subject, or, conversely, if their sporting status is outweighed by their non-sports activities?

It is useful to approach the 'mission' of sports journalism by examining one especially high-profile case of the intersection of sport, glamour and entertainment. Anna Kournikova is one of the world's most famous and wealthy sportspeople. This is despite the fact that she has yet to win a major tennis tournament, and at the time of writing was considering retirement from full-time tennis at the age of 22 because of a chronic back complaint. Kournikova is a mega-celebrity because her image has been calculatedly sexualized by her management (Octagon) and by the news, sports and entertainment media. The pact between media and sports star here is that she will be constantly discussed and photographed irrespective of her on-court competitive performance, and will capitalize on this attention through modelling, endorsements and merchandising. Kournikova's body image clearly attracts public interest (Harris and Clayton 2002), but is it the role of sports journalists to be complicit in the selling of Anna, or should they ask the awkward questions that are central to the professional duties of the Fourth Estate?

In June 2002, Kournikova lost in the first round of Wimbledon – her tenth first round exit of that year. When asked by a BBC reporter whether she should descend to a lower grade of tennis in order to work on her technique, she walked off camera and asked to re-start the interview, and had to be persuaded by an accompanying Women's Tennis Association (WTA) official to resume the interview. The subsequent broadcast of the interview in full created enormous press interest, including several front-page stories, not only because it concerned a sporting celebrity, but because its content was far removed from the conventionally clichéd, anodyne exchanges of most post-match TV sports interviews. The WTA made an official complaint about the incident, which the BBC rejected on the grounds that it was merely practising 'good journalism'.

At such moments, the usually comfortable, symbiotic relationship between the sports industry and the media is exposed. The incident was newsworthy because the generally successful media management of the sports star had broken down. But this was not a watershed moment in sports journalism, and the business-as-usual of media-trained athletes providing sports journalists with predictable 'sound bites' was soon restored. As journalist Paul Kelso (2002) noted at the time:

> Last week's storm is likely to be of the teacup variety – Kournikova's value to the game cannot be overstated. Open the current edition of *Advantage* [tennis] magazine and you will find the first two spreads devoted to Kournikova ads, one for Omega watches and another for Berlei sports bras. In the next 22 pages there are another five pictures of

her (in only one is she carrying a racket) and there are four lifestyle features further back.

> She also sells papers, as [an anonymous] tennis writer acknowledges: 'She is one of those people who transcend the sport. People who know nothing about tennis know her name. She's one of the most famous people on the planet, and that's got to be good for the game. Let's face it, we're all in showbiz.'

Here it is suggested that sport and 'showbiz' have merged, and, presumably, that sports journalism is now part of the 'sportsbiz'. The above-quoted sports writer had also complained that 'the most interesting' women tennis players had been placed off limits for interviews because of the unpredictability of the outcome. It is difficult, therefore, for sports journalists to penetrate the public relations blanket thrown around sports stars by their representative and employer organizations, but if sports journalism is to be worthy of the name, that is precisely its role. Despite systematic media management, however, the world of sport is frequently disrupted by scandals and controversies when, in the English journalistic vernacular, it 'all goes pear-shaped'.

Journalists and sports scandals

Much of what passes for news in sports journalism is highly predictable in form, following the cycle of seasons and circuits, and tracing the well mapped lines of such stock subjects as recruitment, form, strategy, tactics, injury and retirement, and anticipating, describing and then reflecting on sports encounters. This orderly routine can be broken by sports scandals concerning, for example, the use of performance-enhancing drugs, allegations of sexual assault or financial impropriety (Rowe 1997). Sports journalists, however, are rarely prominent in breaking sports scandal stories for two main reasons. First, many seem to fear that they would compromise their relationships with leading sportspeople and organizations with whom they may have come to identify. Second, there is some evidence that sports journalists are not especially well trained to handle stories involving complex, investigative stories. Many sports journalists have only ever worked on the sports desk and, while there are both individual and national variations in this regard (US sports editors and journalists, for example, have higher levels of education than their British counterparts), sports journalists operating in the 'mini-empire' of sport tend to have more limited occupational experiences than those on other 'beats' (Rowe 2004).

Thus, major sports scandals concerning corruption in international sports organizations like the International Olympic Committee (IOC) have tended to be broken by journalists beyond the sports remit. As 'dissident' journalist Andrew Jennings (1996: 13) has argued forcefully:

> The Olympics is a tough beat for reporters who care . . . The [IOC] is
> headquartered far away in a small town in Switzerland and its members
> are scattered world-wide. Helpfully, the committee faxes out thousands
> of press releases asserting its successes; these find their way, without
> much editing, into the news.
>
> Other analysis is provided by a few deferential European reporters in
> the grander broadsheets plus a handful of journalists at the international
> news agencies. Some have tight bonds to their subject . . . It's all very cosy.

According to Jennings (1996: 14), 'insider' sports journalists receive
IOC-paid trips and subsidized 'freelance' public relations publication
payments, and disruption comes only from those beyond the circle:

> Just occasionally journalists outside this loop dish the Olympic dirt.
> Pandemonium! Then denials and evasions get the headlines, the
> unpleasant home truths minimised and marginalised. The committee
> says there are only fifteen journalists in the world capable of reporting
> on it. What a relief and a compliment for the rest of us.

In the revelation of major sports scandals, such as those involving bri-
bery of IOC members (like Salt Lake City's bid for the 2002 Winter Olympic
Games), sports journalists tend not to take a central role until transgressions
have already 'gone public'. For example, the award-winning investigation
into the 2002 financial scandal in Australia involving the Bulldogs rugby
league team was led by two non-sports journalists from the *Sydney Morning
Herald*. One sports journalist whom I interviewed regarded this as a logical
division of labour:

> I think a lot of times the sports journalists are concentrating on their
> round, which is providing the public with information on who's in and
> out of the team, providing the public with entertaining and interesting
> reads about their favourite sportsmen etc. It is hard when you're on a
> beat to set aside time for a special investigation. And that's where
> general reporters can come in . . . Which I think is fine, because the
> general people can devote a lot of time, what is required, to those sorts
> of things. It's a good mixture of coverage I think, if the sports guys
> continue to do their main job . . . I don't see it as a negative slight on
> sports journalists. I see it as more of an apportioning of skills and
> training.
>
> (Tony – all interviewee names are disguised)

There have been many sports scandals recently throughout the world,
including positive drug tests in association football, tennis, athletics, cycling
and other sports, and rape and sexual violence allegations in American
basketball and football, English Premier League football, Australian rugby
league and Australian rules football. Some sports journalists have taken an
active role in covering these scandals but others have clearly taken a position that has sought, in Jennings's (1996: 14) words, to avoid these
'unpleasant home truths [or at least allegations]', and have tried to exert

territorial rights over the 'sports patch' against what they see as the intrusions of social commentators and journalists from other disciplines. It should be acknowledged, though, that the professional ideologies of individual sports journalists vary, and that there are also patterned national variations in their attitudes to critical and investigative sports reporting. For example, Henningham's (1995) research among Australian sports reporters indicated less concern about critically investigative practice than among the US sports editors and journalists sampled by Salwen and Garrison (1998). Furthermore, within national sports media structures there are variations in the working relations between sports journalists and sports associations, clubs and players that influence how they handle scandals and more routine sports subjects. In some sports, for example, sports journalists may be closer to sportspeople than in others. As one interviewed sports journalist argued:

> . . . there are some sports where the group of journalists are seen as more or less fans of the sport. Say in the swimming, for example, there's a bit of a perception with the swimming 'journos' that it's more like a fan club, and there's no end of positives, which is not necessarily a bad thing, but there's no end to the positive stories. And this guy's the greatest, this guy's the greatest, this guy's the greatest. And if there is a bit of a hint of a negative story they won't really want to chase it.
>
> (Terry)

Other journalists may have scruples regarding the inspection of the private lives of sportspeople. One who specializes in cricket discussed in an interview the case of Shane Warne, the leading Australian spin bowler who has been caught up in various scandals and allegations, including contact with bookmakers, making uninvited sexual advances by mobile phone, marital infidelity, and taking a prohibited substance. This journalist was troubled by the pressure from both editors and readers to cover Warne's 'bedroom' conduct:

> I'm no friend of Shane Warne through a number of difficulties I've had over the years with him, working with him closely as a cricket writer, [but] to have his personal life paraded like that when he's got a family with young children, I think is very unfair on him personally. Now it's fair enough to say that he's a public figure and, therefore, he has to cop it. Well, Shane Warne never asked to be a public figure, Shane Warne lives and dies on his performance on the cricket field, and the issue is related around that. And if he misbehaves in any broad sense that does him or his team or cricket in Australia generally harm, then fair enough, that's fair game, that deserves to be exposed, and he deserves to be punished for his misbehaviour. But I think that, at a personal level, when you take it around what surrounds what you do, in his case being a very good cricketer, [and] you take it into the realm of the bedroom, then I guess that's overstepping the mark. Unfortunately my editors and various other people don't think that, and any kind of salacious gossip they

can get on a personality, particularly someone who's as big as Shane Warne, seems to go down a treat.

(Michael)

Here, Michael is describing his desire to contain sports journalism within parameters relating to sporting performance. But the fusion of sport and celebrity culture has made this separation virtually impossible to sustain. Thus, the extraordinary attention given in April 2004 by the British press to the alleged marital infidelity of David Beckham, and its impact on his marriage to Victoria 'Posh Spice' Beckham, is a classic instance of the ungovernable passage of sport from the back to the front page. Yet Posh'n'Becks are the 'property' of global media culture (Cashmore 2002), and the world of sport, it should be remembered, looks very different from the perspective of the local sports round.

Local and partisan sports journalism

Sports journalists can find themselves in very different everyday work situations. Those who cover multiple sports from metropolitan centres have more potential (re)sources, and so are less dependent on a small number of key informants. There are many ways of covering the Beckham phenomenon within journalism, and many journalists on hand to do the job. Most sports journalists, however, cover only one or a limited range of sports, and their 'beat' is largely restricted to a prominent local team in one or more sports. In smaller cities and towns, these journalists are not only highly dependent on limited news sources but are highly visible to tightly packed groups of local fans, who often expect them to support the team's cause. The more locally based a sports journalist in relation to covering sport, the greater are the pressures to become a fan of, and apologist for, prominent local sports entities (Lowes 2004).

For example, in the Australian regional centre of Newcastle, rugby league is the main winter sport, and the Newcastle Knights team garners most newspaper and radio coverage, as well as the largest share of sports sponsorship, marketing and advertising (Rowe and McGuirk 1999). The local journal of record, the *Newcastle Herald*, sponsors the Knights, and routinely carries stories about them on its front page. Since becoming a tabloid in 1998, the newspaper has followed many of the precepts of the form, with frequent textual and photographic coverage of the Knights on the front page, and more stories sprinkled throughout the newspaper in news, gossip and features sections, as well as in editorials and reader letters. The sports pages proper at the end of the newspaper have also expanded. The Saturday edition carries a numerical list of 'newsmakers' mentioned in the newspaper over the previous week, with Newcastle players and their coach always featuring in the top ten during the rugby league season (and frequently outside it). For example, in one week in April 2004 sports stories constituted 265 (26 per cent) of a total of 1,028 stories, with two Knights players and their coach among the top 11 most mentioned personalities, among whom sport accounted for 7 (64 per cent) of the most frequently named people.

The chief football reporter generally writes routine stories about the club that are rarely critical of it, and also runs the 'Footy Fan Forum' on 'The Footy Page' that enables readership feedback. However, after suggesting that the club could not prosper in 2003 in view of a serious injury to its captain, Andrew Johns (widely heralded as the code's best player in the world), a reader complained that:

> 'As a mad, passionate member of the football club, I find it hard to believe that you, who write regularly and are obviously a supporter, could be so negative in your comments after last night's match [against the Warriors]', Audrey wrote.
>
> 'Don't you realise that positive feedback is what is needed for the team and the fans to get through the rest of the season?
>
> The last thing we need is one of our local journalists bagging us. We get enough of that from the Sydney media!'
>
> (Phythian, quoted in Keeble 2003: 123)

Here the competing pressures on the local sports journalist are thrown into sharp relief. He is expected to contribute to the team effort by giving 'positive feedback', partly on the basis that his usual commentary is favourable to the local team (that is, analogous to that of the fan), in contrast to the 'Sydney media', who are seen to hold a metropolitan bias against a provincial club. This construction of the journalist-as-fan makes critical, reflective commentary difficult, however reasonable and muted that critical reflection might be. The local sports journalist's assessment of the Knights' chances was shared by most media commentators and the most unsentimental of all predictors of sports results – the bookmakers – and was vindicated in due course. Here, the rationality associated with journalism and modernity is in conflict with the subjectivist sporting tribalism of fan discourse. It is continually evident in sports across the globe, such as in the confident declarations 'Innocent' on fan banners concerning the three Leicester City football players arrested in Spain for 'sexual aggression' in March 2004 – over 2 months before their acquittal.

Ironically, the aforementioned 'Sydney media' include newspapers from the same ownership stable as the *Newcastle Herald* (John Fairfax), as well as the Rupert Murdoch-owned press. It is notable that, when Newcastle's best known sportsman separated from his wife, it was the Sydney press who broke the story. Claims that such personal issues were unsuitable for coverage in the *Newcastle Herald* were obviously inconsistent given the density of positive off-field stories concerning the player. It is for this reason that, in dealing with sports scandals of varying degrees of seriousness, local sports journalists – and, indeed, sports journalists in general – tend to take a low profile while their colleagues in other journalistic beats (and perhaps from other news organizations with weaker ties to the club or individual concerned) take responsibility for its coverage. As one interviewed sports journalist explained, the local press gives virtually automatic primary voice to its principal sports 'client':

> I think to be in a one-team town, particularly at a provincial level, then it would be very difficult to operate if you weren't to some extent 'on board'. You'd have trouble with access. I may be offending some journalists who do a very good job at provincial level . . . they'll do a good job quoting the coach and all the rest of it, but if an issue blows up . . . it's always going to be the reaction from the home team that's going to be important. The difficulty there is the journalist doing the job in that circumstance, because they are reporting the home team, reporting the reaction. [But] they have failed in their duty, because the wider issue is that the home team has failed for whatever reason to fulfil its responsibilities, and that should be the issue. It's easy for journalists in some of those circumstances to hide behind always quoting someone else. So while you aren't seen to be writing in a biased way yourself, you're always quoting an official to put in the salient points of view, getting their message across. Rather than taking a clear view yourself and saying, 'Well, hang on, this is right and this wrong according to the way I see it, and we'll tackle it this way'. And therefore, they have made a mistake.
>
> (Michael)

Sports journalists, it can been seen, vary in their occupational practice not only in relation to their professional ideologies, but also to their structural location, proximity to, and dependency on, their principal sources. Prominent among their dilemmas, especially in local contexts, is whether to conduct criticism that may be unpopular with their readerships or to practise a populist sports fandom that undermines their claim to reputable journalism.

Conclusion

As Garrie Hutchinson (2002: 330–1) argues in a survey of sports writing:

> The role of journalists in sport today is not just to provide well-turned descriptive phrases but also to investigate and report. This applies, or should, to TV journalists as well as to print journalists – and reporting has been patchy, to say the least. All proprietors of TV networks are deeply involved in the control and marketing of the sports product . . . [which] has created obvious problems for print journalists . . . For journalists, sport in today's media provides many exciting opportunities, and events to write about – it also places them at the sharp end of some pointed ethical and professional questions.

These difficult everyday issues faced by sports journalists are exacerbated, Hutchinson argues, by the increasing convergence of interest – and often common ownership – of media and sport (Rowe 2004). Sports journalists are, at different times and by different people (and sometimes by the same people at different times), expected to be uncritical sports fans and trenchant sports critics. They have witnessed in recent decades their chosen subject become the province of other journalists as it has divided and grown, amoeba-like, to fill sundry expanding media spaces.

In response, some sports journalists have taken to parodying their own brand of 'postmodern' celebrity sports journalism, as in the case of *Sports Illustrated*'s 2002 article concerning Simonya Popova, a young, glamorous Eastern European tennis player. The Kournikova look-alike Popova was revealed to be an invention, but only after the WTA received many media requests for an interview. The WTA regarded the spoof as disrespectful to women's tennis, but it could also be seen as an unconscious indictment by sports journalists of their own professional practice and that of their colleagues anxious to cultivate the next 'sexy' sports celebrity (especially given that the magazine's biggest selling edition is its annual swimsuit issue – Davis 2004). Such ironies are symptomatic of both the successes and failures of journalism's expanding engagement with sport as a form of popular culture with apparently boundless, multi-functional appeal.

❙ References

Allan, S. (1999) *News Culture*. Buckingham: Open University Press.

Andrews, D. L. and Jackson, S. J. (eds) (2001) *Sport Stars: The Cultural Politics of Sporting Celebrity*. London and New York: Routledge.

Bennett, W. L. (2003) *News: The Politics of Illusion*, fifth edition. New York: Longman.

Cashmore, E. (2002) *Beckham*. Cambridge: Polity.

Curran, J. and Seaton, J. (2003) *Power Without Responsibility*, sixth edition. London: Routledge.

Davis, L. R. (2004) The Basic Content: 'Ideally Beautiful and Sexy Women for Men', in D. Rowe (ed.) *Critical Readings: Sport, Culture and the Media*. Maidenhead: Open University Press, pp. 246–60.

Dahlgren, P. and Sparks, C. (eds) (1992) *Journalism and Popular Culture*. London: Sage.

Franklin, B. (1997) *Newszak and News Media*. London: Arnold.

Greenslade, R. (2003) *Press Gang: How Newspapers Make Profits from Propaganda*. Basingstoke: Macmillan.

Harris, J. and Clayton, B. (2002) Femininity, Masculinity, Physicality and the English Tabloid Press: The Case of Anna Kournikova, *International Review for the Sociology of Sport*, 37(3/4): 397–413.

Hartley, J. (1996) *Popular Reality: Journalism, Modernity, Popular Culture*. London: Arnold.

Henningham, J. (1995) A Profile of Australian Sports Journalists, *The ACHPER Healthy Lifestyles Journal*, 42(3): 13–17.

Hutchinson, G. (2002) In Our Own Style: Sports Writing in Australia 1803–1997, in G. Hutchinson (ed.) *The Best Australian Sports Writing 2002*. Melbourne: Black Inc: 312–31.

Jennings, A. (1996) *The New Lords of the Rings: Olympic Corruption and How to Buy Gold Medals*. London: Simon & Schuster.

Keeble, B. (2003) Ardent Fan Bristles at Negative Forecast, *Newcastle Herald*, 23 July: 123.

Kelso, P. (2002) Fame, Set and Match, *Guardian Unlimited*, 1 July: n.p.

Lindsey, E. (2001) Notes from the Sports Desk: Reflections on Race, Class and Gender in British Sports Journalism, in B. Carrington and I. McDonald (eds) *'Race', Sport and British Society*. London and New York: Routledge, pp. 188–98.

Lowes, M. D. (2004) Sports Page: A Case Study in the Manufacture of Sports News for the Daily Press, in D. Rowe (ed.) *Critical Readings: Sport Culture and the Media*. Maidenhead: Open University Press, pp. 129–45.

Lumby, C. (1999) *Gotcha: Life in a Tabloid World*. Sydney: Allen & Unwin.

Rowe, D. (1997) Apollo Undone: The Sports Scandal, in J. Lull and S. Hinerman (eds) *Media Scandals: Morality and Desire in the Popular Culture Marketplace*. New York: Columbia University Press, pp. 203–21.

Rowe, D. (2004) *Sport, Culture and the Media: The Unruly Trinity*, second edition. Maidenhead, UK and Philadelphia, PA: Open University Press.

Rowe, D. and McGuirk, P. (1999) '[D]runk for Three Weeks': Sporting Success and City Image, *International Review for the Sociology of Sport*, 34(2): 125–41.

Salwen, M. and Garrison, B. (1998) Finding their Place in Journalism: Newspaper Sports Journalists' 'professional problems', *Journal of Sport and Social Issues*, 22(1): 88–102.

Sparks, C. and Tulloch, J. (eds) (2000) *Tabloid Tales: Global Perspectives on the Popular Media*. Boulder, CO: Rowman & Littlefield.

Tomlinson, A. (1999) *The Game's Up: Essays in the Cultural Analysis of Sport, Leisure and Popular Culture*. Aldershot: Ashgate.

Turner, G. (2004) *Understanding Celebrity*. London: Sage.

Turner, G., Bonner, F. and Marshall, P. D. (2000) *Fame Games: The Production of Celebrity in Australia*. Melbourne: Cambridge University Press.

Whannel, G. (2001) *Media Sport Stars: Masculinities and Moralities*. London: Routledge.

|10

McJournalism

The local press and the McDonaldization thesis

Bob Franklin

- Is McJournalism producing dumbed-down local newspapers?
- Is efficiency compatible with quality journalism?
- Has high quality local journalism been replaced by what Andrew Marr describes as 'bite sized McNugget journalism'?
- Why are local newspapers flourishing at a time when the numbers of journalists and readers are in decline?

British local newspapers experienced seismic and rapid change in 1995 when the greater part of the local press shifted to tabloid formats. By 1997, only 10 of the 72 local evening papers published in broadsheet (Griffith 1997: 12): 2 years later, the *Yorkshire Evening Post* was among the last converts (Reeves 1999: 18). The move to tabloid generated changes in editorial content as well as page layout and size. A greater editorial emphasis on entertainment, consumer items and reports that refracted news stories through the prism of human interest was evident in a higher story count and shorter, 'frothier' stories, which used bigger headlines, more pictures and a greater use of colour (Franklin 1997: 113). Driven by the increasing competitiveness and corporatization of media markets, these restyled local newspapers emerged bearing all the hallmarks of tabloid journalism. By this process, the local press has become a focus for what has been described as the 'dumbing down debate', which engages both those who 'lament' the decline in traditional journalism and those enthusiasts who wish to celebrate the emergence of more popular cultural forms (Langer 1998).

In this chapter I offer some preliminary theorizing of a different explanation for this evident shift in news reporting. This trend, I suggest, might usefully be understood as part of the wider socio-historical processes of rationalization and bureaucratization first identified by Max Weber (1974). More recently, George Ritzer (1993, 1998, 2002) has adopted the metaphor of a fast food restaurant based on the principles of efficiency, calculability, predictability and control to characterize this intensifying process of rationalization, which characterizes modernity: Ritzer's neologism 'McDonaldization' articulates this trend. Increasing areas of social life are subject to McDonaldization and I wish to argue that the emergence of a highly standardized, packaged journalism might represent a further manifestation of McDonaldization. The high quality local journalism which used to offer a culinary feast, has been replaced by what Andrew Marr denounced as 'bite-sized McNugget journalism' (cited in Franklin 1997: 5) but what might better be described as 'McJournalism'.[1] I begin by outlining Ritzer claims concerning McDonaldization and provide a thumbnail sketch of the British local press, before assessing the explanatory value of McDonaldization for developments in local newspapers.

Ritzer, McDonaldization and rational efficiency

Drawing on Max Weber's suggestion that modern, capitalist societies are characterized by their requirement for the increasing application of rational decision making to new areas of social life, Ritzer (1993, 1998) neologizes the term 'McDonaldization' to characterize the highly controlled, bureaucratic and dehumanized nature of contemporary, particularly American, social life. For Ritzer, the word articulates 'the process by which the principles of the fast-food restaurant are coming to dominate more and more sectors of American society as well as the rest of the world' (Ritzer 1993: 1; Schlosser 2002). The fast-food restaurant built on principles of efficiency, calculability, predictability and control, where *quantity* and *standardization* replace *quality* and *variety* as the indicators of value, serves as a metaphor for this preoccupation with efficiency. Increasing areas of social life are subject to McDonaldization including packaged holidays (Ritzer 1998: 134–50) and universities (Ritzer 1998: 151–63) along with the shops and hotel chains (Ritzer 1993: 88), which bring such striking uniformity to contemporary cityscapes that it becomes difficult to distinguish the built environment of Bangor from Birmingham or Barnsley. It seems irresistible to add the increasingly homogenous local tabloid newspapers to this list, as they articulate an evident corporate style imposed from the centre.

Ritzer's analysis also explores the organization and experience of work by drawing on Braverman's (1974) analysis of the labour process. Work, he suggests, has become increasingly rationalized through bureaucracy, scientific management (Taylorism) and assembly lines (Fordism). Consequently, McDonaldization is leading to the creation of greater numbers of 'McJobs' in which work is highly routinized and thinking is reduced to a minimum while higher level skills, creativity, critique as well as genuine personal contact and interaction are effectively excluded: both producers and, in the service industries, consumers are systematically disempowered (Ritzer 1998: 59–70). Contemporary journalism is increasingly earning a place here.

There are four dimensions to McDonaldization. First, *efficiency*, which involves 'the choice of the optimum means to a given end' (Ritzer 1993: 35). Ritzer identifies two aspects of efficiency. He is concerned with the efficiency with which goods and services are delivered to consumers and, by this reasoning, fast-food restaurants provide more efficient means of obtaining meals than cooking at home from raw ingredients. McDonald's provides the best means for 'getting us from a state of being hungry to a state of being full' (Ritzer 1993: 9). At 'Drive Thru' facilities, the customer consumes the burger without leaving the car. But Ritzer is also concerned with efficiency in the organization of the production of goods and services. Consequently, market forces and relations drive production within a global system.

Second, *calculability* which requires an emphasis on things that can be counted and quantified. The time required for work tasks is carefully calculated and *quantity*, rather than *quality*, becomes the measure of value (Ritzer 1993: 62–82). McDonaldization delivers 'Big Macs' not 'Delicious Macs', large fries not tasty fries, 'Double' or even 'Triple Deckers' but not 'wholesome burgers'.

Third, *predictability* reflecting an emphasis on standardization: in the world of McDonalds, the settings, the food and the behaviour of the staff are identical (Ritzer 1993: 83–99). The food, as well as being 'fast', is absolutely standard and predictable. The Big Mac consumed in Land's End is exactly the same as the gluttonous feast purchased in John O'Groats.

Fourth, *control* by which Ritzer means the close and increasing control of both workers and consumers, typically via the introduction of technology. People are deskilled by both the detailed scripting of behaviour (of both workers and customers) and the use of technologies that make workers 'watchmen' or overseers of production rather than any more active engagement with production: so the frying machine decides when the fries are cooked, the drinks machine delivers precisely the standard amount of 'shake' before switching off (Smart 1999: 6).

Ritzer acknowledges that there are positive outcomes from this process of McDonaldization and hence the global spread of the phenomenon – just like McDonald's (Ritzer 1998: 81–94). But there are 'downsides': 'rational systems often spawn irrationalities' and can trigger *in*efficiency, *un*predictability, *in*calculability and *loss* of control (Ritzer 1998: 121): what Weber termed 'unintended consequences', Ritzer dubs the 'irrationality of rationality'. In the context of the local press, the paradox of constantly declining circulations that coexist with ever rising profits expresses one such irrationality of rationality.

The local press paradox: fewer readers, more profits

The local press in Britain is comprised of a cluster of newspapers distinguished by their size of circulation, periodicity of publication and the proportion of revenue they derive from advertising rather than sales. These local newspapers differ significantly in the financial and journalistic resources they enjoy, which research studies reveal, in turn has implications for their reliance on information subsidies from non-journalistic news organizations, such as organized public relations in local government and business: smaller weekly papers, heavily reliant on press releases enjoy little prospect for independent, investigative or critical journalism (Franklin 2004: 106–11).

In 2004, there were 1,300 local newspapers including 25 morning dailies (19 paid and 6 free), 75 evening papers, 21 Sundays (11 paid, 11 free), 529 paid weeklies and 650 free weeklies. The aggregate figure represents a slight decline in the number of published titles (1,333) since 1990, although the contribution of the various papers to the 'local press mix' has shifted significantly with 17 morning dailies, 73 evening papers, 7 Sundays, 434 paid weeklies and 802 free weeklies published in 1990 (Franklin and Murphy 1998: 10–13; *Press Gazette*, 5 March 2004: 12–13).

Fewer people are reading these newspapers and circulations continue their steady decline from the peak year of 1989 reflecting, at least in part, the expansion of local radio, the spiralling costs of newsprint and growing access to the Internet. Audit Bureau of Circulation (ABC) figures which measure circulation changes (July to December 2003), chart this sustained decline in all sectors except the expansive paid weekly papers: 51 per cent of weeklies enjoyed some, albeit a slight, increase. Only seven of the 75 listed evening papers displayed any increase with each of the 20 largest circulation papers registering decline. Some papers are haemorrhaging readers with the *Birmingham Evening Mail* losing 6.1 per cent of sales across the 6 months monitored: equivalent figures for the *Coventry Evening Telegraph* and the *Liverpool Echo* are 5.9 per cent and 5.3 per cent respectively (*Press Gazette*, 5 March 2004). Similar trends are evident for morning dailies with only three resisting circulation decline: at the *Northern Echo* the 6.7 per cent loss of circulation change represents a dramatic collapse. Only the *Sunday Sentinel* bucked the trend for Sunday papers. The ten largest Sundays, by circulation, registered falling sales: six showed declining circulations of 5 per cent and above. Only the new *Metro* papers, published by Associated Press and distributed free to commuters in the large metropolitan centres, show any prospect for optimism, with all titles revealing growth: *Metro* London increased distribution by 13.2 per cent to 449,616, but the status of such papers is uncertain. Part regional and part national, Associated Press describes them as 'FUN' papers: free urban nationals.

But advertising is buoyant despite declining circulations. In 2002, advertising revenues in the regional press reached £2,870 million, which represented a 21 per cent share of total media advertising revenues: second only to television at 26 per cent but higher than national newspapers (14 per cent), magazines (13 per cent), radio (4 per cent), cinema (1 per cent) and the Internet (1 per cent). In terms of year-on-year percentage increase, moreover, the local press outperformed the general advertising market in 2002 and remains the only medium to have increased advertising expenditure every year for the last decade: from £1,600 million in 1992 to £2,300 million in 1997 and £2,870 million in 2002.

This buoyancy of advertising revenues offers partial explanation for the highly profitable nature of the local press. In 2001, for example, Johnston Press, the fourth largest UK publisher of local papers, enjoyed an operating profit of £90 million on annual turnover of £301 million, representing a very respectable margin of 30 per cent. In 2003, Trinity Mirror, the largest group, returned a profit in its lucrative regional newspaper division of £123.9 million on a turnover of £525 million: a profit margin of 24 per cent (Pondsford 2004: 3).

Two additional reasons explain profitability. First, the low wages paid to journalists. A survey for the Journalism Training Forum found that 18 per cent of journalists earned less than £18,000 and 51 per cent below £25,000. Perhaps unsurprisingly, ITN's Nicholas Owen, addressing the Newspaper Society's conference, described provincial journalists' pay as 'abysmal' (Harcup 2003: 19).

Second, provincial newspaper groups enjoy economies of scale because ownership is concentrated among a very small number of groups. Takeovers and mergers are rife. In 1996, for example, ownership of one-third of all regional newspaper companies changed hands (Franklin and Murphy 1998: 19). Since 1995 more than £6.5 billion has been spent on mergers. In December 2002, Newsquest acquired the *Glasgow Herald*, the *Glasgow Evening Times* and the *Sunday Herald* for £216 million, following its earlier purchase of the Newscom group in May 2000 for £444 million, adding titles with circulations of 499,550 to its holdings. In March 2002, Johnston Press purchased Regional Independent Media's (RIM) 53 titles with aggregate circulations of 1,602,522. An obvious consequence of this merger activity has been a marked reduction of the 200 publishing companies in 1992, to 137 by 1998 and to 96 in 2003. But while 47 of these publishing companies own a single newspaper, the largest 20 groups own 85 per cent of regional titles and control 96 per cent of the weekly circulation: the five largest groups own 76 per cent of newspaper by circulation (http://www.newspapersoc. org.uk/factsandfigures.html).

In summary, the British local press is characterized by a sustained decline in the number of published titles, publishers, readers and circulations although, paradoxically, this decline coexists with robust and expansive advertising revenues and profits.

The growth of McJournalism?

Ritzer notes that McDonald's has become so symbolically significant in America, that a number of organizations have been given nicknames with the prefix 'Mc' to reflect their commitment to the McDonald philosophy. The popular American paper *USA Today*, for example, is nicknamed 'McPaper': the short pithy articles it publishes are known as 'News McNuggets'. But does the McDonaldization thesis, with its emphasis on efficiency, calculability, predictability and control, illuminate recent developments in the local press in the UK and signal the emergence of McJournalism?

Efficiency

McDonaldization is concerned with the efficient delivery of goods and services to the consumer and, consequently, McDonaldization requires newspapers to make news readily accessible to readers. In Britain, local newspapers deploy editorial and typographical techniques to enhance readers' access to news: many of these conform to tabloid formats. A brief scan of newspapers reveals a greater emphasis on big (splash) headlines, WOB headlines, humorous (punny) headlines, more sensational headlines, along with shorter words, fewer words, shorter stories, bigger pictures, colour pictures and more of them. Newspapers increasingly offer readers 'news at a glance' or 'news in brief', which provides a précis of the day's news in a vertical column down the left or right hand side of the page for 'people who are busy'. In the *Metro*, for example, the 'Metro digest' summarizes national news stories, the 'Metro world' offers brief reviews of international news, while the '60-second interview' provides readers with opportunities to get to know a celebrity in just one minute.

The local press is increasingly organized for 'efficiency', which, decoded is a synonym for a press organized according to market principles. A key feature of this quest for efficiency has been the increased concentration of corporate press ownership in the last ten years. As noted above, the largest 20 newspaper groups own 85 per cent of regional titles and own 96 per cent of local newspapers by circulation: the five largest groups – Trinity Mirror, Newsquest, Northcliffe Newspapers, Johnston Press and Archant – own 76 per cent of newspaper by circulation. Their dominance of the local press market is evident from Table 10.1.

Concentration of ownership in large regionally based monopolies has fostered concerns about whether this pattern of industrial organization is in the public interest. When the Competition Commission examined Johnston Press's bid to sell eight East Midlands newspapers to Trinity Mirror in May 2002, for example, it concluded that the sale would be against the interests of the public and advertisers. The Commission expressed concern that 'cluster publishing' might nurture a 'live and let live' philosophy in which regional monopolies – Newsquest in northern Lancashire, Trinity Mirror in the Midlands and north Wales and Johnston Press in southern Scotland and the north-east of England – tacitly agree to share the market by carving up the country and allowing each other free rein in their 'own territory' without any need to compete for readers or advertisers. Cluster publishing is, of course, inimical to quality journalism. In the Commission's words, 'head-to-head competition between different publishers provides a spur which causes newspapers in such areas to be of higher quality than those produced by monopoly publishers' (Reeves 2002: 17). The impact of these 'efficient' patterns of ownership on editorial integrity and homogeneity is evident. The editorial policy of a single

Table 10.1 Twenty largest regional publishing groups by number of titles and circulation

	Total		Dailies (paid and free)		Sundays (paid and free)		Weekly (paid)		Weekly (free)	
	Number of titles	Weekly circulation	Number of titles	Weekly circulation	Number of titles	Weekly circulation	Number of titles	Weekly circulation	Number of titles	Weekly circulation
Top 20 regional press publishers	1,110	65,484,882	96	35,168,757	20	2,074,467	398	5,421,630	596	22,820,028
Other regional press publishers (76)	190	2,691,115	4	418,275	1	120,395	131	876,686	54	1,275,759
Total regional press publishers (96)	1,300	68,175,997	100	35,587,032	21	2,194,862	529	6,298,316	650	24,095,787

Source: Newspaper Society, http:/www.newspapersoc.org.uk

newspaper group may now influence content in more than 240 local papers.

In corporate ownership, moreover, local papers must contribute to group profits by minimizing costs and maximizing revenues. Consequently, trades unions (judged an imperfection in the market according to classical economics) have been progressively derecognized since the mid-1990s with attendant cuts in journalistic staffs, casualization, low wages and poor conditions of service (Leapman 2001: 17).

Across the same period, the introduction of new technology has reinforced these journalistic staffing trends (Gall 1998). Some measures to secure efficiency seem bizarre. Some local newspaper groups, for example, employ centralized teams of subeditors to work on a number of remote titles, rather than employing a local sub for each paper. The centralized subeditor has little, if any, local knowledge of the patch. The efficiency is high but the tie with the local community is severed, while 'little matters like quality, accuracy and integrity . . . don't show up on the balance sheet'. A group editor claimed that subbing a paper 'up to 60 miles away' was like working in 'another country' (Lockwood 1999: 15).

But it is not only the 'processing' of news that is increasingly 'centralized'. Cuts (efficiencies) in the number of journalists employed means newspapers are increasingly reliant on local news agencies and public relations departments for stories: to adopt the jargon of business rhetoric, journalism has been 'outsourced'. The diversity and plurality of views, opinions and information available is reduced to a narrow group of influential and defining sources (Franklin 2004: 109). Agencies also provide a photojournalism service with the same images of events syndicated around the region stamping the dull hand of uniformity on the presentation of news.

Another 'efficiency' has been the decline in journalism training conducted 'in house'. Trainees used to learn not simply practical skills from senior colleagues but the professional culture of journalism and public service. But these senior colleagues have been lost to redundancy and early retirement in the quest for efficiency. The conveyor belt that transmitted values as much as knowledge across professional generations, has been snapped. Training has also been 'outsourced'. Would-be journalists must fund their own training, which is increasingly provided by universities.

Calculability

For Ritzer, calculability implied an emphasis on what can be quantified, in which *quantity* rather than *quality* becomes the measure of value. The media delight in quantifying both their products and the time invested on particular tasks by their workforce. So far as the first is concerned, newspapers are preoccupied with circulation: it is the key indicator of success. Circulation is crucial, of course, because it is related proportionately to cover price and advertising revenues. But circulation has replaced any judgement of quality. Editors claim that if circulation is rising or even holding steady then, 'we must be getting something right'. When circulation is flat, newspaper groups have increasingly resorted to 'dumping' copies with special deals for students, free copies dumped at bus and railway stations. Occasionally, newspapers will make misleading returns to the ABC.

Pagination has also expanded since the mid-1990s reflecting the close gearing ratio that local papers maintain between the number of editorial pages and advertising revenues. The local and regional press has, uniquely across the 1990s, sustained year-on-year increases in advertising revenues (see above). Consequently pagination has grown apace with local newspapers producing larger papers than ever: across 2003, the *Croydon Borough Post* averaged 150 pages each issue while the *Bromley News Shopper* averaged 111 pages (Newspaper Society 2004). Like Big Macs, British newspapers are, in the words of the advertising slogan, 'Bigger than ever, with more news than ever' while few claims are made for quality.

But it is in the management of the production process where the principle of calculability rules and has become rampant. Geneva Overholster, writing in the *American Review of Journalism*, describes the FTE (full time equivalent) system that oversees the production of news in newspapers in the Gannett Group, which owns Newsquest. The FTE system prescribes precisely the amount of time, space and resource which certain categories of stories require for their production. It recommends that an 'AI category story should be 6 inches or less and that the reporter should use one press release and/or one or two cooperative sources, should spend 0.9 hours to produce each story and should deliver 40 such stories each week'. These working protocols are market driven and Overholster comments that 'investors in these companies demand quarter to quarter profit increases and when the local economy does not promote or permit growth, profits have to be squeezed up by cost cutting. In doing so journalism is diminished' (cited in Reeves and Blyth 1999: 15). Newsquest has considered similar practices and has introduced story count guidelines for journalists and page count guidelines for subeditors.

Predictability

The local press increasingly offers a standardized fare of McJournalism with similar editorial contents and formats. The local press is now virtually a tabloid press. In terms of specific content, of course, local papers necessarily publish *local* stories and consequently the particular detail of stories varies between locales. But certain story types prevail in the local press with human interest stories predominating. A number of local editors asked to account for the declining election coverage in their papers in 1997 compared to 1992, mentioned their preference for human interest stories even during the course of the election. 'The pressures of circulation are upon us', an editor explained.

> We would obviously love to have human interest stories day after day because we worry about becoming too boring for the public. They're very much keener about what they will buy. Reporting about schools, councils, that sort of thing, you might have got away with that in the

past, but now you have to look for good stories and the good stories which sell newspapers are tabloid stories. So for a couple of years now there has been big pressure on us to report these tabloid stories.

(cited in Franklin and Parry 1998: 225)

The fact that the paper had been taken over by the Johnston Press Group two years earlier perhaps signals the impetus towards standardization and predictability which group ownership can provide. The *Newcastle Evening Chronicle* describes their editorial style as 'human interest with a hard edge' while 'court and council are a turn off'. A new 'family desk' assumes a 'central role in the newsroom' and reports, health, education, family and consumer issues (Pilling 1998: 187).

Other consequences of group ownership trigger standardized press formats. The economies of centralized subbing have been mentioned. The result is that a single subeditor with little if any knowledge of the local area may impose a uniform feel on local news reported in a number of local papers in the same group. Worse, the same stories and even the same readers' letters may be passed around and published in the different papers in the same press group. A study of local press coverage of the 2001 general election discovered that letters that appeared in one local paper appeared in a sister paper owned by the same group some three weeks later (Franklin and Richardson 2002).

Resource-starved local papers, moreover, like their national counterparts, are increasing reliant on press releases from local government and other local sources. A study of a county council's success in placing stories in the local press revealed that the same press release generated stories in 11 local papers in Northumberland: 19 of the 44 press releases each generated three or more stories in local newspapers (Franklin 2004: 110), but news management by government (locally and nationally) has subsequently developed apace prompting further standardization of news. Journalist Peter Oborne, for example, claims that Alastair Campbell distributed a single press release with Tony Blair's byline, which was published verbatim in 100 different local newspapers: the only word changed was the name of the town in which the paper circulated (Oborne 1999).

There is a further point here, which illuminates the dehumanizing, routine, almost robotic aspects of the work process under McDonaldization. At one point Ritzer's discussion of cooking the burgers at McDonald's provides a metaphor for journalists' growing dependence on press releases from non-news organizations, as well as the de-skilled, repetitive and even unreflective nature of some contemporary local journalism. 'The food arrives [at McDonald's]', Ritzer claims, 'preformed, pre cut, pre sliced and prepared . . . all they [the workers at McDonald's] need to do is, where necessary, cook or often only heat the food and pass it on to the customers' (cited in Smart 1999: 6). In the Northumberland study cited above, journalists also seemed to operate in this passive manner, reading and publishing with only minimal – if any – editing or additional information, the press releases delivered to them 'prepared and preformed' by the County Council:

like the cooks at McDonald's, journalists' professional practice required no more than to 'pass it on to the customers'.

Control

The introduction of new technology, a cause and consequence of staff cuts, has resulted in journalists and production workers losing control of their workplace production. Locally, Eddie Shah pioneered the introduction of the new print technology at the *Warrington Messenger* in 1983: the union response was robust (Goodhart and Wintour 1986). But it was Murdoch's transfer of the *Sun, News of the World, The Times* and *Sunday Times* to Wapping without disruption of production or consultation with the unions that marked a decisive shift in power and control in newspapers. Murdoch sacked 5,000 print workers, cut his production costs substantially and challenged his competitors to employ similar technology or become uncompetitive. Murdoch's unilateral move spoke eloquently to journalists and production workers about their new position in relation to management in the production of news.

Subsequently, new print technology has been established throughout the industry: two consequences follow. First, new technology allows for the convergence of some production tasks and the elimination of others. The role of subs and page layout designers has been challenged by new software which delivers journalists template pages into which they simply write their text: 'QuarkXPress has given every reporter the capability of being an editor' (Bourke 2003: 15). Second, new technology has prompted 'multi-skilling', perhaps better described as the 'deskilling', of journalists (Pilling 1998). Digital convergence requires journalists to combine news gathering and reporting with other tasks: one example 'is the way reporters are being encouraged to carry digital cameras' (Pilling 1998: 191). Additionally, the availability of laptop computers, modems, mobile telephones and digital cameras mean that pictures and reports of events can – and must – be filed within seconds. Speed and efficiency are the obvious benefits of this technology which allows a 1,000-word story to be filed in seconds without a copy taker (the downside of such technology being more evident to copy takers than newspaper managers). But new technology also isolates journalists, makes them individual rather than team workers, removes them from the collective news room culture, facilitates freelance work, reduces journalists' bargaining power, encourages multi-skilling practices and empowers managers against journalists and other production workers: casualization is widespread with fewer staff jobs in the local press than in the recent past.

▎Conclusion

I have tried to suggest that recent developments in the local press might be clarified by employing Ritzer's suggestive metaphor about fast food and

McDonaldization. A new style of journalism, which may be dubbed McJournalism, reflecting the drive for efficiency, calculability, predictability and control via technology is evident in the local press. The manifest paradox – 'the irrationality of rationality' – of this sustained emphasis on these four aspects of McDonaldization is that while readerships, circulations, the number of published titles, publishers, production workers and full-time journalists on staff contracts has experienced a sustained decline since the 1990s, advertising, pagination, profits and turnover have all increased.

Associated Newspaper's *Metro* series seems to exemplify the McDonaldization phenomenon. The Editor of the six regional 'FUN' (free urban newspapers) papers insists the 'commuters' free tabloid *Metro* has spawned a different kind of journalism and journalist'. Its claims for exceptionalism are largely quantitative: size is important! The 'sixth biggest daily paper in the country and the biggest free paper in the world' it has only 'half a dozen news reporters in London and four in Manchester working for the regional editions'. The Metro is 'basically a subs' paper' with a high story count informed by the ' "F*** me Doris" factor so beloved of Kelvin MacKenzie when he edited the *Sun*'. In sum, the editor claims,

> what we are doing is soundbite journalism. We are giving people very compact news stories. We don't have on-the-road reporters. Our reporters are Internet literate and do a lot of casting around on websites. We are reinventing what it means to be a news reporter.
>
> (Morgan 2001: 14)

In truth the *Metro* is a larger scale version of the old 'slip edition' in which an identical and common core of centrally produced news and agency copy has different smatterings of local news wrapped around it to create a number of local editions: the essential feature of the paper remains the homogeneity of the central news core.

McJournalism delivers predictable and standardized newspapers. While market theorists claim diversity and quality as the essential products of competition, the reality is McJournalism and McPapers with similar stories and even pictures reflecting a growing reliance on agency copy. The reduced numbers of journalists, the influence of local advertisers, the increasing reliance on information subsidies from local government and other organizations with active public relations staffs means that, from Land's End to John O'Groats, McJournalism delivers the same flavourless mush.

Two consequences follow from the emergence of McJournalism. First, there is evidence of what might be termed an increased 'spoon feeding' of news to readers in ever more accessible formats exemplified by the changes in the presentation of news in local, but also national, newspapers. Second, there is evidence of increased 'force feeding' of readers with a relentlessly *uniform* and *predictable* diet of news presented in ever more *uniform* formats. Predictable news, of course, is an oxymoron: another irrationality of the rational. Price wars, special offers, relaunches and free supplements have become perennial components in local newspapers' marketing strategies, but they have failed to stem the long-term decline in readership. Perhaps unsurprisingly, the key 'irrational' outcome of McJournalism is that customers are no longer willing to enter the restaurant. There are lots of empty seats: special offers have failed to seduce the customers back to try the newly launched dishes. A more fundamental dietary change is necessary.

Note

1   I have coined the word 'McJournalism' to describe the practices and products of journalism under the conditions of McDonaldization.

References

Bourke, D. (2003) The Charge of the Frees, *Press Gazette*, 28 February, p. 16.

Braverman, H. (1974) *Labour and Monopoly Capital: The degradation of work / the 20th Century*. New York: Monthly Review Press.

Franklin, B. (1997) *Newszak and News Media*. London: Arnold.

Franklin, B. (2004) *Packaging Politics: Political Communication in Britain's Media Democracy*, second edition. London: Arnold.

Franklin, B. and Murphy, D. (1998) *Making the Local News; Local Journalism in Context*. London: Routledge.

Franklin, B. and Parry, J. (1998) Old Habits Die Hard: Journalisms' Changing Professional Commitments and Local Newspaper Reporting of the 1997 General Election, in B. Franklin and D. Murphy (eds) *Making The Local News: Local Journalism in Context*. London: Routledge, pp. 209–27.

Franklin, B. and Pilling, R. (1998) Taming the Tabloids: Markets, Moguls and Media Regulation, in M. Kieran (ed.) *Media Ethics*. London: Routledge, pp. 111–23.

Franklin, B. and Richardson, J. (2002) A Journalist's Duty? Continuity and Change in Local Newspapers. Coverage of Recent UK General Elections, *Journalism Studies* 3(1): 35–52.

Gall, G. (1998) Industrial Relations and the Local Press: The Continuing Employers' Offensive, in B. Franklin and D. Murphy (eds) *Making The Local News: Local Journalism in Context*. London: Routledge, pp. 91–104.

Goodhart, D. and Wintour, P. (1986) *Eddie Shah and the Newspaper Revolution*. London: Coronet.

Griffiths, D. (1997) The Irresistible Rise of the Tabloid, *Press Gazette*, 1 August, p. 12.

Harcup, T. (2003) 'Priced Out Of A Job', *Press Gazette.* 27 June, p. 19.

Langer, J. (1998) *Tabloid Television: Popular Journalism and the 'Other News'*. London: Routledge.

Leapman, J. (2001) Iceberg Dead Ahead! *Press Gazette*, 9 February, p. 17.

Lockwood, D. (1999) A Substandard Service, *Press Gazette*, 16 July, p. 15.

Morgan, J. (2001) Welcome to Metroland, *Press Gazette*, 12 January, pp. 14–15.

Newspaper Society (2004) http://www.newspapersoc.org.uk, accessed 15 March 2004.

Oborne, P. (1999) *Alastair Campbell, New Labour and the Rise of the Media Class*. London: Aurum Press.

Pilling, R. (1998) The Changing Role of the Local Journalist: From Faithful Chronicler of the Parish Pump to Multi-skilled Compiler of an Electronic Database, in B. Franklin and D. Murphy (eds) *Making The Local News: Local Journalism in Context*. London: Routledge, pp. 183–95.

Pondsford, D. (2004) 'Record Results for Johnston Press', *Press Gazette*, 19 March, p. 3.

Reeves, I. (1999) The Last To Go, *Press Gazette*, 24 September, p. 18.

Reeves, I. (2002) Share and Share Alike, *Press Gazette*, 17 May, p. 17.

Reeves, I. and Blyth, J. (1999) Back Over Here, *Press Gazette*, 2 July, p. 15.

Ritzer, G. (1993) *The McDonaldization of Society*. London: Pine Forge/Sage.

Ritzer, G. (1998) *The McDonaldization Thesis*. London: Sage.

Ritzer, G. (2002) *McDonaldization: The Reader*. London: Pine Forge/Sage.

Schlosser, E. (2002) *Fast Food Nation: What the All American Meal is Doing to the World*. London: Penguin.

Smart, B. (1999) *Resisting McDonaldization*. London: Sage.

Weber, M. (1974) trans Parsons, T. *The Protestant Ethic and the Spirit of Capitalism*. London: Unwin University Books.

|11

The emerging chaos of global news culture

Brian McNair

- What has been the impact of new information and communication technologies on global news culture?

- Do the assumptions of materialist sociology hold true in the new conditions of the twenty-first century?

- Are the contemporary news media to be viewed as agents of elite control, or of a growing cultural chaos?

- In the era of the war on terror, can theories and concepts developed for the Cold War retain their validity for journalism studies?

We inhabitants of the twenty-first century live in an environment of communicative turbulence – a cultural chaos[1] brought into being by the proliferation of media channels and the volume of information of all kinds, which flows up, down and through them. Exponential growth in the quantity of information in circulation, alongside other trends (see below) leading to change in the way we relate, as individuals and societies to that information, suggest the need for what I have previously characterized as a 'new' sociology of journalism (McNair 1998, 2003), equipped to make sense of a very different set of conditions from those in which the British media studies tradition – and journalism studies in particular – was formed. By 'new' in this context I do not mean to imply wholesale rejection of the old, so much as a perspectival re-orientation away from the long-standing focus of materialist scholars on media as instruments of control concentrated in the hands of dominant elites, towards a view of them as autonomous and increasingly unruly agencies driven by economic, technological, political, ideological and cultural forces over which those elites, including even the proprietors of big media capital, have relatively little control.

From relative autonomy to relative control

The concept of autonomy – albeit relative – has long been central to materialist accounts of the ideological role of the media. For theorists in this tradition the notion of relative autonomy was used to explain deviations from the presumed default position of a pro-systemic bias in ideological apparatuses such as the media. Media organizations, and the institutions of the cultural sphere in general, were recognized to enjoy a certain amount of independence in respect of elite groups, while being *determined in the last instance* by the economic needs of capital, and the reproductive requirements of the capitalist mode of production viewed more broadly. The conditions of ideological reproduction of a fundamentally exploitative system would always assert themselves in the end, implying a deep structural conservatism on the part of the media. Observable failures of control – Woodward and Bernstein's exposure of the Watergate scandal, for example – had to be explained in terms that could be presented as compatible with materialist assumptions about the exercise of power in advanced capitalism. In Britain, for example, Ralph Miliband argued that 'impartiality and objectivity are quite artificial', operating only 'in regard to political formulations which are part of a basic, underlying consensus' (Miliband 1972: 200). American scholars described 'arenas' or 'spheres' of 'legitimate controversy' (Hallin 1986; Schudson 1995), by means of which dissent was managed and contained. Efforts to identify and explain the ideological control mechanisms operative in capitalist societies drove theoretical development in media and journalism studies, often under the heading of 'radical' or 'critical theory'. The *control paradigm* is my term for the scholarly mindset, or intellectual worldview that has underpinned those efforts.

The persuasive power of the control paradigm is not difficult to explain. The intellectual environment in which the founding texts of media sociology were written was characterized by rigid ideological bipolarity (expressed in divisions between left and right, communism and capitalism, East and West), and a limited number of media channels disseminating news, analysis and commentary to relatively passive publics (in so far as they consumed, but could not produce or interact with media in the manner taken for granted by today's net-savvy citizens). This was the world before globalization (if not cultural imperialism); before the rise of environmentalism on to the political agenda, or the mainstreaming of feminism and gay rights – movements which fractured traditional left-right dichotomies structured by competing class-based ideologies; before the fall of the Berlin Wall, the Moscow coup attempt of August 1991, and the velvet revolutions; before the emergence of the Internet.

It was, one might suggest, a simpler world, still recognizable by radical or critical theorists as the capitalism dissected by Marx and Engels in the *Communist Manifesto* of 1848 (Marx and Engels 1998), on the basis of which they formulated the materialist political philosophy that would be so central to Western media studies in the twentieth century. Great trades union-led struggles, such as the 1984–5 miners' strike, still erupted in advanced capitalist societies with some regularity. Around the world, wars and civil conflicts were still rooted in and defined by the superpower conflict, made sense of as episodes and skirmishes in the larger struggle between communism and capitalism. Until *glasnost* and *perestroika* exposed the realities of Soviet power, past and present, Western capitalism still had a systemic rival with claims to present a viable alternative to the exploitation and injustice of the free market system. Marxism-Leninism as practised in the Warsaw Pact countries of eastern and central Europe, parts of Asia and Africa, south America and Cuba remained for many a flawed, but essentially well-intentioned and socially progressive attempt to provide humanity with an alternative to capitalism. Maoist China, nominally socialist but divergent from the ideological path of the USSR and its allies, still had ahead of it the massacre of Tien An Mien Square and the rapid transition to the hybrid but hugely successful form of free market capitalism that will see it become the world's second largest economy by 2015. Yugoslavia was still a 'socialist' country, not yet broken into warring ethnic tribes.

This was a world of seemingly permanent political structures and divides, held in place, materialist theorists argued, by various types of control apparatus. In the nominally socialist world the preferred instruments were *repressive* – jails, psychiatric hospitals, totalitarian surveillance of all dissidence, crude propaganda and strict censorship of all media in line with Lenin's theory of proletarian dictatorship and his dismissal of press freedom as a bourgeois illusion (Lenin 1977). In advanced capitalist countries, more affluent and consumer-oriented but still riven with inequality and injustice, the control mechanisms, it was argued, were principally cultural – the media, education, family and the churches. These were Althusser's *ideological state apparatuses*, crucial to what he described as the 'reproduction of the ability to manipulate the ruling ideology correctly for the agents of exploitation' (Althusser 1978: 132). The media were responsible for 'cramming every citizen with daily doses of nationalism, chauvinism, liberalism, moralism, etc.' (Althusser 1978: 144), and for disseminating images that disguised 'real' (exploitative and oppressive) social relations to the people. Stuart Hall's Gramsci-influenced work attributed to the media the role of winning the people's consent to the 'preferred readings' of dominant elites, getting them to 'decode within the dominant [ideological] framework' (Hall 1980: 344).

This was the intellectual environment in which I, like other media sociologists of my generation, was formed. You see its influence on the 1970s work of the Glasgow University Media Group, or the studies of the Birmingham Centre for Contemporary Cultural Studies on news and ethnicity, gender and youth. Crude media bias was not asserted in these studies. Rather, ideological skewing was argued to arise from structural or 'culturalist' factors – organizational routines and professional codes, the value-laden preferences of media professionals for elite-led accounts, or *primary definitions* of events.

From control to chaos

Could such a paradigm retain its usefulness in the advanced capitalist societies of the twenty-first century? Adherents to the control paradigm will answer that question in the affirmative, describing the ideological role of the media in terms little different from those developed decades ago for a very different social context. Critical media sociology has continued to view journalism in liberal democracies as instruments at the disposal of the socially dominant, as the bearers of a kind of false consciousness or brainwashing (however much such terms are avoided in recognition of their paternalistic connotations) imposed from above, and which play a key role in a variety of social phenomena deemed negative by the critic. Whether in the sophisticated form of the theory of dominant ideology, or in Chomsky and Herman's more conspiratorial 'propaganda' thesis, the model of top-down control of the masses by organized and unified elites has been applied to the media of the post-Cold War era as much as it was to the Cold War. One writer asserts, for example, that 'the cultural product of the international television news agencies serves to perpetuate a western hegemony hostile to developing nations' (Paterson 1998: 95). Others have condemned what they perceive to be the global 'implantation of the commercial model of communication', viewing the media as 'missionaries of capitalism' (Herman and McChesney 1997). A recent study of domestic UK news asserts that 'conservatism over the theme of monarchy typifies the British press' (Blain and O'Donnell 2003: 3), and that 'royal and monarchical media accounts' are 'an obvious stratagem of distraction and ideological reinforcement' (Blain and O'Donnell 2003: 59). This study was published before the scandal of November 2003, during which the alleged sexual practices of HRH Prince Charles were the subject of global media speculation for days on end, and before the *Mirror* newspaper's successful infiltration that same year of the Royal household at Buckingham Palace with an undercover reporter, whose reports subsequently became the basis for an extended period of less than respectful royal coverage. A 'distraction' such coverage may legitimately be judged, but 'ideological reinforcement' seems problematic, unless one believes that the survival of British capitalism is strengthened by the depiction of its present head of state as a figure of fun, and its future king as a sexual deviant. Royal coverage in most of the British print and broadcast media, and especially the right-wing tabloids (and especially the newspapers of the arch-capitalist Murdoch) has, since the marriage of Charles and Diana in 1981, been consistently subversive of the respect and deference in which the monarchy had been held in the UK throughout most of the twentieth century.

In foreign affairs, coverage of the post-September 11 'war on terror', the Israeli-Palestinian conflict and the Coalition invasion of Iraq in 2003 had all, as this book went to press, been accused of pro-Western, pro-American, pro-UK government and even pro-Israeli bias.[2]

In the late twentieth century, at the height of the cold war, in the era of

Ronald Reagan and Margaret Thatcher, such analyses were compelling. The rigorous exposure of double standards in US reportage of Soviet dissidents and central American death squads presented by Chomsky and Herman in *The Political Economy of Human Rights* (1979) made sense if media organizations were recognized as propaganda apparatuses of a national security state engaged in a global conflict with communism. But in the post-Cold War, post-September 11 environment, the evidence of media output suggests a more complex picture. Michael Schudson (1995: 4) described the propaganda model as 'misleading and mischievous'. Abercombie *et al.* (1990: 250) challenged the dominant ideology thesis, arguing that 'the existence of a postmodern culture [defined by these authors as "the fragmentation and diversification of modern cultures by the forces of consumerism and global markets"] means that by definition there cannot be a single, dominant, or coherent ideology'. The thrust of such writings was to assert that while elites exist, clearly, they find it difficult to act as unified blocs, or to exercise effective power over the media. And even if they did exercise such power, the media's impact on audiences is far from straightforward.

A more fundamental objection to the control paradigm attacks its implication that the media are required as ideological instruments of control to support hierarchical structures and elite dominance in the face of mass inequality and exploitation, or at least the perception among the masses that there is something to be gained by replacing or removing ruling elites. If the existence of such inequality was a key driving force behind the formation of historical materialism in the nineteenth century, and remains a factor in many developing capitalist countries, it applies less obviously to advanced capitalism, where living standards for the great majority have improved steadily since the Second World War. Control is not required in such circumstances, because consent is freely given (if not without complaint). The media are thus freer to exercise a social role other than that of control or ideological dominance.

Theoretical objections aside, the evidence of contemporary media output presents a further challenge to the control paradigm. Mainstream news coverage of the activities of Bush, Blair and their respective administrations, after the initial wave of media patriotism following on September 11 (Zelizer and Allan 2002) has been highly critical. As has coverage of Israeli policy on Palestine, from the 2002 assault on Jenin (a massacre of up to 500 people was reported by the BBC and other highly respected news outlets) to the announcement of its planned withdrawal from the Gaza strip in April 2004. Criticism of governing elites has become routine, making the management of domestic and global public opinion for the governments of the US-led coalition increasingly difficult. Negative stories (from the Coalition point of view) have included accusations of murder, torture and abuse of inmates in Abu Ghraib prison, substantiated by photographic evidence; cover up over the causes and conduct of war; allegations of relationships between the Bush family and the Saudi ruling elite; and suggestions that 'poodle' Tony Blair has deceived Parliament, broken international law and ridden roughshod over popular opposition.

Criticism, when it comes, has often been at the top of the news agenda. Since 11 September 2001, and especially since the build up to and execution of war in Iraq by the US- and British-led coalition, mainstream political journalism in both countries has told a tale of alleged governmental deceit, lies, betrayal, lack of trust and immorality. On this central issue of the twenty-first century the efforts of ruling elites on both sides of the Atlantic to control media coverage of the reasons for war in Iraq, to set the terms of the debate around such issues as weapons of mass destruction, the ethics of regime change, or the performance of the Coalition after Saddam Hussein's eviction from office, have been singularly unsuccessful, to the extent that they have themselves frequently become the story, as in coverage of the 2003 Hutton inquiry.

The control paradigm views the appearance of sustained media criticism of governing elites, even at a time of warfare and in conditions of global emergency, as less damaging to dominant interests than it appears – not representative of how the media work in a national security state. The *chaos paradigm* proposed here views media in general, and the media of the mainstream in particular, as tending increasingly to the disruptive, the subversive and iconoclastic in their relationship to power, functioning whether deliberately or not as unwitting transmitters of news, analysis and commentary that embraces and connects the national, transnational and global spheres of public discourse, with unpredictable and largely uncontrollable outcomes. It assumes that, in contemporary conditions, independence and autonomy are the default positions of the media with respect to power in advanced capitalism, and that successful control of the media by elites increasingly represents not the norm but the deviation, a state of *relative control*, which has to be worked for through the application of public relations techniques (spin), direct censorship and 'flak'. Control is constantly worked for, as BBC bosses know only too well from their dealings with Alistair Campbell and the Downing Street communications apparatus, but never with any guarantee of success.

The roots of chaos

The assumption of straightforward elite control over the institutions of media and culture was never without need of qualification, as already noted, and has been accepted (if never satisfactorily reconciled with materialist assumptions about how the world is ordered) by scholars from Althusser to Chomsky. But long-term trends along four axes, I would suggest, have created a cultural environment that can be characterized as qualitatively different – more chaotic – than any we have known before.

1. Politics: democracy and the culture of access

It has long been conceded, even by the sternest critics of capitalism, that the steady global expansion of liberal democracy in recent decades, and the establishment of universal suffrage as a basic democratic principle, has made governing elites, ruling classes and dominant groups everywhere responsive to mass opinion and feelings (or, at least, sensitive to the need to be *seen* to be responsive). To provide an obvious illustration – the war on terror, and the occupation of Iraq, cannot be prosecuted without consideration of electoral outcomes, as the Spanish government discovered to its cost in March 2004, and the Bush and Blair governments are only too aware.

Alongside the growth of democratic institutions, advanced capitalist societies (and none more so than the UK) have evolved political cultures of public debate with elites, exercised through what I have called *mediated access* (McNair *et al.* 2003). This takes the form of non-elite participation in radio phone-ins, talk shows and studio debates of the type exemplified by BBC television's *Question Time*, or Tony Blair's pre-Iraqi war appearances on live TV to answer hostile questions from angry members of the public. In these ways, institutional democracy is complemented by new forms of mediated accountability. Such opportunities may not of themselves solve the problems of democratic legitimacy and low electoral turnouts afflicting Britain and other advanced capitalist countries, nor need they have a measureable impact on short-term policy formation. They do, however, create a political environ-ment of substantially greater volatility and uncertainty than was faced by previous generations of governing elite. Expectations of elite accessability (extending to Clintonesque revelations of personal impropriety or unethical conduct) have changed and while the political establishments of different countries have responded to this in different ways, none can ignore it.

2. Technology

On their own, these developments would justify a revision of materialist and structuralist assumptions about how power is exercised in capitalism. Their impact is amplified, however, by the emergence of new information and communication technologies, from the launch of CNN in the early 1980s to the growth of the blogosphere today. In late 2003 the proportion of UK households with access to the Internet passed the 50 per cent mark for the first time, making it a truly mass medium. That same year, Internet access in China reached the 300 million mark, with a further half billion regular users anticipated by 2008. Everywhere in the advanced capitalist world, and in many developing countries too, the exponential expansion of journalistic discourse communicated through cable, computer and satellite technologies is pronounced.

The rate of flow of this information, the immediacy and unpredictability of its content, and its cognitive impact (dependent on individuals' belief in the truth and reliablity of their news), are a root cause of the cultural chaos observed on such occasions as the 9/11 attacks, the Clinton-Lewinsky scandal, the Cheriegate affair of December 2002 in the UK, or the occupation of Iraq. Just as the regular drip-drip of a household tap differs from the turbulent flow of a rain-swollen river, such a crowded, pressurized media environment is more unpredictable, less easy to get the measure of, than that of a few short years ago. The global availability of real-time satellite news, from Al Jazeera and Al Arabiya as well as BBC, Sky and CNN, alongside a sprawling virtual universe of online media, means that political elites in democratic societies (and also in authoritarian states such as China, when confronted with a crisis such as the SARS outbreak of 2003, for example) must respond to events at speeds that might conflict with the demands of good government. Greg McLaughlin, writing before the September 11 attacks brought channels such as Al Jazeera to the fore, asks: 'what happens if television short-circuits the policy-making nexus and taps into a groundswell of public support for intervention that policy makers cannot spin and control, or that they may wish not to consider' (McLaughlin 2002: 192). What happens, indeed?[3]

For a recent example of this 'chaos' in action, consider President Bush's appearance on Arab satellite news channels in early May 2004, in an attempt to deflect criticisms of the US military that had been provoked by the publication of photographs of torture and prisoner abuse a few days before. Without digital cameras, and the rapid global dissemination of the photographs made possible by new media technologies, and the availability of satellite channels for presenting the US administration's propaganda counter-offensive, the story would not have evolved in that way. The My Lai massacre took years to be recognized as the outrage it was. The Iraqi prisoner abuse scandal was the subject of angry global debate, necessitating a rare public display of presidential contrition within days.

3. Economics

In an earlier era, when there were many fewer media outlets, much less global in their reach, imposing elite control on coverage of such events was easier (if never without the risk of failure). But in a global media market of many news providers, competitive realities determine that bad news will out. In the global news market of the twenty-first century quality journalism is not a luxury dispensed at the whim of proprietors, but a marketing necessity. Quality journalism means, among other things, the visible demonstration of reliability, objectivity, authority, independence and diversity. Many organizations fail to meet these criteria, but the majority of serious players, regardless of proprietorial bias, have no choice but to do so. In a world where Al Jazeera can communicate its take on events to hundreds of millions of Arab viewers, Western-based outlets cannot be satisfied with jingoistic propaganda, even if that is what proprietors might wish them to produce. For a profit-hungry, commercially focused, globally targeted news media, speed and exclusivity are hugely important, and a scoop is a scoop, even if it involves American newspapers and satellite channels telling the world about US troop abuses of Iraqi prisoners.

4. Ideology

Cultural chaos is further encouraged, finally, by the collapse of the ideological dividing lines which have followed the end of the Cold War. There is, clearly, a sense in which US and British government claims about the threat posed to the world by Saddam Hussein, and in particular the now notorious claim that he possessed weapons of mass destruction poised to strike at his enemies within 45 minutes, can be read as the re-emergence, post-communism, of the same rhetoric and imagery used to colour the Soviet threat 20 years before (McNair 1988). This, indeed, is the reading suggested by an application of the control paradigm to the post-September 11 events – that they represent business as usual for US-British imperialism and the media which prop it up with pro-systemic propaganda. Threat inflation, selective use of dubious intelligence, apocalyptic warnings of imminent catastrophe if the enemy were left to his own devices – all these techniques were used by Ronald Reagan and Margaret Thatcher in their time to justify development and deployment of new weapons like Cruise missiles and Trident submarines. Stock footage of the Soviet military parading marching through Red Square in the 1980s was echoed in similar images of Saddam's army parading its (illusory) might in Baghdad two decades later.

But there is a significant difference between the two periods. The Soviet threat, such as it was, was rarely questioned in the mainstream media of the Reagan-Thatcher era. The nature of the Iraqi threat, as I have suggested, was subject to critical media scrutiny from the moment invasion began to look likely. Journalistic consensus around the reality of the Iraqi 'threat' lacked solidity, not just because of the existence of a faster, more expansive and more competitive news media constantly interrogating it, but because there was no longer a simple left-right structure to the public debate. The Cold War, and all those images of the enemy which it generated on both sides, arose from conflict between two competing models of socio-economic organization, each with claims to moral and economic superiority. In Western countries this ideological competition was reflected in the left-right, Labour/Conservative, Republican/Democrat divide. The war on terror, on the other hand, and the war on Saddam Hussein, which has been presented to global publics as a necessary part of it, is a conflict between progress and reaction of a type that transcends the twentieth century's ideological divisions and blurs the left-right divide. Clinton bombed Afghanistan before Bush (and was criticized for not doing so effectively enough). John Major, as a Conservative prime minister, invaded Iraq in 1991, with the support of the Soviets, the Chinese and most of the Arab countries. The 2003 Iraqi war lacked that breadth of international support but was similarly irreducible to a left-right divide of the Cold War type. In such conditions the lines separating and policing the spheres of consent from legitimate and illegitimate dissent have become blurred and porous. In Britain, leftish journalists such as David Aaronovitch, John Lloyd and Anthony Andrews find themselves occupying much of the same terrain as the hated 'neo-cons' and neo-imperialists in the Bush administration.[4]

Conclusion

Ideological realignment, competitive realities imposed on media organizations by globalized news markets and the demands of increasingly media literate and democratically empowered audiences, and the communicative possibilities of new technologies, have ushered in what we might call an era of *dissolutions* – the erosion of temporal, spatial, ideological, cultural and social barriers that have structured capitalism for centuries – and generated the conditions for a paradigm shift, a re-orientation from control to chaos in the default position of the sociological imagination. While dominance and control of media and their outputs remain key objectives of those who are or would be in ruling or elite positions, it is necessary to pay more attention to how the *routine* workings of the media act to destabilize established authority and power, and thus to impact on broader social and political processes.

Before the rise of the Internet to its present level of saturation McKenzie Wark (1994) discussed cultural globalization in terms of 'the unpredictable movement of information', noting that 'the immediacy of information can create crises'. Paul Virilio (1998) has written of 'the sudden bewildering Babel clamour of the world-city, the untimely mix of the global and the local'. Piers Robinson and others have been working for some time on 'the CNN effect' (Robinson 2002; Gowing 1994; Bennett and Pletz 1994; Natsios 1996; Hamelink 1998; Nacos *et al.* 2000; Robinson 2002; Volkmer 2002). Zelizer and Allan's (2002) edited collection on *Journalism After September 11* contains several essays which depart from the critical orthodoxy. Simon Cottle identifies a 'communicative paradigm', within which 'the accent shifts to a more politically contingent and communicatively less settled or predictable outcome' (Cottle 2003: 17).

Some observers, myself included, are optimistic about the trends described in this chapter, and their implications both for liberal democracies, and for the long-term dismantling of authoritarian societies around the world (Atkins 2002; Kalathil and Boas 2003; El-Nawawy and Iskandar 2002). Others view cultural chaos negatively, as in Todd Gitlin's complaint about 'the travesty of human existence' brought on by the 'media unlimited', which provide the title for his 2002 study,[5] or Zygmunt Bauman's reference to a world 'under siege' (Bauman 2002). Jean Baudrillard speaks of global culture as 'becoming a kind of lowest common denominator' in which 'all differences are annulled'.[6]

Critical scrutiny of elite power remains a key task of media sociology, but in a world where the only alternatives to established capitalist power are the totalitarianisms of state socialism and medievalist religion, the critical project – and materialist political philosophy more broadly – must move beyond the rejectionism and cultural pessimism of twentieth-century thinking to embrace the possibility that significant social progress can be an outcome of capitalist evolution in the century just begun. The recognition of cultural chaos, and the development of a sociology of journalism which might help make sense of it, is part of that process.

Notes

1   In using a phrase such as *cultural chaos* I am aware of the dangers of importing terms developed by the natural sciences into social science and humanities scholarship. Social 'scientists' have traditionally understood that the objects of their intellectual labours are fundamentally different from those of physicists or astronomers. The latter can recreate and simulate phenomena in vacuum chambers and particle accelerators. They can isolate, observe and experiment on them with a degree of empirical precision that sociologists cannot match, testing hypotheses, developing laws, making predictions that are likely to be just as valid in one region of time and space as another. Social science, on the other hand, necessarily engages with phenomena shaped by human emotion, perceptual relativism, subjectivity and cultural specificity, which exhibit randomness and contingency in their evolution. It is precisely for that reason, however, that models and metaphors drawn from the emerging science of chaos – a science that identifies features such as sensitivity to initial conditions, uncertainty and connectedness as important to the study of all non-linear systems, be they natural or of human origin – may help social scientists develop new insights into such phenomena as the evolution of news agendas, the spread of panics and scares, as well as the forces driving policy formation. For a relatively accessible introduction to the science of chaos, see Gleick (1996).
2   See for example, Philo, G., Bad News from Israel: Media Coverage of the Israeli/Palestinian Conflict (www.gla.ac.uk/departments/sociology/Israel.pdf).
3   Piers Robinson's (2002) study of the 'CNN effect', and Susan Moeller's (1999) *Compassion Fatigue* explore in different ways the impacts of real time news on western public opinion and policy making.
4   See for example Andrews, A. (2004) Thatcher's Legacy: No More Us and Them, *Guardian*, 5 May.
5   In an interview on American radio about his book, *Media Unlimited: How the Torrent of Images and Sounds Overwhelms our Lives* (2002).
6   From An interview with Jean Baudrillard, *European Journal of Social Theory*, 5(4): 521–30.

References

Abercrombie, N., Hill, S. and Turner, B. (eds) (1990) *Dominant Ideologies*. London: Unwin Hyman.
Althusser, L. (1978) *Lenin and Philosophy and Other Essays*. London: Verso.
Atkins, W. (2002) *The Politics of Southeast Asia's New Media*. London: RoutledgeCurzon.
Bauman, Z. (2002) *Society Under Siege*. Cambridge: Polity.

Bennett, W. L. and Pletz, D. L. (eds) (1994) *Taken by Storm: the Media, Public Opinion and US Foreign Policy in the Gulf War*. Chicago: University of Chicago Press.

Blain, N. and O'Donnell, H. (2003) *Media, Monarchy and Power*. Bristol: Intellect.

Boyd-Barrett, O. and Rantanen, T. (eds) (1998) *The Globalization of News*. London: Sage.

Chomsky, N. and Herman E. (1979) *The Political Economy of Human Rights*. Boston: South End Press.

Cottle, S. (ed.) (2003) *News, Public Relations and Power*. London: Sage.

Girardet, E. R. (1996) Reporting humanitarianism: are the new electronic media making a difference? in R. I. Rotberg and T. G. Weiss (eds) *From Massacres to Genocide: the Media, Public Policy and Humanitarian Crises*. Washington, DC: The Brookings Institution.

Gitlin, T. (2002) *Media Unlimited: How the Torrent of Sounds and Images Overwhelms our Lives*. New York: Henry Holt & Company.

Gleick, J. (1996) *Chaos: the Amazing Science of the Unpredictable*. London: Minerva.

Gowing, N. (1994) *Real-time Television Coverage of Armed Conflicts and Diplomatic Crises*. Cambridge, MA: Harvard University Press.

Hall, S. (1980) Encoding/decoding, in S. Hall, D. Hobson, A. Lowe and P. Willis (eds) *Culture, Media, Language*. London: Hutchinson.

Hallin, D. (1986) *The 'Uncensored War': the Media and Vietnam*. New York: Oxford University Press.

Hamelink, C. J. (1998) World communication: conflicting aspirations for the twenty-first century, in K. Brant *et al.* (eds) *The Media in Question*. London: Sage.

Herman, E. and McChesney, R. (1997) *The Global Media: the New Missionaries of Global Capitalism*. London: Cassell.

Kalathil, S. and Boas, T. C. (2003) *Open Networks, Closed Regimes: the Impact of the Internet on Authoritarian Rule*. Washington, D.C.: Carnegie Endowment for International Peace.

Lenin, V. U. (1977) *State and Revolution*. Moscow: Progress Publishers.

Marx, K. and Engels, F. (1998) *The Communist Manifesto*. London: Verso.

Moeller, S. (1999) *Compassion Fatigue: How the Media Sell Disease, Famine, War and Death*. London: Routledge.

Miliband, R. (1972) *The State In Capitalist Society*. London: Quartet.

McLaughlin, G. (2002) *The War Correspondent*. London: Pluto.

McNair, B. (1988) *Images of the Enemy*. London: Routledge.

McNair, B. (1998) *The Sociology of Journalism*. London: Arnold.

McNair, B. (2000) *Journalism and Democracy*. London: Routledge.

McNair, B. (2003) From Control to Chaos: Towards a New Sociology of Journalism, *Media, Culture and Society*, 25(4): 547–55.

McNair, B., Hibberd, M. and Schlesinger, P. (2003) *Mediated Access*. Luton: University of Luton Press.

Nacos, B. L., Shapiro, R. Y. and Isemia, P. (eds) (2000) *Decisionmaking in a Glass House: Mass Media, Public Opinion and American and European Foreign Policy in the Twenty-first Century*. Lanham: Rowman & Littlefield.

El-Nawawy, M. and Iskandar, A. (2002) *Al-Jazeera: how the free Arab news network scooped the world and changed the Middle East*. Washington: Westview Press.

Natsios, A. (1996) Illusions of Influence: the CNN Effect in Complex Emergencies, in R. I. Rotberg and T. G. Weiss (eds) *From Massacres to Genocide: the Media,*

Public Policy and Humanitarian Crises. Washington, D.C.: The Brookings Institution, pp. 149–68.

Paterson, C. (1998) Global battlefields, in O. Boyd-Barratt and T. Rantanen (eds) *The Globalization of News.* London: Sage, pp. 79–103.

Robinson, P. (2002) *The CNN Effect: the Myth of News, Foreign Policy and Intervention.* London and New York: Routledge.

Rotberg, R. I. and Weiss, T. G. (eds) (1996) *From Massacres to Genocide: the Media, Public Policy and Humanitarian Crises.* Washington, D.C.: The Brookings Institution.

Schudson, M. (1995) *The Power of News.* Cambridge, MA: Harvard University Press.

Virilio, P. (1998) *Open Sky.* London: Verso.

Volkmer, I. (2002) Journalism and Political Crises in the Global Network Society, in B. Zelizer and S. Allan (eds) *Journalism After September 11.* London and New York: Routledge.

Wark, M. (1994) *Virtual Geography.* Bloomington: Indiana University Press.

Zelizer, B. and Allan, S. (eds) (2002) *Journalism After September 11.* London and New York: Routledge.

PART III

Journalism's realities

|12

Journalism through the camera's eye

Barbie Zelizer

- What does journalism look like when it comes through the camera's eye?
- How do we evaluate journalism through the camera's eye?
- What problems ensue when journalism comes through the camera's eye?
- What does this say more generally about the workings and authority of journalism?

No one has yet been able to pinpoint definitively who coined the notion that a picture is worth a thousand words. But regardless of whom it was or the circumstances under which it was coined, its potential application to journalism was certainly not part of the notion's original formulation. And therein lies the misfortune, for journalism might have been different had more thought been devoted early on to its relationship with pictures. Instead, journalism has evolved without that question ever being sufficiently addressed, and the history, evolution and practice of journalism around the world have all developed alongside a long list of conflicting assumptions about how the image is supposed to work in news. Contemporary journalism is filled with images – still photographs, graphics, televised and cable video, and even interactive visual sequences on the Internet. Yet how many words those visuals are worth, if any at all, remains an unspoken issue in contemporary thinking about the incorporation of images in news. How to account for journalism when it comes through the camera's eye is thereby a critical topic when considering how journalism works.

What does journalism look like when it comes through the camera's eye?

For many of us who came of age in a mediated era, seeing is believing. Perhaps nowhere is that as pertinent as when applied to news, where notions about trust, believability and credibility in the public sphere rest in part on the capacity to present and see evidence of what is being claimed. In that regard a long list of image-making technologies has come to populate the relays of local, national and global news organizations around the world, including drawings, lithographs, televisual and cable images, and interactive online relays. Of all the imaging opportunities, however, it is the photograph that changes the stakes of journalism to the greatest degree. Photographs operate in a decidedly singular fashion alongside the words of journalistic accounts. By definition, they rely on an unspoken ocularcentric bias of Western civilization to be understood sufficiently, a bias that holds them to be largely affective, emotion driven, and generating gestalt-like experiences in their viewers. Images that are composite, more schematic than detailed, conventionalized and simplified work well as relays of news. At the same time, photographs differ from other imaging technologies: they freeze action in a way that moving images cannot; their materiality allows audiences to contemplate them at leisure and at length; and they have long been held to facilitate an appeal to the emotions that transforms them into powerful and memorable vehicles. As a choice of news relay, then, photographs occupy a front-row position in the rolodex of vehicles by which journalism reaches its audiences.

When journalism comes through the camera's eye, it takes on numerous forms. Just like words, images help journalists address circumstances that are wholly unpredictable, are fraught with tension and stressful judgement, and involve the problematic co-presence of high stakes and uneven or even low resources. What journalists decide to do with the photographs that are incorporated as part of news thus always invokes more than just the photograph itself. Negotiations over selection, placement, prominence and size always involve more than just the photographer who takes the shot and the photo-editor who positions it on the page. What is worthy of depiction, how, and why are always issues with many routes to resolution, which are weighed by various individuals.

Journalism through the camera's eye thereby has many shapes. Photographs can be discretely focused on individuals and contained settings, or they can broadly encompass vast landscapes and wide-ranging physical scenes. The angle, lighting and distance with which a photograph is shot are key in that they convey a sense of power or powerlessness, forbiddingness or intimacy, even credibility or untrustworthiness just by virtue of how and where the camera is held. The photographer chooses to shoot his or her images in black-and-white or colour, although the images are not always shown in a way that matches their initial shooting. They can be strategically ill-focused, lending a soft, fuzzy aura to the target of depiction, or they can provide a hard, relentless reflection of what the camera sees. Images come in varying sizes and shapes, and they can be shot, cropped and shaped in ways that are impacted both by the circumstances by which they are selected as well as the values and preferences of the photographer.

Photographs can also be presented in a variety of ways. When presented alone, they signify importance, though the reasons for their centrality are not always self-evident. They can be displayed as individual images, singly appended to a page of news-text, or grouped together with numerous other images that are collected around common themes and contexts. Images can appear on the front pages of newspapers or covers of news magazines – boldly prominent as the beacon of a single day's or week's news – or they can be readily contextualized as a larger part of a photographic display that itself alternately takes the shape of double or triple page spreads, fold-out or detachable supplements, or special pictorial or photographic issues. Photographic images travel onward to other media too; they appear in Web galleries or as the focus of broadcast and cable televisual line ups.

Dependent on the ways in which photographs are selected and presented, they exist in varying relationships with the news stories at their side. Other practices of display – whether or not to credit, how and in what fashion to title and/or caption, where to affix a photo on a page, what other photos to affix alongside it – are central here. Sometimes images show precisely what the news story reports – an athlete's triumphant cross of the finish line or the embrace of two relatives reunited after years of separation by war. Other times they signal a broader circumstance or state of being – the joy brought on by the coming of spring or the relief of being rescued after a natural disaster. And yet other times they communicate in tandem with other images, showing sequences of action as wide ranging as medical procedures undertaken in war zones, executions in process, or, the dismantling of a suicide bomb.

When seen through the camera's eye, journalism becomes more vivid, more accessible, more visible, and potentially understood with greater ease by a wider group of people than would be the case were photographs not part of news. Conversely, however, the presumed ease with which journalism can be accessed through images hides the basic fact that news photos are the work of selection and construction. As such, they require constant scrutiny from the publics they reach. Images can be vivid about the least important dimension of a news story and can provide access to the news in a way that does not reflect what news audiences ultimately need to know. Images, then, are seductive in that they appear to make the news more available, but they are dangerous in that they couch that availability in a series of practices by which publics are ill-equipped to access what is beyond the camera's eye.

How do we evaluate journalism through the camera's eye?

A large part of evaluating journalism when it comes through the camera's eye takes shape in conjunction with what we think we know about how images work. In that much of journalism evolves with the aim of attending to the public interest through information, many of the popular and professional evaluations of journalistic photographs are driven by the impact that they are thought to wield on the public. News images, for many, are evidence. And thus the extent to which they shape public opinion – if at all and under which circumstances – is key to much of such thinking about how news images work.

In that regard, images continually creep into ongoing discussions about the trappings of the larger world. They have been held responsible for a myriad of public events, including the efforts of documentary photographers in shaping understanding about the Depression (Goldberg 1991), the waging of war (Moeller 1989), the dispelling of public disbelief regarding the atrocities of the Holocaust (Zelizer 1998), arguments for and against the assassination of US President John F. Kennedy in 1963 (Zelizer 1992), the eroding of US public support for the war in Vietnam (Hallin 1986), the swaying of public sentiments regarding the continued US presence in Somalia during the early 1990s (Perlmutter 1998) and the absence of public response to the Falklands War (Taylor 1991). Images are thought to have effects – on public sentiment and attitudes, and on the public policy that follows in their stead. A few years ago, the noted social psychologist Albert Bandura linked the display of the famous Nick Ut photograph – of a girl running naked in a Vietnamese village after her clothes were burned off by napalm – to the military ban on cameras in battlefield areas to block the publication of disturbing images of death and destruction (Bandura 1999). During the beginning of the recent war in Afghanistan, CNN chief Walter Issacson was said to have instructed his staff to avoid displaying an excess of gruesome images of the war (Kurtz 2001: C1). In short, images are widely regarded at least in some circles as having authority. In each case, the assumption has been that images matter as a reflection of the world at large. They are not typically seen as constructions – as the result of actions taken by individual photographers, their corresponding photo editors, and the larger institutional setting that engages both – but as mirrors of the events that they depict. A related assumption posits that when news increases in magnitude or importance, pictures come to the fore. As one observer said of American journalism, 'it is a tradition . . . that when the event or history is raised to a level of great importance, we use pictures to reflect that importance' (Bill Marinow cited in Nesbitt 2001: 23). Finally, an assumption has prevailed that seeing photos – of atrocities, of natural disasters, of circumstances both difficult and heartrending – is enough to promote action or responsiveness of some kind.

Three groups have been most invested in articulating these assumptions about the value of images and their concomitant authority:

- Publics see images as a way of coming to grips with the news. Such a notion has antecedents in the ocularcentric bias of our culture, by which seeing remains an important way of determining proof in the contemporary age. A widespread popular notion equates seeing with believing, understanding with perspective. It affords the belief that pictures somehow help us grapple with the world in a more manageable, authentic and trustworthy fashion. Pictures, then, enable publics to come to grips to an extent with the world beyond their grasp in a way that renders it more readily understandable. Moreover, certain members of the public reserve special value for images. Abraham Lincoln is said to have credited his electoral victory to photographer Mathew Brady, who shortened his neck and made him appear more youthful (Goldberg 1991). And yet, publics have definitive assumptions about what should and should not be shown in news images. In March 2003, 57 per cent of the US population felt that the US media should not show pictures of captured US soldiers in Iraq (*Time*/CNN Poll 2003).

- Images are valued by journalists, who appreciate the message of 'eyewitness' authority, the notion of 'having been there' and the idea that 'we were there and you were not' that a photograph implies by virtue of its display. Commonly called photographic verisimilitude and associated with realism, the image helps journalism credential its own aims of accounting for the events of the world as they happen. In one photographer's view, the draw to pictures is undeniable: 'Many people ask me "why do you take these pictures?" . . . It's not a case of "There but for the grace of God go I"; it's a case of "I've been there"' (McCullin 1987: 11). In this regard, images help journalists do a better job of being journalists, and journalists readily rely on images to help substantiate the stories they are responsible for telling.

- Images are valued by newspaper publishers and chief executives of media organizations, who recognize that images compel public attention. Following large-scale crises, images literally come to the fore of the journalistic record. Following September 11, the *New York Times* experienced a 'sea change' in its use of images (Philip Gefter cited in Hirsch 2002), by which its pages displayed more than double the number of images it tended to display in non-crisis times (Zelizer 2002). For the first few days after the *Challenger* explosion, the *New York Times* published up to 30 images per day, thereafter reduced to a mere six images per day (Zelizer 2002), while after the *Columbia* explosion, images of the disintegrating space shuttle appeared time and again across newspapers, news magazines and even as stills on television. During the beginning of the war in Iraq, cable news organizations around the world turned to photographic galleries and interactive visual displays, showing, in the words of US news anchor Dan Rather, that there was a 'literal flood of live pictures from the battlefield' (quoted in Hilbrand and Shister 2003: A20). Certain TV news networks even featured slide shows of the photographic work of certain individuals, profiling the photographers' images against background music. And yet here too the media echoed a belief in not showing photographs of captured soldiers during the war in Iraq. As a spokeswoman for the

Independent said in March 2003, 'we are not keen on showing US or UK prisoners of war' (cited in Lawson 2003: n.d.).

Each of these groups has been consistent in its assumption that seeing is believing and its related claims. What this means is that images are accorded recognition as a viable and authoritative vehicle of news relay among both professionals and the public. At the same time, seeing is only preferred under certain circumstances.

However, the recognition given images as automatic or at least predictable transformers or facilitators of public opinion has not been matched by what scholars have established about the workings of images. From scholars of photography and photographic representation (Sekula 1984; Barthes 1977, 1981; Hall 1974), we know that images work in curious ways. Photography's specific attributes – its materiality, ease of access, frozen capture of time, an affective and often gestalt-driven view of the world that is thought to bypass the intellect and communicate directly with the emotions – help shape its power. Photographs are also thought to evolve through a twinned power of denotative and connotative force. The denotative side of images references the image's ability to account for the image as it is, commonly called its indexicality or referentiality. Associated with photographic verisimilitude and realism, the denotative side of images helps convey the world as it supposedly is. At its side, images also function through a connotative force, by which images help lend meaning to the contingent details that are being depicted. Associated with symbolism, universality and generic meaning, connotation is what allows images to contextualize concrete details and make them understandable.

These two forces, however, do not work equally as part of news. Denotation is valued over connotation, and links with the presumed effect of images in depicting public events. Images are thought to provide depictions of the world as 'it is,' offering a concrete and grounded depiction of the events underlying the news. In this regard, they lend journalists eyewitness status, helping to establish that 'they were there'. Thus, the photograph's denotative power is as important for journalism establishing its claim to the real as it is for the power of the image itself. In other words, photography's denotative power helps journalists do their job as journalists.

This is not to say that connotation does not figure in the shaping and understanding of photographs. Even if the two forces of the photograph are valued differently, journalists engage in a slew of practices surrounding images that attend explicitly and implicitly to connotation. Framing, positioning, titling and captioning a photo can have much to do with connotation. Iconic images, for instance, are singled out and reproduced time and again by news organizations, who recognize the value in treating the JFK assassination through an image depicting the graveside salute of his young son or the repeated display of the aeroplanes hitting the World Trade Center in an effort to come to grips with September 11. Shown over time not for their denotative qualities, it is their capacity to capture the symbolic meaning of the events they depict that is central here. Similarly, the difference between collectively titling four images *Icons of Starvation* versus titling a specific image with the name of the person about to die from malnutrition and delineating where he or she is situated makes a powerfully distinct statement about what a news photograph is for. In each case, connotation, rather than denotation, is what generates the photo's power.

What all of this suggests is that photographs are like an emperor caught without his clothes. Though recognized at least in the popular imagination as powerful and authoritative, photographs remain a vehicle for news relay that is unaddressed by the community most relevant in determining their use – journalists. Today, some 160 years after the ascent of photography in news, the visuals of journalism are the source of inattention by the journalistic world. How to use images in the news, how or whether to caption or credit them, how to affix them to the words at their side remain unanswered questions in the use of visuals in the news. Even in discussions of images, the image receives little if any presence on the front stage of attention. In Bandura's article, mentioned above, nowhere did he detail the precise name of the image or name of the photographer who took it, though he went on at some length about the role it played in changing military policy regarding cameras in the battlefield. When coupled with the long-standing belief in the power of images that publics, journalists and publishers seem to accord images, there is need to assess critically what role images play in journalism.

What problems ensue when journalism comes through the camera's eye?

It is no surprise, then, that problems with the authority of news images arise wherever images are used. Deriving from the unusual combination of a lack of standards for how to use images and a strong almost undisputable regard for images, the resulting dissonance rears its head particularly when publics have the greatest need for information, as in the circumstances following crisis, war, natural disasters and the like. At such times, photographs come to the forefront of documentation. And yet it is not along the lines of newsworthiness that they necessarily do so.

Moreover, the creeping growth of image manipulation leaves questions, particularly in a digital age where the original can no longer be compared with its copy. Whether it is *Time* magazine's decision to blacken the colour of O. J. Simpson's skin or remove evidence of a pilot's genitals as he was being dragged through Mogadishu, real questions about editorial intervention and photography remain. What kind of truth value is attached to photographs remains unaddressed, despite the fact that journalism continues to depend on that truth-value for its ability to account for the world.

This is exacerbated by the fact that newspapers, news magazines and other media regularly turn over their column inches and airtime to still photographs. The question thus arises as to how these photographs in effect matter. Do they give the public the information it needs, which is the basics of the presumed impact images are thought to have? Even following September 11, publics did not always receive new photos of new aspects of the circumstances that followed as much as repetitive, familiar and predictable shots. For instance, one magazine showed 18 separate shots of people running from the World Trade Center in its issue following the event ('September 11, 2001' 2001). During the war in Iraq, one *New York Times* article showed not one but three pictures of Iraqis uncovering the graves of their relatives, all on one page (pictures appended to Fisher 2003: A10).

Pictures evade newsworthiness in other ways. During wartime, for instance, images tend to depict events and objects that are patriotic and bear connections with the nation-state, civic pride and heroic sacrifice. Wars that may be different in tenor and circumstances are linked through familiar images. Not depicted typically are those sides of war that offset the prevailing assumptions about how war is to be waged: thus, there are few or no images of human gore, one's own war dead or POWs, damage to the opposing side, military operations that have gone poorly, or the effect of one's own war on civilians of the other side (Zelizer 2004). What appears, too, are images that recycle pictures from earlier wars – instances of flag-raising depicted both the US forces at Iwo Jima during the Second World War, after September 11, and Afghanistan. Pictures of soldiers cradling infants injured on the side of their 'enemies' were used to depict the Allied forces during the Second World War, the Lebanese civil war during the early 1980s, and US forces in Iraq in 2003. Depictions showing soldiers and civilians bearing witness to atrocity appeared as depictions of a wide range of wars, including the Second World War, Cambodia, Bosnia, Rwanda, Afghanistan and Iraq. In such pictures, familiar depictions showed individuals or groups of people looking at evidence of war's human loss – mounds of corpses, stacks of skulls, shattered bodies.

Sometimes the pictures show very little. Many pictures of civilians on September 11 showed them bearing witness to the burning towers, though no towers were seen in the images. Soldiers in Iraq in 2003 were shown looking at images of dead and captured US POWs on Al Jazeera, although no POWs were shown in the images. In each case, viewers of the images needed to supply the context surrounding the image in order to understand it.

What does this say more generally about the workings and authority of journalism?

That images would provide a lasting problem for journalism practitioners was articulated early on by resistant reporters, such as the *Time* editors who looked askance at photography and disdainfully pronounced it as a 'mechanical side-line to the serious business of fact narration – a social inferior' (*Time* editors 1936: 20). As early as 1935, British reporters declared photographers' work 'not journalism' and argued that the press photographer's admission into journalistic organizations was 'indefensible' (Grimley 1935: 54). Given the level of image saturation in contemporary news, this is worth considering anew. Have images lived up to the somewhat desultory potential that journalists originally predicted, or has journalism failed to figure out what to do with its own increasingly central reliance on the image as a tool, however unarticulated, of news relay?

The authority of news images thus presents itself time and again like an emperor without clothes. In need of address, it grows consistently as the technologies for news relay make its reasoned consideration ill-timed, burdensome and ultimately unnecessary. What we need to recognize, however, is that the delay in addressing images in news, and the authority we accrue them, works to the disadvantage of all involved in their use and their reception. It prohibits the public from receiving visual information that they can use to reliably understand public events in a more informed fashion. It leaves journalists using images in unthoughtful and uneven ways, often undermining both the value of the image and the story at its side. And it prevents the publishers and media executives from using images to their full potential, not as adjuncts to words but as full partners in news relay.

At the same time, the ways in which photographs work as part of news suggest that journalism relies on a vehicle of information relay that is problematic. It is unevenly reliable, generates ambivalent and often contradictory assessments, and is insufficiently connected to journalism. In this sense, the problems and issues surrounding journalistic images serve as a litmus test for the workings more generally of journalism. It is time to consider more fully how images work in journalism, not only for the sake of the image but for that of journalism too.

References

Bandura, A. (1999) Moral Disengagement in the Perpetration of Inhumanities, *Personality and Social Psychology Review* 3(3); 193–209.

Barthes, R. (1981) *Camera Lucida*. London: Hill & Wang.

Barthes, R. (1977) The Rhetoric of the Image, in *Image/Music/Text*. New York: Hill & Wang.

Fisher, I. (2003) Threat Gone, Iraqis Unearth Hussein's Nameless Victims, *New York Times*, 25 April: A1, A10.

Goldberg, V. (1991) *The Power of Photography*. New York: Abbeville Press.

Grimley, E. (1935) Not Journalists, *Journal*, March: 54.

Hall, S. (1974) The Determinations of News Photographs, in S. Cohen and J. Young (eds) *The Manufacture of News*. London: Sage.

Hallin, D. (1986) *The 'Uncensored War': The Media and Vietnam*. New York: Oxford University Press.

Hilbrand, D. and Shister, G. (2003) A Flood of Images into Homes, *Philadelphia Inquirer*, 27 March: A1, A20.

Hirsch, M. (2002) The Day Time Stopped, *Chronicle of Higher Education*, 25 January: B11.

Kurtz, H. (2001) CNN Chief Orders 'Balance' in War News, *Washington Post*, 31 October: C1.

Lawson, A. (n.d.) Editors Show Restraint with War Images, *Guardian* online, posted at http://media.guardian.co.uk/print/0,3858,4636103–111303,00.html.

McCullin, D. (1987) Notes By a Photographer, in E. Meijer and J. Swart (eds) *The Photographic Memory: Press Photography – Twelve Insights*. London: Quiller Press and the World Press Photo Foundation, pp. 11–26.

Moeller, S. (1989) *Shooting War*. New York: Basic Books.

Nesbitt, P. (2001) Tragedy in Photos: A New Standard? In American Press Institute, *Crisis Journalism: A Handbook for Media Response*. Reston, VA: American Press Institute, pp. 23–5.

Perlmutter, D. (1998) *Photojournalism and Foreign Policy. Icons of Outrage in International Crises*. Westport, CT: Praeger.

Sekula, A. (1984) On the Invention of Photographic Meaning, in *Photography Against the Grain*. Halifax: Press of the Nova Scotia College of Arts and Design.

September 11, 2001 (2001) *People*, 24 September.

Taylor, J. (1991) *War Photography: Realism in the British Press*. London: Routledge.

Time/CNN Poll. Conducted by Yankelovitch Associates, 28 March 2003.

Time editors (1936) *Four Hours a Year*. New York: Time Inc.

Zelizer, B. (1992) *Covering the Body: The Kennedy Assassination, the Media, and the Shaping of Collective Memory*. Chicago: University of Chicago Press.

Zelizer, B. (1995) Journalism's 'Last' Stand: Wirephoto and the Discourse of Resistance, *Journal of Communication* 45(2): 78–92.

Zelizer, B. (1998) *Remembering to Forget: Holocaust Memory Through the Camera's Eye*. Chicago: University of Chicago Press.

Zelizer, B. (2002) Photography, Journalism, and Trauma, in B. Zelizer and S. Allan (eds) *Journalism After September 11*. London and New York: Routledge, pp. 48–68.

Zelizer, B. (2004) When War is Reduced to a Photograph, in S. Allan and B. Zelizer (eds) *Reporting War: Journalism in Wartime*. London and New York: Routledge, pp. 115–35.

Mighty dread
Journalism and moral panics

Chas Critcher

- What is a moral panic?
- How does journalism contribute to the generation of moral panics?
- Which conditions are required for a moral panic to develop?
- Why are Britain and the US especially prone to experiencing moral panics?

The centrality of news media to moral panics

The most often quoted description of a moral panic remains the opening paragraph of Stan Cohen's 1973 book *Folk Devils and Moral Panics*:

> Societies appear to be subject, every now and then, to periods of moral panic. (1) A condition, episode, person or group of persons emerges to become defined as a threat to societal values and interests; (2) its nature is presented in a stylized and stereotypical fashion by the mass media; (3) the moral barricades are manned by editors, bishops, politicians and other right-thinking people; (4) socially accredited experts pronounce their diagnoses and solutions; (5) ways of coping are evolved or (more often) resorted to; (6) the condition then disappears, submerges or deteriorates and becomes more visible. Sometimes the object of the panic is quite novel and at other times it is something which has been in existence long enough, but suddenly appears in the limelight. Sometimes the panic passes over and is forgotten, except in folk-lore and collective memory; at other times it has more serious and long-lasting repercussions and might produce such changes as those in legal and social policy or even in the way the society conceives itself.
>
> (Cohen 1973: 9, numbers inserted)

Cohen's book used an extended case study of social reaction in the 1960s to two British youth subcultures, Mods and Rockers. In his attempt to trace the origins of a massive overreaction to the supposed 'threat' posed by the influx of such young people to south coast resorts on Bank Holidays, Cohen placed the news media at the centre of analysis:

> The student of moral enterprise cannot but pay particular attention to the role of the mass media in defining and shaping social problems. The media have long operated as agents of moral indignation in their own right: even if they are not self-consciously engaged in crusading or muck-raking, their very reporting of certain facts can be sufficient to generate concern, anxiety, indignation or panic. When such feelings coincide with a perception that particular values need to be protected, the pre-conditions for new rule creation or social problem definition are present.
>
> (Cohen 1973: 16)

Since Cohen's pioneering work there have been numerous studies of moral panics, although not all have used that precise term. In both the US and the UK – reviewed in Goode and Ben-Yehuda (1994) and Thompson (1998) respectively – there have been studies of, among other topics, violent street crime, recreational and addictive drugs, AIDS and child abuse in all its forms. Not all these studies have followed Cohen in emphasizing the central role of the news media. In the US, moral panic studies have been dominated by social constructionism. This perspective concentrates on how social problems are constructed into major public issues requiring action from the authorities. It places at the centre of analysis the activities of 'claims makers', organized groups that campaign for public recognition of, and political action about, what they perceive as a particularly threatening issue. They seek publicity through the media, which influence their cause by deciding how much attention to give to it. Where the media do pay such attention, they will also affect how the public views the issue and thus pressurize politicians to take action. But the media are not themselves seen to exert an independent influence on the progress of a moral panic. They are its channel, not its source. By contrast, British studies of moral panics see the news media as the most important single factor in the creation of moral panics. They are seen as less dependent upon the campaigning activities of claims makers, more able and willing to attempt to instigate a moral panic on their own account, regardless of whether groups already exist campaigning on the issue.

These differences of emphasis are, I have suggested (Critcher 2003: 124) partly attributable to the media and political systems in each country. Both media and political power are more highly centralized in Britain than in the US, so the relationship between them is more direct and transparent. The multiplicity of local media and political institutions in the US renders media power less direct and visible. Thus it is not surprising to find British scholars observing and theorizing such blatant media influence while American scholars observe and theorize a complex interplay between claims makers, media and political structures. Relatedly, there are different intellectual traditions among social scientists. British scholars are more critically engaged with the powers and authority of the state, while Americans take a more liberal view of the political process as the outcome of a competition among interest groups.

All this makes hazardous any attempt to generalize across nations about the role of the news media in moral panics. Moreover, there are variations in both countries in what we mean by the news media. There are important distinctions, for example, between national and local media, between broadcasting and the press, between hard news and investigative or feature journalism. Such considerations should qualify, though need not invalidate, generalizations about the role of the news media in moral panics.

Questioning the media role

Elsewhere (Critcher 2003), I have argued that Cohen's model, and the six stages it implies, has proved robust. It is a remarkably accurate description of what happens in a fully-fledged moral panic. The most obvious recent example – in the US, the UK and beyond – is the serial moral panic about paedophilia, where each of Cohen's stages was apparent, at least in broad outline. Generally we can describe what will happen, even though it is not always apparent why. This applies most of all to the role of the news media. We can identify what needs to happen for a moral panic to succeed but it is often less clear why sometimes these requirements are met and sometimes they are not.

Nevertheless, from the work of Cohen and others, we know that a moral panic requires:

• recognizing a new and threatening social problem;

• labelling, defining and interpreting the problem and its perpetrators;

• developing an agenda about the problem – its causes and resolutions;

• legitimizing the views of claims makers and experts;

• demanding and securing relevant action from political elites.

In modern, democratic societies these processes can only be realized with the assistance of the news media. Their role may vary. They may themselves seek to instigate a moral panic, mainly articulate the claims of interest groups or mediate between claims makers and their opponents. Yet their overall function remains strategic; for a moral panic to happen, the news media must actively participate in realizing its conditions. It is thus possible to specify some essential questions about the role of the news media in moral panics. Each is derived from one of the requirements of a moral panic.

1. Why and how are some events interpreted by the news media as symbolizing a wider social problem or issue?

2. How are new social problems or issues labelled, defined and interpreted?

3. What kind of agenda is developed by news media and how does it become common across them?

4. In what ways do the news media make use of claims makers or experts in its discussion of the problem?

5. How does the news media agenda gain support among influential political elites, sufficient to bring about policy changes?

I shall first answer each question in turn, then briefly illustrate the argument with a case study of the brief eruption of 'gun culture' as a potential moral panic in Britain in early 2003. Finally, I consider frameworks needed to account for the overall process.

Answering the questions about the news media

1. Why and how are some events interpreted by the news media as symbolizing a wider social problem or issue?

Cohen originally specified how 'a condition, episode, person or group of persons' becomes defined as a 'threat to societal values and interests'. This is essentially the problem of when, how and why moral panics start, to which there are no easy answers. The nearest we have is the idea of 'key events' (Kepplinger and Habermeier 1995) which come to symbolize and crystallize a wider threat. Such key events take various forms. They might be: a tragic death; a crime, reported when it occurred, during and after the trial or all three; an official inquiry or report of some kind; a statement by a political figure or a pressure group; a public scandal or disclosure by a whistleblower. (All of these, for example, have been evident in the moral panic about immigration evident in Britain in mid-2004.) Such events, it might be thought, need to be newsworthy in themselves, according to established criteria of newsworthiness. However, and this is something that news value models do not always recognize, a key event may become news less because of its intrinsic qualities than because it is taken to be symbolic: it stands for more than what it is.

2. How are new social problems or issues labelled, defined and interpreted?

Once recognized as a new problem, then, in Cohen's words, 'its nature is presented in a stylized and stereotypical fashion by the mass media'. Cohen details the processes involved in what he calls the 'inventory': stylization and stereotyping, exaggeration, distortion, prediction and symbolization, sensitization, creation of folk devils. This is where the news media operate most independently of other actors: they need no support or sanction to do this, although they will accept what comes their way. Crucial here is the invention of a new name or label for the condition and those responsible for it: 'paedophilia' is an obvious example. With remarkable rapidity, this becomes the accepted term for the condition, all the more connotatively powerful for never having been precisely defined. Definition is not needed because it is achieved through stereotyping: paedophilia is what paedophiles are or do. Thus stereotyped, the condition is exaggerated in its prevalence and distorted in its nature. Sensitization involves ferreting around for other events that do or can be made to fit the stereotype. Symbolization becomes the means by which we can recognize both the condition or its perpetrators and the wider threat that it or they pose. From this can be developed predictions about what will happen unless effective action is taken now against this threat. At the core of is these processes is the creation of a folk devil, the source and embodiment of the problem.

3. What kind of agenda is developed by news media and how does it become common across them?

An agenda is both a definition of the problem and a prescription of the remedy. Any moral panic develops a call for action, normally changes in the law or its application. Here the news media implicitly or explicitly endorse the programmes of active campaigners. They advocate political action for legal reform.

This campaigning role seems to be intrinsic to the media except where regulation of broadcasting explicitly forbids it, as is the case in Britain though not in the US. However, a moral panic requires virtually all the news media to adopt the same agenda. It may first appear confined to one newspaper or locality but must then, if it is to gain national recognition, become the agenda of the media system as a whole. We can sometimes see this happening. In the US, local concerns about ritual abuse spread to the whole nation (deYoung 1998). In Britain, the agenda of one Sunday newspaper for reform of sex offender laws eventually became the agenda of all news media (Critcher 2002). In both instances, the spread of the agenda was aided by sensational cases involving respectively the alleged abuse and the undoubted murder of young children. The media also have a tendency to report on each other: broadcasting and the press constantly monitor each others' stories and campaigns. There also appear to be some media that have more capacity to initiate this process than others. In Britain I have argued that one national newspaper, the *Daily Mail*, appears to have extraordinary influence. In the US, newsweeklies appear to have similar influence. But this diffusion of an agenda throughout the news media does not always happen and we are some way from understanding which conditions encourage or discourage it.

4. In what ways do the news media make use of claims makers or experts in its discussion of the problem?

In assessing the significance of a news event, journalism needs some cues that there is indeed a story behind the event, a 'frightening new strain of' something or other that is deviant and/or criminal. Such confirmation may be sought from news sources but often there is no need. If a newspaper has itself been campaigning on the issue, finding stories for its news pages and advocating action in its editorial columns, then that will be enough. 'This paper has for a long time been calling attention to the dangers posed by . . .' As an alternative or supplement, the journalist can turn to those already concerned about the issue. However new it appears to be, there is likely to be a group of some kind that has been campaigning about it, from organizations of victims or sufferers to general purpose groups that monitor the morals of the nation – although the latter are far less prominent in Britain than in the US. If the victims or sufferers belong to a distinct group, then there will be organizations committed to their welfare. The journalist will know where to go for comments on, for example, the welfare of children or teenagers or the elderly.

Often, though not invariably, there may be a group with the specific goal of publicizing the threat, be it the evils of violence on television, the misuse of drugs, the excesses of immigration. If the agendas of such groups and the newspaper coincide, then symbiosis exists: the newspaper will want the statistics, assertions and case histories which the organization will be only too happy to provide. According to Cohen, such publicity brings to the moral barricades 'editors, bishops, politicians and other right-thinking people', those whom Becker (1963) once called 'moral entrepreneurs'. More-or-less simultaneously, experts are invited to comment. Experts do not seem to need many credentials, other than being described as such by the newspaper. On medical and scientific issues there sometimes appear genuine experts whose professional lives involve detailed study of the condition. Media friendly psychiatrists and psychologists are more common, remarkably willing to pronounce the truth about any new condition immediately it appears. But in practice expertise seems to be on the retreat. Not only has trust in experts of all kinds generally declined but they are unlikely to subscribe to the simplistic diagnoses and remedies favoured by the press. Preferred, because they do share this perspective, are claims makers whom the media accredit with expertise on the issue, despite their vested interests. Newspaper columnists or television pundits will also habitually cite that well-known opponent of expertise, common sense.

Experts remain unnecessary to moral panics and may be avoided if they implicitly challenge the premises of the panic. However, on some rare issues where authoritative experts can claim a monopoly of knowledge they may forestall the moral panic and establish jurisdiction over the issue. AIDS was such an instance. We need to understand more how and why the news media grant expert status to some, often despite their vested interests, while denying such status to others, despite their professional credentials.

5. How does the news media agenda gain support among influential political elites, sufficient to bring about policy changes?

An important precondition for effective action can be derived from one of Goode and Ben-Yehuda's (1994) five defining characteristics of a moral panic. This is the need for a clear consensus among elites. The nature and extent of opposition to the panic may be important here, among politicians, 'counter claims makers' or sections of the media. If it is strong enough, the course of the moral panic may be disrupted. There needs to be a unanimous media view about the urgency of the problem, backed up by pressure group activity, endorsed by politicians from the ruling party or opposition. Together, these require a response from government.

Such a response comes when, as Cohen notes, 'ways of coping are evolved or (more often) resorted to'. The precise reaction of government is matter of political calculation: whether the issue will prove ephemeral; whether it is felt to be significant to the electorate; whether it can appear to be resolved by measures that will cost the government little in material resources and gain it much in symbolic status. On both sides of the Atlantic, quite radical changes in the legal and criminal justice system have been instigated on the basis of what have proved to be fleeting events. Such changes in the law or in the procedures of agencies of social control are the normal outcomes of moral panics. At this point news media congratulate the government for its eventual action and, of course, themselves for having represented the public interest so determinedly. If the action is accepted to be effective then the whole panic, or at least one episode of it, has effectively achieved closure, unless or until a new key event revives it. Such closure is a product of the news attention cycle and the narrative form of news reportage (Critcher 2003).

In Cohen's final stage, the condition then 'disappears, submerges or deteriorates and becomes more visible'. Its legacy may only be as a footnote in social history or it may have affected legal and social policy. It may reappear later, becoming a serial panic. It may even, says Cohen, have effects on the way society conceives itself. Such effects will be discussed in the Conclusion.

An example: gun culture in Britain

I have deliberately given few actual examples, since I wanted to explore an abstract schema of media processes, in principle applicable to all putative moral panics. I have previously applied Cohen's model to a wide range of examples (Critcher 2003). Except for paedophilia, now a permanent serial panic, many of these have now dated. A more recent example occurred in early 2003 in the UK. A specific crime was interpreted by the news media as indexing a problem of 'gun culture' in Britain's inner cities (see Chiricos 1996 for an earlier equivalent in the US). While this did not develop into a moral panic proper, it does illustrate many of the news media processes identified so far.

On New Year's Eve 2002, two young African Caribbean women were shot dead outside a party in Lozells, an inner city area in Birmingham. In a society where gun crime is comparatively rare and gun ownership highly regulated, any fatal shooting is likely to attract news attention. It was not, however, the use of guns or even the fatalities that determined newsworthiness because, as media coverage subsequently noted, there had been a spate of underreported shootings in several inner city areas across Britain, associated with conflict among drug gangs. What shaped the newsworthiness of the Birmingham shooting was the nature of the victims. Young and female, they were taken to be innocents, literally caught in the cross fire of a conflict in which they had no part. Photographs of the girls, dressed up and laughing, underwrote this interpretation.

Even then, this event might have passed quickly from news view, had it not been for what it was taken to represent. It made dramatically visible a previously hidden problem. In line with the moral panic model, this new problem had to be given a name, one which was pithy, reusable and highly connotative. The initial definition of the event as an instance of 'gun crime' was quickly abandoned, as the news media settled on a significantly richer term: 'gun culture'. Derived from the US, its usage served a number of functions, intentional or not. It established that this incident was more than simply a trend in criminal behaviour, the use of guns, but that guns had become part of a whole way of life, which sanctioned their usage. Thus much follow-up coverage concentrated less on the event itself than on the alleged 'culture' that had produced it. This was ethnically defined, implicitly excluding from gun culture the use of firearms by white criminals. Both conservative and liberal analysts agreed that gun use was encouraged by black street culture which offered solutions to the problems of identity among disaffected black youth. Its dress and music, especially gangsta rap, encouraged the belief that maintaining face was crucial, with immediate and dramatic response to any suggestion that a member had been 'disrespected'. Adding to this the turf wars over the drug trade and the known ruthlessness of those involved, there emerged a quite clear portrait of the problem of 'gun culture' residing in, and thus becoming the problem of, the black community. The use of 'culture' effectively depoliticized the problem. The causes were not to be found in the political and economic structures of the predominantly white society but in the habits and lifestyles of the black community.

This cultural perspective appeared alongside, but did not displace, traditional law and order narratives. Senior police officers were cited on the extent and nature of the problem, the effectiveness of police response and the 'wall of silence' among witnesses. The ongoing dispute about police powers to stop and search suspects was revived, especially their reluctance to stop young black men for fear of accusations of racism. The government was about to institute a minimum five-year sentence for simple possession of a firearm, the effectiveness of which was debated and evaluated. Other experts here were few and far between, though journalists did consult local people in Lozells, including supposed black community leaders, about disaffected black youth and their tendency to gravitate towards drug gangs. A junior government Minister attacked the nihilistic lyrics of gangsta rap which provoked hostile response from black DJs.

But, after a few days' coverage, the issue petered out. It did not develop into a recognizable moral panic. Several reasons may be suggested for this. One is that additional legislative action could not easily be proposed. Britain already had the strongest gun controls in Europe; the five-year minimum sentence would constitute a suitably draconian response. Though gun crimes continued among black gangs, including murders, these were 'black on black' crimes that did not directly threaten the white community. No other innocent victims appeared. Defining the problem in term of a 'gun culture' located the problem firmly within the black communities themselves, with white society only involved in policing their activities and more generally in social engineering to reclaim disaffected black youth. The latter did not lend itself to any simplistic calls for immediate action. In moral panic terms, the folk devil was curiously absent, diffused into culture and lifestyle: no gun-toting, drug-crazed black youth appeared to threaten society at large. No new measures could be advocated. Legal changes were imminent, while social policies remained vague and long-term.

Of the moral panic conditions identified earlier, this example confirms the presence of some and the absence of others. As expected, a dramatic news event was taken as symbolizing a wider problem, one endorsed by the police as the significant claims makers and experts. The debate drew in politicians and commentators on or from the black community. But the scope of the threat was confined to black people in inner cities. Moreover, the simplistic solution of heavier sentencing for firearms possession had already been adopted by the government. In such circumstances, media attention, though intense, proved ephemeral.

News, agendas and fear

When we understand news practices, we understand most, though not all, of what we need to know about how moral panics work. The features that make an event newsworthy are also those that have potential for moral panic development. To cite only some from Galtung and Ruge's (1981) classic list, events that are unexpected, negative, momentous, personalized and unambiguous are likely to contrast the abnormal with the normal and thus lead down the road of good and evil. What we know about journalists' use of sources suggests that the vested interests of pressure groups and politicians are likely to be treated as expert testimonies justifying definitions of threat and calls for action. However, we have also noted that this does not always happen; otherwise Britain and the US would be permanently caught up in one moral panic or another. The crucial development seems to be that moment when one or more events are taken as an index of a wider and larger problem. Only then emerges the need to name, define and remedy the threat. So understanding how and why specific news events are given this symbolic power may be the key to unlock the remaining secrets of moral panic formation in the news media.

However, understanding news alone will not enable us to understand the political impact of moral panics or other media-based discussions of social problems. For that we need a wider perspective – one that interrelates news media with politicians and public opinion. One such perspective is provided by the agenda-setting approach (Dearing and Rogers 1992). This suggests the existence of three agendas, those of the media, politicians and the public. To become a national problem requiring intervention, an issue must be prominent simultaneously on all three agendas. Current knowledge, based on a range of case studies, suggests that the news media are the predominant influence. They have the power to influence public opinion and thus pressure politicians into action. If they unanimously and consistently present issue X as Britain's/America's number one social problem, then audiences will assume this to be so, even if they do not necessarily agree with the proposed solutions. If politicians, ever sensitive to news media, pick up this message themselves and believe that their constituents are doing likewise, then it is in their interest to be seen to act as the guardians of the national's morals. Debates in the British Parliament or Congressional hearings in America will confirm the reality of the threat and the appropriateness of the proposed remedies. This will receive coverage in the news media, provoking columnists and chat-show hosts to comment further. Thus will be achieved the level of concern and degree of consensus identified by Goode and Ben-Yehuda (1994) as vital to moral panics.

But, we must insist again, this does not always happen. At any one time, there are many more issues being campaigned about than can possibly attract the attention of the news media, politicians and the public. As agenda-setting theorists note, each agenda – media, public and politicians – has a limited carrying capacity. It can only deal with a few issues at the same time. A new issue can only be taken on board if a current one is jettisoned. Inbuilt into the system is a permanent turnover of social problems. If we ask which are more or less likely to move up these agendas, then we return once more to the process of symbolization. Events seem to need to symbolize wider issues and the issues themselves to symbolize something about the state of the nation.

Of the available explanations of this symbolic power, one of the most convincing is the idea that we live increasingly in a culture of fear. Furedi (1997) in Britain and Glassner (1999) in the US have argued that for complex reasons we trust our institutions, our leaders and thus ultimately each other, less and less. We seem to inhabit a risky world of dangerous strangers. The news media may reflect and enlarge our sense of risk. If the news concentrates on what or who is deviant, abnormal, threatening, unpredictable, dangerous (Reiner 2002), then it is possible to forget that we are actually most of the time reasonably safe. We can become convinced that this safety is precarious, likely to be destroyed at any time by unknowable threats. This is perhaps a recognizable climate at a time when the Western world in general, and Britain and the US in particular, feel under daily threat of terrorist attacks from Islamic fundamentalists. Yet it may not be so different in its psychology from other recent moments, when in the US thousands of children were supposedly being abducted or murdered or when, in Britain, bogus asylum seekers were flooding into the country unhindered. For both issues, the news media were at the forefront of claims that such threats were real. If we ask how journalism contributes to moral panics, we can point to newsmaking practices and the processes of agenda setting as crucial influences. But it may be that its most significant, enduring and intractable contribution is in fostering this climate of fear and creating the folk devils that give it shape. Here is today's news: be afraid.

References

Becker, H. (1963) *Outsiders: Studies in the Sociology of Deviance*. New York: Free Press.

Chiricos, T. (1996) Moral Panic as Ideology: Drugs, Violence, Race and Punishment in America, in M. J. Lynch and E. Britt Patterson (eds) *Justice with Prejudice: Race and Criminal Justice in America*. Guilderland, New York: Harrow & Heston.

Cohen, S. (1973) *Folk Devils and Moral Panics*. St. Albans: Paladin.

Critcher, C. (2002) Media, Government and Moral Panic: the Politics of Paedophilia in Britain 2000–1, *Journalism Studies*, 3(4): 520–34.

Critcher, C. (2003) *Moral Panics and the Media*. Maidenhead and New York: Open University Press.

Dearing, J. W. and Rogers, E. M. (1992) *Communication Concepts 6: Agenda-Setting*. Thousand Oaks: Sage.

deYoung, M. (1998) Another Look at Moral Panics: the Case of Satanic Day Care Centers, *Deviant Behavior*, 19(3): 257–78.

Furedi, F. (1997) *Culture of Fear: Risk-taking and the Morality of Low Expectation*. London: Cassell.

Galtung, J. and Ruge, M. (1981) Structuring and Selecting News, in S. Cohen and J. Young (eds) *The Manufacture of News: Deviance, Social Problems and the Mass Media*. London: Constable.

Glassner, B. (1999) *The Culture of Fear: Why Americans are Afraid of the Wrong Things*. New York: Basic Books.

Goode, E. and Ben-Yehuda, N. (1994) *Moral Panics: the Social Construction of Deviance*. Oxford: Blackwell.

Kepplinger, H. M. and Habermeier, J. H. (1995) The Impact of Key Events Upon the Presentation of Reality, *European Journal of Communication*, 10(3): 371–90.

Reiner, R. (2002) Media Made Criminality: the Representation of Crime in the Mass Media, in M. Maguire, M. Morgan and R. Reiner (eds) *The Oxford Handbook of Criminology*. Oxford: Oxford University Press.

Thompson, K. (1998) *Moral Panics*. London: Routledge.

14

Communication or spin? Source-media relations in science journalism

Alison Anderson, Alan Petersen and Matthew David

- How do pluralist, critical and risk theories interpret power relations within source-media interactions?
- Can there ever be a 'correct' or 'accurate' news portrayal of science?
- Are recent attempts by scientists to improve their media reporting evidence of openness or spin?

This chapter examines the contribution that the study of source-media interactions has made, and can make, to contemporary science journalism. It examines some theories pertaining to source-journalist dynamics and recent evidence on science news production processes, making particular reference to findings on medical genetics news. It is argued that the study of how science news is produced, and in particular how scientists and journalists see their respective roles in the news production process, is crucial to understanding both the public representation of science and the formation of policy. Recent controversies about the nature and accuracy of reporting in relation to issues such as cloning, embryonic stem cells, and nanotechnology have highlighted the need for journalists to develop an in-depth understanding of the social processes influencing their practice.

Mapping the field

Since the mid-1990s the interaction between news sources and the news media has become an increasingly important area of research within journalism studies. With the growth of the public relations industry, and the politics of 'spin', more attention has focused upon the ways in which contending voices seek to get their message across through the news media. The significance of understanding source-media relations was emphasized in the UK in 2003 to 2004 with the controversy surrounding news reporting on the dossier which claimed Iraq possessed stockpiles of weapons of mass destruction. Arguments about the accuracy or otherwise of news coverage of the government's interpretation of intelligence reports in making the case for war against Iraq became crucial in the evidence of Lord Hutton's inquiry into the events leading to the death of weapons inspector, Dr David Kelly. Recognizing the importance of understanding news production processes, scholars have increasingly turned their attention to the activity of news sources and their relationship with the news media. A rich vein of research has focused on how organizations utilize news media in order to challenge the portrayal of issues. These include health (Conrad 1999; Miller and Williams 1993; Nisbet and Lewenstein 2002), the environment (Anderson 1997), criminal justice (Ericson *et al.* 1989; Schlesinger and Tumber 1994) and trade unionism (Davis 2000). The question of the degree to which competing groups and organizations are able to make their voices heard, and successfully gain access to the news media is a key issue for the sociology of journalism. Moreover, issues of news media access are central to addressing broader concerns about citizenship and democracy.

News production and source strategies

Both liberal democratic theory and the various strands of critical theory share a central underlying concern with issues of news representation and source access. Questions concerning whose voices are given prominence, whose voices are silenced or marginalized, and the role of the media in representing 'public opinion', is the subject of intense debate. The pluralist model of power suggested by liberal democratic theory assumes that the existence of a range of pressure groups and interest groups ensures that the public can access a range of views, with no one organization/group consistently dominating for any length of time. This model suffers from a number of major limitations, such as over-emphasizing individual autonomy and under-estimating the constraints of material resources, but it does usefully draw attention to the relative fluidity of power and the ways in which organizations mobilize symbolic and material resources (see Anderson 1997; Manning 2001). In particular, the pluralist model draws attention to the skilful and strategic use of political and symbolic resources, and contestation and conflict among campaigning groups. Recognizing the limitations of the pluralist model, in the 1970s, media scholars began to focus on the structural biases of the media that privilege certain views and voices. Some neo-Marxist (for instance Gramscian) approaches, for example, have concentrated upon macro-structure media-state interactions that benefit the powerful. However, this has led them to underestimate the extent to which there is competition and conflict among campaigning groups vying to gain news media access.

A seminal study by Hall *et al.* (1978), *Policing the Crisis: Mugging, the State and Law and Order*, advances the argument that powerful 'accredited' sources, such as government departments, legal institutions, the police and established interest groups close to government, enjoy privileged access to the media. They are seen to command greater access to the media by virtue of their claims to expert knowledge, their powerful position in society and their representative status. News agendas are seen as almost always shaped by the frameworks provided by these privileged sources. Hall *et al.* suggest that such sources become over-accessed by the media and, as a consequence, become 'primary definers' of issues.

The extent to which news routines continue to be structured so that there is a systematic over-accessing of the views of the powerful forms a key debate within the sociology of journalism. Over recent years a number of qualifications to Hall *et al*'s notion of 'primary definition' have emerged from a range of perspectives. The critique was led by Philip Schlesinger (1990) who, while supporting the general argument that the news media tend to reproduce the definitions of the powerful, argued for a more nuanced, less media-centric, approach to studying news sources. He suggested that there were more opportunities for politically marginalized sources to gain entry to the news than is acknowledged by Hall's theory. As Schlesinger points out, the notion that 'primary definers' necessarily secure advantaged access to the news media has its problems:

> . . . it is necessary that sources be conceived as occupying fields in which *competition for access* to the media takes place, but in which material and symbolic advantages are unequally distributed. But the most advantaged do not secure a primary definition in virtue of their positions alone. Rather, if they do so, it is because of successful *strategic action* in an imperfectly competitive field.
>
> (Schlesinger 1990: 77 original emphasis)

To briefly summarize, Schlesinger (1990) identifies five major limitations with the 'primary definer' thesis: First, it fails to account for longer-term shifts in access to media. Second, it fails to account for inequalities of access within the 'accredited' sources themselves. Third, it tends to assume a one-way flow of definitions from privileged sources to the media. Fourth, patterns of source access are deduced from quantitative content analysis that conceals the behind-the-scenes activities of news sources. And fifth, it implies that there is a consensus among official sources, leaving no room for cases where there is a conflict of interest among institutional representatives. Off-the-record briefings are a major source of news.

A number of empirical studies have sought to investigate further the degree to which definitions are contested and negotiated, and have focused on the news media strategies employed by a variety of politically marginal organizations. These include areas such as environmentalism (Anderson 1997; 2003), health (Miller and Williams 1993), taxation policy (Deacon and Golding 1994), the voluntary sector (Deacon 2003), the Northern Ireland crisis (Miller 1993), and labour relations (Manning 1998). This body of work suggests that, under certain circumstances, it is possible to successfully contest definitions of the powerful. Until relatively recently the role of non-official sources in constructing political agendas has been under-researched. Little research has considered the relative differences *between* non-official sources with studies tending to treat them as one category. Indeed, the categories of 'official' and 'non-official' sources are themselves problematic, because both categories embrace a huge diversity of groups and organizations with varying degrees of political and cultural capital. By empirically analysing the success or otherwise of the media strategies of politically marginal groups, we can learn a great deal about the institutional disadvantages that they face, as well as the factors that advantage institutionally powerful sources in getting their views across (Schlesinger 1990).

Changing historical conditions influence views on the legitimacy of different sources and offer novel opportunities for accessing and influencing media. According to some sociologists, in late modernity – characterised by 'reflexivity', risk consciousness and uncertainty, and reliance on abstract systems and expertise – the question of how the media report science and technology becomes crucial to the development and maintenance of public trust (Beck 1992; Giddens 1991). This is especially the case in media reporting of technologies involving 'high consequence' risks, such as environmental pollution and health effects (as with Bhopal and Chernobyl). In relation to the nuclear power industry, Helga Nowotny (1977: 249) documented the erosion in the 1970s of the 'cognitive immunity' previously largely accorded by and in the mass media to scientists in this industry. When pressed, scientists could not provide the certainty of 'proof' assumed to be required in law. What distinguished the 1970s from previous media coverage was not the knowledge available to scientists, but the kinds of questions being asked by journalists of scientists, and the availability of counter voices within science willing to contradict the mainstream view of nuclear safety. In print and broadcast output, both scientists and journalists challenged scientific expertise in the nuclear field as either partial or insecure.

These changes emerged together with the rise of new social movements and the *decline* of trust in technocratic authority. Ulrich Beck extended his analysis from the nuclear field in Germany to a general theory of science, media and society. The increased willingness of 'technocratic' gatekeepers (journalists, scientists, politicians, lawyers, engineers, insurance calculators) to publicly exploit differences within other sections of the 'technocratic' elite, is what Beck (1992, 1995) calls 'the sub-politics of technocracy'. When such disputes resonate with the insecurity of those outside the technocracy, and people experience increasing 'individualized' and flexible lives without the comfort of an 'authority' to trust, Beck suggests we have entered a 'Risk Society'. It is important to recognize that the increased contestability of scientific 'expertise' is a co-production between scientists and journalists, each reacting and contributing to wider social changes in the position and production of authority. However, for all the increased pluralism of Beck's 'sub-politics of technocracy', it still largely comprises disputes between elite groups (David and Wilkinson 2002).

Issues of inequalities in access to the news media are particularly pertinent when considering how controversies over science and technology are represented in the news media. Ulrich Beck (1992) has drawn attention to the crucial role that the media play in articulating competing rationality claims. This suggests a need to critically examine how particular news sources are presented as self-evidently 'credible' and 'authoritative'. Science journalism tends to be source driven and source framed. News media coverage is, to a large extent, the outcome of a battle among a selective range of news sources. However, studies of science journalism have tended to focus upon news media representation of scientific debates rather than getting behind the scenes to examine news production processes. In relation to genetics, Conrad (1999: 286) noted that: 'Who the sources are and how they are used in science reporting have been examined in only a few studies.' Relatively few researchers have examined, in depth, processes of contestation and negotiation among news sources that impact upon science coverage. Ethnographic case studies that follow through particular issues, by tracing the initial framing activities of news sources through interviews and/or observational studies, are particularly valuable. These shed light on [behind-the-scenes] factors that affect news sources' success or failure in gaining favourable coverage over a sustained period of time. The following sections of this chapter on news sources within science journalism highlight a range of key questions concerning their strategic and definitional power, making particular reference to research on the new genetics. In particular, this work raises important questions about how news sources come to be defined as 'legitimate', 'credible' and 'authoritative', and how far alternative or oppositional voices are constrained by the routine demands of news work.

News sources and media framing of science

Research undertaken to date suggests that journalists' use of sources is shaped by a variety of factors, including professional and pragmatic demands, existing knowledge of an issue, the existence of contacts in the field, and commercial pressures. Part of the professional orientation of journalists is to cultivate 'credible', 'trustworthy' and 'legitimate' sources in the field, not least to safeguard their reportorial integrity. In practice, journalists obtain material from a range of sources, including press releases, press conferences, information and public relations officers, professional society meetings, scientific journals and interviews (Nelkin 1995: 105). However, journalists often do not have the time, means or expertise to seek independent verification of facts (Anderson 2002, 2003; Dunwoody, 1999; Miller and Riechart 2000), and are sometimes overly reliant on pre-packaged information over which they have little control (Goodell 1986; Petersen 2001; Logan 1991; Manning 2001). When interviewed, journalists have identified a variety of factors that may affect news media coverage. These include level of understanding of the issues, time and space limitations, news format requirements, editorial control, the presence or absence of the 'human interest' factor, and the lack of policy activity on the issue (Anderson 2000; Cunningham-Burley *et al.* 1998; Kitzinger and Reilly 1997; Kitzinger *et al.* 2003; Nelkin 1995; Steinbrook 2000). Commercial pressures encourage newspaper organizations to connect with issues and themes that are likely to be familiar and relevant to readers (Allan 2002; Anderson 1997; Conrad 1999; Hansen 1994; Kitzinger 2000; Kitzinger and Reilly 1997). The quest for dramatic stories encourages journalists to focus on 'breaking news' and discourages the coverage of long-term issues or issues that require technical expertise (Nelkin 1995: 105). Issues deemed to be controversial are regarded as especially 'newsworthy' (Hansen 1994). Such factors serve to 'frame' stories in ways that are likely to connect with readers' interests, but sometimes appear to non-journalists to 'distort' or 'mis-represent' science.

Evidence such as the above has led some writers to suggest that journalism and science occupy two separate cultures. The notion of 'two cultures' implies that scientists and journalists inhabit distinct worlds, and always necessarily hold different views and aims. The corollary is that science reporting involves a process of translating or popularizing science fact for lay readers/audiences. However, recent research in the reporting of science suggests a more complex set of interaction processes (Lewenstein 1995). For a start, the model of science popularization implies a clear separation between 'science' and 'popularization', which denies the input of popular views into the research process and the simplification that is an intrinsic part of scientific communication (Hilgartner 1990: 523–4). Journalists are also often specialists in their field and, in some cases, are trained scientists. This model also overlooks the ways in which scientists, and other interest groups, may attempt to control news at various stages of its production through, for example, regulating the flow of information (through press releases, news conferences, news 'leaks', etc.), and the promotion of particular imagery and claims (choice of particular language and rhetorical devices). Michael Mulkay's (1997) account of the passing in 1990 of the Human Fertilization and Embryology Act illustrates this. Mulkay examines the interaction of interest groups and their attempts to present the issue of embryo research in either a positive or negative light. Supporters were eventually able to succeed in winning the vote by forging an alliance of like-minded parties, comprising the scientific, business and medical communities, as well as members of government, who came to see the public's interests as best represented by the acceptance of embryo research. It is not enough to simply observe how journalists 'frame' an issue, but rather to examine the social relations of news production.

Scientists, as sources, potentially exert a great deal of control over the news production process. Although journalists may choose the topic for a news story, scientists have the opportunity to help define the boundaries from which story choices are made (Dunwoody 1999: 63; Friedman *et al.* 1986; Peters 1995). Many stories are source generated – some estimates put it as many as half or more of newspaper stories – so scientists are able to strategically package news items for journalists (Nisbet and Lewenstein

2002: 362). Scientists are frequently quoted or cited in news stories on medical genetics, which may help explain the generally positive portrayal of issues, found in a number of recent studies (Conrad 2001; Gutteling *et al.* 2002: 118–19; Kitzinger *et al.* 2003: 29; Petersen 2001: 1263–5; Smart 2003). Many scientists are aware that the continuity of their research funding is heavily reliant on public support that can be influenced by media coverage of science research. Hence, many are keen to use the media to promote a positive image of research and of scientists (Nelkin 1985, 1994). By controlling the timing of news releases, and by choosing particular language and metaphors, scientists may seek to shape public discourse and influence the direction of policy (see, for example Nelkin 1985). With controversial issues, scientists have an opportunity to play a major role in influencing public understandings of science, not least through their ability to select voices (Dunwoody 1999: 69). They may use conflicting opinion and uncertainty to their advantage, as a rhetorical tool. That is, they may use the occasion to highlight the validity of their own work and the uncertainties of others with whom they disagree (Dunwoody 1999: 73).

Being aware that they are never fully in control of the 'frame' into which their work and words are placed, many scientists 'blame' the media for its representations of science, which are frequently portrayed as overly simplistic or wrong. Interview-based research into genetic scientists' interactions with journalists (Wilkinson 2004, unpublished) suggests that scientists frequently see themselves as being misrepresented. Wilkinson's research highlights a significant degree of anxiety among scientists that the position of scientists as 'experts' is often over-extended by reporters, allowing journalists to gain 'newsworthy' quotes from alleged authorities whose 'expertise' in the specific field on which they are being quoted would be considered tenuous by researchers working directly in that area. This research also suggests that many scientists believe faulty media portrayals of science are a significant cause of a distrust of science among the 'lay' public. The tendency to blame journalists for introducing contestable evidence and claims, and for using misleading simplifications and reductionist language, however, hides the active part played by scientists in the production of 'populist' accounts of their own research. Scientists have been found to use popular imagery and metaphors, and a causal language (such as 'a gene for . . .') in science journals such as *Nature* and *Science*, which science correspondents frequently use as key sources for accessing complex and specialist scientific debates (Petersen 1999). Genetic reductionism may be introduced in the use of terms such as 'transmission', used for example in Hamer *et al.*'s (1993) article, 'A linkage between DNA markers on the X chromosome and male sexual orientation' – subsequently portrayed as heralding the 'gay gene' discovery – which otherwise used a scrupulous language of correlation rather than causation (Miller 1995). The use of particular descriptions and metaphors in quotations (for example the 'code' and the 'map') may be a way in which scientists seek to frame the portrayal of science, and thus maximize its perceived value, as an explanatory force and/or its curative potential (Petersen 2001: 1261–2; David 2005; Mulkay

1997). In other words, scientists are not simply the victims of simplifications and reductions, but rather active participants in the production of 'popular' conceptions of their own work.

Conclusion

Recent controversies surrounding the nature and accuracy of reporting on issues such as cloning, embryonic stem cells and nanotechnology, have emphasized the importance of understanding source-media relations in studies of science news. Many scientists have expressed concern that the media often 'hype', 'misrepresent' or 'distort' research, thereby reinforcing public mistrust in science and creating a backlash against potentially useful research. Thus, public concerns about human cloning in the wake of the reporting of the birth of the cloned sheep, Dolly, it is believed, can mobilize politicians and the public against research into the therapeutic uses of cloning technology (Petersen 2002). Similarly, portrayals of 'designer babies' in reports on treatments involving embryonic stem cells (for example, the Hashmi and Whittaker cases in the UK), it is argued, can lead to a public reaction against the development of useful new stem cell-based treatments (David and Kirkhope 2005). In an effort to overcome these perceived problems in science news reporting, in the UK, scientists, through the Royal Society, have sought to develop guidelines to assist journalists and scientists in reporting science and health issues (http://www. royalsoc.ac.uk/ files/statfiles/document-105.pdf). In relation to media reporting on cloning specifically, the Royal Society has also published 'a checklist of tips for the public', containing 'ten key questions to help non-specialists assess the validity of claims' (www.royalsoc.ac.uk/news/).

Efforts such as these may go some way towards developing a consensus on what constitutes 'quality' science news reporting, and perhaps nurturing a better understanding between scientists, journalists and publics about the factors likely to influence coverage. However, it suggests that there could be a 'correct' or 'accurate' reporting of science, which denies the fact that both news and science are always social productions and involve conflicting claims about 'truth'. Despite differences between the above theories of source-media relations in views on the nature of power, all emphasize that what gets in the news and how news is portrayed is a product of struggles between groups with competing definitions of reality. Increasingly, scholars of journalism and media studies have begun to view the media as a site where contending 'claims makers' seek to impose their definition of reality in order to shape public policy (see Hansen 2000). In a mass-mediated society, understanding news production processes is integral to understanding what counts as valid, useful science and of why publics and policy makers are willing to support certain kinds of scientific research and particular technologies. In their efforts to control science communications and reporting practices, scientists have shown recognition of this fact. Clearly, journalists can benefit greatly from a deeper understanding of source-media relations, of how these relations shape their practice of science reporting and their contributions to the public representation of science.

Acknowledgements

We would like to thank Stuart Allan and Clare Wilkinson for their respective contributions to developing the material upon which this chapter is based.

References

Allan, S. (2002) *Media, Risk and Science*. Buckingham: Open University Press.

Anderson, A. (1991) Source Strategies and the Communication of Environmental Affairs, *Media, Culture and Society*, 13: 459–76.

Anderson, A. (1993) Source-media Relations: the Production of the Environmental Agenda, in A. Hansen (ed.) *The Mass Media and Environmental Issues*. Leicester: Leicester University Press.

Anderson, A. (1997) *Media, Culture and the Environment*. London: UCL.

Anderson, A. (2000) Environmental Pressure Politics and the Risk Society, in S. Allan, B. Adam and C. Carter (eds) *Environmental Risks and the Media*. London: Routledge.

Anderson, A. (2002) In Search of the Holy Grail: Media Discourse and the New Human Genetics, *New Genetics and Society*, 21(3): 327–37.

Anderson, A. (2003) Environmental Activism and News Media, in S. Cottle (ed.) *News, Public Relations and Power*. London: Sage.

Beck, U. (1992) *Risk Society: Towards a New Modernity*. London: Sage.

Beck, U. (1995) *Ecological Politics in an Age of Risk*. Cambridge: Polity.

Conrad, P. (1999) Use of Expertise: Sources, Quotes, and Voice in the Reporting of Genetics in the News, *Public Understanding of Science*, 8: 285–302.

Conrad, P. (2001) Genetic Optimism: Framing Genes and Mental Illness in the News, *Culture, Medicine and Psychiatry*, 25: 225–47.

Cunningham-Burley, S., Amos, A. and Kerr, A. (1998) *The Social and Cultural Impact of the New Genetics*. Edinburgh: Department of Public Health Sciences, Medical School, University of Edinburgh.

David, M. (2005) *Science in Society*. London: Palgrave.

David, M. and Kirkhope, J. (2005) Cloning, Stem Cells and the Meaning of Life, *Current Sociology*, 52(2): 245–64.

David, M. and Wilkinson, I. (2002) Critical Theory or Self-critical Society, *Critical Horizons*, 3(1): 131–58.

Davis, A. (2000) Public Relations, News Production and Changing Patterns of Source Access in British National Media, *Media, Culture and Society*, 22(1): 39–59.

Deacon, D. (2003) Non-governmental Organizations and the Media, in S. Cottle (ed.) *News, Public Relations and Power*. London: Sage.

Deacon, D. and Golding, P. (1994) *Taxation and Representation: The Media, Political Communication and the Poll Tax*. London: John Libbey.

Dunwoody, S. (1999) Scientists, Journalists, and the Meaning of Uncertainty, in S. Friedman, S. Dunwoody and C. L. Rogers (eds) *Communicating Uncertainty: Media Coverage of New and Controversial Science*. New York: Lawrence Erlbaum.

Ericson, R. V., Baranek, P. M. and Chan, J. B. (1989) *Negotiating Control*. Milton Keynes: Open University Press.

Friedman, S. M., Dunwoody, S. and Rogers, C. L. (1986) *Scientists and Journalists*. Washington DC: AAAS.

Giddens, A. (1991) *Modernity and Self-Identity: Self and Society in the Late Modern Age*. Cambridge: Polity.

Goodell, R. (1986) How to Kill a Controversy: The Case of Recombinant DNA, in S. Friedman, S. Dunwoody and C. Rogers (eds) *Scientists and Journalists: Reporting Science as News*. New York: Free Press.

Gutteling, J. M. *et al.* (2002) Media Coverage 1973–1996: Trends and Dynamics, in M. W. Bauer and G. Gaskell (eds) *Biotechnology: The Making of a Global Controversy*. Cambridge: Cambridge University Press.

Hall, S., Critcher, C., Jefferson, T., Clarke, J. and Roberts, B. (1978) *Policing the Crisis: Mugging, the State and Law and Order*. London: Macmillan.

Hamer, D. H., Hu, S., Magnuson, V. L., Hu, N. and Pattatucci, A. M. (1993) A Linkage Between DNA Markers on the X Chromosome and Male Sexual Orientation, *Science*, 261 (16 July): 321–7.

Hansen, A. (1994) Journalistic Practices and Science Reporting in the British Press, *Public Understanding of Science*, 3: 111–34.

Hansen, A. (2000) Claims-making and Framing in British Newspaper Coverage of the 'Brent Spar' Controversy, in S. Allan, B. Adam and C. Carter (eds) *Environmental Risks and the Media*. London and New York: Routledge.

Hargreaves, I, Lewis, J. and Spears, T. (2003) *Towards a Better Map: Science, the Public and the Media*. London: ESRC.

Hargreaves, I. and Ferguson, G. (2000) *Who's Misunderstanding Whom? Bridging the Gulf of Understanding between the Public, Media and Science*. London: ESRC/ British Academy.

Hilgartner, S. (1990) The Dominant View of Popularisation: Conceptual Problems, Political Uses, *Social Studies of Science*, 20: 519–39.

Kitzinger, J. (2000) Media Templates: Patterns of Association and the (Re)construction of Meaning over Time, *Media, Culture and Society*, 22: 61–84.

Kitzinger, J., Henderson, L., Smart, A. and Eldridge, J. (2003) *Media Coverage of the Ethical and Social Implications of Human Genetic Research*. Final Report for the Wellcome Trust (February 2003) Award no: GR058105MA.

Kitzinger, J. and Reilly, J. (1997) The Rise and Fall of Risk Reporting, *European Journal of Communication*, 12(3): 319–50.

Lewenstein, B. V. (1995) Science and Media, in S. Jasanoff, G. E. Markle, J. C. Petersen and T. Pinch (eds) *Handbook of Science and Technology Studies*. Thousand Oaks: Sage.

Logan, R. A. (1991) Popularization Versus Secularization: Media Coverage of Health, in L. Wilkins and P. Patterson (eds) *Risky Business: Communicating Issues of Science, Risk and Public Policy*. New York: Greenwood.

Manning, P. (1998) *Spinning for Labour: Trade Unions and the New Media Environment*. Aldershot: Ashgate.

Manning, P. (2001) *News and News Sources: A Critical Introduction*. London: Sage.

Miller, D. (1993) 'Official Sources' and 'Primary Definition': the Case of Northern Ireland, *Media, Culture and Society*, 15(3): 385–406.

Miller, D. (1995) Introducing the 'Gay Gene': Media and Scientific Representations, *Public Understanding of Science*, 4: 269–84.

Miller, D. and Williams, K. (1993) Negotiating HIV/AIDS Information: Agendas, Media Strategies and the News, in J. Eldridge (ed.) *Getting the Message. News, Truth and Power*. London: Routledge.

Miller, M. M. and Riechert, B. P. (2000) Interest Group Strategies and Journalistic Norms: News Media Framing of Environmental Issues, in S. Allan, B. Adam and C. Carter (eds) *Environmental Risks and the Media*. London: Routledge.

Mulkay, M. (1997) *The Embryo Research Debate: Science and the Politics of Reproduction*. Cambridge: Cambridge University Press.

Nelkin, D. (1985) Managing Biomedical News, *Social Research*, 52(3): 625–46.

Nelkin, D. (1994) Promotional Metaphors and their Popular Appeal, *Public Understanding of Science*, 3(1): 25–31.

Nelkin, D. (1995) *Selling Science: How the Press Covers Science and Technology*, second edition. New York: W. H. Freeman.

Nisbet, M. C. and Lewenstein, B. V. (2002) Biotechnology and the American Media: the Policy Process and the Elite Press, 1970 to 1999, *Science Communication*, 23(4): 359–91.

Nowotny, H. (1977) Scientific Purity and Nuclear Danger: the Case of Risk Assessment, in E. Mendelsohn, P. Weingart and R. Whitley (eds) *The Social Production of Scientific Knowledge, Sociology of the Sciences Yearbook I*. Dordrecht and Boston: Reidel Publishing Company.

Peters, H. P. (1995) The Interaction of Journalists and Scientific Experts: Co-operation and Conflict between Two Professional Cultures, *Media, Culture and Society*, 17(1): 31–48.

Petersen, A. (1999) The Portrayal of Research into Genetic-based Differences of Sex and Sexual Orientation: a Study of 'Popular' Science Journals, 1980–1997, *Journal of Communication Inquiry*, 23(2): 163–82.

Petersen, A. (2001) Biofantasies: Genetics and Medicine in the Print News Media, *Social Science and Medicine*, 52: 1255–68.

Petersen, A. (2002) Replicating our Bodies, Losing our Selves: News Reporting of Human Cloning in the Wake of Dolly, *Body and Society*, 8(4): 71–90.

Reed, R. (2001) (Un-)Professional Discourse: Journalists' and Scientists' Stories about Science in the Media?, *Journalism*, 2(3): 279–98.

Schlesinger, P. (1990) Rethinking the Sociology of Journalism, in M. Ferguson (ed.) *Public Communication*. London: Sage.

Schlesinger, P. and Tumber, H. (1994) *Reporting Crime: The Media Politics of Criminal Justice*. Oxford: Clarendon Press.

Smart, A. (2003) Reporting the Dawn of the Post-genomic Era: Who Wants to Live Forever, *Sociology of Health and Illness*, 25(1): 24–49.

Steinbrook, R. (2000) Medical Journals and Medical Reporting, *The New England Journal of Medicine*, 342(22): 1668–71.

Wilkinson, C. (2004) unpublished PhD thesis in progress, Multiple Experts: Scientific, Medical, Media and Public Discourses on New Genetics, School of Sociology, Politics and Law, University of Plymouth. Presented for discussion and referred to here with permission from the author.

15

Risk reporting

Why can't they ever get it right?

Susanna Hornig Priest

- What should journalists report about risks?
- Is it better to ignore an uncertain risk and avoid panic, or to report it anyway?
- If scientists can't figure out a risk, how can journalists?

Almost everyone seems to complain about journalistic reporting of risks. Scientific experts complain that the science is inaccurate or incomplete, or else that it is presented as being more certain than it is. Public officials complain that unnecessary panic is being created, or else that people are not being warned adequately. Advocacy groups complain that particular issues or problems in which they have an interest are not getting enough attention; corporations complain that their technologies and products are represented as being too risky – and are getting too much attention. Media consumers complain that they cannot figure out what they should and should not be concerned about, and that frequent reversals in interpretation of the scientific evidence confuse them even more. Journalism scholars complain that media coverage is too dependent on 'official sources' for their views, and that science journalism in particular is obsessed with immediate 'breakthroughs' in science at the expense of longer-term trends and developments.

Risk is not only a technical concept, it is also a social concept. In fact, some social theorists (see, for example, Beck 1992) have proposed that post-industrial societies can be reconceptualized as 'risk societies' in which – fundamental problems of daily survival having been, for many people, already addressed – avoidance of risk is the new organizing principle. Risks come from many elements unique to such societies – from the technologies of modernization (in manufacturing, energy production, transportation); from associated environmental contamination; from mechanized, large-scale agricultural production; from changing diets and lifestyles in the face of our vastly improved but still incomplete knowledge of heredity and nutrition;

from violent crime associated with these mobile, competitive, urbanized societies; from the diseases of ageing now that many major infectious diseases that used to kill people at younger ages are largely under control; from war in a globalized economic order. Older risks from natural disaster remain, partially mitigated (and occasionally exacerbated) by newer technologies such as earthquake-proof buildings and bridges and early warning systems for tornadoes and hurricanes.

Risks, clearly, are all around us. A world in which journalists ignored risks would be unacceptable. But how should risks be reported, and is it possible to report them without sensationalizing them and still have stories that will attract readers and audiences? Will too much risk reporting cause people to turn away from an 'overload' of threatening messages? Nearly everyone seems to agree that it is part of the news media's job in contemporary society to alert the citizenry to potential risks, even though there is little or no consensus about how this should be done. The classical list of media functions original proposed by Lasswell (1948) included environmental surveillance, correlation of societal response, and transmission of heritage. Clearly, risk has been part of the job for some time.

Risk reporting might most clearly constitute surveillance, the issuing of alerts and warnings about situations that people may see as threatening. This can also work in reverse. When I open my local paper and see little serious news of interest beyond the immediate community, I am somewhat reassured because I sense that if a major national or global catastrophe was imminent it would surely have displaced the news of our city council meetings, the construction of a golf course or shopping area, and the hiring of a new principal for the junior high school. I can depend on the news media, even a local small-town paper, to bring me news of most major risks, although there is always a chance local interests might suppress a report or the journalists' sophistication not be up to the task. Will the golf course change stream run-off patterns and create drainage problems? Is the city acting responsibly in setting aside new land for a garbage dump rather than considering alternatives such as recycling? Is the new principal going to address the number of unvaccinated students in our public schools? I am not so sure these things will be covered as they should be, but I have a fair confidence major immediate threats will be identified.

Of course, correlation of societal response and the transmission of heritage, including the values we bring to bear on understanding and interpreting a risk, are more complex. Announcements of what a government agency is doing in response to an earthquake or hurricane, for example, are quite prominent in news accounts (Hornig [Priest] *et al.* 1991). These let people know about how society is responding and indirectly suggest that everything is under control. The values we should bring to bear on interpreting risk information and evaluating the acceptability of a risk are even more likely to be conveyed implicitly rather than explicitly. When the local paper suggests that the golf course and the shopping centre are a good thing, they are conveying social values (with which I may or may not fully agree) – for example, that having a golf course in place of untamed land is an aesthetic positive and that economic development is always and necessarily a good thing.

Risk and human social values

Risk is certainly a matter of values. Some years ago I attended a conference on values in agriculture. The conference was held in western Pennsylvania and a field trip was arranged to a local Amish farm. The Amish people, to varying degrees that reflect the preferences of local leaders, reject modern technology (automobiles, tractors, in some cases electricity) but are successful farmers. This particular group of Amish also rejected most scientific medicine, preferring alternatives such as herbal treatments. Someone in our group interested in nutrition asked about their rate of heart disease, given that they reported a fairly high-fat diet. Their answer was they commonly died (presumably of heart disease) in their fifties, they *expected* to die in their fifties, and they felt *God wanted them to die*, in many cases, at about that age, leaving a smaller number of older individuals to lead and teach the next generation. What was the problem? In their view there wasn't one. Even such seemingly basic human desires as wanting to live a long as well as a healthy life, in other words, represent value choices that are not universally shared.

Which risks we find acceptable – or which are preferable to other risks – is largely a question of such value-based choices, not scientific absolutes. Further, there is commonly a large amount of uncertainty about the science behind risk analysis. Nutrition is a good example here, as well. As of this moment, controversy rages over the health effects of low-fat versus low-carbohydrate diets; whether dietary fat and cholesterol are actually the major heart disease 'culprits' after all; the scientific (and the political) meaning of the 'food pyramid' graphic that the US Department of Agriculture has adopted to stress a grain-based rather than a protein-based diet; the adequacy of food labelling policies for nutritional matters; and the reasons behind the explosion of deadly obesity, perhaps the newest and biggest pandemic in the developed world. Under these circumstances, what scientific truths should people turn to on which to base their day-to-day decisions? In fact it appears that patterns of trust in particular social institutions, institutions that people may feel represent their own worldviews and beliefs, are a better predictor of some risk-related attitudes and choices than scientific knowledge (Priest *et al.* 2003), although scientific knowledge also plays a role (Sturgis and Allum 2004). In situations of uncertainty or controversy, people must decide who to believe. It stands to reason they will tend to believe those they see as sharing their own values.

In addition, not all injuries or deaths are equal, in terms of human values. We may have more sympathy for injury to a child, who has a long life yet to live and does not have much control over external circumstances, than for an adult. Risk to a child can be highly emotional, as when the entire US seemed to hold their breath for days waiting for the 1987 rescue of 'Baby

Jessica' from the abandoned Texas well into which she had fallen. Other deaths are emotional because of symbolic circumstances, as in the 1999 deaths of 12 Texas A&M University students killed building a giant bonfire in an annual tradition dating from 1909; this event received worldwide media coverage, sympathy and concern, but the deaths of hundreds of other Texas high school students who were killed in highway traffic accidents during that year went largely unnoticed outside their local communities. (In 1997 alone, according to the National Transportation Safety Board, over 800 people were killed in Texas crashes involving drivers age 20 or younger; Hall 1999.)

Risk and uncertainty

Risk estimates are often characterized by pervasive uncertainty. Will nuclear power plants destroy us, or save us? Is hormone replacement therapy helpful, or harmful? There is rarely a single 'correct' scientific answer. Sociologist Bruno Latour (1987) has distinguished between 'emerging' or uncertain science, about which scientific and medical consensus has not – or has not yet – emerged, and science that is settled and widely accepted. News accounts, by their nature, are almost always about science that is 'emerging' in this sense. Newsroom values dictate this; it is 'emerging' science that is seen as newsworthy because this is what people are seen as wanting to know about. But in risk reporting this can be a problem. It is difficult enough, after the fact, to say that the use of the pesticide Alar on apples, or exposure to airborne SARS virus, or shaking hands with someone with AIDS, or eating British beef *is* or *is not* unreasonably risky. Months or years later, science may have the answer, or at least a partial answer, to these and similar questions, though the definition of 'unreasonably' remains a matter of judgement. But journalists have to live for today, not wait for hindsight or patient research to clear up the confusion.

Scientists, on the other hand, are often reluctant to take positions when the evidence about a risk is still uncertain. Some journalists use a well-known trick in such cases: they ask the scientist about personal involvement with the risk, forcing a subjective decision even in the face of uncertainty. Would you eat the fish, they ask? Would you let your children swim in this lake? Scientists who cannot say for certain what the scientific evidence supports are often willing and able to answer such questions. Like the rest of us, they have to make their own decisions in the face of uncertainty and cannot always wait for all of the evidence to be brought in and evaluated. This is so even though in their role as scientific experts they feel they must be more cautious. But their reluctance to commit to a public position on matters related to risk complicates journalists' task.

Paradoxical probabilities

In many situations, individual risk and decision making and collective risk and decision making are not the same. This happens in situations like the so-called 'tragedy of the commons' (Hardin 1968) in which an environmental resource is shared. In this now-famous example, a group of villagers share a pasture. If each grazes his or her cow only a certain amount, the pasture will remain healthy. But the temptation is always there for some farmers to graze their cows beyond the share that would be prudent. If only a few farmers do this, there will be a benefit for some and there may not be a problem for everyone, but if everyone thinks that 'it is only my cow that will get extra the grass', then the pasture will be ruined and all the farmers – and cows – will suffer. Many other cases of environmental or natural resource threats involve a risk to the individual that may be quite small but a risk to the group that is much more substantive.

A similar but not quite identical case of difference between individual and collective risk is presented by relatively small risks to the individual that represent, in the aggregate, near certainty of at least some harm to some individuals, but (unlike the 'tragedy') not necessarily harm to everyone. For example, I could probably get away with not wearing my seatbelt today, but I know with fair certainty that if everyone in the world suddenly stopped wearing seatbelts, a large number of additional people would be killed or injured. Such behaviours can be managed, although it is not always easy. The idea of not wearing a seatbelt makes people uncomfortable but this is partly because wearing them has become (as a result of deliberate communication campaigns) a social norm, a shared expectation for appropriate behaviour, the violation of which may cause an individual to feel guilty or to be rejected by others. Even 'bad guys' in Hollywood movies always buckle on their seat belts before they try a high-speed escape from the police!

A medication that may pose a tiny risk of harm to a given individual may pose a substantial risk that if thousands of people take the drug some of them will almost certainly be harmed. What should news accounts advise people to do? Conversely, a relatively rare disease or condition may strike a small group or 'cluster' of people in a given location in a short period of time, as has happened recently for women with breast cancer in Long Island, New York. How many such instances have to occur before the events are considered evidence there is an underlying, non-random cause, even if we have not yet found it? But could this particular risk (while it certainly appears to be statistically 'real') receive too much attention in a predominantly middle-class area with active advocacy organizations? How much is 'too much'? Perhaps this can best be understood in comparison to cases of risks elsewhere, involving different populations, such as an apparent increase in the rate of anencephaly, a fatal birth defect, among Hispanic South Texas babies discovered in 1991 – a problem that might have been attributable to poor nutrition; air or water pollution from local manufacturing or nearby agriculture; upstream Rio Grande River contamination; viral infection;

genetics; or random chance. (The most recent reports, over a decade later, have linked the phenomenon to toxins produced by a corn fungus and consumed in tortillas – Walberg 2004.) How should journalists discuss these events? It is not much of a solution to suggest the news media should only report the 'facts' and not give opinions. Whatever they say (or avoid saying) will be influential. And the implied explanations inevitably matter to the political interests of a broad range of stakeholders (including allegedly polluting industries and the makers of suspect chemicals) and advocates. Stereotypes are highly relevant in both cases: poor Mexican women are easily accused of nutritional ignorance; rich New York housewives of being neurotic.

Like all social problems, issues involving risk and its reporting can be analysed in at least three ways, based on three major paradigms in social theory. The first paradigm involves recognition of the role of personal and societal values (not just scientific understanding) in defining which risks we pay attention to and which we do not. The second paradigm involves recognition of the role of social structure and associated institutions and practices (including those of the media themselves) in defining and managing risks. The third paradigm, which I would argue is often less prominent than it deserves to be, involves recognition of the importance of conflict and power in determining who will bear risks and which risks society will choose to address and resolve. Each paradigm has implications for how journalists deal with news of risks.

▌ The risk perception paradigm

The roots of the idea that human values enter into perceptions of risk are generally attributed to the work of Paul Slovic and others (Slovic 2000 reviews this work.) Slovic and his colleagues have demonstrated that a number of psychological factors enter into the perception of risk, in particular the idea of a 'dread risk' that poses a threat of death or serious harm to many people at once being less acceptable, psychologically, than something that causes the same number of deaths or harmful events a few at a time. This concept of 'dread risk' has become a part of the common language of risk analysis and risk communication specialists. It helped promote the idea that when experts and the lay public disagree, it may not be because valid information is not available to both groups but because they apply different values in its interpretation.

But Slovic's ideas, as originally put forth, had several limitations. The first was the failure to deal adequately with the relationship between risk 'perception' and the 'actual' or scientific risk, that is, a hypothetical risk as seen from a probabilistic, scientific perspective (Bradbury 1989). No definition of risk is completely value-free, so the distinction between 'actual' and 'perceived' risk sometimes confuses things more than it clarifies them. The term 'perception' implies 'distortion', and the distinction can also be used (though, in fairness, not typically by Slovic) to discount popular worries about risks where these reflect value choices or concerns not generally shared with the scientific and medical establishment. On the other hand, this psychometric approach has been very effective in pointing out that public perceptions of risk are not always simply errors in understanding of relevant scientific data but may instead represent 'rational' thinking, even where that rationality leads to conclusions that are not based on science.

A second limitation of the original psychometric approach is the fact that risk is not just an individual matter but a collective or social one. Social dynamics cannot be reduced to individual consciousness or individual behaviour. Values do not belong just to individuals in isolation but are closely associated with cultural norms, beliefs, expectations and attitudes, all of which are socially shared. In fact, it is this shared set of values and beliefs that generally defines the identity of a culture, society or smaller social group. Risk perception is like public opinion in the sense that it is a collective perception. Stranded on a desert island, no one could have a 'public' opinion; the formation of public opinion depends on knowing something about what others think and situating one's own position (mentally) among those of others. Similarly, risk perception depends on shared values and how the actions of social institutions with respect to risks are understood – whether the institutions are trusted, whether the risks are fairly or unfairly distributed, whether appropriate actions to reduce or mitigate the risks are being taken by responsible parties, and so on.

The news media have a tremendously important role to play in alerting the public to issues and actions of this kind. Most sources for news stories represent institutions, rather than speaking strictly as individuals; journalists need to recognize the role such sources play in providing media with resources for framing issues and for representing the motivations of social actors in particular ways. Journalism is highly dependent on information subsidies from such sources, especially in technical areas (Gandy 1982). This is unlikely to change; it is institutional sources that will have the most up-to-date technical information and the earliest knowledge of risks. But all institutions are stakeholders in risk-related issues with which they are engaged, and journalists need to understand this.

Social structure and amplification

Social institutions, in addition to having significant influence over the news media, play other key roles in what has been called the social amplification of risk (see Pidgeon *et al.* 2003, for discussion). According to this theory, risk can be amplified, meaning made to appear larger, or attenuated, meaning made to appear smaller, because of the actions of various social institutions such as advocacy groups, government agencies, corporations and the news media themselves. This theory is somewhat parallel to agenda-building theory in media studies (Lang and Lang 1983), which states that it is not just the media that set the political or public agenda but a number of social institutions working in concert. The prominent appearance of an issue (whether about a risk or anything else) in the news media, on the political stage and in public thinking results from a complex social process involving multiple institutions. Risks work the same way as other political issues; their prominence depends on the outcome of complex interactions among a variety of social actors. Multiple institutions, including the less formal organizations characteristic of early stage social movements, determine which risks will be noticed.

Like the psychometric paradigm, this explanation tends to make an unexamined assumption that the process starts with an 'actual risk' that exists before institutions act on it, and then is raised or lowered by the actions of those institutions. Of course, there is rarely a clearly visible 'actual risk' that we can discern without the intervention of social institutions. We can imagine that there might be a hypothetical undistorted risk estimate lurking somewhere just beyond our field of vision, but all of those risk estimates that we can actually come into contact with have been constructed by social actors, usually working within larger institutions – including the institutions of science. And, of course, science itself and its agenda are not value free either, even before political, corporate and advocacy groups add their own spins on the nature and importance of a risk. This is not to say that science is wrong, but neither is it always value free. Journalists must be aware of the institutionally constructed character of risk.

Another problem with amplification theory is that it has not yet reached the stage where it fully explains or predicts how the social system will produce a particular outcome, whether an amplification or an attenuation, of a particular kind of risk. If the risk seems to grow larger as a result of public discussion, the risk has been amplified; if it seems to recede into the distance, it has been attenuated. It is clear that it is not just scientific evidence about the magnitude of a risk that controls this process, but what processes decide which risks behave which way? In order to account for this it is essential to think about the distribution of power in society. Not all social institutions and actors are equal in their ability to influence the course of events. Any risk involves multiple stakeholders, from the scientists, doctors, engineers or risk analysts who first defined the nature of the risk to the various interests who advocate for its being redefined later on.

Stakeholder interests and the social distribution of risk

The third major social explanation of risk more directly considers the social distribution of risks and the conflicts among stakeholders with different interests and different degrees of power over both how risks are distributed and how they are defined. Insurance companies want safer cars; car manufacturers want to make a profit, though if making safer cars can help them do so they will probably be all for it. Environmental and health advocates want fewer or safer chemicals to be used in agriculture and manufacturing; farmers and manufacturers again want profits but want to be perceived as socially responsible, if only for business reasons. Minority groups want environmental justice; that is, they want environmental and health risks to be evenly distributed rather than disproportionately burdening lower income, higher minority neighbourhoods. Advocates for the elimination of risks caused by particular diseases (muscular dystrophy, for example), social problems (domestic violence, for example), or problematic behaviours (drinking and driving, for example) compete among themselves for the attention of the media, politicians and the public. Public health officials want tobacco use discontinued; tobacco interests lobby for redefining smoking as a 'right' of individuals. The presence and activity of these competing interests is a sign of a healthy pluralistic democracy, but these various groups do not have equal power to determine social outcomes.

Global warming presents a pressing major example of a struggle over the social distribution of risk and of the *costs* or potential consequences if risk becomes reality. Like many environmental issues, global warming as a 'tragedy of the commons' dimension: I can drive my car without causing global warming, but we cannot *all* drive cars without causing global warming. (This assumes for the moment that this is the only cause with which we need to be concerned; of course, the real situation is more complex and industrial activity is another significant source of concern.) At present, people in the richer, more developed countries drive more cars. But everyone will certainly suffer if the globe heats up so much that agricultural productivity is threatened in some areas. In fact the poorer, less-developed countries where the ability of local agriculture to feed the nearby population is less certain and where storage and distribution systems are less efficient will undoubtedly bear a greater share of any eventual costs in terms of widespread food or other shortages. The developed world probably has a better chance to adapt agriculture and certainly has a better food distribution and storage system. Yet international agreements in this area have been difficult to reach because it is exactly the better developed and more powerful nations who would have to alter their practices the most if global warming is to be curbed, and yet who may perceive themselves (accurately or not) to be at lesser risk.

It is easy to think of other examples of unequally distributed risk. Some such differences are natural and not socially determined. It is largely women who fall victim to breast cancer and only men who get prostate cancer, but other risks are distributed in ways that clearly reflect the class structure and ethnic divisions within society. The risk of being a victim of street crime falls disproportionately on minorities and lower income people who must live in higher crime neighbourhoods – the same neighbourhoods where many have claimed toxic waste dumps are more likely to be located. The risk of dying from a preventable disease falls disproportionately on those who cannot afford or have no access to health insurance, including the unemployed and those whose jobs do not provide health benefits. The undereducated are less aware of best practices in prevention of health and the economically disadvantaged are less able to implement them; what good does it do to be advised to eat lean meat or five servings a day of fresh fruits and vegetables if you cannot afford them? Sugary drinks and deep-fried foods tend to be cheaper. The risks of post-industrial society are not shared equally.

What can journalism provide?

Journalists need to recognize the social and political character of risk. This means that they must question the purely scientific definitions of a risk and ask themselves who benefits and who loses in a particular risk situation and how particular definitions of the risk may change this equation. They must realize that their own treatment of risks, together with public perceptions that depend on a host of psychological and cultural factors, will contribute to the process through which some risks are addressed and others ignored, with winners and losers among the institutional stakeholders. It is not really enough to say that journalism should report the 'objective' facts and let people make up their own minds.

This is not in any way to suggest that science is irrelevant or that journalism should ignore scientific reality. A risk does not go away because people choose not to pay attention to it or do not believe it exists. Smoking, like standing on the tracks in front of a moving train, is a risk no one should be advised to take – or ignore. Risks represent something beyond mere politics; they represent the possibility that real people can really be harmed, sometimes by something that really might have been prevented if the news media had done their job better. Conversely, excessive amplification is a risk in itself, diverting societal resources from other issues and sometimes causing unnecessary anxiety and even more substantive harm. But recognizing the scientific dimensions of a risk, which are themselves socially constructed, is only the beginning.

What is a 'reasonable' risk to take, and what is 'unreasonable'? The answers to these questions are matters of judgement and depend heavily on social values and priorities. These issues should be matters of public debate. It is the journalist's job to inform and stimulate this debate and to help people identify what is at stake. This debate cannot take place *despite* science, but it must take place *alongside* it. Instead of seeing science as the centre of a risk debate and a variety of sociocultural factors as being 'on the margins', it might be more useful in many cases to think of society as the centre and science as on the margins – providing input to a debate that takes place among other actors, on other grounds than science itself. Lasswell was right that the media's role involves more than surveillance. Journalism must also help shape society's response to identified threats and acknowledge the human social values that are in play in deciding what to do about risks.

References

Beck, U. (1992) *Risk Society: Towards a New Modernity*. Translated from the German by Mark Ritter. London: Sage.

Bradbury, J. A. (1989) The policy implications of differing concepts of risk, *Science, Technology, and Human Values*, 14: 380–9.

Gandy, O. H. (1982) *Beyond Agenda-setting: Information Subsidies and Public Policy*. Norwood, NJ: Ablex.

Hall, J. (1999) Remarks before the Second Annual North Texas Transportation Safety Summit, Irvine, 18 August. Accessed on 17 May, 2004, from http://www.ntsb.gov/speeches/former/hall/jhc990818.htm.

Hardin, G. (1968) The Tragedy of the Commons, *Science*, 162(3859): 1243–8.

Hornig [Priest], S., Walters, L. and Templin, J. (1991) Voices in the News: Newspaper Coverage of Hurricane Hugo and the Loma Prieta Earthquake, *Newspaper Research Journal* 12(3): 32–45.

Lang, G. E. and Lang, K. (1983) *The Battle for Public Opinion: The President, the Press and the Polls during Watergate*. New York: Columbia University Press.

Lasswell, H. (1948) The Structure and Function of Communication in Society, in L. Bryson (ed.) *The Communication of Ideas*. New York: Institute for Religious and Social Studies. (Reprinted 1964 by Cooper Square Publishers.)

Latour, B. (1987) *Science in Action: How to Follow Scientists and Engineers through Society*. Cambridge, MA.: Harvard University Press.

Pidgeon, N., Kasperson, R. E. and Slovic, P. (eds) (2003) *The Social Amplification of Risk*. New York: Cambridge University Press.

Priest, S. H., Bonfadelli, H. and Rusanen, M. (2003) The 'Trust Gap' Hypothesis: Predicting Support for Biotechnology Across National Cultures as a Function of Trust in Actors, *Risk Analysis*, 23(4): 751–66.

Slovic, P. (2000) *The Perception of Risk*. London: Earthscan Publications.

Sturgis, P. and Allum, N. (2004) Science in Society: Re-evaluating the Deficit Model of Public Attitudes. *Public Understanding of Science*, 13:55–74.

Wahlberg, D. (2004) Corn Fungus Linked to Fatal Birth Defects, *The Atlanta Journal Constitution*, 4 April.

16

News talk

Interaction in the broadcast news interview

Ian Hutchby

- What are the special features of news interview talk for an overhearing audience?
- How do news interviewers maintain a neutralistic stance?
- How do interviewers seek to challenge those in the public eye?
- What happens when interviewees refuse to observe the conventions of the news interview?

One significant environment in which journalists operate is that of broadcast news. Broadcast news bulletins are occasions for talk – some of it monologic, as when a news reader delivers headlines and leads direct to camera (or microphone in the case of radio), but much of it in the form of social interaction, whether between studio journalist and outside correspondent via live link, between two or more newscasters in the studio, or between broadcast journalists and public figures or other newsworthy actors in the context of a news interview. Increasingly, the more interactive formats for broadcast news talk are coming to outweigh the monologic contributions of the standard newsreader, or 'anchor'. Key agenda-setting news broadcasts such as BBC radio's *Today* programme or BBC television's *Newsnight* routinely consist of a series of interviews, each prefaced with little more than a brief contextualizing statement from one of the anchors. In the US, long-running high profile shows such as ABC's *Nightline* have similarly been organized around a series of live interviews. Indeed, even in the case of standard news bulletin broadcasts, recent years have seen a significant growth in the 'dual anchor' format, such that the newsreader's task itself becomes situated within a broader context of interactional talk.

The result of this is that broadcast news messages are increasingly being generated in and through the production of talk-in-interaction. This encourages us to examine news interviews not just in terms of their role in the manufacture of news, but also in terms of their structural characteristics as contexts which shape and constrain the very content of news messages. As Heritage, Clayman and Zimmerman (1988: 78–80) put it:

> The consistent growth in the use of social interaction as a medium through which the news is presented suggests that it has become increasingly unrealistic to analyse the structure and content of news messages independent of the interactional medium within which they are generated. For, although the medium may not be the message, the interactional structures through which broadcast news is conveyed must necessarily contribute to the content and appearance of news messages.

The aim of this chapter is to introduce research which has investigated the interactional medium for news generation represented by the broadcast news interview. The studies to be discussed adopt the methodological perspective of conversation analysis. The chapter begins with a brief overview of the main tenets of that method (for a comprehensive introduction, see Hutchby and Wooffitt 1998). Then, turning to an examination of the ways in which news is framed and constructed in the course of broadcast interviews, the chapter is organized around the key question of how journalists seek to challenge politicians and other figures in the public interest, while maintaining a suitably neutral journalistic stance. A range of work in conversation analysis is introduced which sheds light on this question.

Conversation analysis

Conversation analysis (CA) seeks to build a naturalistic, observation-based empirical science of human social interaction. Recordings of naturally occurring conversations are analysed in order to discover how participants understand and respond to one another in their turns at talk, with a principal focus being on how sequences of activities are generated. The main objective of CA is to uncover the socio-linguistic competencies underlying the production and interpretation of talk in organized sequences of social interaction. Conversation analysis thereby represents a major bridge between more formally linguistic analysis in fields such as pragmatics (see Levinson 1983), and the sociological investigation of human sociality.

Conversation analysis emerged in the pioneering researches of Harvey Sacks into the structural organization of everyday language use, at the University of California in the 1960s (see Sacks 1992). Sacks was partly influenced by Harold Garfinkel's research into everyday methods of practical reasoning, known as ethnomethodology (Garfinkel 1967), and also by Erving Goffman's explorations of the structural properties of face-to-face interaction (Goffman 1961). Building on these influences, Sacks initiated a radical research programme designed to investigate the levels of social order, which could be revealed in the everyday practice of talking.

The main tenet of CA is that ordinary conversation is not a trivial, random, unorganized phenomenon of little interest to sociologists but a deeply ordered, structurally organized social practice. Its second tenet is that this order can best be explored through the use of audio and video recordings of naturally occurring data, which can be looked at repeatedly, transcribed and analysed in depth. As Sacks wrote, describing his commitment to working with tape-recorded conversations:

> Such materials had a single virtue, that I could replay them. I could transcribe them somewhat and study them extendedly – however long it might take. The tape-recorded materials constituted a 'good enough' record of what had happened. Other things, to be sure, happened, but at least what was on the tape had happened.
>
> (Sacks 1984: 26)

Through engaging with what is observable in their transcripts of recorded talk, conversation analysts take a unique approach to the study of ordinary language. This approach focuses on what Sacks called the 'machinery' of conversational turn taking. By that he meant, first of all, the methods by which persons are able to manage the routine exchange of turns while at the same time minimizing gap and overlap between their individual contributions: the ways that talk-in-interaction is *coordinated*. Secondly, the sequential patterns and structures associated with the management of *social activities* in conversation: from telling jokes and stories (Sacks 1978; Jefferson 1978) to opening and closing telephone conversations (Schegloff 1979; Schegloff and Sacks 1973); from making invitations (Drew 1984) to managing disagreements (Pomerantz 1984); indeed any of the myriad activities that are accomplished in the exchange of talk-in-interaction.

The main aim of CA, then, is to reveal how the technical aspects of speech exchange represent structured, socially organized resources by which participants perform and coordinate activities through talk-in-interaction. Talk is treated as a vehicle for social action; and also as the principal means by which social organization in person-to-person interaction is mutually constructed and sustained. Hence it is a strategic site in which social agents' orientation to and evocation of the social contexts of their interaction can be empirically investigated.

This concern with social context has a particular relevance for the present chapter. Although CA began with an interest in the organization of ordinary conversation, it has also been applied within a broader framework to analyse the distinctive methods of turn-taking and activity organization found in specialized settings such as courts of law (Atkinson and Drew 1979), classrooms (McHoul 1978), radio and television talk shows (Hutchby 1996), doctors' surgeries (Heath 1992), public speeches (Atkinson 1984) and many others (Drew and Heritage 1992), including broadcast news interviews (Clayman and Heritage 2002).

In studies of such 'institutional' settings, CA has developed a distinctive perspective on how participants themselves play a central role in establishing and reproducing the 'context-specific' nature of their interaction. At root, this is based on the idea that different forms of talk should be viewed as a continuum ranging from the relatively unconstrained turn-taking of mundane conversation, through various levels of formality, to ceremonial occasions in which not only who speaks and in what sequential order, but also what they will say, are pre-arranged (for instance, in wedding ceremonies) (Sacks *et al.* 1974). By selectively reducing or otherwise transforming the full scope of conversational practices, concentrating on some and withholding others, participants can be seen to display an orientation to particular institutional norms as relevant for their current state of interaction. In many institutional settings, therefore, including the broadcast news interview, 'the institutional character of the interaction is embodied first and foremost in its *form* – most notably in turn-taking systems which depart substantially from the way in which turn-taking is managed in conversation' (Heritage and Greatbatch 1991: 95).

Studies of broadcast news interviews have focused on the ways in which participants orient to a strict turn-taking format. That format centrally involves chains of question-answer sequences and the incumbents of particular roles – the interviewer and the interviewee – are normatively constrained in the types of turns they may take, the expectation being that interviewers restrict themselves to asking 'questions', while interviewees correspondingly restrict themselves to providing 'answers' (Greatbatch 1988). This is, of course, very different from turn-taking in mundane conversation, where roles are not restricted to those of questioner and answerer, and where the type and order of turns in a given interaction may freely vary. During the course of an interview, normative rules operate which mean that attempts to move outside the boundaries of the question-answer framework may be subject to sanction.

However, the question-answer pre-allocation format is only a *minimal* characterization of the speech exchange system for news interviews. As Atkinson and Drew (1979) pointed out in their study of another question-answer speech exchange system, courtroom cross-examination, any of a range of actions may be done in a given turn, provided that they are done in the *form* of a question or answer. News interviews are not sterile occasions in which, purely and simply, questions get asked and answers are given. They are interactional events in which broadcast journalists may seek to challenge politicians and other public figures and in which those public figures may, in turn, seek to resist such challenges; they are unfolding real-time happenings in which broadcast journalists may pursue one agenda while public figures make it their business to pursue quite another; in short they are domains of contestation in which the contest is played out through the exchange of turns that are at least minimally recognizable as questions and answers.

Within this broad framework, a wide variety of aspects of news interview conduct have been analysed. These range from the basic ways in which the turn-taking format is managed (Greatbatch 1988), to the means by which interviewees shift the agendas that interviewers seek to pursue (Greatbatch 1988); from the ways in which interviewers display their journalistic objectivity in questions (Clayman 1988, 1992), to the means by which debate and disagreement are managed in the context of panel interviews (Greatbatch 1992). Recently, Clayman and Heritage (2002) have published the first full-length treatment of news interviews from a conversation analytic stand-point. The remainder of this chapter will illustrate selected aspects of this work.

Aspects of news interview conduct

One of the key issues addressed by conversation analysts stems from the fact that, in their role as questioners, interviewers are required to avoid stating their views or opinions on the news. Rather, their task is to elicit the stance, opinion or account of the one being questioned, but to do so at least technically without bias or prejudice. This is bound up with the professional journalistic ethos of neutrality, in which journalists (including broadcast journalists) are seen as acting in the interests of a wider public in extracting information from individuals in the news. But from a conversation analytic point of view, such a practice is of additional interest because it is bound up with the means by which broadcast news interviews are produced for the benefit of an overhearing audience (Heritage 1985). This involves the withholding by interviewers of certain kinds of turns that routinely occur in question–answer sequences in other contexts of social interaction.

In many types of question–answer adjacency pair, in ordinary conversation as well as institutional settings such as classroom teaching (McHoul 1978), there occurs a third position slot in which the questioner acknowledges or evaluates the answer. Thus, in standard information-seeking questions, we may find the sequence *question–answer–acknowledgement*, while in the kind of knowledge-testing questions asked by teachers we may find the sequence *question–answer–evaluation*. In news interviews, there is generally no third turn acknowledgement or evaluation; rather, the standard sequence is *question–answer–next question* . . . and so on. (One possible exception to this, the case of *question–answer–formulation*, is discussed below.) The general avoidance of third-position acknowledgements and evaluations thus acts as one of a number of noteworthy features of the question–answer chaining sequence that is specific to news interviews.

It is also the case that news interviewers routinely and systematically minimize their use of the kind of continuers, receipt tokens and news-markers (such as 'uh huh', 'right', 'yeah', 'oh really?' and so on) that are regularly found in ordinary conversational turn-taking (Heritage 1985). Such items do the work of situating their producer as the intended, and attentive, primary recipient of the talk being produced by an interlocutor (Schegloff 1982). Hence, by withholding their production, news interviewers effectively preserve a sense in which it is the audience, rather than themselves, who are the primary recipients of the interviewee's talk.

As Heritage (1985: 100) summarizes it, the withholding of acknowledgements, evaluations and continuers is significant in the design of talk for an overhearing audience for two main reasons:

> First, their production would identify prior talk as news for questioners (who are usually fully briefed beforehand or may be required to appear

so) rather than the overhearing audience . . . for whom it is, putatively, news. Second, by their production of these receipt objects . . . questioners identify themselves as the primary recipients of the talk they elicit [and] audiences could . . . come to view themselves as literally the overhearers of colloquies that, rather than being produced for them, were being produced and treated as private.

All this does not mean that interviewers do not possess opinions, or that they do not sometimes find ways of inflecting their questions so as to evaluate an interviewee's response or convey a particular stance on an issue or on the conduct of an interviewee's talk on the issue. For this reason, Clayman (1992) stresses that we should prefer the term 'neutralism' over 'neutrality' in discussions of news interview talk. While 'neutrality' implies that the interviewer *is*, somehow, a neutral conduit using questions to extract relevant information from interviewees (an interpretation often favoured by news professionals themselves), 'neutralism' foregrounds the fact that news interviewers actually *achieve* the status of 'being neutral' through a set of specialized discourse practices (see also Greatbatch 1998).

One such practice is the 'footing shift'. Goffman (1981) used the concept of footing to describe the varying ways in which speakers are able to take up positions of proximity or distance with respect to the sentiments expressed in an utterance. Distinguishing between the *animator* (the producer of the utterance), the *author* (the person whose words are actually being uttered) and the *principal* (the person whose viewpoint, stance, belief and so forth, the utterance expresses), Goffman noted that at any moment in talk, the animator can exhibit differing degrees of authorship and principalship regarding the words he or she is speaking.

Clayman (1992) adopted this concept to examine how broadcast news interviewers use footing shifts in order to give the appearance of formal neutrality. The following examples illustrate.

(1) From Clayman (1992: 169). (IR = interviewer, IE = interviewee)

```
 1      IR:   Senator, (0.5) uh: President Reagan's elected
 2            thirteen months ago: an enormous landslide. (0.8)
 3→           It is s::aid that his programs are in trouble,
 4            though he seems to be terribly popular with
 5            the American people. (0.6)
 6→           It is said by some people at thuh White House
 7            we could get those programs through if only we
 8            ha:d perhaps more:. hh effective leadership
 9            on on thuh hill an' I [suppose] indirectly=
10      IE:                        [hhhheh ]
11      IR:   =that might (0.5) relate t'you as well:. (0.6)
12            Uh what d'you think thuh problem is really.
13→           is=it (0.2) thuh leadership as it might be
14            claimed up on thuh hill, er is it thuh
15            programs themselves.
```

Here, the interviewer begins by stating a statistical fact about President Reagan's election victory (lines 1–2), and at that point he takes up the footing of animator, author and principal. But when he comes to more controversial issues (challenging the effectiveness of the President's programmes and his leadership), he shifts footing so that he is no longer author, and principalship becomes ambivalent (line 3 and line 6). In other words, he *redistributes authorship* for the position that lies behind his eventual question. Note that even when the question gets asked (lines 13–15), after the statement-formulated preamble, the footing shift is sustained: 'the leadership *as it might be claimed* up on the hill . . .'

The next extract shows how interviewers may repair their turns in order to insert a footing shift which turns the utterance from one in which they begin by expressing an opinion, to one where that opinion is attributed to others.

(2) From Clayman (1992: 171)

```
1      IR:   How d'you sum up thuh me:ssage. that this
2            decision is sending to thuh Soviets?
3      IE:   .hhh Well as I started- to say:: it is ay- one
4            of: warning an' opportunity. Thuh warning
5            is (.) you'd better comply: to arms control::
6            agreements if arms control is going to have
7            any chance of succeeding in thuh future.
8            Unilateral compliance by thuh United States
9            just not in thuh works . . .
((Some lines omitted))
10→    IR:   But isn't this- uh::: critics uh on thuh
11           conservative- side of thuh political argument
12           have argued thet this is::. abiding by thuh
13           treaty is:. unilateral (.) observance (.)
14           uh:: or compliance. (.) by thuh United States.
```

Having begun, in line 10, to ask a question the wording of which heavily implies that he will be both author and principal of the view behind the question, the interviewer breaks off and then initiates self-repair in order, once again, to redistribute authorship, this time to 'critics . . . on thuh conservative- side'.

Clayman's (1992) argument is that the use of footing shifts enables the interviewer to fulfil two professional tasks simultaneously: to be adversarial while remaining formally neutral. Interviewers routinely use footing shifts when they want to put forward provocative viewpoints for discussion, when they want to counter an interviewee and put the other side of an argument, or when they want to foster disagreement among interviewees on panel programmes. If they did any of these things while retaining a footing of animator, author and principal, they would inevitably be taking up positions on these issues. With the footing shift they can avoid this.

Another technique for producing talk that is critical and challenging towards interviewees, and which is also bound up with the production of talk for an overhearing audience, is that of 'formulating' the gist or upshot of the interviewee's remarks, usually in pursuit of some controversial or newsworthy aspect. Heritage (1985: 100) describes the practice of formulating as:

> summarizing, glossing, or developing the gist of an informant's earlier statements. Although it is relatively rare in conversation, it is common in institutionalized, audience-directed interaction [where it] is most commonly undertaken by questioners.

This practice of summarizing or glossing is used as a means of packaging or repackaging the central point made in an interviewee's turn for the benefit of the overhearing audience. In Heritage's (1985) study of formulations in news interviews, he found that the practice could be used both in a relatively benign, summarizing role ('cooperative recyclings'), and also as a means by which the interviewer seeks to evaluate or criticize the interviewee's remarks ('inferentially elaborative probes'). The following extract provides an illustration of the latter type of use:

(3) TVN: Tea

```
 1      IE:   What in fact happened was that in the course of last
 2            year, .hh the price went up really very sharply, .hhh
 3            and uh the blenders did take advantage of this: uh
 4            to obviously to raise their prices to retailers. (0.7)
 5            .hhh They haven't been so quick in reducing their
 6            prices when the world market prices come down. (0.3)
 7            .hh And so this means that price in the sh- the
 8            prices in the shops have stayed up .hh really rather
 9            higher than we'd like to see them.
10            (0.7)
11→     IR:   So you- you're really accusing them of profiteering.
12      IE:   .hhh No they're in business to make money that's
13            perfectly sensible.=We're also saying that uh: .hh
14            it's not a trade which is competitive as we would
15            like it.=There're four (0.2) blenders which have
16            together eighty five percent of the market .hhh
17            and uh we're not saying that they (.) move in
18            concert or anything like that but we'd like the
19            trade to be a bit more competitive.=
20→     IR:   =But you're giving them: a heavy instruction (.) as
21            it were to (.) to reduce their prices.
22      IE:   .hh What we're saying is we think that prices
23            could come down without the blenders losing their
24            profit margins
```

The interviewee here is the Chairman of the Price Commission, who is being interviewed about the Commission's report on tea prices. Looking at the two arrowed IR turns (lines 11 and 20), what we find is an emergent dispute over what IE can be taken as 'actually saying'. In line 11, for instance, the interviewer formulates the long turn in lines 1–9 as 'accusing (the blenders) of profiteering'. Since the interviewee had not himself used the term 'profiteering', this formulation can be described as inferentially elaborating a claim proposed to be implicit in IE's remarks.

A central sequential feature of formulations is that they make relevant in the next turn a response in which a recipient either agrees or disagrees with the version being put forward. In this case, IE disagrees with the 'profiteering' formulation (line 12) and moves on to address another issue, lack of competitiveness. In line 20, the interviewer formulates these remarks, again using much stronger terms than the interviewee; and once again (in lines 22–24), IE puts forward a weaker version of his argument than the 'heavy instruction . . . to reduce prices' referred to in the formulation. The formulations therefore attempt to 'restate the interviewee's position by making overt reference to what might be treated as implicated or presupposed by that position' (Heritage 1985: 110).

As remarked earlier, news interviews involve 'specific and significant narrowings and respecifications of the range of options that are operative in conversational interaction' (Heritage 1989: 34). These narrowings and respecifications are managed ongoingly, and collaboratively, by participants themselves. Significantly, that also goes for *departures* from the news interview conventions, such as when interviewers either adopt a more argumentative line of questioning, or are oriented to by interviewees as moving outside the bounds of formal neutrality. Both in the US and the UK, there are well-known interviewers who are widely perceived to be adopting an intentionally adversarial style of questioning: for example, Jeremy Paxman or John Humphrys of the BBC, or Dan Rather of CBS. This is not something that is specifically tied to recent trends in broadcasting. As Schudson (1984) shows, in an enlightening history of news interview practices from the mid-nineteenth century onwards, there have always been conflicting views of what the news interview should really be for, as well as different approaches both to the carrying out of interviews by journalists, and to participation in interviews by public figures. Certain interviewers have always seen their job as more about 'pressing for the truth' than 'letting the interviewee get their point across'. ITV's Sir Robin Day, for instance, was well known in Britain in the 1960s and 1970s for asking questions, live on air, which could cause politicians to walk out on the interview.

For conversation analysis, interest in these cases stems not so much from their role in public controversy but from the question of what happens when the normative conventions of the news interview as an interactional occasion break down. For example, an interviewee may attempt to avoid answering a particular question (as happened in one interview between

Jeremy Paxman and then Home Secretary Michael Howard, in which Paxman asked the same question – and Howard avoided answering it – more than 20 times); or the interviewee may so object to a line of questioning that he or she literally gets up and walks out of the studio (as happened with government Minister John Nott during the 1980s Falklands war, or ex-Prime Minister James Callaghan in an interview with Brian Walden).

Examining these kinds of breakdown in interview conduct is relevant because it tells us more about the very norms and conventions that are relied upon to get standard news interviews done. In other words, by looking at how participants break the rules, we can confirm that those rules are there to be relied on in the first place. To illustrate this I will make some observations on one high-profile American case, a 1988 interview between Dan Rather of CBS News and Vice-President George Bush Snr. The cause of the breakdown here was that Bush sought to restrict the interview topic to his presidential candidacy while Rather, seeing himself as acting in the public interest, sought to question Bush on his involvement in a secret arms-dealing affair that had recently come to light (known as the Iran-Contra affair). The result is that the entire 9 minute interview descends into what was generally perceived to be an argument (or according to the popular American press, a 'slugfest') characterized by constant interruptions and overlapping talk, ended abruptly by Rather cutting Bush off in mid-sentence.

This case is a useful one not just because it is so striking, but because there exists a further collection of studies in which conversation analysts examine the interview in great depth (Clayman and Whalen 1988/9; Nofsinger 1988/9; Pomerantz 1988/9; Schegloff 1988/9). These studies, which the reader is encouraged to consult, revealed how the publicly perceived 'confrontation' between the two men in fact emerged from a series of departures from the otherwise collaboratively sustained conventions of the interview. Close analysis showed how, while the consistently overlapping talk could be described as orderly in terms of the turn-taking system for ordinary conversation (Sacks *et al.* 1974), it was not orderly in terms of the turn-taking system for news interviews.

Let us just look at one example. It shows how the interviewer in this case conducts himself according to one of the established conventions of news interviews: that is, a question may be prefaced with one or more contextualizing statements which serve to 'frame' the question both for the interviewee and for the overhearing audience. However, the interviewee does not observe this convention, instead persistently seeking to 'answer' the statements rather than waiting for the question. Throughout the interview, this led to cycles of interruptive and otherwise overlapping talk in which the interviewer sought to pursue the production of his unasked question while the interviewee pursued the production of his pre-emptive 'answers'.

(4) Rather-Bush: 94–125 (IR is Dan Rather; IE is Vice-President George Bush Snr)

1	IE:	. . . I've answered <u>every</u> question <u>put</u> be<u>fore</u> me.=Now if
2		<u>you</u> have a <u>que</u>stion, .hh [(<u>what</u> is it.)]
4	IR:	[I <u>do</u> ha]ve one.
5	IE:	Ple[ase]
6	IR:	[Ah-] I h<u>a</u>ve one. .hh[hh <u>You</u> have <u>sa</u>id that- if <u>yo</u>]u=
7	IE:	[Please fire a<u>wa</u>y heh-hah]
8	IR:	=had <u>know</u>::n, you said tha' if <u>y</u>ou had known this was
9		an <u>a</u>rms for hostag[es <u>sw</u>]<u>ap</u>, .hh that you would've=
10	IE:	[Y e s]
11	IR:	=opposed it. .hhhh You <u>a</u>lso [said thet-]
12→	IE:	[E x a c t]ly
13	IR:	[[that <u>you</u> did NOT KNOW thet y-]
14→	IE:	[[(m- may- may I-) may I] <u>a</u>nswer that.
15		(0.4)
16	IE:	Th[uh right ( )-]
17→	IR:	[That wasn't a] question.=it w[as a statement eh-]
18→	IE:	[<u>Yes</u> it was a]
19→		statement [and I'll <u>a</u>nswer it. Thuh President]=
20→	IR:	[<u>Let</u> me ask the <u>que</u>stion if I may <u>fir</u>st]
21	IE:	=<u>crea</u>ted this program, .h has <u>te</u>stified er <u>s:ta</u>ted
22		publicly, (.) he <u>did not think</u> it was <u>a</u>rms fer <u>ho</u>stages.
23		.hh [and it was only <u>la</u>ter thet- and th]<u>a</u>t's me=
24	IR:	[That's thuh <u>Pres</u>ident Mr Vice President]
25	IE:	=(.hh)[<u>Cuz</u>] I went al<u>o</u>ng with it because ya know why Dan?
26	IR:	[We-]
27	IR:	.hh because <u>I</u>: [worried when I saw Mister:]=
28	IR:	[That <u>wa</u>sn' thuh <u>qu</u>estion Mr Vice President]
29	IE:	=.hh Mister <u>Buck</u>ley, (.) uh: heard about Mister Buckley
30		being <u>tor:</u>tured ta <u>dea</u>th. Later admitted as (a) CIA chief.
31		.hh So if <u>I</u> erred, I erred on thuh <u>side</u> of <u>tryin</u>' tuh get
32		those hostages <u>outta</u> there.

To repeat, the two conventions that we need to summarize in order to see what is going on in this extract are:

- Interviewers should use statements only in the framework of a question (for example as prefaces).

- Interviewees should refrain from speaking until a question has been asked (treat statements as prefatory to questions).

Note that the extract begins with the IE instructing IR, if he 'ha[s] a question' to 'please fire a<u>wa</u>y' (lines 1–2 and 7). Rather's attempted line of questioning so far has been to establish that Bush, though he denies it, was somehow involved in the secret deal brokered by the US secret service to deliver arms to anti-government forces in Nicaragua in exchange for the release of American hostages in Iran. He begins, in lines 6–11, to form up a question along similar lines using a technique that Pomerantz (1988/9), in her analysis of other parts of the same broadcast, has described: namely to get the IE to agree to two contradictory factual statements, and then ask a question which invites the IE to deal with the contradiction foregrounded in the statements just agreed to. In this, therefore, the IR appears to be observing norm (1) above. However, in line 14 IE breaches the corresponding norm (2), by interrupting IR's second factual statement ('you <u>a</u>lso said thet- that <u>you</u> did NOT KNOW . . .', lines 11–13) with an attempt to 'answer' the first ('may I <u>a</u>nswer that'). Notice how, in the following turns, both parties display their hitherto tacit knowledge of the very norms that are being breached, and on which the properties of this occasion as an 'interview' rely: in line 17 IR says 'That wasn't a <u>question</u>.=it was a statement' and, in line 20, '<u>L</u>et me ask the <u>question</u> if I may <u>first</u>'; while IE clearly displays that he is moving outside the question–answer turn-taking framework in his intervening utterance: '<u>Yes</u> it was a <u>statement</u> and I'll <u>answer</u> it' (lines 18–19).

The extract above gives just a glimpse of the way that this interview, in the course of its 9-minute broadcast, came to be widely perceived as a confrontation between the two participants. As Clayman and Whalen (1988/9: 242–3) describe it, media commentary at the time focused on the personalities of the protagonists: Rather being seen as 'combative' and 'volatile', while Bush 'appeared surprisingly forceful and aggressive, and was widely felt to have dispelled his "wimp" image'. However, by the application of CA to the turn-by-turn unfolding of the event, we are able to take a different perspective on the movement between 'interview' and 'confrontation'. This involves determining

> how the participants shaped the encounter from within; [isolating] the specific social practices they employed in its development. Since contributions to interaction are contingent upon the independent actions of others, they cannot be treated as the straightforward behavioural realisation of preplanned political strategies or psychological predispositions. Whatever prior agendas or predispositions there may have been, the actual course of the encounter must be treated as an emergent and fundamentally *interactional* achievement.
>
> (Clayman and Whalen 1988/9: 243)

From a conversation analytic perspective, therefore, this encounter and others like it are primarily interesting as deviant cases: ones in which the participants deviate from the normative conventions that underpin broadcast news interviews *as* interviews in the first place. As in other types of deviant case analysis, examining how the interaction changes its shape in the absence of those conventions only serves to reinforce the main point of CA studies: that specific turn-taking practices are crucial factors in the ability of broadcast journalists and public figures to produce news interviews as recognizable occasions for the production of news talk 'on the air'.

References

Atkinson, J. M. (1984) *Our Masters' Voices: The Language and Body Language of Politics*. London: Routledge.

Atkinson, J. M. and Drew, P. (1979) *Order in Court*. London: Macmillan.

Clayman, S. (1988) Displaying Neutrality in Television News Interviews, *Social Problems*, 35: 474–92.

Clayman, S. (1992) Footing in the Achievement of Neutrality: The Case of News Interview Discourse. In P. Drew and J. Heritage. (eds), *Talk At Work*. Cambridge: Cambridge University Press.

Clayman, S. and Heritage, J. (2002) *The News Interview*. Cambridge: Cambridge University Press.

Clayman, S. and Whalen, J. (1988/9) When the Medium becomes the Message: The Case of the Rather-Bush Encounter, *Research on Language and Social Interaction*, 22: 241–72.

Drew, P. (1984) Speakers' Reportings in Invitation Sequences. In J. M. Atkinson and J. Heritage (eds), *Structures of Social Action: Studies in Conversation Analysis*. Cambridge: Cambridge University Press.

Drew, P. and Heritage, J. (eds) (1992) *Talk At Work*. Cambridge: Cambridge University Press.

Garfinkel, H. (1967) *Studies in Ethnomethodology*. Englewood Cliffs: Prentice-Hall.

Goffman, E. (1961) *Encounters*. New York: Bobbs-Merrill.

Goffman, E. (1981) *Forms of Talk*. Oxford: Blackwell.

Greatbatch, D. (1988) A Turn-taking System for British News Interviews. *Language in Society*, 17: 401–30.

Greatbatch, D. (1992) On the Management of Disagreement between News Interviewees. In P. Drew and J. Heritage (eds) *Talk At Work*. Cambridge: Cambridge University Press.

Greatbatch, D. (1998) Conversation Analysis: Neutralism in British News Interviews, in A. Bell and P. Garrett (eds), *Approaches to Media Discourse*. Oxford: Blackwell.

Heath, C. (1992) The Delivery and Reception of Diagnosis in the General Practice Consultation, in P. Drew and J. Heritage (eds) *Talk At Work*. Cambridge: Cambridge University Press.

Heritage, J. (1985) Analyzing News Interviews: Aspects of the Production of Talk for an Overhearing Audience, in T. van Dijk (ed.) *Handbook of Discourse Analysis, Volume 3: Discourse and Dialogue*. London: Academic Press.

Heritage, J. (1989) Current Developments in Conversation Analysis, in D. Roger and P. Bull (eds), *Conversation*. Clevedon: Multilingual Matters.

Heritage, J., Clayman, S. and Zimmerman, D. (1988) Discourse and Message Analysis: The Micro-structure of Mass Media Messages. In R. P. Hawkins, J. M. Wiemann and S. Pingree (eds) *Advancing Communication Science: Merging Mass and Interpersonal Processes*. London: Sage.

Heritage, J. and Greatbatch, D. (1991) On the Institutional Character of Institutional Talk: The Case of News Interviews. In D. Boden and D. Zimmerman (eds) *Talk and Social Structure*. Cambridge: Polity.

Hutchby, I. (1996) *Confrontation Talk: Arguments, Asymmetries and Power on Talk Radio*. Mahwah, NJ: Lawrence Erlbaum Associates.

Hutchby, I. and Wooffitt, R. (1998) *Conversation Analysis*. Cambridge: Polity.

Jefferson, G. (1978) Sequential Aspects of Storytelling in Conversation. In J. Schenkein (ed.) *Studies in the Organisation of Conversational Interaction*. New York: Academic Press.

Levinson, S. (1983) *Pragmatics*. Cambridge: Cambridge University Press.

McHoul, A. (1978) The Organisation of Turns at Formal Talk in the Classroom, *Language in Society*, 19: 183–213.

Nofsinger, R. (1988/9) Let's Talk about the Record: Contending over Topic Redirection in the Rather/Bush Interview, *Research on Language and Social Interaction*, 22: 273–92.

Pomerantz, A. (1984) Agreeing and Disagreeing with Assessments: Some Features of Preferred/Dispreferred Turn-shapes. In J. M. Atkinson and J. Heritage (eds) *Structures of Social Action: Studies in Conversation Analysis*. Cambridge: Cambridge University Press.

Pomerantz, A. (1988/9) Constructing Skepticism: Four Devices used to Engender the Audience's Skepticism, *Research on Language and Social Interaction*, 22: 293–314.

Sacks, H. (1978) Some Technical Considerations of a Dirty Joke. In J. Schenkein (ed.) *Studies in the Organisation of Conversational Interaction*. New York: Academic Press.

Sacks, H. (1984) Notes on Methodology. In J. M. Atkinson and J. Heritage (eds), *Structures of Social Action: Studies in Conversation Analysis*. Cambridge: Cambridge University Press.

Sacks, H. (1992) *Lectures on Conversation*. Oxford: Blackwell.

Sacks, H., Schegloff, E. A. and Jefferson, G. (1974) A Simplest Systematics for the Organisation of Turn-taking for Conversation, *Language*, 50: 696–735.

Schegloff, E. A. (1979) Identification and Recognition in Telephone Conversation Openings, in G. Psathas (ed.) *Everyday Language*. Hillsdale, NJ: Lawrence Erlbaum Associates.

Schegloff, E. A. (1982) Discourse as an Interactional Achievement: Some Uses of 'Uh Huh' and Other Things that Come between Sentences, in D. Tannen (ed.) *Analysing Discourse: Text and Talk*. Washington, DC: Georgetown University Press.

Schegloff, E. A. (1988/9) From Interview to Confrontation: Observations on The Bush/Rather Encounter, *Research on Language and Social Interaction*, 22: 215–40.

Schegloff, E. A. and Sacks, H. (1973) Opening Up Closings, *Semiotica*, 7: 289–327.

Schudson, M. (1984) Question Authority: A History of the News Interview in American Journalism, 1860s–1930s, *Media, Culture and Society*, 16: 565–587.

|17

'A fresh peach is easier to bruise'

Children and traumatic news[1]

Cynthia Carter and Máire Messenger Davies

- What have journalism researchers had to say about children's relationship to traumatic news?
- Why are parents often encouraged to protect their children from frightening news stories?
- How do certain cultural constructions of childhood shape journalism research and what assumptions are made about the child news audience?
- In what ways are children used as symbols in traumatic news?
- How do children respond to the news coverage of frightening events?

Journalism researchers have rarely attached much importance to studying the relationship of children and young people to the news. Few studies have sought to understand the ways in which certain ideological models of childhood innocence and vulnerability shape journalistic assumptions, the ways in which young people tend to be represented in the news, how child audiences make sense of it, or even what sort of provision is made for children's print, broadcast and online news in the first place. Meanwhile, adult broadcast and print news organizations in the UK and US have found it to be increasingly difficult to attract sufficiently large numbers of younger audiences during a period that has also seen a steady decline in many young people's interest in electoral politics. Both of these developments are worrying political leaders and journalists alike. Without a sufficiently informed citizenry, how best to ensure the future health of democratic politics?

For all the talk about wanting to reinvigorate political debate and participation few journalists appear to appreciate the need for forms of news that might encourage in young people a sense of belonging and engagement with the world from the earliest years of their lives. Nor have most journalism scholars thought that this issue warrants rigorous scholarly analysis (exceptions include Barnhurst and Wartella 1991; Carter 2004; Davies 2004; Lemish 1998; Lester-Roushanzamir and Raman 1999). There appears to be a taken-for-granted assumption that political interest and activity start, like magic, when people reach the age of political enfranchisement in their late teenage years. A prevailing view seems to be that children are not interested in politics nor do they have sensible opinions about what is happening in the world before age 18. Even where citizenship (UK) or civics (USA) education has become embedded within secondary school educational structures, so far little has been done to encourage children's engagement with the news and therefore with the most important debates that centrally engage and connect citizens and political representatives in the public sphere (see Buckingham 2000).

In this chapter we focus on the questions posed above and the concerns that they raise for us. We begin to address these questions, firstly, by exploring research that looks at children's emotional or fright reactions to the news, which represents the most substantive body of work in this field. In the second section, we turn to examine the cultural models of childhood that underpin research on children's emotional responses to the news. From there we consider the ways in which children are used as particular types of symbols in traumatic news stories – to signify, for instance, innocence, vulnerability, victimhood and weakness.[2] In the final section, we assess some of the assumptions that shape journalists' thinking about the interests and needs of child news audiences.

Researching children and traumatic news

The limited body of research examining children and their relationships to the news has tended to centre for analysis individual emotional responses and fears generated by frightening stories (for example, war, conflict, child abduction and murder). This research, which methodologically speaking, routinely employs quantitative surveys and interviews with children to generate data on children's fright reactions, can be grouped into two broad conceptual approaches. Research that fits into the first one often examines things like the influence of a child's age on the intensity of their (negative) emotional response to the news or will focus on a child's level of news consumption (if children are heavy news consumers, are they more or less likely to be frightened?) as a determinant of their (negative) emotional reactions. Studies grounded in the second approach tend to be interested in children's (negative and positive) emotional and intellectual responses to the news, assuming that reactions will vary according to a child's educational, social, economic and cultural background.

Conceptually, the first approach is based on models of childhood emerging from developmental psychology where importance is placed on finding out how frightening news might negatively affect children and even damage them emotionally and psychologically. This emphasis has been decisive in encouraging researchers to highlight, for example, which age groups are most likely to become emotionally traumatized. A central aim of such research is to identify the most vulnerable age categories so that psychological protection is age appropriate.

Some researchers have argued that very young children are the most likely to feel distressed by frightening news because they are unable to contextualize the violence (Cantor 2001, 2002; Cantor and Nathanson 1996; Hoffner and Haefner 1993). That is to say, they are said to be more affected by frightening images than words or text as they tend to be unable to understand verbal or written explanations for why violent actions have occurred. Against this, other scholars conclude that children in older age groups are most at risk from experiencing negative emotional responses precisely because they are better able to understand the consequences of the stories that are being reported (Cantor *et al.* 1993; Smith and Wilson 2002). Still others have found no relationship between the age of children and their level of fear, concluding that other factors (gender, social status and so forth) may be more important in determining responses (Wober and Young 1993).

With this point in mind, some researchers have sought to find out whether gender is a salient factor in children's emotional responses (Cairns 1990) or if there might be a correlation between the age and gender of a child; for example, some studies conclude that younger girls are most likely of all groups of children to be upset by the news (Van der Molen *et al.* 2002). Others have centred for analysis the influence of parental reactions to traumatic news upon their children (Hoffner and Haefner 1993; Van der Voort *et al.* 1993). Yet another focus has been on the amount of television news children watch; so far, results have not been able to prove nor disprove the cultivation theory argument that heavy viewers would be most upset by traumatic news as it would make them think that the world is a more violent place than it is in reality (Hoffner and Haefner 1994; Morrison and MacGregor 1993).

What these researchers have in common is an agreement that psychological development of the individual child shapes their reactions to the news. As such, their responses need to be closely monitored and measured. These data, it is argued, provide empirical evidence for parents, teachers, public health officials and policy makers that will enable them to know how best to protect children of different ages from being emotionally damaged by exposure to terrifying news stories (Van der Molen 2004). 'Expert' advice from medical and psychological associations, parental pressure groups and governmental agencies tends to uniformly recommend that adults should find ways to manage children's fears so as to protect them from potential psychological harm (Kaiser Family Foundation 2003; National Center for Children Exposed to Violence 2003). This may include severely limiting their exposure to television news if an adult decides that this is appropriate (Cantor 2001). Based, as it is, on cognitive psychology models of child development, the 'appropriate' response as a parent, teacher or other significant adult in a child's life is to treat children's reactions as individualized responses that can be handled at the personal and age-appropriate level through personalized care and counselling.

This line of argument tends to assume that children are largely unable to understand what is being reported in the news and are therefore emotionally ill-equipped to cope with it. This is a view that has been persuasive and pervasive, particularly in the US. Founded on ideological assumptions about childhood innocence and vulnerability (a conceptual construction that we address in the next section of this chapter), it has become widely accepted as the most appropriate model for understanding children's responses to traumatic news. Responsibility for dealing with such reactions is often placed on the shoulders of parents who are urged to ask their children if they have any questions (answers are to be appropriate to the particular age of the child) and to provide reassurance that they are safe personally. That said, the parental role is not necessarily to provide a full explanation of such events, nor to provide analysis or critique of how they are reported in the news. Instead, they are directed to monitor their child's emotional responses and to look out for psychological and physiological symptoms that he or she may be suffering (bad dreams, crying, insomnia, irritability and so forth). The central concern is to mitigate any psychological and behavioural negative effects traumatic news may have on children (Cantor 2001).

The second conceptual approach to which we referred earlier in this chapter, where researchers seek to better understand children's emotional and intellectual responses to shocking news, comes to a different set of conclusions from those outlined for the first approach. Influenced by critical models of childhood that regard the child as a citizen in the making, researchers working within this second approach assume that children are able and willing to understand and cope with traumatic news if it is clearly and sensitively explained to them. Critical news researchers have tended to emphasize the need not for less coverage of these events nor, indeed, to sanitize unnecessarily how they are represented, but instead to provide more and better explanation so that child audiences can better understand the issues.

While some news media critics argue that some traumatic stories are better off not being told to children at all because they are too distressing, the importance of facing up to the facts and keeping oneself informed, Buckingham (1996) maintains, is much more important than the possible risks of being upset or frightened (see also Buckingham 2000; Lemish 1998). Ongoing debates around what to show or not to show to children and young people, in Buckingham's (1996) view, are deeply political. Responses to traumatic news, he says

> cannot be simply relegated to the domain of 'mere emotions'. On the contrary, there is a sense in which such emotions are a central part of children's developing understanding of the social and political world . . . familiar divisions between the emotional, the cognitive and the social can obscure the genuine complexity of what is taking place.
>
> (Buckingham 1996: 209)

Conceptually, the developmental psychology emphasis on children's negative emotional responses to frightening news depoliticizes the events to which children are reacting. By robbing those responses of their political context, children's responses are seen to be personal and treatable with parental intervention (to limit exposure to frightening news) and, where necessary, psychological counselling by experts.

Clearly, there are important theoretical and political issues for critical journalism studies that are raised by research on children's emotional responses to traumatic news. In the next section, we examine how certain social and cultural constructions of childhood or models of childhood have influenced this field of academic study, as well as those that are assumed or promoted in journalistic accounts of frightening news events. The section that follows picks up on this last point, specifically looking at examples of the ways in which children tend to be used for signification purposes in stories about war and conflict – largely as naive, vulnerable, and as victims.

Theoretical constructions of childhood: agency and victimhood

Over a two-year period, we interviewed children at a primary school in Glasgow, Scotland, asking them to tell us what they think about adult and children's news and how they respond to traumatic news stories.[3] Like other research that involves consulting children about adult socio-political issues, it draws attention to a broader theoretical consideration. That is, the way in which even quite young children constitute themselves as subjects and as agents, generating a sense of selfhood and autonomy that is an indispensable attribute of citizenship (see Carter and Allan 2005; Davies 2001). Contemporary academic accounts of childhood following Aries' (1961) seminal *Centuries of Childhood* emphasize the social constructedness of the concept (see James and Prout 1990).

Notions of the child as 'innocent', 'becoming', and hence, 'incompetent', are seen by some revisionist scholars as romantic mythologizing. Such ideas are seen as not applicable to childhoods in non-Western societies, nor to children in pre-industrial Western societies, where they were expected to work and contribute economically to the household. The idea of childhood as 'innocent' and 'undeveloped' also conflicts with the post-modern notion of pre-adolescent children as 'tweens', with adult consumer aspirations. This robust academic approach, while legitimately emphasizing, for example, the economic status of children in non-Western societies and their competence in performing many 'adult' tasks (see Qvortrup 1990) can be in danger of overlooking their very real vulnerability. There is no question that children, being smaller and weaker than adults, are especially vulnerable, at risk and defenceless in war situations. The suffering, mutilated, bereaved or dead child victim is not an invention of media representation. Neither is the child warrior simply a construct, even though such representations may leave out important political and ideological contexts. Nevertheless, the representation of children in the news as suffering victims is not a justification for denying them a voice in political discourse.

As discussed above, much media research on children (and media and culture do not figure largely in the historical and sociological revision of childhood) has taken a negative perspective – suggesting that not only are children and young people passive victims but they are also gullible consumers, violent imitators of bad behaviour and apathetic about current affairs. In contrast, we assume that children *are* aware of and interested in news representations of various kinds, particularly of traumatic events, like the Iraq war, and that they are likely to have strong opinions and feelings about these events. In other words, our construction of the child news audience assumes active agency on their part. But this is not how children tend to be represented in news stories – especially in those about war and trauma.

Signifying children

Generally speaking, it is fair to suggest that representations of children in the media are typically used in at least two – somewhat opposed – ways in news coverage of traumatic events. The first is primarily illustrative. That is to say, as Holland (2004) has pointed out, pictorial representations of childhood are widely used to illustrate the underlying ideologies of Western society towards children. Holland's work indicates the ways in which child images – for instance lines of uniformed school children – can be used to demonstrate an ideological construction of political order, or how art images, often recycled through advertising, can be employed to illustrate social constructions of innocence or of sexualization. Suffering children are among the most frequently chosen subjects of images of war, famine and genocide. They serve the dual purpose of arousing adult sympathy and humanizing the brutality of war, and creating more compelling representations to potential adult news audiences (see Davies 2004, for further discussions of the ambivalence of children in news images).

A notorious example, shown on the cover of the G2 section of the *Guardian* of 8 August 2003, accompanied a news story by Esther Addley. The injured child in the photograph, Ali Ismaeel Abbas, an 11-year-old Iraqi boy, had lost both his arms and 14 members of his family in a bomb attack on Baghdad on 6 April 2003. Addley described how Ali was going to 'fly to the UK to be fitted for prosthetic arms and begin up to six months of physiotherapy . . . an extraordinarily happy ending for the little boy whose doctors at one point told journalists "it would be better if he died".' When simply presented as a 'story' with a 'happy ending', the political significance of Ali's story was diminished and his family became just one among several thousand other Iraqi families whose members have been killed and injured but whose stories are not reported in the Western news media. The story of how Ali was treated by the media illustrates the way in which this suffering child became a symbol for something other than himself – an example of how the humanitarian instincts of the British people who contributed to a fund for his treatment and the miracle-working high-tech of Western medicine can reassure us that even the very worst excesses of war can be overcome – they can have 'a happy ending'. Compounding this representation of Ali as a symbol of the suffering child was the absence of his voice telling us what had happened to him. Like the majority of children used to illustrate news stories about war and disaster, Ali was not interviewed or quoted in the *Guardian* article; he was not allowed to tell his own 'story'.

Journalists themselves can be fully aware of their own contribution to such ambivalent representations. For example, Libby Brooks (2003) pointed out in a *Guardian* article in April 2003 that emotive appeals in aid of suffering children are a way of 'granting ourselves the absolution that comes with witnessing their victimhood and acting on it' (see also Davies and Mosdell 2001). Brooks makes the point that war coverage doesn't only present children as 'wholly blameless'. As she points out, children are sometimes war perpetrators too, with the AK47 being treated like 'a toy of choice', as she put it.

The child interviewees we spoke to in our research in Glasgow noticed the duality of children's representation in the media. As one 12-year-old boy put it: 'It is usually sick children or children in poverty that are shown in children's news, like the two seriously injured Iraqi children that were saved in Kuwait.' A 12-year-old girl strongly objected: 'Children are shown as a responsibility in adult news . . . something which commits teenage crimes and eats unhealthily. THIS IS NOT RIGHT.' Another 12-year-old boy pointed out: 'Children are only seen as hoolagins [*sic*] in adult news.'[4]

The second role children play in relationship to the news is illustrated by the 12 year olds' remarks above. This is a conception of children as news audiences with opinions and concerns of their own, which are often divergent from those of adults (see Buckingham 2000). The journalistic discourse around children and young people as news audiences and potential voters rarely represents such forthright opinions from young people. Such discourses are often negative and belittling, as, for example, Stephen Cushion's (2003) analysis of the news media's representation of young people protesting against the Iraq war suggests. Young protesters' concerns were trivialized in headlines such as 'It beats doing your homework.' Our research with children in Glasgow supports this point, and maintains that young people are not satisfied with a representation of themselves and their contemporaries in the media as innocent victims, as 'hoolagins' [*sic*] or as truants 'bunking off' school when they attempt to demonstrate political involvement and activism.[5]

In *Consenting Children*, Davies and Mosdell (2001) discuss a number of ways in which children were represented in adult television programming. Examining children's portrayal in the news, the authors' reading suggests that passivity and emotionalism were recurrent characteristics of these portrayals. 'Passivity' is defined as a lack of participation of the child in the events so that, even where children are prominently on display, they are not interviewed, or even described as significant participants. Instead, they appear to be used largely for emotional responses – that is, to appeal to adults' feelings and to influence their views.

Davies (2004), as part of her research on children's responses to traumatic news, carried out an analysis of 83 TV war stories in March 2003. Children were featured in 27 (33 per cent) of them. Among these 27 items there was only one example of children/young people being active agents – as war protesters. All other examples showed children as 'patients' both grammatically and medically; they were lying down; being treated; being carried or being held by the hand. No child spoke on camera. This representation of childhood contrasts with the kinds of responses that children and young people give when they are actually consulted, as our next section indicates.

Journalistic assumptions about the child audience

Young people expect to have their views about the world taken seriously but are painfully aware that adults seem largely uninterested in what they have to say. Others complain that adults tend to be too inclined to want to protect them from traumatic news, effectively withholding information that they believe might be too upsetting to children. This point was made most clearly by 10-year-old Cara-Leigh from Arlesey on *Newsround*'s Web site: 'I am very scared about the war with Iraq, because President Bush and Tony Blair are not giving our selves, CHILDREN a chance to speak about it, because it may change our lives' (posted 25 March 2003; emphasis in the original). In societies that purport to be democratic, young people must be made to feel actively connected to the events taking place around them, and empowered to make their voices heard.

While children and young people often insist upon knowing what is happening in the world, even when the news is upsetting, journalists have tended to be divided in their views about what is appropriate to show to child audiences. Former Editor of *Newsround*, Nick Heathcote, claims that it is important for the programme to primarily consist of good news. In his view, children are already exposed to a large amount of negative news, and there is a danger that this will make them feel that there is no hope for the future. Great care must be taken when reporting traumatic news to children, he adds. Says Heathcote, 'children have the right to be upset, but we have to accept that their experience of the world is limited. A fresh peach is easier to bruise' (cited in Dodd 1994).

Former Deputy Director of *Newsround*, Marshall Corwin takes a similar view, noting that the programme is able to make bad news seem less frightening because it is being reported by the familiar, friendly faces of *Newsround* presenters. Claims Corwin, 'Very occasionally we get complaints saying we shouldn't be reporting wars; but we believe that it's our duty, and children have the right to understand the world if they are going to be part of it' (cited in Grant 1996: T6).[6]

More recently, Nicky Parkinson, head of Nickelodeon UK, explained that their children's news programme, *Nick News* (which ceased production in 2003), didn't cover September 11 because 'We took the view that with the saturation coverage elsewhere, we were there to provide some respite for children' (cited in Hirst 2002: 7). In contrast, *Newsround* Executive Producer, Roy Milani, insisted that it was important for children's news to provide coverage precisely because adult news had left many children upset and confused. According to Milani, 'It is our job to put the stories in perspective and make them clearly understandable to children . . . we don't think we can shy away from these subjects' (cited in Hirst 2002: 7).

Conclusions

Our brief review of research on children and traumatic news raises important questions for news producers and for journalism studies scholars. How are editorial decisions taken about representations of children, especially suffering children? In what circumstances are children's images preferable to alternatives, such as an elderly person or a suffering soldier? What are the ethics of using such representations? What steps are taken to get consent from the participants concerned, or their parents and guardians? The use of images of suffering children has political and propaganda implications. One logical conclusion of such emotive representations could be to invite an anti-war, response: war should be stopped because, for example, children are getting killed and maimed. This potential agenda was spotted by one of our child interviewees in Glasgow: 'At the time of war in Iraq, children were shown in hospital near to death, which made us feel: why did we go to war if we are hurting innocent children?' (girl, 12).[7] For this girl, the message of showing children suffering leads logically to the view that war is wrong.

The repeated image of childhood as one of persistent victimhood and lack of autonomy creates a problem for journalists. If they want to use children as routine signifiers for the pity and horror of war, to arouse adult sympathy and to generate human interest in order to focus the attention of viewers and readers, such emotive images of childhood may conflict with journalists' stated desire to have active and informed young viewers and readers who will one day watch their programmes and buy their papers.

If adults want children to take an interest in news and thereby become informed citizens, one way of helping them is to encourage journalists to show children in a wide variety of roles in the news. At the moment, they are not represented in this way. Wartime, especially, is an occasion for mobilizing the political awareness and consciences of the young – the lack of which is often lamented by journalistic commentators when commenting on low turnouts in elections, or on the alleged 'apathy' and 'hedonism' of today's young people. Effective news coverage both of and for children does not only show the traumatic effects of war. It also offers insights into effective ways of taking political action.

Notes

1 This quotation comes from Nick Heathcote (cited in Dodd 1994), former Editor of Children's BBC news programme *Newsround*. In Heathcote's view, the programme should tell children the truth about what is happening in the world, but that when covering upsetting news it has a responsibility to report it in a way that does not make children feel like there is no hope for the future. *Newsround* was first broadcast on 4 April 1972, anchored by former BBC Bristol journalist John Craven. Today it is the only news programme of its kind in the UK, and the most watched children's programme (over one million viewers tuned in during 2001; see Atwal *et al.* 2003). In 2001, *Newsround* launched its Web site.

2 Children are also sometimes used as symbols for evil, as in the UK case of the two 10-year-old boys, Robert Thompson and Jon Venables, who in 1993 killed the 2-year-old James Bulger. That said, this negative symbolization of children is largely confined to stories about petty crime, truancy and bullying. Most stories encourage readers to see these children as 'not normal', thereby keeping intact assumptions about innate childhood innocence and vulnerability.

3 We are pleased to acknowledge that some of the ideas developed in this chapter have benefited from our collaborative field research on children and news initially funded by the Cardiff School of Journalism, Media and Cultural Studies, with colleagues Dr Stuart Allan (University of the West of England, Bristol), Dr Karin Wahl-Jorgensen (Cardiff University) and Frances Meredith (Cardiff University). Our thanks go to the British Academy for funding the Children and News Archive housed in the Bute Library, Cardiff University, which is one of the results of this research collaboration. For further information about the archive, see http://www.cf.ac.uk/jomec/research/firsted.html. Cynthia Carter would like to thank the Arts and Humanities Research Board for extended study leave support that enabled her to conduct the research upon which this chapter is based.

4 Selected responses from interviews at Hillhead Primary School, Glasgow, June 2003.

5 From interviews at Hillhead, June 2003.

6 This view is shared by current *Newsround* editor, Ian Prince, as outlined in his presentation on children's news at the Prix Jeunesse Awards, Munich, June 2004.

7 From an interview at Hillhead, June 2003.

References

Aries, P. (1961) *Centuries of Childhood*. London: Pimlico Press.

Atwal, K., Millwood-Hargrave, A. and Sancho, J. (2003) *What Children Watch: An Analysis of Children's Programme Provision between 1997–2001, and Children's Views*. London: Broadcasting Standards Commission and the Independent Television Commission.

Barnhurst, K. G. and Wartella, E. (1991) Newspaper and Citizenship: Young Adults' Subjective Experience of Newspapers, *Critical Studies in Mass Communication*, 8, 195–209.

Brooks, L. (2003) Guilt and Innocents, *The Guardian*, 26 April.

Buckingham, D. (1996) *Moving Images: Understanding Children's Emotional Responses to Television*. Manchester and New York: Manchester University Press.

Buckingham, D. (2000) *The Making of Citizens: Young People, News and Politics*. London: Routledge.

Cairns, E. (1990) Impact of Television News Exposure on Children's Perceptions of Violence in Northern Ireland, *The Journal of Social Psychology*, 130(4): 447–52.

Cantor, J. (2001) Helping Children Cope: Advice in the Aftermath of the Terrorist Attacks on America, http://www.joannecantor.com/terror_adv.htm (accessed 19 April 2004).

Cantor, J. (2002) The Psychological Effects of Media Violence on Children and Adolescents. Paper presented at the Colloquium on Television and Violence in Society, Centre d'études sur le media, HEC Montréal, Canada, 19 April, http://www.joannecantor.com/montrealpap_fin.htm (accessed 3 March 2004).

Cantor, J., Mares, M. and Oliver, M. B. (1993) Parents' and Children's Emotional Reactions to TV Coverage of the Gulf War, in B. S. Greenberg and W. Gantz (eds) *Desert Storm and the Mass Media*. Cresskill, NJ: Hampton Press, pp. 325–40.

Cantor, J. and Nathanson, A. I. (1996) Children's Fright Reactions to Television News, *Journal of Communication*, 46: 139–52.

Carter, C. (2004) Scary News: Children's Responses to News of War, *Mediactive*, 3: 67–84.

Carter, C. and Allan, S. (2005) Young People's Voices: Citizenship, Media Education and Online News, in A. Williams and C. Thurlow (eds) *Communication in Adolescence: Perspectives on Language and Social Interaction in the Teenage Years*. London: Peter Lang.

Cushion, S. (2003) '*Well it beats doing your homework*' – Representing Protests Against the War in Iraq: Young People, Politics and Apathy. Paper presented to the MeCCSA Conference, Sussex University, 20 December.

Davies, M. M. (2001) '*Dear BBC': Children, Television Storytelling and the Public Sphere*. Cambridge: Cambridge University Press.

Davies, M. M. (2004) Innocent Victims: Active Citizens, *Mediactive*, 3: 55–66.

Davies, M. M. and Mosdell, N. (2001) *Consenting Children? The Use of Children in Non-fiction Television Programmes*. London: Broadcasting Standards Commission.

Dodd, V. (1994) John Craven May be Long Gone but *Newsround* is Still Going Strong, *Scotsman*, 16 March.

Grant, L. (1996) How to Handle Horror, *Guardian*, 12 June: T6.

Hirst, C. (2002) Watch out John Craven, here's Jimmy Neutron, *Independent on Sunday*, 1 September: 7.

Hoffner, C. and Haefner, M. J. (1993) Children's Affective Responses to News Coverage of the War, in B. S. Greenberg and W. Gantz (eds) *Desert Storm and the Mass Media*. Cresskill, NJ: Hampton Press, pp. 364–80.

Hoffner, C. and Haefner, M. J. (1994) Children's news interest during the Gulf War: the role of negative affect, *Journal of Broadcast and Electronic Media*, 38(2): 193–204.

Holland, P. (2001) Living for Libido or *Child's Play IV* – the Imagery of Childhood and the Call for Censorship, in M. Barker and J. Petley (eds) *Ill Effects: The Media Violence Debate*, second edition. London: Routledge, pp. 78–86.

Holland, P. (2004) *Picturing Childhood: The Myth of The Child in Popular Imagery.* London: IB Tauris.

James, A. and Prout, A. (1990) *Constructing and Reconstructing Childhood: Contemporary Issues in the Sociological Study of Childhood.* London: Falmer Press.

Kaiser Family Foundation (2003) Children and the news: coping with terrorism, war and everyday violence, http://www.kff.org/entmedia/loader.cfm?url=/commonspot/security/getfile.cfm&PageID=14268 (accessed 6 April 2004).

Lemish, D. (1998) What is News? A Cross-cultural Examination of Kindergarteners' Understanding of News, *Communication: The European Journal of Communication Research*, 23: 491–504.

Lester-Roushanzamir, E. P. and Raman, U. (1999) The Global Village in Atlanta: A Textual Analysis of Olympic News Coverage for Children in the *Atlanta Journal-Constitution, Journalism and Mass Communication Quarterly*, 76(4): 699–712.

Morrison, D. and MacGregor, B. (1993) Anxiety, War and Children: the Role of Television, in B. S. Greenberg and W. Gantz (eds) *Desert Storm and the Mass Media*, Cresskill, NJ: Hampton Press, pp. 353–63.

National Center for Children Exposed to Violence (2003) Children and terrorism, http://www.nccev.org/violence/children_terrorism.htm (accessed 17 May 2004).

Qvortrup, J. (1990) A Voice for Children in Statistical and Social Accounting: a Plea for Children's Right to be Heard, in A. James and A. Prout (eds) *Constructing and Reconstructing Childhood: Contemporary Issues in the Sociological Study of Childhood.* London: Falmer Press.

Smith, S. L. and Wilson, B. J. (2002) Children's Comprehension of and Fear Reactions to Television News, *Media Psychology*, 4: 1–26.

Van der Molen, J. H. W. (2004) Violence and Suffering in Television News: Toward a Broader Conception of Harmful Television Content for Children, *Pediatrics*, 113(6): 1771–5.

Van der Molen, J. H. W., Valkenburg, P. M. and Peeters, A. L. (2002) Television News and Fear: a Child Survey, *Communications*, 27: 303–17.

Van der Voort, T. H. A., Van Lil, J. E. and Vooijs, M. W. (1993) Parent and Child Emotional Involvement in the Netherlands, in B. S. Greenberg and W. Gantz (eds) *Desert Storm and the Mass Media*. Cresskill, NJ: Hampton Press, pp. 341–52.

Wober, M. and Young, B. M. (1993) British Children's Knowledge of, Emotional Reactions to, and Ways of Making Sense of the War, in B. S. Greenberg and W. Gantz (eds) *Desert Storm and the Mass Media*, Cresskill, NJ: Hampton Press, 381–90.

PART IV
Journalism and the politics of othering

|18

Talking war

How journalism responded to the events of 9/11

Martin Montgomery

- How and when did the talk of war begin after 9/11?
- What other forms of description were available?
- Did journalism lose its critical distance from public figures?

This chapter examines ways in which journalism responded in the immediate aftermath of the events of 9/11 by examining verbal reactions in 'the public sphere' (Habermas 1989) and by focusing in particular on how the talk turned to war. In doing so, it explores the interface between journalism and significant public figures such as the US President, his spokesperson and the Secretary of State. Drawing upon data from newspaper headlines, broadcast interviews, briefings and presidential addresses it will chart the transition for 'terror' to 'war', from immediate reaction to more developed response. It will show that the term *war* – which was to prove so decisive – emerged very early. Initially, however, the term was used as a figure of speech, uncertainly and awkwardly, before coming to be the decisive expression for articulating a public response. In the transition from shifting, heteroglossic and equivocal uses to its elevation as the dominant term of description, journalism played a central and – quite literally – a defining role. On the one hand, by a process of discursive amplification the press in newspaper headlines of 11 and 12 September came to highlight the term. On the other hand, in adversarial encounters, in interviews and briefings, journalists called its use into question. Once *war* became established, however, as the dominant term of description, it re-organized the discursive fields through which responses to the destruction of the twin towers could be articulated and led them in a fateful direction. Even though other expressions were available, which could have provided competing currencies of description, *war* quickly came to dominate public discourse and ultimately thereby to dominate events.

Journalism, as *the* significant shaping practice within the public sphere, inevitably works with words as its raw material. Whatever keeps the public sphere in place and works to change it, discourse constitutes the elementary forms of its interchange. Journalists as a profession have various ways of encapsulating the core concerns of their craft. *Write it tight and get it right* might be one neat formulation of their central commitments to precision, accuracy, compression, economy and speed. We can see this as the particular inflection for the public sphere of those underlying maxims of communication first formulated by the linguistic philosopher Grice – the maxim of quality and the maxim of quantity (Grice 1975). The first of these may by summed up as 'do not say what you know to be untrue' (*get it right*) and the second as 'make your contribution as informative as is required for the current purposes of the exchange' (*write it tight*).

Immediate reactions to 9/11: finding words for events

As is well known, the events of 11 September were instantly mediated (and re-mediated) to a mass audience. But although the events – first one and then a second aircraft striking the World Trade Center – were almost instantly visible through images televised to a mass audience, they posed at the outset a problem of verbal description. This has two dimensions. Firstly, the problem of selecting the relevant paradigm of description; and secondly the problem of accumulating enough information to decide which possible paradigm might be relevant.

Reporting an event involving large-scale destruction and fatalities will draw upon established paradigms that influence the course of subsequent coverage. Two obvious paradigms consist of: (a) 'human error/accident disasters' (Chernobyl, for example); and (b) 'natural disasters' (such as hurricanes or earthquakes). The trajectory of coverage will differ under either paradigm. In the first case a dominant theme of coverage is 'what went wrong' and the associated ascription of blame. In the second case a dominant theme is the scale of the disaster and the heroism/resilience of rescuers/survivors. In the immediate aftermath of an event such as 9/11, journalists must select a paradigm often on the basis of fragmentary and changing information.

In the case of broadcasters, in the face of a breaking news story they must interpret an unfolding event for a large audience with only scarce information. The first collision with the World Trade Center could quite feasibly have been presented as an accident; and CNN, for instance, did speculate about the possibility of problems with the guidance system of American Airlines Flight 11. But, as Scannell (2003) shows, CNN was also careful as the event unfolded to limit itself to what the visual evidence could support.

Ex 1

Well you can see these pictures

It's obviously something relatively devastating has happened

And again unconfirmed reports that a plane has crashed into one of the towers there

We are efforting more information on this subject as it becomes available to you.

(Scannell 2003)

Once the second tower had been hit, however, the event would have to be reclassified as in some way deliberate or planned; and description would begin to move from the paradigm of accident to one of attack or assault with implications of fatalities in the hundreds. Again, however, as Scannell (2003) shows, whatever the pressures of the moment, CNN continued to restrain its account to what could be seen on camera or what could be supported by the eye-witness accounts of those with different vantage points on the scene.

Ex 2

We can see a billowing smoke rising and I'll tell you that I can't see that second tower. But there was a cascade of sparks and fire.

(Scannell 2003)

Within minutes, of course, the towers would collapse and the commentary begins to suggest a pattern behind the scene of devastation.

Ex 3

But just look at that

That is about as frightening a scene as you will ever see

Again this is going on in two cities

We have a report that there is a fire at the State Department as well and that is being evacuated

So we've got fires at the Pentagon (.) evacuated

The White House (.) evacuated on the basis of what the secret service described as a credible terrorist threat

We have two explosions (.) we have two planes hitting the World Trade Centre here in New York

And what this second explosion was that took place about (.)

A part of that would be the south tower has apparently collapsed.

(Scannell 2003)

CNN at an early stage begins to display a caption in its coverage, 'America under attack'. But their difficulty, and that of other live continuous news outlets, is primarily in the first instance a problem of description – how to render what is happening/has happened in words that are adequate to the scene. More specifically they have to furnish a description that conforms to the maxim of quality (Grice 1975): 'do not say what you know to be untrue'; and, more particularly, do not put into the public domain something which might prove to be drastically wrong. Both Scannell (2003) and

Carey (2002) make the point that, despite the problems of description, within only a few hours of the event major broadcasters such as ABC in the US and the BBC in the UK had arrived at a fairly comprehensive account of the disaster, the contours of which remained subsequently unchanged. But journalists – broadcasters, news agencies – have to struggle to 'get it right'.

Adequacy of response to an unfolding scene and the maxim of quantity

If, initially, the problem of description is mainly one of 'quality' – of accuracy, of 'getting it right', of not saying what will turn out to be untrue – it soon becomes in Gricean terms a problem of 'quantity': *make your contribution as informative as is required for the current purposes of the exchange* (Grice 1975).

This core principle can be re-stated for the public sphere as the *principle of discursive amplification*:

> Do not simply re-iterate what has been said before: make a stronger statement rather than a weaker one if the audience is interested in the extra information that could be conveyed by the stronger.

News coverage by definition must purvey 'new' stories; and, when many journalists in a variety of media converge on the same event, they cannot simply re-iterate what has already been said. They must seek to provide not only 'the latest' (and we could say 'the strongest') but also 'the exclusive' version of it, thereby distinguishing their report from others in the information market. Indeed, any speaker/writer reacting in public to the events must assume within the space of a few hours that hardly anyone in the audience can be ignorant of the basic parameters of the disaster. For this reason an utterance such as

Ex 4

Two passenger airliners have separately crashed into the twin towers of the World Trade Centre and a third passenger airliner has crashed into the Pentagon.

(constructed example)

soon becomes inadequate because it simply reiterates what everyone can by now be already assumed to know. Any utterance in the aftermath quickly needs to supply 'new' as well as 'given' information. One strategy for journalists and public figures alike is to move up a scale producing utterances of greater strength and scope.

Descriptions – most especially in the public sphere, where many expressions may be circulating about the same event – can be understood as involving scalar expressions, ranging from weak to strong. Consider Tables 18.1 and 18.2.

Table 18.1

	the World Trade Centre
	Manhattan
	New York
An attack/assault on	America
	the people of America
	democracy
	civilization
	humanity

Table 18.2

A bad act
A wicked act
An evil act
A barbaric act
An act of war

In each table the first expressions in the series, as they apply in a temporally unfolding context, quickly become unusable: whatever point on the scale from which an expression is selected must soon give way to pressure from a perceived stronger point. The movement from 'weaker' to 'stronger' may take place in a variety of ways. It may be from smaller in scope to larger ('attack on New York' → 'attack on America') from concrete to abstract ('attack on America' → 'attack on freedom') from weakly evaluative to strongly evaluative ('day of devastation' → 'day of infamy'). In the case of Table 18.1, for instance, it is noticeable that progress along the scale entails a movement from the literal to the metaphorical (by synecdoche) where the World Trade Center comes to stand for the district (Manhattan) which comes to stand for the City (New York) and the City for the Nation and the Nation for Humanity: that is, the terms of literal description are quickly exhausted by the requirement to make the strongest relevant claim.

This process can clearly be seen at work in the statements both of journalists and the public figures to whom they turned for comment. First of all, let us consider the press, as captured in headlines across America.[1]

Fixing the terms of description: newspaper headlines on 11 and 12 September

If the problem of the live broadcaster is the maxim of quality, 'efforting more information to you' (CNN) and *getting it right*, the problem faced by newspapers is somewhat different. Headlines, especially, make features of an event salient and thematize them in irrevocable ways.[2]

Even as early as day one, 11 September itself, many newspapers managed to produce editions devoted to the attacks on the World Trade Center. Headlines with *attack* as the nodal term[3] accounted for over 40 per cent of all headlines on the first day of the tragedy. The single-word headline *Attack* or *Attacked* occurred 14 times – and it also figured in expanded versions such as *America attacked* (13 times), *U.S. attacked* (13 times) and *Under attack* (nine times) as well as in versions such as *U.S./America under attack* (13 times). *Attack* was the dominant concept.

The second dominant concept was *terror*. This was, indeed, the most common free-standing headline, occurring 21 times. It also occurred in combinations such as *Terror attack(s)* (three times), *Terrorist acts/attacks* (five times) and *Day of terror* (six times). Overall, *terror* as a nodal term accounted for 30 per cent of all headlines datelined 11 September. Thus, between them, these two concepts – *terror* and *attack* – account for nearly three-quarters of all headlines on the first day.

The remaining quarter is composed of a medley of node terms such as *Horror, Chaos, Disaster, Infamy, Unthinkable, Devastation, Bastards* and expansions such as *Day of Horror. War* occurs four times in expressions such as *Act(s) of War* or *Rumours of War.*

The consistency of reaction – the pervasive repetition of nodal terms – is striking, even allowing for syndication and the necessary reliance on common sources. And the same consistency carries over into the satellite concepts. Over a third of all headlines on this first day figured *America(n)* or *U.S.* as in *Attack on America* (11 times) or *U.S. attacked* (13 times) (possibly derived from CNN's caption, *America under attack*), as well as headlines such as *Assault on America, American Tragedy, War on America.*

The emphasis on *America/U.S.* – as a secondary but all-pervasive concept – constitutes a quite particular way of mapping the details of the event, especially of identifying the target, goal or location of the attack. It is one selection from a whole array of possibilities, the full extent of which may be seen from the following attested examples:

Hijacked Jets Destroy Towers
Attacks Level Trade Center
Terrorists Attack World Trade Centre, Pentagon
Terror Hits Pentagon, World Trade Center
Terrorists Strike N.Y., Washington
Terrorists hit N.Y., D.C.
Terror Strikes New York, D.C.
Terrorists hit U.S. (2)
Terror Attacks Strike the U.S.
Terror Strikes at Pulse of U.S.
Attack on America (11)
Struck at Home
Freedom under Fire

This list of alternative formulations forms a paradigm of possibilities moving from the concrete to the abstract. Indeed they display the kinds of routes through which the principle of discursive amplification (*make a stronger statement rather than a weaker*) can be expressed. Thus, although it is literally and factually the case that hijacked jets have destroyed the twin towers of the World Trade Center, we can see how, by a process of substitution or metaphorical extension, these concrete entities in a reflex application of the principle come to stand for abstract notions of America, the United States and freedom itself. And it is noticeable that the more abstract formulation is broadly preferred. Thus, when the target or goal of the attack is formulated in the headline this is much more commonly in general or abstract terms rather than particular ones. The same point can be made about agency. One or two headlines are relatively specific (*Hijacked Jets Destroy Towers* or *Terrorists Attack World Trade Centre, Pentagon*) but more usually if the action is referred to an origin, then it is encoded in abstract terms – for example, *Terror hits home*.

With the dawn of the second day, several hours have now elapsed since the destruction of the twin towers and many papers are now producing their second or perhaps third edition. However, with the lapse of time a wider range of responses than on the first day now begins to be elaborated. The most common response, '*Terror*', is carried over from before; but it now accounts for 18 per cent rather than 30 per cent of the headlines. '*Attack*' also figures prominently, but it has dropped from over 40 per cent to 12 per cent. New nodal concepts begin to squeeze out previously dominant nodal concepts and diversify the original fairly uniform reaction – thus *Evil* (8.5 per cent) and *War* (11 per cent) make their appearance. Secondary or satellite concepts are *America/U.S.* (featuring in 13 per cent of headlines), *Nation* (in 10 per cent) and *Day* (in 9 per cent). Roughly half of all headlines drew on the concepts of *terror*, *attack*, *evil* and *war*, either singly or in combination with each other or with the secondary concepts of *America, nation, day*. Examples would be:

> *Evil*
> *Day of Evil*
> *War*
> *Act of War*
> *Attack*
> *Attack on America*
> *Terror*
> *Day of Terror*

The remaining headlines in a variety of forms strike a common, sombre, note: *Infamy* (eight times) *Horror* (four), *Outrage, Tragedy, State of Shock, We Mourn, Unyielding Anger*. These mostly express an emotional state and/or a moral reaction. In addition, however, considerations of the death toll and questions of responsibility begin to be raised, as for example in *Death Count Begins* and *Who did this?*

Broadly, however, if the prototypical headline for the first day was *Terror attack on America*, by the second day this had become elaborated along the following lines: *Evil terrorist attacks are war against America*.

In retrospect these headlines may seem inevitable: how else could the events be described? But it is important to recognize that they are discursive workings and re-workings of reality and these re-workings raise many important issues.

Firstly, although there were potentially many ways to map the field of the event, on the first day only two versions dominated the coverage.[4] The consistency of press response might be explained in various ways,[5] but no simple explanation seems sufficient to explain how the terms of the description unfolded. They were not shaped, for example, in the first instance by members of the government, most of whom were unavailable for comment. President Bush was from an early stage almost incommunicado in flight aboard Air Force One. He makes one extremely brief statement (ten sentences or so) before leaving the Emma Booker Elementary School, Sarasota, at 9.30 a.m. E.D.T and an equally brief one on touchdown at Barksdale Air Force Base, Louisiana. His first considered public statement was his evening broadcast to the nation at 8.30 p.m. E.D.T. Meanwhile, Vice President Cheney had retired to a White House bunker. Secretary of State Powell was flying back from South America having immediately cut short attendance at a conference of Latin American governments. So it seems unlikely that the press nationwide were following strong cues from government spokespersons.

The broadcast media, as far as the press were concerned, did provide first-hand footage of the unfolding event. But in the earliest stages the terms of description in broadcast commentary were changing as the event unfolded (until CNN's caption, 'America under attack'). So when the press came to fix the semantic contours of the event in headlines on the first day they had little more than visual footage and eyewitness accounts to go on. This makes the uniformity of their response all the more striking and suggests that once the tragedy had unfolded it quickly declared a public, common meaning for itself almost from the outset.

Once the initial terms of the description had become established, however, various discursive pressures came to bear. For one thing, headlines are a competitive form of rhetoric. They are intended to distinguish one newspaper from another rather than repeat what everyone else is saying. For another thing, successive editions of the same paper cannot simply reiterate their own previous headline (or, for that matter, a close competitor's headline). Thus, between day one and day two individual newspapers search for alternative expressions even though unwittingly they may come to choose the same terms as their competitors, as can be seen in examples in Table 18.3.

Secondly, although the term *war* existed alongside three or four other nodal terms in newspaper headlines on the second day, it had a salience that far exceeded its numerical weight. For instance, the term as an element of press reaction is picked up and relayed back to public figures for comment, as will be evident when we consider other sections of the mediated public sphere such as press conferences with Ari Fleischer and broadcast interviews involving Secretary of State Powell.

Table 18.3

September 11 DAY ONE	September 12 DAY TWO	September 13 DAY THREE
San Jose Mercury News Attack	Acts of War	
Tusa World Attack on America	A Day of Infamy	Acts of War
Anchorage Daily News Horrifying	Terror	Acts of War
Augusta Chronicle Attacks Paralyze U.S.	Act of War	
The Charlotte Observer Terror	Attack on America	
Courier Post U.S. Attacked	Act of War	
Dallas Morning News Day of Terror	War at Home	

Indeed, if broadcasters and the press face problems of description early on in the aftermath of large scale disaster, this soon becomes, for figures with accredited status within the public sphere, a problem of reaction – what do I/ we feel about what has happened and what should be done about it. The most obvious source for official reaction in the face of the disaster is the President.

President G. W. Bush's public utterances

Bush's main statement on 11 September is his televised address to the nation on the evening of the attacks. In this address he refers to them as 'acts of terror', 'acts of mass murder', 'terrorist attacks', 'these evil attacks', as we can see in the following excerpts:

Ex 5

(a) Good evening. Today, our fellow citizens, our way of life, our very freedom came under attack in *a series of deliberate and deadly terrorist acts* . . . Thousands of lives were suddenly ended by *evil, despicable acts of terror*.

(b) *These acts of mass murder* were intended to frighten our nation into chaos and retreat. But they have failed; our country is strong.

(c) *Terrorist attacks* can shake the foundations of our biggest buildings, but they cannot touch the foundation of America.

(d) The search is underway for those who are behind *these evil acts*.

(e) I appreciate so very much the members of Congress who have joined me in strongly condemning *these attacks*.

(f) We stand together to win the war against terrorism

(President's televised address to the nation: 11 September 2001)

The initial formulation is at the level of 'acts' (5.a and b), which then becomes 'attacks' (5.c) A single reference to war comes near the end of the address ('we stand together to win *the war against terrorism*' 5.f), but this is couched in metaphorical terms, analogous to expressions such as *war on want, war on poverty, war on drugs*.

However, there is an explicit hardening of this reference over the next two days. On 12 September, day two, the President speaks as follows in a short public statement made at the opening of a meeting of his national security team and explicitly reformulates what has happened as an act of war:

Ex 6

The deliberate and deadly attacks which were carried out yesterday against our country were *more than acts of terror. They were acts of war.* This will require our country to unite in steadfast determination and resolve. *Freedom and democracy are under attack.*

(Televised opening of meeting with national security team: 12 September 2001)

However, by 13 September – day three – this becomes a trajectory of response in which the initial emphasis on acts has now been assimilated to a larger picture in which 'war has been waged against us'

Ex 7

War has been waged against us by stealth and deceit and murder. This nation is peaceful, but fierce when stirred to anger. This conflict was begun on the timing and terms of others. It will end in a way, and at an hour, of our choosing.

(13 September 2001)

Even at this point it should be noted that Bush's utterances avoid describing America's response as one of war: unnamed others are held to be conducting a war against America but America's response is not referred to precisely as 'war'. War has been waged against America. But America's response is not described in precisely symmetrical terms.

These are scripted comments from Bush. There is no direct interchange between Bush and journalists in the days immediately following 11 September. His comments do, however, resonate throughout the public sphere.

Press mediation of Bush's statements: newspaper headlines on 12 September

Their impact, indeed, was profound. Out of 163 headlines on 12 September close to one-third of them are clearly derived from one or other Presidential address. In some cases this is made clear through attribution, as in:

Bush: 'Today, our nation saw evil'

In other cases citation marks are used, but without explicit attribution, though the wording may be found to correspond exactly with the text of one or other address, as in:

'Our Nation Saw Evil' (six times)
'Bring them to justice'
'Unyielding Anger'
'Acts of War' (three times)

Elsewhere, sub-editors adopt forms of indirect quotation or summary but with Bush clearly acknowledged as the source, as in:

Bush says good will prevail
Bush vows revenge (two times)

Sometimes the quotation is precise:

Acts of Mass Murder

Sometimes it is less exact:

'Freedom itself was attacked'

Thus, in the newspapers of 12 September there was much quotation from, and allusion to, the two Presidential addresses, ranging from 'evil' (13 times overall) to 'freedom (being) under attack' (three times) (as well as frequent citation of America/US/the nation in satellite positions). The term with the most resonance, however, was *war*. This was adopted in quotation no less than 15 times in headlines on 12 September alone.

As we have seen, what Bush said on the morning of 12 September was

Ex 7
    The deliberate and deadly attacks which were carried out yesterday against our country were more than acts of terror. They were acts of war . . . But we will not allow this enemy to win the war . . .

In headlines this became variously:

'Acts of War' (three times)
Acts of War (twice)
'An Act of War' (three times)
An Act of War
Act of War (four times)

'Act of War'
'This is War'

Thus, while a great deal of what Bush said in his two addresses came to be echoed in the headlines, the phrase that was most decisively echoed was his reference to war.

There is no doubt then that all these references to *war* can be traced directly back to Bush. It does not follow from that, however, that every reference to war derives from Bush. One semantic thread in the headlines that we have not much discussed is the self-conscious recognition by journalists of the events as somehow epochal and apocalyptic. Almost from the moment of the attacks 11 September becomes a historic transition point. The following headlines, for instance, are from the day itself.

A Day of Terror
Day of Terror (seven times)
Day of Horror
Darkest Day (twice)
Day of Hell
A Day of Devastation
A New Day of Infamy

By 12 September this thread becomes even more pronounced:

Day of Death
The Day After (twice)
Our Worst Day
The Longest Day
Day of Terror (three times)
A Day of Infamy (twice)
A New Day of Infamy (twice)
New Day of Infamy
INFAMY (twice)

The references to infamy directly echo, not President Bush in fact, but President Roosevelt's address to Congress on the day following the Japanese attack on Pearl Harbor when he began:

Yesterday, December 7, 1941 – a date which will live in infamy – the United States of America was suddenly and deliberately attacked by naval and air forces of the Empire of Japan.

Thus the 9/11 references to a new day of infamy rest upon a historical parallel and suggest the emergence instantly in the public sphere of a sense of the event as epochal. It is worth noting also, of course, how President Roosevelt closed his address to Congress in 1941.

I ask that Congress declare that since the unprovoked and dastardly attack by Japan on Sunday, December 7, a state of war has existed between the United States and the Japanese Empire.

The resemblances between the attack on Pearl Harbor in 1941 and the attacks on the Twin Towers and the Pentagon on 9/11 are many, particularly at the level of shock, surprise, loss of life, explosive destruction and the sense of unprovoked attacks. What is less obvious, perhaps, is the way in which the historical analogy, once articulated, provided a ready frame for the emerging discourse of war. It is understandable that whatever the American President said in the immediate aftermath of 9/11 would be widely reported – all the more so in the American press. That his references to war, however, should be so immediately highlighted in headlines suggests that the press were already predisposed to single them out for attention and repetition, fuelled by the principle of discursive amplification. At the same time, it must be stressed that on-the-record public presidential utterances have by this point only invoked war as a term of description of what has been done ('an act of war against us') not as a term of response. This may be obscured in the brevity of a headline such as *'This is War'* but other sections of the public sphere are not prepared to let the term pass unscrutinized. Two kinds of immediate public scrutiny took place: (a) broadcast interviews of senior administration figures; (b) press briefings including question-answer sessions with journalists.

Public utterances of Secretary of State Powell

Powell was at a conference of Southern American states on the morning of 11 September. He flew back almost immediately, giving a press briefing on board his plane in which he referred to what had happened as *this cowardly attack* and as *a well coordinated, extensive assault*. (Both the Pentagon and the World Trade Center had by this time been hit.) On day two, 12 September, he gave several interviews – to NBC, ABC, National Public Radio and CNN among others. 'War', proves to be a constant theme of the exchanges. NBC, for instance, refer to a poll in which '92 percent said they would support it [military action in retaliation] even if it meant entering a war', before asking 'is the US Government prepared to enter a war against these terrorists and wouldn't that entail committing ground troops to find them, weed them out?' ABC approach the theme as follows:

Ex 8

But we know there is so much anger welling up in the country right now. I've got the Daily News here, the New York Daily News, which has a headline: 'It's War.' First of all, is it war, as you see it? And if it's Usama bin Laden, what is going to work against him?

National Public Radio raise the issue as follows:

Ex 9

Secretary Powell, the newspaper headlines in New York today, a lot of them, screamed the word 'war.' I wonder, is that appropriate? Do we regard this as the equivalent to war?

Three things are striking about these references to war. Firstly, it is the questioner who introduces the term and offers it to Powell for comment. Secondly, they do so on the basis of its prior circulation in the public sphere through opinion polls, for instance, or headlines. Thus, the term has already become established within a day of the attacks. Thirdly, the questioner typically requests clarification about the use of the term and its implications: 'is [the word] war appropriate?', 'is it war, as you see it?', 'wouldn't that entail committing ground troops?' It is not immediately obvious to the questioners what it can mean.

Scrutiny of the term becomes even more scrupulous the next day, 13 September. Here is a multiple question from one journalist at an on-the-record briefing by Powell to the press

Ex 10

You spoke about building a coalition and you talk about tools such as the NATO Article V and the UN resolution, are you speaking about war in a legal sense? Are you ready to declare war on this candidate, Usama bin Laden? Or another candidate? And are you expecting these organizations to join you much as you did during the Gulf War in such a war? And are you worried that using the language of war would carry with it specific guidelines as per war that you're not willing or able to follow?

Powell's answers are overwhelmingly circumspect. Initially, he avoids using the term. He says: 'we want to respond'; 'you don't attack America like this and get away with it'; the President 'will look at every option he has available to him to respond militarily'; 'let's not think that one single counter-attack will rid the world of terrorism'; but he avoids saying: 'yes, we are at war.' When finally he does use the term he attributes it to others. It is 'the American people', for instance, who understand 'that this is a war', says Powell, adding that this understanding may not correspond to a legal definition. And when Powell accepts in the face of a question that he too sees it as a war he immediately qualifies the statement with the formulation 'we've got to respond *as if* it is a war'. So Powell displaces ownership of the expression away from himself to others. And he also shifts the originating action of war away from his own side to an invisible, unnamed protagonist while simultaneously extending the scope of the target: it's a war not just against the United States. 'It's a war against civilization. It's a war against all nations that believe in democracy.'

Indeed, in his own discourse, this key White House figure (and no other figure from the White House engaged with the public through the media to anything like the same extent in the 24 hours following the attacks), the lineage of description moved from describing the events as *an attack, attacks, an assault*, initially on *innocent people*, the *World Trade Center* and the *Pentagon*. It then moves to extend the focus of the attack to the nation, as in *a well-coordinated, extensive assault against the United States* or *you don't attack America like this and get away with it*.

Finally, however, this vocabulary allows for the notion of response to be articulated in terms of *counter-attack*:

Ex 11

> Let's not think that one single counter-attack will rid the world of terrorism of the kind we saw yesterday. This is going to take a multi-faceted attack along many dimensions: diplomatic, military, intelligence, law enforcement.

It is from this discursive platform, so to speak, that *attacks* become upgraded to *acts of war*, as in:

Ex 12

> yes, we believe that acts of war have been committed against the American people, and we will respond accordingly

The trajectory of description may be summarized broadly as follows:

1. Cowardly attack against innocent people
   ↓
2. Extensive assault against the United States
   ↓
3. Acts of war against the American people

Thus, we can summarize Powell's public utterances as also prone to discursive amplification – as moving up a scale of intensity of reaction that seeks not to minimize the enormity of the event but to keep in step with the scale of public response fed back to him by journalists in an extended round of interviews. By the time the term has become pervasively established it is noticeable that Powell refers the expression to the President as the ultimate source: 'the President is speaking about war'; 'the President believes that it was an act of war against us'.

In general the path of the term through the public sphere starts primarily with Bush at 8.30 in the evening of 11 September and again in an amplified fashion at 10.30 E.D.T the next morning. Newspapers highlight it in headlines and it becomes material for scrutiny in interviews and briefings with the press. While Bush, himself, only speaks in scripted situations, there were, however, daily briefings by his spokesperson Ari Fleischer.

Press reaction to the Bush statements: press briefings with presidential spokesperson – Ari Fleischer

Broadcast interviews with public figures, especially politicians, tend to be adversarial in mode (see Clayman and Heritage 2002). White House press briefings tend to be all the more so (Smith 1990). A major focus of adversarial questioning in the days that followed 9/11 was the term *war*. Journalists invoke prior usage by key actors (such as the President or the Secretary of State) in another context and pose questions to Fleischer about how such usage works. Thus

Ex 13

Q Ari, in terms of the President's statement this morning *that this was an act of war*, ... Was it a threat against the head of this country that elevated it to that level?

(12 September 2001, press briefing)

Ex 14

Q But why not use *the word 'war'* last night in his televised address to the nation? What changed overnight to ratchet up that rhetoric?

(12 September 2001, press briefing)

Several further questions focus precisely on the issue of language.

Ex 15

Q Ari, given the President's language today, is there any discussion here of asking Congress for *a declaration of war*?

(12 September 2001, press briefing)

In this context, at least, the press corps appear to have been alert to the implications of references to war. Subsequent questions at the same briefing ask

Ex 16

Q ... how can you *declare war* against a nation when you don't know the nation involved?

(12 September 2001, press briefing)

Ex 17

Q You don't *declare war* against an individual, surely.

(12 September 2001, press briefing)

Does an act of war lead to a declaration of war? Or, as another journalist puts it, does the President need a declaration of war to go after known terrorists?

Ex 18

Q Does he feel he has to have *a declaration of war* to go after known terrorists?

(12 September 2001, press briefing)

Ex 19

Q Ari, can I ask again, by saying that *these are acts of war*, what exactly does that mean practically, when the President says that? Where does that take him?

(12 September 2001, press briefing)

In these exchanges, attempts to clarify the sense and implication of any reference to 'war' lead the press corps to offer candidate frameworks of interpretation in which the expression has narrow or precise definitions. One way of doing this is to embed the term in a legal or constitutional discourse in order to give the term a candidate, narrower sense. In effect, a journalist, by suggesting the relevance of the legal framework, opens up further questions in which the implications of this framework can be pursued. This step goes further than merely narrowing the meaning of the expression. For, if the legal framework applies, then we are bound by its terms – and certain implications will by definition follow.

Fleischer develops three kinds of response to questions about the use of the term, 'war'.

- There is no precedent for the events of 11 September. Language is struggling to catch up with reality so the available vocabulary only imperfectly applies. See for example his comment 'this is also a different situation from situations our nation has faced in the past . . . And it is a *different type of war than it was*, say, when you knew the capital of the country that attacked you.'

- Legal/constitutional discussions are in process. Nothing has yet been finalized, so the terms have not been fixed: 'And the President will continue to work with Congress on any appropriate measures at the appropriate time . . . So we will continue to work with the Congress on appropriate language on the appropriate time.' And again later, 'that's why I indicated that we would continue to work with the Congress on appropriate language at the appropriate time.' And further 'Again, anything dealing with Congress is something that the President will work Congress on, appropriate language at the appropriate time' (*sic*).

- A third line of response from Fleischer invokes the President's own personal manner of speaking. Because the President uses 'ordinary language' not 'technical language', his utterances should be judged in non-specialist terms: thus . . . 'the United States was attacked. American soil was attacked. And the President will describe this, as he always has and he always does, in a frank and forthright fashion.' And elsewhere: 'The words the President used speak for themselves.' This is an implicit appeal to everyday norms. Fleischer can be seen as trying to return the term 'war' from the domain of specialist, professional, military-legal concerns to the taken-for-granted domain of the 'lifeworld': the President is a plain man speaking plain language. The populist dimension of this kind of response is even more evident in the following reaction from Fleischer: 'I think the American people know that when the United States is attacked in the manner it was attacked, *this is an act of war*. And I think there is no other way to describe it. And I think that's what the American people expect from their President, is a President who will talk with them straight and direct about it.'[6]

Clearly questions of consistency might be raised about trying to maintain all these positions simultaneously: if the words the President used speak for themselves, then why is it difficult to match words with the event, and why is it necessary to work on the appropriate language with Congress? The potential for contradiction does not prevent Fleischer trying to combine two kinds of response in consecutive exchanges.

It is impossible to read the transcripts from the 12 September White

House press briefing without a sense of the difficulty posed to the participants by references to war. Whatever the difficulties, however, it is by now clearly established as the key term through which public response is being articulated. Indeed, lengthy exchanges take place next day (13 September) at the White House press briefing between Fleischer and the press corps, which now explore in further detail the legal ramifications of the term. In order to give the flavour of the exchanges I quote some of the questions.

> Ex 20
> Q Can I do a follow on that, Ari, please? *If it is actual war*, as the President and others in the administration have declared, does he indeed not need a *congressional approval to wage war* on anyone?

> Ex 21
> Q Ari, just one more. *Can there be war without a formal national enemy?*

> Ex 22
> Q Ari, *the word 'war'* is being bandied around here so much. But that word, in and of itself, carries such a constitutional connotation, et cetera, and creates a confrontation with Congress, or whatever. Is it possible we'll see a ratcheting down of the rhetoric with the administration?

The crux of the discussion by now has become what kind of resolution will be drafted for Congressional approval: since the President holds the title of Commander in Chief does he need a resolution for any military action; is there a difference between military action and war; to what extent does the War Powers Act apply in this particular case, and so on? It is clear, however, that the three kinds of response offered by Fleischer a day earlier are now narrowed down to one: 'we're working with Congress on the language.' And the term 'war' has become embedded decisively – in this arena of the public sphere, anyway – in a discourse of law and constitutional process. In other words, the US is going to war and the legal and constitutional implications of this are being addressed.

Conclusions

What we see, therefore, at the level of public discourse is the term *war* (as in 'act of war') emerging by discursive amplification out of the difficulties of describing a tragic and horrific event. It then begins to echo and re-echo within the public sphere partly because it lends itself easily to well-established figurative as well as literal usages. Indeed, its first mentions are *not* literal but manifestly figurative, as in Bush's first address to the nation, 'we stand together to win the war against terrorism'. Once established, its status is problematic to public figures such as Powell or Fleischer in their exchanges with journalists. Powell, for instance, tends to handle the term pseudo-analogically, *as if*, at arms length. For Fleischer, it is demanded by the unprecedented nature of the attack, it speaks for itself; and if not, then the White House 'is working with Congress on the appropriate language'. Within hours of the attacks on the World Trade Center, *war* has developed a discursive momentum, a trajectory as Silberstein (2002) calls it, which will culminate later in the tragedies of Afghanistan and Iraq. In all of this it is most important to note that discursive mechanisms are driving events as much as events, administrations or powers are driving the discourse. Newspapers, for instance, do not simply ventriloquize the President's utterances. They do so selectively. In his first relatively extended address after the collapse of the twin towers, for instance, Bush refers to what has happened in various ways: as 'evil, despicable acts of terror', for example, and as 'acts of mass murder'. The next day there are 30 references to 'terror' in headlines, 14 references to 'evil' but only one reference, by direct quotation, to 'acts of mass murder'. Thus, some formulations resonate through the public sphere; others do not. *War, evil, terror* and *attack* all resonate within press headlines. *Mass murder* does not. *War* is a focus of questions to Powell and to the President's press spokesperson. Forensic issues do not provide anything like the same initial focus.

It is not just that *war* flooded out the other available terms of response. It did so in defiance of precedent. Previous atrocities by non-state terrorist groups such as the IRA, the Italian Red Brigades, the Baader-Meinhof group, ETA, the PLO, had mostly an apparently clear line of responsibility. The group in question would claim the action, as part of military-type hostilities against the State or a system and would seek to justify its violence in terms of a military campaign made necessary by the collapse of politics. States have responded, however, denying any claims to military-political status on the part of such groups, insisting instead on treating them as in breach of civil and criminal law. Indeed, there have, for instance, been intense and protracted struggles over prisoner status with terror groups attempting to claim for themselves special rights to military detention. In all of this a basic asymmetry of approach has been maintained. The terrorist group resorts to violence against the State as part of an armed struggle for political ends (equality, independence, the overthrow of capitalism). The state invokes criminal law in response.

In the case of 9/11, however, a strange reversal occurs. No group claims responsibility so the origins of the action are shadowy. No demands seem to be made and the meaning of the event has to be inferred from its details. Into this semantic vacuum the State steps and attributes responsibility to a shadowy group who it describes as being at war. The action thereby is lifted out of the domain of criminality into the domain of warfare. On this occasion the State, which normally refuses to grant warlike status to terrorist actions, now grants it when no request was made.

And clearly a great deal hangs by this choice. A world of difference exists between the dominant paradigm for considering the events of 11 September as 'an act of war' and an alternative paradigm such as 'mass murder'. Quite simply, 'mass murder' identifies the act in criminal terms, locating it within a particular set of jurisdictions, made subject to the internal operations of a sovereign state's systems. It is the subject of police enquiry and investigation. The criminals must be identified and brought to justice. Individual responsibility and guilt must be established and sentence passed. It defines the terms of the response within the domain of police investigation, criminal justice and the safeguards of law.

In the event, of course, in the case of 11 September there were many difficulties with the legal/forensic route. The immediate perpetrators were identified quite early but had killed themselves in the performance of the crime; so there was no way they could be brought to justice. Others who may be associated with the crime with different degrees of complicity are difficult to hold to account: their identity is in doubt; their whereabouts are in doubt; and even if this information can be provided, they are quite likely to be living somewhere beyond the jurisdiction of the US courts.

The discourse of war – as we have seen – offers a quite different route. Actions and reactions are understood in military terms operating at the level of the sovereign state and its relations with other states (or state-like entities).[7] In this context, death and injury are considered unavoidable from the outset of hostilities – whether in terms of innocent or military fatalities, civilian casualties and so on. Under military discipline questions of responsibility become dispersed and attenuated. Criminal justice becomes suspended. As Sontag (2004) has observed: 'those held in the extra-legal American penal empire are "detainees" . . . An interminable war inevitably suggests the appropriateness of interminable detention.'

The purpose of this chapter has been to demonstrate that the discourse of war became established in significant areas of the public sphere with great rapidity after the tragedy of 11 September. There were other ways of talking about the event but none gained such general currency so rapidly as talk of war. But the discourse of war unfolded – even if the time frame was narrow – with difficulty. It was not clear what *war* meant and journalists posed searching questions about its applicability. Can there be war without a formal national enemy? How can you *declare war* against a nation when you don't know the nation involved? 'You can't declare war against an individual, surely?' Does the President feel he has to have *a declaration of war* to go after known terrorists? Once the talk of war had become established, a national enemy had then to be identified – first Afghanistan (or the Taliban), then Iraq (or the regime). In the first instance there was at least some apparent association via Osama bin-Laden and Al-Quaeda with the Twin Towers. In the case of Iraq there is no connection.

There has been much commentary (see, for example Baudrillard 2002 and Zizek 2002) regarding the different character of 9/11 compared with previous terrorist outrages. But it is not just the action itself that is new. It is also the reaction, the new symmetry between action and reaction, and how the talk turned to war within hours of the event. Condaleeza Rice has commented recently: 'the attacks that day meant the idea of the nation being at war was no longer a figure of speech.' This is disingenuous. The first resort to the term *war* after 9/11 was precisely as a figure of speech. Amplified in headlines it quickly became something else, although some journalists who used it also questioned it and neither they nor other public figures could be clear what it meant. Nonetheless a momentum was building that would lead tragically to Baghdad, Fallujah, Najaf and Abu Ghraib prison. Stumbled into as a figure of speech to respond to a horrific event, the rhetoric paved the way to a literal war – but one whose connection with 9/11 has only ever been loosely justified in rhetoric and never in fact. In this process journalism was both resistant and complicit.

Notes

1 Data on headlines are drawn from an invaluable comprehensive archive at http://www.september11news.com, which provides 181 cover pages from across the US for 11 September, 163 for 12 September and 13 for 13 September.

2 Headlines here are treated as a discursive system, in which certain rules implicitly govern their construction. See Montgomery *et al.* (2000: 333–43).

3 In treating the cover or front pages of the US press immediately after 11 September, I distinguish between nodal lexical items and satellite lexical items. Key terms, such as *attack* appeared frequently as self-standing lexical items. But other terms such as *America* also played an important role in mapping the event and responding to it, though they did not figure as self-standing items. In other words *America* (a satellite term) was not possible as a headline, but *Attack* was, as was *Attack on America*.

4 Although there were about 80 different headlines across America (in 181 newspapers), there was an enormous amount of repetition and a very small number of terms – *Terror, Attack, America/US* – were overwhelmingly repeated.

5 For example, (a) journalists were in thrall to a limited number of sources; or (b) journalists were influenced by US government spokespersons who uniformly dispersed the same message(s); or (c) the event(s) had an intended meaning that was immediately clear at the outset; or (d) journalists share between them the same sense-making practices and so independently but more or less simultaneously adopted the same interpretations of the event. The problem with all these explanations is that while they may explain the uniformity of response on day one they cannot explain the variation in response on day two.

6 This is rather different from Powell's rather more intellectual attempt to avoid legal definitions by trying to define the word in new or different ways: 'I am speaking about *war*; the President is speaking about *war* as a way of focusing the energy of America and the energy of the international community against this kind of activity. And *war* in some cases may be military action, but it can also be . . .'

7 Others have developed in detail the argument that terrorism should be dealt with as a crime. See, for instance, Barker (2003: 112), 'The war on terrorism discounts the political side of terrorism . . . A better response would vigorously combat terrorism as a crime.' See also Chomsky (2003: 187–217). The point at issue here is more local and particular – how the notion of war became mobilized in response to 9/11 to the exclusion of other kinds of response.

References

Barker, J. (2003) *Terrorism*. London: New Internationalist Publications.

Baudrillard, J. (2002) *The Spirit of Terrorism*. London: Verso.

Carey, J. (2002) American Journalism On, Before and After September 11, in B. Zelizer and S. Allan (eds) *Journalism after September 11*. London: Routledge.

Chomsky, N. (2003) *Hegemony or Survival*. London: Hamish Hamilton.

Clayman, S. and Heritage, J. (2002) *The News Interview*. Cambridge: Cambridge University Press.

Cole, P. and Morgan, J. (eds) (1975) *Syntax and Semantics 3: Speech Acts*. New York: Academic Press.

Grice, H. P. (1975) The Logic of Conversation, in P. Cole and J. Morgan (eds) *Syntax and Semantics 3: Speech Acts*. New York: Academic Press, pp. 41–58.

Habermas, J. (1989) *The Structural Transformation of the Public Sphere*. Cambridge: Polity Press.

Montgomery, M., Durant, A., Fabb, N., Furniss T. and Mills, S. (2000) *Ways of Reading*, second edition. London: Routledge.

Scannell, P. (2003) 'Broadcasting 9/11' working paper for broadcast task seminar held at Ross Priory, Scotland.

Silberstein, S. (2002) *War of Words*. London: Routledge.

Smith, C. T. (1990) *Presidential Press Conferences: A Critical Approach*. New York: Praeger.

Sontag, S. (2004) What have we done? *Guardian G2*, 24 April, pp. 1–5.

Zelizer, B. and Allan, S. (eds) (2002) *Journalism after September 11*. London: Routledge.

Zizek, S. (2002) *Welcome to the Desert of the Real*. London: Verso.

|19

Banal journalism

The centrality of the 'us-them' binary in news discourse

Prasun Sonwalkar

- Whose interests do the news media uphold?
- Why do journalists fail to go beyond sporadic reportage of events and issues involving minorities?
- Even if individual journalists recognize the limited range of events and issues they cover, how do their cultural/ethnic background and socialization in newsrooms influence any remedial measures?
- Is news coverage dependent on journalists' perception of *who* is affected, involved or interested?
- What lies beneath the commonplace terminology of 'us' and 'them' that features so prominently in newsroom discourse, as well as news content?

Pick up any newspaper or watch any television bulletin. You will see a range of news items, impressively produced, with (usually) well written text, compelling images and eye-catching graphics. Sure, it is 'news' concerning, say, the 'war on terrorism', David Beckham, John Kerry, a rise in house prices, and so forth but it will probably not really surprise you. The range of events and issues presented day after day in newspapers and bulletins is inevitably in the realm of the expected. It is habit-forming, almost addictive (is the media the new opium of the masses?). Over days, months and years, you get used to a particular newspaper, to its style, to the range of events and issues it covers. It grows on you – you know that it will always give you what you expect. Indeed, it rarely provides fare that is out of the routine.

Scratch the surface or read between the lines, however, and a different picture of journalism emerges. It is not so much a case of the way certain issues, events and sections of society are 'represented' by journalists. In fact, the very presence of news about the life situations of a large segment of population in any society is in question. A closer look reveals that focusing on what is usually *not* covered in the news media – events and issues involving various minorities (ethnic, religious, sexual, class and so forth) and their perspectives – may help unpack the way a society is ordered and how journalism facilitates, nurtures and perpetuates dominant value systems. The news media need to be seen by students of journalism studies as an index of cultural power geometry in a society, and how it influences the roots and routes of news production.

The events and issues that rarely figure in news content may be termed the media's 'sphere of invisibility' or what Tuchman (1978) called 'symbolic annihilation'. The selectivity of news largely goes unnoticed because it is routinely presented as normal, day after day. Located within the discourse of production of news, this chapter makes a case for a closer examination of the point of encoding, one stage before raw information becomes news, which later goes on to have 'effects' on readers/viewers.

It is important to perceive journalism as a project that is steeped in intentional and unintentional biases at various levels: selection, language, images, framing, presentation and representation. Like nationalism, journalism is Janus-faced; it purports to adhere to the ideals of modernity but in practice diurnally wallows in being politically incorrect. Of course, journalists would be the first to deny that they primarily cater to the dominant sections of society or that their exertions are invariably dependent on official sources. To some extent, the denials ring true, because it is rare for any journalist to be openly prejudiced towards certain values or sections of society. But the fact remains that news is a 'human construction' (Hall 1982: 148); journalists can scarcely remain untouched by the social and cultural environment in which they function. The bias in news discourse is so institutionalized, naturalized and normalized that it seems benign, boring – and banal.

Caught up in the web of events, tight deadlines and the inherent disposability of their daily output, journalists are rarely able to realize that they routinely ignore large parts of human existence or that willy nilly their exertions end up catering to the elite sections of society. This is the larger 'story' of mainstream journalism. I state this as much from an academic perspective as that of a practitioner, having been part of the whirl for over two decades. The biases are mostly unstated, but not always. Before taking over as the *Times of India*'s correspondent in insurgency-ridden northeast India – a region and its people that are routinely seen as the 'other' in the Indian public sphere – a senior editor remarked to me, not entirely in cynical jest: 'Treat them with the contempt they deserve.'

Banal journalism

Following Billig's (1995) notion of 'banal nationalism', I argue that most of what passes off as mainstream journalism in democratic societies can be called *banal journalism*. One way to unpack this brand of journalism is to use the optic of the socio-cultural binary of 'us' and 'them'. These terms are apparently simple notions; they are invoked in routine conversation and figure often in newspaper headlines. But they reify a deep-rooted and complex structure of values, beliefs, themes and prejudices prevailing in a socio-cultural environment. Announcing the 'war on terrorism' after 11 September, President Bush declared: 'You are either with *us* or against *us* in the fight against terror' (CNN 2001; emphasis added). Here, I want to explore this seemingly simplistic binary and see if it is at all possible for journalists, as Gans (1980: 182) suggests, to 'leave their conscious personal values at home'.

I suggest that mainstream journalism, or banal journalism, is predicated on this key binary of 'us' and 'them'. The newspaper you read or the television bulletin you watch, play similar roles as Billig's surreptitious, limpid flag: 'The metonymic image of banal nationalism is not a flag which is being consciously waved with fervent passion; it is the flag hanging unnoticed on the public building' (Billig 1995: 8). The newspaper may be lying carelessly on the drawing table, the bulletin may be on air as you go about your chores, but you know that that they will always present what is of interest to you, to 'us'. Banal journalism flags the 'us' daily in news columns and television content, without most of us realizing that there is a vast reality out there that is rarely considered newsworthy, even if it involves much violence and terrorism (Sonwalkar 2004).

But banality does not imply being benign – it is not synonymous with harmlessness (Arendt 1963). Banal journalism is hegemonic; it caters to the 'us' and presents one view as *the* worldview of an entire society or nation. After 11 September, this omnipresent but unstated sense of 'us' and 'them' came out of the closet. As Said (2001) observed:

> There really is a feeling being manufactured by their media and the government that a collective 'we' exists and that 'we' all act and feel together, as witnessed by such perhaps unimportant surface phenomena as flag-flying and the use of the collective 'we' by journalists in describing events all over the world in which the US is involved. We bombed, we said, we decided, we acted, we feel, we believe, etc. Of course, this has only marginally to do with reality, which is far more complicated and far less reassuring.
>
> (Said 2001)

The binary informed much of the editorial content in the Western media as 'we' tried to make sense of the event triggered by 'them' (Sreberny 2002). I believe that various academic formulations of news and news values can all be conflated into the notion that *news is essentially about 'us'*, howsoever politically incorrect it may sound. This implies the existence of its subtle but discernible part and counterpart, 'them'. In multicultural democratic societies, the existence and influence of such dichotomies can scarcely be denied. It is hardly a secret which sections of society hold the reins of social, political, economic and cultural power. Since journalists hail from middle-class, educated segments of society, the journalistic community cannot be untouched by the divisive functions of the socio-cultural binary, notwithstanding the demands and claims of being professional and objective in their work routines. According to former editor of the *Guardian*, Alistair Hetherington (1985: 8), the instinctual news value of most journalists simply is: 'Does it interest me?'

A journalist's personal sense of location vis-à-vis the wider socio-cultural environment is crucial to understanding the cut and thrust of journalism practices. At the same time, it is important to *a priori* acknowledge that the sense of 'us' and 'them' is a fact of life in all multicultural societies. This sense is produced or constructed, it is not a given, and is causally linked to the process of nation formation. Despite impressive legal and executive instruments drawn up by multicultural societies such as Britain, the United States or India, who wields power and which sections of society are institutionally at the receiving end, is hardly a secret. As Hartman and Husband (1981: 274) observed, 'there are elements in the British cultural tradition that are derogatory to non-whites', which explains much of the British news coverage dominated by the life situations of the Christian, Anglo-Saxon, white and middle-class sections of the population.

The 'us' symbolizes what is popularly called the 'national mainstream'. The 'mainstream' may be defined as a relative commonality of outlook and values that the media believes exists in its target audience, which it also circularly cultivates among its readers/viewers. The 'us' naturally elides with these dominant sections of society. Journalists are drawn from the 'national mainstream' and circularly cater to this section of society and its value system. Thus, events and issues that do not fall within the paradigm of interest to this section are unlikely to be considered by journalists as news-worthy. Sore that the influential English-language Indian national press routinely ignores the life situation of people in insurgency-ridden northeast, a senior government official (NRK) said: 'There are three major aspects of human relationships: love me, hate me and ignore me. The third is the most painful. At least, recognize my existence' (Sonwalkar 2003: 175).

Shoemaker and Reese (1996: 64) observed that it is the 'individual' aspect of news production that lies at the core of the many levels of influences on media content. This 'individual' aspect, like others, is framed within the broad social structure and is subject to the prevailing socio-cultural power geometry. Hence, '. . . none of these actors – the individual, the organization or the social institution – can escape the fact that it is tied to and draws sustenance from the social system' (Shoemaker 1991: 75). I argue that at the encoding stage itself, an event or issue first has to cross the filter of this binary before it is considered newsworthy. Professional values such as objectivity, accuracy, ethics or impartiality run secondary to this primary 'gate'. However, I must hasten to add that this terminology of 'us' and 'them' should not be seen as pejorative, conspiratorial or insular; the journalist may well reply: 'But that's the way things are.' The attempt here is to take Hall's (1982: 234) idea of a 'deep structure' functioning as a selective device in news production a step further, and to identify one set of the structure's possible attributes.

▌Binary in news literature

There is a determinism implicit in earlier studies of news production, suggestive of a mechanical process, that if events accord with certain 'news values', they are more likely to become news. This implies a simple input-output, 'cause' (event) and 'effect' (media coverage) equation, as it were. In such a perspective, journalists are seen as cogs in the wheel of news production, mechanically converting information that accords with news values into news content. In such a view – almost reminiscent of the discredited 'hypodermic needle' theory, but in relation to journalists instead of readers – journalists are seen as robots, without a mind of their own, as passive recipients of external event-stimuli.

Figuratively, the relationship implied in the discourse may be presented as in Figure 19.1.

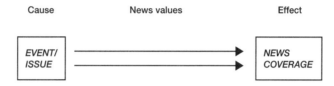

Figure 19.1

There is no room envisaged for the possibility of several events and issues *not* amounting to news even though they may accord with several news values. In such a situation, the 'us-them' binary is helpful in explaining the 'symbolic annihilation' and 'areas of invisibility' in the media. In fact, this binary has some resonance in earlier studies of news production. For example, Hartley (1982) explained the news value of 'meaningfulness' thus:

> *Meaningfulness* (a) Cultural proximity: events that accord with the cultural background of the news-gatherers will be seen as more meaningful than others, and so more liable to be selected. This works in two ways. First, Islamic, third-world and oriental events may not be seen as self-evidently meaningful to Western reporters unlike European, American or even Russian events. Second, within *'our'* culture, events connected with underprivileged or ethnic groups, with regions remote from centralized bases of news organisations, or with specifically working-class culture, will be seen as less intrinsically meaningful than those associated with central, official, literate culture. (b) Relevance: events in far-off cultures, classes or regions will nevertheless become newsworthy if they impinge on the news-gatherer's *'home culture'* – usually in the form of a threat; as with OPEC and the (mostly Arab) countries with oil – their lifestyles, customs and beliefs are suddenly fascinating for Western journalists.
>
> (Hartley 1982: 77; emphasis added)

Allan's (2004) more recent formulation is pertinent:

Cultural specificity: events which conform to the 'maps of meaning' shared by newsworker and news audience have a greater likelihood of being selected, a form of ethnocentrism which gives priority to news about *'people like us'* at the expense of those who *'don't share our way of life'*.

(Allan 2004: 58; emphasis added)

Van Dijk's (1988) observation that 'negativity' is the 'best known' news value, also implies the 'us-them' binary:

(Negative) information is a test of general norms and values. Especially when deviance of various types is involved, it provides *ingroup* members with information about *outgroups or outcasts* and the application of a consensus of social norms and values that helps define and confirm the *own group*.

(Van Dijk 1988: 123; emphasis added)

The binary connects specifically with Schudson's (2000) 'cultural' approach to production of news. The news value of cultural proximity (meaningfulness) is embedded in this approach, and looks at the media as an institution that operates within a given culture or a symbolic system, which shapes the news and in relation to which reporters perform their duties. Based on the Gramscian concept of hegemony, this approach argues that a ruling ideology is not imposed but appears to exist by virtue of an arrived-at consensus. In other words, hegemony works by way of discourse and is embedded in political and economic power (Hall 1982). This approach can also be called a humanist approach because it views journalists and news workers as subjective individuals infused with their own cultures, strengths and weaknesses, and not as cold, robot-like individuals who are supposed to drop their identities the moment they step into their professional shoes.

The media are seen as working within the sphere of consensus in a society (Hallin 1989). According to Hall (1977, 1982), the media simply bring unusual events to the 'map of meaning' so that the audiences may make sense of them – this assumes the existence of a cultural map of the social world that forms the basis of the audience's knowledge. Newspaper sections reflect this cultural map: politics, nation, international, sports, economy/business and so forth. With this arrangement, some spheres, institutions, events and issues come to be privileged. Hall *et al.* (1981) argued that the classification, ranking and ordering of events in themselves indicate clear preferences and interpretations. Certain contexts are rendered 'meaningful' whereas 'normal' and 'abnormal' behaviour is also constructed, which strengthens a common culture. Thus, a particular image of a society is constructed as representing the interests of all; the groups and voices outside this consensus are seen as deviant, dissident or mad. As Van Dijk (1988) perceptively observed, 'the macrodimensions of social structure, history, or culture are enacted or translated at the microlevel of news discourse and its processing'.

Although most journalists try to be objective, impartial and fair in their professional endeavours, their exertions are invariably conducted within a socio-cultural framework, which determines the nature and limits of their activities. A sense of *we-ness* pervades their output from the primary stage of selection, encoding and transmission; this 'we-ness' is largely unstated and unarticulated, but lurks in the background as journalists go about performing their professional activities. A clearer picture of news production (or non-production) emerges when the unstated is brought to the surface. The 'we-ness' is most evident in the coverage of foreign events and issues, as Nossek (2005) observed in a discussion about international political violence:

> (When) political violence is reported and covered, there is already a prior definition by the journalist of the event as some kind of political violence – say, war, terrorism, or a violent demonstration – that predates the reporter's own professional definition. Thus, professional norms become secondary to the national identity of the correspondent covering the story for the newspaper. The definition requires the journalist to decide instantly whether or not it is *our* war of *theirs*, etc. The definition, and the immediate stance adopted as a result, will influence whether the event is selected as news and the way it is covered.
>
> (Nossek 2005; emphasis added)

When the entire nation is taken as the 'us', it is mostly unproblematic to define who might constitute the 'them' – other nations. But within a nation, the location (local, regional, national) and the category of a publication (general, financial, specialist) also defines what journalists may consider to be of interest and newsworthy to 'us', the target audience. For example, journalists of a 'national' newspaper based in the capital may privilege events within the nation according to their sense of 'us', and perceive events and issues of other countries as 'their' events. Only if this sense of 'us' is involved or affected in other countries would the events be deemed newsworthy (for example, the coverage in the London-based national press of British nationals arrested in Gulf countries; or the coverage in the Indian press about achievements of Indian IT expatriates in the west, and so forth). Likewise, journalists working on local newspapers may have a different and more local conception of 'us' and 'them'.

Theorizing 'us' and 'them'

Among the many levels at which the sense of 'us' and 'them' is constructed, we shall look at two: individual and nation. The first point to note about the binary is that it is not rigid, but shifts according to locale, focus and perspective (Sreberny 2002; Elias 1994; Elliott 1986; Shils 1975). For example, the Scots in Edinburgh may consider themselves as the 'us' and the English as 'them', but the situation reverses when viewed from London;

similarly, Hindus and Muslims in India may alternately view each other as 'us' and 'them'. This discursive nature of the binary, however, does not question its existence; it exists in most societies even if it is not spelt out in clear terms: 'a sense of *we-ness* and *they-ness* . . . appears to run through all human societies' (Elliott 1986: 1; emphasis in original). Journalists, breathing the same socio-cultural air, can scarcely remain untouched by the prevailing sense of we-ness and they-ness.

Newsroom conversation is invariably replete with the use of words such as 'us' and 'them'. But they should not be disparaged because they are commonplace, as Elliott (1986: 6) pointed out, because 'they effectively describe the collective feelings or attitudes of individuals who regard themselves as belonging to nations, subnations, social classes, religious sects or any other identity types with a sense of distinctiveness of their own'. The binary features prominently not only in newsroom discourse among news workers but also in news content. The binary – among other binaries (gender, ethnic, religious, sexual, class, caste, and so forth) – enters media discourse as part of the inherent selectivity in the process of news production, but overt examples are also common. Announcing a series of articles on British Islam after 11 September, a full-page announcement in the *Guardian* wondered: 'How much do *we* know about *them*?' (emphasis added). The newspaper did not identify the social groups it considered the 'we' or 'them', but it was evidently addressing its majority white, middle-class, Christian readership, and openly categorizing Muslims as the socio-cultural 'they' of British society. The question seemed to deny the possibility of British Muslims being considered part of the readership of the *Guardian* or the British mainstream. After 11 September, there was a rash of articles in the Western press that openly invoked the parochial sense of 'we' and 'they' (Sreberny 2002). This implies clear identification with certain groups or sections of society.

Journalists are individuals and subject to the same pulls and pressures of identity as others. The problematic of identity has always haunted mankind: Who am I? Where do I belong? Who are my people with whom I can interact? As Smelser (1981: 281) observed, 'The primary good that we distribute to one another is membership in some human community.' A desire to belong, or membership of society, is one of the fundamental characteristics of humankind. It is not rare for journalists to openly identify with their countries (or religion, ethnicity, gender, and so forth). For example, during times of crisis they contribute to the welter of patriotism; for example, the American press's jingoistic coverage of the action in Iraq in 2003 or the Indian press's fervent patriotism during the 1999 conflict in Kargil when India and Pakistan almost went to yet another war. According to Elliott (1986: 11–12):

> (Group) consciousness or a sense of *we-ness* simply springs from the individual's identification with familiars as opposed to strangers . . . (The) essence of *societas* is the sense of *we-ness* which, however, need not be a totality in itself, but may be expressed at different levels and at different strengths.

Every society has a core, or what Shils (1975: 3) termed 'a phenomenon of the realm of values and beliefs. It is the center of the order of symbols, of values and beliefs, which govern the society.' He made the additional point that such a centre is the 'ultimate and irreducible'. In Britain, the centre may well be identified as the white, English, Anglo-Saxon and Christian sections of society while in India, it may constitute the affairs of the Hindi-speaking, Hindu-Muslim majority. Almost all journalists in the London-based 'national' press or the Delhi-based Indian 'national' press are drawn from these sections of society, which indicates certain preferences in recruitment and the desire to uphold and perpetuate certain values in a society, or what Elliott (1986) called 'we-ness' and 'they-ness':

> People only display attitudes of *us* due to an acquired sense of *we-ness* determined largely by a sense of *they-ness* in relation to others . . . (Group) consciousness involves social attachments going beyond personal ones and immediate relatives and friends to embrace unknown individuals conceived to be own kind whom one may not know personally at all . . . except that they are conceived to be own people to whom one belongs, by virtue of shared language, accent, religion or nation. To such people, or the country where they live, one feels a sense of attachment of even greater intensity than for single individuals on whose behalf one would rarely be prepared to die. Group attachment, therefore, imports loyalty and allegiance to *us* in the face of outsiders. (One) notes the correlation of *us* and *them* and the prevalence of both ingroup and outgroup behaviour at the same time.
>
> (Elliott 1986: 8–9)

The sense of 'us' and 'them' is developed through socialization with familiars and strangers as well as through educational texts and the media that reflect the prevailing power relations in society. Discussing Elias's work, Mennell (1992: 121) argued that branding one group as inferior and making it stick was a function of a specific figuration formed by two groups with one another: 'The centrepiece of such a figuration is an uneven, tensile balance of power . . . They are uneven because one group has succeeded in monopolising some power resource.' Elias (1970) suggested that it was impossible to conceive of an individual separate from the socio-cultural environment, but he also recognized that the constituents or the definition of 'us' and 'them' may change over time.

> One's sense of personal identity is closely connected with the 'we' and 'they' relationship of one's group, and with one's position within those units which one speaks as 'we' and 'they'. Yet the pronouns do not always refer to the same people. The figurations to which they currently refer can change in the course of a lifetime, just as any person does himself. This is true not only of all people considered separately, but of all groups and even of all societies. Their members universally say 'we' of themselves and 'they' of other people; but they may say 'we' and 'they' of different people as time goes by.
>
> (Elias 1970: 128)

This discursive binary not only helps understand a society's power geometry but also frames much of the discourse of nations and nationalism. As Smith (1991: 9) noted, 'The homeland becomes a repository of historic memories and associations, the places where "our" sages, saints and heroes lived, worked, prayed and fought. All this makes the homeland unique.' National consciousness involves collective feelings of own kind shared by a majority of the inhabitants, if not all. Elliott (1986) suggested that this consciousness is merely one among several types of group identification, 'the causes of which are basically psychological . . . it is the identification of individuals which matters and their psychological sense of *us* and *them*' (Elliott 1986: 113, 114; emphasis in original). At the macro level, all members of a nation may consider themselves as 'us' and members of other nations as 'them'. But due to the global reality of 'people belonging to groups within groups within groups' (Mennell 1992: 177), the 'us-them' dichotomy problematizes power relations within a nation. The dichotomy is central to the construction of nationhood, as Nag (2001) observed:

> Nations have always been concerned about 'us' as against 'them'. Nations are obsessed with 'self' and discriminate 'the other'. The construction of the national self has always been only vis-à-vis 'the other'. The basis of such construction is differentiation. The 'self' consisted of people who share common cultural characteristics and such commonalities could be measured only by contrasting against those who do not. Thus construction of nationhood is a narcissist practice while nation-building was all about building walls around the 'self' and distancing from 'the other'.
>
> (Nag 2001)

If nations were always formed by focusing on the 'self', and discriminating against the other, the situation has not changed much despite years of governance informed by the principles of modernity. Almost every modern state is characterized by cultural diversity, Parekh (1994: 199) noted, which amounts to 'the presence of different and sometimes incompatible ways of life that seek in their own different ways to preserve themselves.' Thus, the uneven power relations within a nation make the reification and persistence of the socio-cultural binary a *sine qua non* of most nation-states, even though it may not be routinely articulated. The thesis of multiculturalism itself is premised on the belief that minority cultures do not get their due in societies that are dominated by particular socio-cultural groups. As Billig (1995: 175) observed, 'National identities are rooted within a powerful social structure, which reproduces hegemonic relations of inequity.' Journalists, in their routines, help perpetuate such 'hegemonic relations of inequity'.

Conclusion

Below the normative discourses of democracy, multiculturalism and nationalism lies a discursive web of relations reified in the binary of 'us' and 'them'. It is based on material as well as psychological factors. The binary can be a key tool to explore and identify group perceptions and consciousness and, in turn, help unravel banal journalism and explain the coverage and non-coverage of a society's 'other'. Events and issues involving the minorities are likely to be considered newsworthy only if they are seen by journalists as affecting or being of interest to the 'we'.

Usually, the life situations of the minorities may be reflected sporadically as event-centred reportage, but without political, historical and cultural contexts. The binary pervades inter-personal and professional discourse in newsrooms where the affairs of the dominant sections are routinely privileged. A Delhi-based special correspondent of a major Indian newspaper, who wanted to travel to the northeast to cover insurgency-related events, was told by seniors: 'Who is bothered? Why do you bother?' (Sonwalkar 2004: 217). Before an event or issue is considered newsworthy, journalists, by default, ask themselves: *who* is affected? Would it interest *our* readers/ viewers? Only those that do are deemed worthy of coverage.

Revising the earlier equation of news production (Figure 19.1), a more accurate depiction of banal journalism would be that given in Figure 19.2.

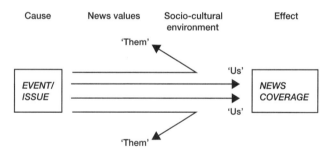

Figure 19.2 Banal journalism.

Thus, even if an event or an issue were to theoretically satisfy the news values, they may not amount to news when passing through the filter of the 'socio-cultural environment' in which the news production takes place. Unless the issue or event is seen as involving, affecting or as being of interest to the 'us', it is unlikely to be considered newsworthy. There is a clear relationship between journalists' professional attitudes and prevailing socio-cultural ethos. As journalists go about their routines, this relationship lurks in the background and, at best, manifests itself in a constant tension between professional norms and their individual socio-cultural backgrounds.

The notion of 'banal journalism' is useful to characterize several such visible and invisible spaces in news discourse. Based on the binary of 'we' and 'they' it can help unravel and explain what lies between the lines and what does not. Much of what passes off as mainstream journalism – with its many spaces of symbolic annihilation – is banal journalism. It is wedded to the status quo and uses the syntax of hegemony. Being an integral part of the power structure, the news media reflect the priorities of the dominant power groupings and in the process, help reinforce prevailing power relations in a given society/culture. Much of what passes off as mainstream journalism has several spaces of symbolic annihilation, and these are presented in a routine, natural and banal manner.

Banal journalism allocates value to events and issues (including those involving violence and terrorism) by preferring some to others. It limits the range of issues and events covered by ignoring alternative perspectives. Banal journalism makes the interests of the 'we' seem routine, and simultaneously it makes the marginalization or exclusion of the 'other' appear natural. Only when events and issues conform to the themes and practices of banal journalism are they accorded media coverage. In many ways, it is based on the real 'imagined community' of the nation: what the journalists understand and *imagine* constitute the 'us' and 'them'. This kind of journalism declares commitment to the ideals of modernity but rarely practises them. In fact, its success lies in the very denial of its existence by news workers. Banal journalism symbolizes the ways in which journalism is actually practised; not the way it ought to be practised.

It is important to note that the culture in which journalism is practised also shapes the worldview of its practitioners. Newsroom banter, irreverence towards authority, doggedness in pursuing a story, cynicism, iconoclasm, brief attention spans, the 'publish and forget' attitude, the constant rush to meet deadlines, and so forth – all contribute to the formation and perpetuation of certain common personality traits in journalists. The social life of most journalists is also invariably confined to professional colleagues; they rarely break away from their established social and professional networks involving colleagues, politicians, bureaucrats, the corporate world and the like. It is in these networks that the banal binary is deeply institutionalized and which makes it all the more difficult to break away from the comfort zone of the circle of reason – as journalists see it.

▌ References

Allan, S. (2004) *News Culture*, Second Edition. Maidenhead: Open University Press.

Arendt, H. (1963) *Eichmann in Jerusalem: A Report on the Banality of Evil.* New York: Viking Press.

Billig, M. (1995) *Banal Nationalism*. London: Sage.

CNN (2001) Bush Says it is Time for Action, 6 November.

Elias, N. (1970) *What is Sociology?* London: Hutchinson.

Elias, N. (1994) *The Established and the Outsiders: A Sociological Enquiry Into Community Problems*. London: Sage.

Elliott, W. A. (1986) *Us and Them: A Study of Group Consciousness*. Aberdeen: Aberdeen University Press.

Gans, H. (1980) *Deciding What's News*. London: Constable.

Hall, S. (1977) Culture, the Media and the Ideological Effect, in J. Curran, M. Gurevitch and J. Wollacott (eds) *Mass Communication and Society*. London: Edward Arnold, 315–348.

Hall, S. (1982) The Rediscovery of Ideology: Return of the Repressed in Media Studies, in M. Gurevitch, T. Bennett, J. Curran and J. Woollacott (eds) *Culture, Society and the Media*. London: Methuen.

Hall, S., Critcher, C., Jefferson, T., Clarke, J. and Roberts, B. (1981) The Social Production of News, in S. Cohen and J. Young (eds) *The Manufacture of News*. Beverly Hills: Sage.

Hallin, D. C. (1989) *The 'Uncensored War': Media and Vietnam*. London: University of California Press.

Hartley, J. (1982) *Understanding News*. London: Routledge.

Hartman, P. and Husband, C. (1981) The Mass Media and Racial Conflict, in S. Cohen and J. Young (eds) *The Manufacture of News: Social Problems, Deviance and the Mass Media*. Beverly Hills: Sage.

Hetherington, A. (1985) *News, Newspapers and Television*. London: Macmillan.

Mennell, S. (1992) *Norbert Elias: An Introduction*. Oxford: Blackwell.

Nag, S. (2001) Nationhood and Displacement in Indian Subcontinent, in *Economic and Political Weekly*, 22 December.

Nossek, H. (2005) Our News and Their News: On the Role of National Identity in the Definition of Political Violence and Terrorism as News, in H. Nossek, P. Sonwalkar and A. Sreberny (eds) *News Media and Political Violence*. Cresskill, NJ: Hampton Press.

Parekh, B. (1994) Cultural Diversity and Liberal Democracy, in D. Beetham (ed.) *Defining and Measuring Democracy*. London: Sage.

Said, E. (2001) Suicidal Ignorance, *Al-Ahram Weekly Online*, Issue 560, 15–21 November; www.ahram.org/weekly/2001/560/op2.htm.

Schudson, M. (2000) The Sociology of News Production Revisited (Again), in J. Curran and M. Gurevitch (eds) *Mass Media and Society*. London: Arnold.

Shils, E. (1975) *Centre and Periphery: Essays in Macrosociology*. Chicago: University of Chicago Press.

Shoemaker, P. J. (1991) *Gatekeeping*. London: Sage.

Shoemaker, P. and Reese, S. D. (1996) *Mediating the Message: Theories of Influence on Mass Media Content*. New York: Longman.

Smelser, N. J. (1981) *Sociology*. Cambridge: Cambridge University Press.

Smith, A. (1991) *National Identity*. London: Sage.

Sonwalkar, P. (2003) Violence as Non-Communication: The News Differential of Kashmir and Northeast Conflicts in the Indian National Press. Unpublished PhD thesis, University of Leicester.

Sonwalkar, P. (2004) Out of Sight, Out of Mind? The Non-Coverage of Small Wars and Insurgencies, in S. Allan and B. Zelizer (eds) *Reporting War: Journalism in Wartime*. London: Routledge.

Sreberny, A. (2002) Trauma Talk: Reconfiguring the Inside and Outside, in B. Zelizer and S. Allan (eds) *Journalism After September 11*. London: Routledge.

Tuchman, G. (1978) The Newspaper as a Social Movement's Resource, in G. Tuchman, J. Bennet and A. K. Daniels (eds) *Hearth and Home: Images of Women in Mass Media*. New York: Oxford University Press.

Van Dijk, T. (1988) *News as Discourse*. Hove: Lawrence Erlbaum Associates.

20

Racialized 'othering'

The representation of asylum seekers in news media

Olga Guedes Bailey and Ramaswami Harindranath

- How does journalistic practice contribute to a process of 'othering' of refugees and asylum seekers?
- What role do the labels such as 'illegal' and 'bogus' play in the politics of immigration control?
- What are the challenges confronting journalists reporting on asylum seekers in the context of globalization?

An incident occurred off Australian territorial waters on 26 August 2001 that had significant consequences in the Australian parliamentary elections held that year. A Norwegian ship, the *Tampa*, rescued 433 survivors, mostly asylum seekers, from a sinking Indonesian ferry and took them to Christmas Island, part of Australian territory. Categorizing the rescued passengers of the *Tampa* as 'boatpeople' and 'illegal immigrants', the ruling Liberal Party sought to appeal to sections of the electorate by having Australian Special Forces board the ship in an attempt to stop the passengers from disembarking on Christmas Island – and thus being in a position to apply for asylum. What is of interest to our present concerns, however, is the role of the press in what subsequently came to be referred to as the *Tampa* affair. Some of the popular newspapers carried stories which reproduced the language of the government, as indicated in the headline in the front page of the *Herald Sun* on 31 August 2001: 'BACK OFF: Howard rejects UN call to take illegals'.

The complicity of the press with the government's position has since been noted by a few scholars. For example, Ward (2002: 22) writing in the *Australian Journalism Review* sees the affair as an instance of 'wedge politics' from which can be learned a lesson in political journalism: 'these events were part of a carefully calculated Liberal Party strategy to revive its flagging electoral stocks ahead of an imminent federal election.' Despite his careful analysis of the context of the incident, however, his claim that 'had this point been understood, the journalists may have framed the Tampa story differently, realising that their description of the Tampa passengers as illegal immigrants assisted the Liberals' cause' (Ward 2002: 23) appears to place too much retrospective faith in journalistic disinterestedness. The implication here is that had journalists been more sensitive to the issue of 'wedge politics' they may have presented the story from a different perspective, a claim that is difficult to justify and defend.

This is not to suggest that all journalists are overtly racist or anti-refugees. What we want to argue in this essay is that, firstly, such depictions of asylum seekers, far from being isolated cases, form a pattern that demonstrates a form of racism which has become part of a commonly held vision of national security and sovereignty. This form of racism is not overt but is constitutive of an attitude to 'foreigners', particularly refugees, and is therefore far more insidious. Our argument is that such rhetoric of national sovereignty points to the apparent paradox within what has come to be known as 'globalization': that is, the celebration of 'global culture' and porous borders on the one hand, and the simultaneous consolidation of national borders, on the other. For example, if developments such as transport technology have contributed to more people travelling between and across countries than ever before, the tightening of immigration control increasingly imposes restrictions on the mobility of certain communities – clear indications of a 'power geometry' (Massey 1994). It is our basic contention that representations of asylum seekers as undesirable aliens has to be considered within the context of this paradox.

Dog whistle journalism, the 'other', and the politics of representation

The tightening of national border control raises questions about the categories of 'desirable' immigrant and 'legal' as opposed to 'bogus' refugees. The latter distinction is further complicated by the small proportion of those seeking asylum attempting to manipulate the conditions to their advantage, and whose claim on the status as asylum seekers is questionable. However, it is precisely when the practices of this small minority of those claiming asylum are used either to stigmatize *all* asylum seekers as 'bogus' and unwarranted, or to justify draconian immigration policies, that the role of the press needs to be scrutinized.

The issue of the representation of refugees and asylum seekers has two sets of related implications for journalistic practice, namely, news discourse and its relationship to power, and the framing of news on asylum seekers in a global context, transcending narrowly defined national interests. In terms of news discourse, broadly speaking media representations are seen as significant in the cultural (and therefore political) sphere precisely because they actively *construct* meaning, and do not merely *reflect* social reality. Hall (1982), for instance, has argued that the media make things mean through the active processes of selection, presentation, structuring and shaping of events; in other words media representations ascribe meaning to events. Significantly, as he has suggested more recently, representation works through marking a difference with the 'other', whether the difference is on the basis of gender, sexuality, 'race' or nationality (Hall 1997). What this means is that 'difference is constructed both through language, in the form of binary oppositions such as man/woman, black/white, legal/illegal, British/foreigner; and also through 'symbolic boundaries': 'marking "difference" leads us, symbolically, to close ranks, shore up culture and to stigmatize and expel anything which is defined as impure, abnormal' (Hall 1997: 237). This symbolic marking of 'difference' is intrinsic to unchallenged assumptions, which are commonplace in a particular national culture, on the basis of which the castigation of 'illegal' immigrants and 'bogus' refugees, for instance, is naturalized.

The use of such terms as 'boat people' or 'asylum seekers' therefore come loaded with particular sets of meaning that resonate with such *naturalized* sets of racially based difference when used in conjunction with qualifiers such as 'bogus'. It should be noted that this process of naturalization leaves scope for challenging existing constructions of meaning. In other words, such representations of refugees are not 'fixed'; they can and are being contested. What is significant for our purposes is what Ward (2002) refers to as 'dog whistle journalism': 'the discussion of policy issues in an outwardly reasonable language, but one using words and phrases that are calculated to carry a different message to the target audience' (Ward 2002: 28). The question of a 'target audience' raises issues that fall outside the immediate scope of this essay, but the use of 'outwardly reasonable language' brings up the matter of journalistic discourse and the politics of representation. In other words, is there a relationship between journalistic discourse on asylum seekers and refugee communities on the one hand, and on the other the justification of discriminatory immigration policies? Crucially, how do discursive strategies in journalism contribute to the legitimation of control, or otherwise 'naturalize' social relations?

Analysing the politics of journalistic representation involves examining language. As Shapiro (1989) has observed

> given that our understanding of conflict, war, or more generally, the space within which international politics is deployed is always mediated by modes of representation and thus by all the various mechanisms involved in text construction – grammars, rhetorics, and narrativity – we must operate with a view of politics that is sensitive to textuality.
>
> (Shapiro 1989: 319)

With reference to both domestic and international politics – and, in the case of asylum seekers the combination of the two – the fact that policies are mediated requires us to pay close attention to aspects of linguistic representation, and the ways in which uncritical use of available terms can reproduce and sustain naturalized forms of racism and through that the politics of exclusion. Conversely, criticism of such representations involves using representational strategies and linguistic terms which challenge and undermine those familiar expressions.

That is a challenge in itself, but if we were to widen the argument to include debates on globalization and the representation of the racialized other, the situation becomes a great deal more complex web of several important issues. 'Globalization' is an amorphous and much-debated term but the specific dimension of it that we are interested in here relates to the argument that through mainly the breakdown of trade barriers and developments in transport and communication technologies, the world appears to have shrunk, and there has emerged a 'global culture' that incorporates and celebrates heterogeneous cultural forms and practices. Not only have such developments reorganized the relations between the national and the global, but it is argued that borders between nation-states have become porous, more permeable. Two points are particularly significant to our present concerns: the complexity that has resulted from the deepening interconnectedness between different nations, cultures and peoples on the one hand, and on the other the question of who benefits from porous borders and who is restricted (the 'power geometry' referred to earlier). Both these are relevant to the representation of asylum seekers and refugees.

One of the main challenges facing contemporary representations of asylum seekers in the news is addressing the particular in terms of the universal. In the present case this requires the presentation of the experiences of an excluded community of exiles in particular localities in terms of wider issues such as the question of human rights and the ethics of caring and support, and to do so without contributing to the process of 'othering'. While academic debates on globalization have underlined the 'politics of recognition' that is fundamental to an acknowledgement of plural cultures and multiple identities, the politics of media representation of refugees and asylum seekers have had to contend with two complementary moves: the persistent othering and a hierarchization of cultures and ethnicities that deconstructs the logic of multicultural global and national cultures, and the invocation (in both political and media spheres) of national borders which alienate (and treat as 'alien') populations who do not possess the necessary symbols of national belonging.

As the Tampa affair alluded to at the beginning of the essay suggests, the process of 'marking difference' between the national (Australia) and the 'other' – asylum seekers criminalized as 'illegal immigrants' or alienated as 'boatpeople' implicitly, in dog-whistle style, mobilize discourses of desirable and undesirable immigration. For instance the *Herald Sun* on 3 September 2001 ran the headline: 'SET TO GO: Voters endorse PM's tough stand. Illegals are ready to be transferred', referring to its own poll on the Tampa affair, and to the government's decision to send a Navy ship to remove the asylum seekers from the Tampa.

Binary oppositions constantly simplify complex situations, whether in debates about terrorism, which invokes the other as evil, or about refugees, which reach back to colonial representations of non-Western populations as duplicitous and dangerous to Western values. The argument informing this chapter is constructed on the idea that journalism has not fully embraced the other. This seems at odds with the pressing awareness of cultural globalism, which has brought with it a necessary consciousness of the differences of the local in relation to the global – that is, the need to think the local and the global as aspects of the same reality which helps reposition each of them in more nuanced ways.

The next two sections of this chapter present a review of a few of the important studies on news and the racial other, followed by a brief analysis of a recent example of news on asylum seekers from the BBC. As we shall see, the coverage of issues such as refugees and asylum seekers, when presented in the context of the need to strengthen national borders, invoke separatist discourses that clearly distinguish between the 'us' within the nation-state and 'them', the outsider, foreigner, the 'bogus' refugee. A caveat is required here: the analysis presented in the following sections draws selectively from the coverage of the issue by the BBC; the sample is used here to locate conceptual issues meriting further elaboration, and not as an indication of the BBC's stance on the issue.

▋ 'Othering' in journalism

The case of the 'other' is illustrative of the fact that journalism has not yet managed to respond fully to the challenges raised by the transnational patterns of communication and mobility that characterize our contemporary, deterritorialized world. National borders continue to figure strongly when it comes to news representations of the other, in particular refugees and asylum seekers, in which the dichotomy of 'us versus them' persist.

What is crucial here is the continuous process of 'selective articulation' by which the media literally 'make sense' out of the world surround us. Portrayals of refugees and asylum seekers in the news continue to separate the 'us' separate from the 'other'.[1] It can be argued that the 'other' is defined by the major news media Western organizations that decide what is news, and what is normal/ordinary/expected/unexpected – the application of 'news values'. As Ginneken (1998) argues, the quasi-consensual ideology of major Western countries contributes to the selection of news:

> news production and news consumption can also be seen as a twenty-four-hour ideological repair shop for our world and our world views. Possible anomalies are identified, checked and 'normalised', so that the ideological machine keeps running smoothly.
>
> (Ginneken 1998: 32)

Galtung and Ruge's (1981) 'news values' model[2] is seminal in terms of raising the issue of how events become news, especially on how overseas events become news, underlining the imbalance in foreign news reporting in their case study of Norwegian press. However, their conception of news values was developed in a different media landscape, where the division of the world into 'centre versus periphery', and the sovereignty of the nation-state had a much stronger role in defining the other than in the current global landscape. Moreover, the media have implemented a worldview of exclusion in which different cultures and societies are defined as 'foreign'. As pointed out by Volkmer (1999), 'the modern world-view gave order to world communication and its effectiveness by employing terms like "First World" or "Third World" in designating communication structures' (Volkmer 1999: 104). In a more recent work, she has elaborated this view in the light of the events of 11 September 2001 and their implication for global journalism. She suggests that the consequences of the attack on the US had challenged the dominant world order of the West (Volkmer 2002) based on the model of 'core-periphery'. Volkmer's views of a possible re-organization of the world order of the West would be more in tune with Canclini's (1992) observation that the world cannot be understood in the rather monolithic terms that the core-periphery dualism suggests.

The issue of refugee and asylum seekers in British media has not received as much attention in the literature as race and ethnicity. However, the purported challenge to national sovereignty and identity resulting from the recent increase in the movement of refugees fleeing conflicts zones, as well as the events of 11 September have brought the issue back on the public agenda and the academic forum. Most studies on the British press coverage of asylum seekers and refugees (Tomasi 1993; Brosius and Eps 1995; Coleman 1995; Clark 1998, Ali and Gibb 1999) emphasize the common sense of the press framework for news of this 'other' as either 'problem' or 'invisible'. For example, the most significant outcome of Kaye's (2001) analysis of representations of asylum seekers and refugees in the British press in the 1990s is that the term 'asylum seekers' itself has been degraded through its use as a signifier for illegality and bogusness. Another British study (Kundnani 2001) concludes that racist ideology is generated and reproduced in relation to asylum seekers through the framing of news stories predominantly in terms of suspicion and deterrence: can we trust them and how do we keep them out?

With regard to research on television news and asylum seekers, most studies demonstrate the persistence of stereotypes similar to those in the press (Hartmann and Husband 1974; Gordon and Rosenberg 1989; Van Dijk 1991, 2000). For example, the Glasgow University Media Group's research on the language and visuals of a sample of news reports on migration and race in February 1995 showed that 'news was sometimes xenophobic in tone, which reinforced our identity and their exclusion and, perhaps more importantly, provided a rationale for the apparent need for exclusion' (Glasgow Media Group 1997: 46). A similar framework of portraying of asylum seekers and refugees in an 'anti-foreigners' agenda can be observed in studies of asylum seekers and media representation elsewhere. Examples abound but for our purpose we refer to two studies from Australia media, which, combined with the analysis of British media, suggest that a 'transnational' racialized regime of representation is in place.

In an examination of the discursive construction of asylum seekers in Australia Saxton (2003), suggests that media reports and public discussions of asylum seekers draw on nationalist discourses along themes of familiarity, security and a sense of community of 'us' and our 'home', which exclude asylum seekers. One of the main conclusions of the study is that 'nationalist discourse prescribes the boundaries of inclusion and exclusion for "others", and is employed to legitimate oppressive and marginalizing practices towards minorities' (Saxton 2003: 122).

Similarly, Klocker and Dunn's (2003) analysis of Australian media releases in 2001 and 2002 points out that, although there were periods in the study in which the media were sympathetic towards asylum seekers, the overall view was that the media represented asylum seekers in a rather negative form. He also implies that at times the media relied on government discourse to construct asylum as a threat to the interests of readers and viewers, linking the issue to crime, violence and 'difference'.

Asylum seekers and 'the immigration headache'

The current study[3] on the representation of asylum seekers and refugees in the BBC and Channel Four[4] news programmes has shown that the framing of news granted a negative meaning to this 'other', relating them to criminality, problems and as a threat to the 'fortress Europe'. Moreover, the two channels analysed put strong emphasis on a frame of reference centred on the legal and political aspects of the issue, which seems to follow the government agenda rather than challenging it. That is, most news on this issue centred around government policies and regulations for border control and deterrence of asylum seekers.

This research suggests that news about refugees is often limited to few events: social problems (housing, employment, welfare); political opinions (politicians commenting on new policies or suggesting solutions); government policy (new laws restricting asylum seekers' access); cultural difference (mostly in terms of deviance and criminality); public perception (in general based on misconceptions of welfare support for asylum seekers and refugees) and incidents of violence. This list confirms the findings of Van Dijk's (2000) discursive analysis of British newspapers representation of asylum seekers. Overall, one could argue that the conclusions drawn by these studies suggests that there is an 'inferential racism'[5] at work in the news representation of asylum seekers which can be seen as a form of 'sanitized' racist discourse.

Let us briefly consider a concrete example of the use of linguistic terms in a television news text to illustrate the framing of asylum news. The news report analysed is an extract from BBC1's *Six O'clock News* on 27 October 2003. The news item is about new asylum laws, and given the audience of the programme, millions of British viewers may have watched this piece.

The news is presented with the headline 'Asylum Law', followed by the newscaster's voice: 'When asylum seekers reach Britain they will face criminal charges under new measures announced today'.

The headline is combined with images of clearly 'non-European' passengers arriving at Heathrow airport and being watched by cameras monitored by migration officers in a separate room. The officers are closely looking at the screens and checking the images with photos of foreign individuals as if looking for someone specific. This is followed by images of people having their passports checked as they leave the plane, and then a young black couple showing their passports at the migration desk. It could be argued that this attempt at 'othering' through the combination of words and images already sets in motion the frame of criminality within which the apparent asylum seekers are placed, both institutionally and discursively. In addition, it is possible to read the construction of a subliminal message of the 'fortress' England: there are several 'doors' to be crossed before one can 'arrive' in England, implying that the 'soft touch' of British asylum laws are about to end.

This possible interpretation is reinforced, in our view, by the Immigration Minister, Beverly Hughes, who states, when interviewed by the reporter, that the measures 'Aim at reducing the number of *bogus* asylum application. Other possible measures include a new limit on appeals and a tighter control on those who give unscrupulous advice to asylum seekers.'

The reporter using a specific military register then establishes the metaphor of a 'war' on immigrants:

> There is a new *weaponry* in the *armoury* of the immigration service at Heathrow intelligence unit. CCTV now allows them to track passengers all the way from the gate. Many asylum seekers hand false travel documents on arrival or dispose of them to hide their through nationality.

The item moves on to the issue of reducing numbers of appeal, making the point about the inefficacy of the government in dealing with the situation by interviewing a black man seeking asylum who, we are informed, went to 14 asylum hearings and two appeals.

The images move on to an 'immigration court' where the news item comes to an end with the reporter, again, presenting the asylum issue as a problem, by the use of words such as 'headache' and his emphasis on the number of government bills in a short period. 'The immigration issue still a headache for politicians. If there will be another asylum bill, it will be the third in just five years.'

The analysis suggests that the news frame is constructed in a scenario where Britain is being invaded and 'we' need 'weaponry' to stop the flow of immigrants. In a similar fashion to the 'dog-whistle' treatment of the *Tampa* passengers, this framing of asylum seekers as a 'headache', and as requiring strict policing is, on one level, an account of the measures adopted to protect borders. The 'othering' at the beginning of the news story, along with the term 'bogus', however, combine to racially criminalize a group of individuals, while 'weaponry' and 'armoury' invoke associations with the guarding of national space from foreign invasion.

This both confirms Saxton's (2003) argument, and supports findings by other studies on television representations of immigrants (Philo and Beattie 1999; Van Dijk 2000), which point out to alarming similarities in the ways the media, in the last decade or so, have been 'manufacturing' news on immigrants. The use of similar news frames over the years, such as the use of statistics on immigration, and specific terms such as 'bogus' and 'illegal', is quite frequent in television news. Even more damaging is the lack of engagement with the experiences of refugees and other communities of exile, that is, the consistent absence of reports presenting the refugees' case. The wider context is rarely explored: issues such as the reasons for seeking asylum, the everyday difficulties encountered by refugees in their 'host' countries are mostly ignored, contributing to the dehumanization of refugees (Manning 2003). As we have seen, there is little distinction in the news analysed in the literature, between 'asylum seekers', 'illegal immigrants' and 'refugees'. The real motivation of the people attempting to seek asylum is lost, and while the terms 'refugee' and 'asylum seeker' suggest that these people are seeking protection from threat, terms such as 'illegal' and 'bogus' undermine their legitimate requests for asylum by criminalizing them (Saxton 2003). The news media then seem to create an unfair construction of asylum seekers who are not 'bogus' or of those who have not being warranted permission to stay, putting under the same negative 'umbrella' all different types of migrants, including economic and highly skilled ones.

It is important to acknowledge that the outcomes of the studies discussed here are 'snapshots' of reality. They not necessarily reflect an essentialist position of the media in representing asylum seekers. Putting it in a different way, the news construction of asylum seekers as 'other' takes place in a changeable political and social landscape where the struggle and negotiation of meaning is always under scrutiny by different social actors. Therefore the processes of 'naturalization' of migration news is contradictory and, in many ways, contested which may alter the production of asylum seekers meaning in the news outcome at different times and contexts.

It is a truism to suggest that the media play a critical role in providing information to people about the world surrounding us, and that they help to shape our perception of social and political issues. Given that members of the public, in all likelihood, will have little direct contact with asylum seekers the mediated nature of public discourse concerning asylum seekers as the 'other' assumes a special significance, which in turn implicates the linguistic and visual construction of such representations. As often argued, the result of this constant process of 'othering' in the news is the promotion and consolidation of 'a racist "commonsense" which serves to justify and help maintain racial inequalities' (Gordon and Rosenberg 1989: 38). Although this does not imply that the audience necessarily accepts such representation uncritically, there is enough support to claim that dominant representations play a significant role in influencing people's perceptions of minority groups and that dominant news frameworks in particular help to structure perception of the key issues in race relations.

(Pilkington 2003: 185)

In this context, it is important to recognize that some progress has been made in representational practices in the media (Ross 1996; Van Dijk 1991). The positive media representations of minorities underlines the possibility of establishing a more balanced media representation of asylum seekers, as a way forward to break the dichotomy of 'us versus them', hence providing the public with less stereotypical, naturalized versions of immigrants. In this respect, BBC Television is well aware of its responsibilities as a public service broadcaster that has a strong commitment to fair and balanced representation of minorities.

Conclusion

Studies such as Van Dijk (2000) and Saxton (2003) suggest that, despite the coverage of a range of events, both local and international, before and after the events of 11 September 2001, the portrayal of 'asylum seekers' is remarkably consistent. Rather than be presented as people who are trying to escape threat, they are, in most cases, represented as *the* threat. It is a representation based on fear of 'them' as a threat to 'our' national security and ways of life. The persistence of such divisive frames contributes to racialized 'wedge' politics and to the justification of policies that approve or deny entry into countries on the basis of narrowly defined 'national interests'. To reiterate an earlier point, it is important to note that such representations are not unchallenged or uncontested. What we have attempted to show in this chapter is the need for sensitivity in journalistic practice when reporting on asylum seekers, and by extension, other 'foreigners'.

As mentioned earlier, rapid developments in communication satellites and computer networks since the early 1990s have reorganized global space, 'shrinking' it through near instantaneous communication, one consequence of which has been the much trumpeted permeability of national borders. As we have seen, however, news reports on asylum seekers and refugees constantly resurrect national boundaries, portraying such exilic communities as a threat to the sovereignty and security of the nation. Journalistic practice has had to re-orient its approach to the new environment in which the relations between the national and the global have been reordered. This new position for journalists should ideally re-establish journalistic frames of reference from the national and the local level – which sustain discourses of foreignness that ride on binary oppositions between 'us' and 'them' – to the global, in which the 'other' takes on a different significance. As Volkmer rightly argues while news framed in the modern paradigm used to consist in the distribution of national affairs within the borders of a defined nation-state, globalization has led to a more complex counter development – disappearance of national state interests within a global 'news' community – while at the same time increasing the perspectives of domestic news.

(Volkmer 1999: 93)

It is this 'disappearance of the national' that provides journalists with the opportunity to challenge existing patterns of representation by addressing the issue of asylum in terms of universal rights of individuals and communities, and by accommodating within the frames of reference the localized experiences of such communities of exile. This requires journalism as a practice to transcend the rhetoric of nationalism, and be prepared to seriously consider the reporting of such issues as addressing the global theme of rights and values, and not as threats to national interests.

Notes

1   The category of the 'other' embraces a wide rubric of racial, cultural and ethnic and linguistic groups, including the legal reference to terms of asylum seekers. Here 'other' refers to its use in the binary opposition of the 'us versus them', specifically regarding misrepresentation of 'asylum seekers'. The term asylum seeker will be used as a collective term for a person who comes to another country in order to claim legal status as a refugee. The person seeking asylum may or may not meet the requirements for refugee status. This is a crucial point in relation to news representation, as 'asylum seekers' become a reified category equated to 'bogus' asylum, which obscures the differences that exist between genuine and non-genuine asylum seekers.

2   The 'structure of foreign news' was a study carried out by Johan Galtung and Mari Holmboe Ruge (1981). They were interested in how major crises (in the Third World periphery) were reported in Norway (First World periphery). In order to find out they developed a content analysis of how the Congo (Zaire), Cuba and Cyprus crises of the early 1960s have been reported in the Norwegian capital. List of news values: frequency, threshold, meaningfulness, consonance, unexpectedness, continuity, composition, reference to elite nations, elite people, reference to persons, and reference to something negative (Galtung and Ruge 1981: 64–91).

3   The research aimed to analyse the texts of news television report on issues related to asylum seekers regarding the construction of a frame of 'inferential racism'. For a period of one year (2003) most news that appeared on the three main BBC and Channel Four news programmes related to asylum seekers were recorded (BBC1: 1 o'clock news (lunch time) 6 o'clock news (evening), 10 o'clock news (evening); BBC2 Newsnight, at 10.30 p.m.) and Channel 4 (7 o'clock evening news). The method employed in this study was discourse and thematic analysis, looking at the language and journalistic strategies used to construct 'asylum seekers'.

4   The BBC1 news coverage 'aims to stand out for the quality of its analysis and

original reporting. Its goal is to help people make sense of what is going on in the world, by covering a broad agenda and using clear narrative and plain English' (www.bbc.co/statement of programme policy 2003/4). It is important to note that the BBC and Channel Four, which have an ethos of public service, operates a policy of 'more balanced media content, and a code of practice designed to avoid ethnic stereotyping'.

5   'Inferential racism' is in place when 'coverage is seemingly balanced but premises are inscribed as a set of unquestioned assumptions' (Pilkington 2003: 185).

▌References

Ali, Y. and Gibb, P. (1999) Le racisme, le droit d'asile et la press britannique, *Migrations Societe*, 11(62): 123–34.

BBC (1995) *People and Programmes*. London, BBC Publications.

Brosius, H. B. and Eps, P. (1995) Prototyping through Key Events: News Selection in the Case of Violence against Aliens and Asylum Seekers in Germany, *European Journal of Communication*, 10(3): 391–412.

Canclini, G. N. (1992) Cultural Conversion. In G. Yudice, J. Franco and J. Flores (eds) *On Edge: the Crisis of Contemporary Latin American Culture*. Minneapolis: University of Minnesota Press.

Clark, C. (1998) Counting Backwards: the Roma 'Numbers Game' in Central and Eastern Europe, *Radical Statistics*, 69: 35–46.

Coleman, P. (1995) Survey of Asylum Coverage in the National Daily Press, *The Runnymede Bulletin*, 291: 6–7.

Coole, C. (2002) A Warm Welcome? Scottish and UK Media Reporting of Asylum-seekers Murder, *Media, Culture and Society*, 24: 839–52.

Cottle, S. (2000) Media Research and Ethnic Minorities: mapping the field, in S. Cottle (ed.) *Ethnic Minorities and the Media*. Buckingham and Philadelphia: Open University Press.

Entman, R. (1992) Blacks in the News: Television, Modern Racism, and Cultural Change, *Journalism Quarterly*, 69(2): 341–61.

Fabian, J. (1983) *Time and the Other*. New York: Columbia University Press.

Galtung, J. and Ruge, M. (1981) Structuring and Selecting News, in S. Cohen and J. Young (eds) *The Manufacture of News*, revised edition. London: Constable.

Gans, H. (1991) *Deciding What is News*. New York: Pantheon.

Ginneken, J. (1998) *Understanding Global News*. London: Sage.

Glasgow Media Group (1997) *Race, Migration and Media*. Glasgow: GMG.

Gordon, P. and Rosemberg, D. (1989) *Daily Racism: The Press and Black People in Britain*. London: Runneymede Trust.

Hall, S. (1982) The Rediscovery of Ideology: Return of the Repressed in Media Studies, in M. Guervitch, T. Bennett, J. Curran and J. Woollacott (eds) *Culture, Society, and the Media*. London: Routledge.

Hall, S. (1992) The West and Rest: discourse and power, in S. Hall and B. Gieben (eds) *Formations of Modernity*. Cambridge: Polity.

Hall, S. (1997) The Spectacle of the 'Other', in S. Hall (ed.) *Representation: Cultural Representations and Signifying Practices*. London: Sage.

Hall, S. (2000) The Multi-cultural Question, in B. Hesse (ed.) *Un/settled Multiculturalism*. London: Zed.

Hartmann, P. and Husband, C. (1974) *Racism and the Mass Media*. London, Davis-Ponter.

Kaye, R. (1998) UK Media Portrayal of Asylum Seekers, in K. Koser and H. Lutz, (eds) *The New Migration in Europe: Social Constructions and Social Realities*. Basingstoke: Macmillan.

Kaye, R. (2001) Blaming the Victim, in R. King and N. Wood (eds) *Media and Migration*. London: Routledge.

Klocker, N. and Dunn, K.M. (2003) Who's Driving the Asylum Debate? Newspaper and Government Representations of Asylum Seekers, *Media International Australia Incorporating Culture and Policy*, 109 (November): 71–92.

Kundnani, A. (2001) In a Foreign Land: The New Popular Racism, *Race and Class*, 43: 41–60.

Law, I. (2000) *Race in the News*. Basingstoke: Palgrave.

Manning, P. (2003) Arabic and Muslim People in Sydney's Daily Newspapers, Before and After September 11, *Media International Australia Incorporating Culture and Policy*, 109 (November).

Massey, D. (1994) *Space, Place, and Gender*. Oxford: Oxford University Press.

Pearson, K. A., Parry, B. and Squires, J. (eds) (1997) *Cultural Readings of Imperialism*. New York, St Martin's Press.

Philo, G. and Beattie, L. (1999) Race, Migration and Media, in G. Philo (ed.) *Message Received*. London: Longman.

Pilkington, A. (2003) *Racial Disadvantage and Ethnic Diversity in Britain*. London: Palgrave.

Ross, K. (1996) *Black and White Media*. Cambridge: Polity.

Rowe, M. (2000) Asylum Seekers in the UK. *Politics Review*, 10(2): 26–7.

Saxton, A. (2003) I Certainly Don't Want People Like That Here: The Discursive Construction of 'Asylum Seekers', *Media International Australia Incorporating Culture and Policy*, 109 (November): 109–20.

Schuster, L. (2002) Asylum and the Lessons of History, *Race and Class*, 44(2): 40–56.

Shapiro, M. (1989) Textualising Global Politics, in M. Wetherell, S. Taylor, and S. Yates, (eds) (2001) *Discourse Theory and Practice: A Reader*. London: Sage.

Solomos, J. (2003) *Race and Racism in Britain*, third edition. London, Palgrave/Macmillan.

Tomasi, S. (1993) Today's Refugees and the Media, *Migration World*, 20(5): 21–3.

Turner, B. S. (1994) *Orientalism, Postmodernism and Globalism*. London, Routledge.

Van Dijk, T. (1991) *Racism and the Press*. London, Routledge.

Van Dijk, T. (2000) New(s) Racism: a Discourse Analytical Approach, in S. Cottle (ed.) *Ethnic Minorities and the Media*. Buckingham: Open University Press.

Volkmer, I. (1999) *News in the Global Sphere: a Study of CNN and its Impact on Global Communication*. Bedfordshire: University of Luton Press.

Volkmer, I. (2002) Journalism and Political Crisis in the Network Society, in B. Zelizer and S. Allan, *Journalism After September 11*. London: Routledge.

Ward, I. (2002) The *Tampa*, Wedge Politics, and a Lesson for Political Journalism, *Australian Journalism Review*, 24(1): 454.

|21

Women in the boyzone

Gender, news and *her*story

Karen Ross

- Why do men dominate the news: men's thoughts, men's actions, men's toys?
- Why are there so few female war reporters?
- Why does the dream (news presenter) team comprise young attractive woman and older indifferently attractive man?
- Why did the *Sun* continue to include 'tits 'n' bums' on page 3 when it had a woman editor?
- Why are there so few women in senior positions in news organizations?

This chapter is concerned with the problematic relationship that women have with news media, both as subjects and sources of news stories as well as their experiences and status as practitioners within news industries. I want to explore some of the issues that regularly irritate me as a consumer of news media and, in so doing, answer some important questions about why we get the news *they* want to give us rather the news *we* want to hear, read and see. Do we get the news we deserve? I don't think so. So, what else do I want to know?

I begin this chapter by discussing the ways in which women are routinely portrayed in news media, including a consideration of self-reflexive studies undertaken by sections of the news media themselves, before moving to consider the experiences of women working in news organizations. Finally, I consider some of the ways in which women journalists are attempting to challenge the macho hegemony of the newsroom. I want to argue that journalism is an irrevocably engendered profession (as so many others), which self-consciously (despite protestations to the contrary) perpetuates stereotypical renditions of masculinity and femininity where men make decisions and women suffer the consequences. Importantly, I suggest that women are most noticeable in news media by their conspicuous *absence* or at least spectacular marginalization: where are women's voices in the protests against the occupation of Iraq or the reinstatement of Taliban rule in Afghanistan? Where they *are* the focus of news interest, it is sometimes as aberrant women who confound gender expectations (for example, women who kill), but most frequently as passive victims, usually of male violence or else as sex object or eye candy, tropes that reduce women to somewhat less than the sum of our parts. The blatant sexism of some of the tabloid press, for example, the British tabloid *Sunday Sport*'s regular pull-out of almost-nude women with its attendant slogan – ''Ave it!' – provides an apposite comment on the place of women in the news: we are there to be *had*.

Subject: woman

The ways in which women are represented in news media send important messages to the viewing, listening and reading public about women's place, women's role and women's lives. The media, and in particular television, with its huge audience share, are arguably the primary definers and shapers of the news agenda and perform a crucial cultural function in their gendered framing of public issues and in the gendered discourses they persistently promote. If news media fail to report the views of women judges or women parliamentarians or women business leaders but *always* report on violent crimes against women, then it is hardly surprising that the public fail to realize that women do, in fact, occupy significant roles in society or, equally, that men are much more likely to be victims of serious crime than women.

Since the mid-1990s, successive studies have attempted to map and analyse the ways in which women are portrayed in factual media, and that *her*story is not especially positive, showing as it does a pattern of marginal presence on the one hand and stereotyping on the other. In 1995, the Global Media Monitoring Project (GMMP) undertook a simultaneous monitoring of news media on one day across 71 countries in order to explore patterns of gender representation in news. In that study, it was discovered that globally, 19 per cent of individuals featured in news stories were women and that the most popular roles they occupied were as victims, mothers and wives (Media Watch 1995). Five years later, a second monitoring exercise undertaken with more or less the same number of countries and 50,000+ separate news items, found that the focus of women-oriented stories were almost identical to the previous study and that the proportion of women featured in news stories had actually gone down by 1 per cent (WACC 2000). Once again, the 'woman-as-victim' trope was the most popular. In both those studies, radio, TV and the press were monitored nationally, regionally and locally: there were few points of departure across the news landscape. In 1999, the European Commission conducted a pan-European analysis of gender and news representation and the rather gloomy conclusion of the report repeats the low volume of women's appearances in the media across all genres, and argues that women are over-represented as victims, usually of violence (see also Carter and Weaver 2003; Kitzinger 2004), often sexual in nature.[1] In 2003, a Southern African study was undertaken, using the GMMP model – the Gender and Media Baseline Study, which covered 12 countries.[2] That study found that women are 'grossly under-represented and misrepresented both in the newsrooms and editorial content of Southern Africa [and that] there are still cases of blatantly sexist reporting that portrays women as objects and temptresses' (www.genderlinks.org.za). What all these studies demonstrate, incontrovertibly, is that the media's framing (in every sense of the word) of women in highly restricted and mostly negative ways is not simply the consequence of the idiosyncrasies of this newspaper or that TV channel or that radio station but rather is a *global* phenomenon that has endured over time. How can we account for this? I would suggest that the only way in which to understand these findings is to argue that they demonstrate the macho and misogynistic nature of journalism as a practice. Is that a fair assessment? Well, what other explanations might there be which could account for the global and enduring nature of these skewed findings?

If we turn our attention to who speaks in news media, there is a similarly sad story. Any number of studies undertaken over the past ten years all point in the same direction. Neves's (1994) work on Belgian television news shows, for example, found that only men read the news during weekdays, that 97 per cent of current affairs interviewees and 80 per cent of all 'expert' witnesses asked to comment in TV news reports were men. Neves's findings are mirrored by any number of later studies of TV news (see for example, Leibler and Smith 1997 – US; Cann and Mohr 2001 – Australia), whose findings are almost identical. Often media apologists argue that one of the main reasons women don't feature as much as men in news discourse is because women don't occupy high status positions in society, as politicians, as government spokespeople, as business leaders and CEOs and so on. While this assertion can itself be challenged (see Ross 2002; Lemish 2004) – women parliamentarians for example do manage to attract media attention, but often it is for their sartorial style and domestic arrangements rather than their policy positions – 'ordinary' women are denied a voice as well. Where women should, in principle, have the same opportunity of speaking as men, for example, in vox pops during elections, they are still much *less* likely to be asked their views than men. In my own study of the radio phone-in show, *Election Call*, in 2001, around one-third of the callers were women (Ross 2004) and a much larger study of citizens and public access programming showed an even lower percentage of women contributing to such shows (McNair *et al.* 2003). When covering extreme situations such as war and terrorism, the resulting content demonstrates an even more stark concentration on the male figure, and news reporting of terrorism in the US in 2001 prompted one women journalist to suggest that women had been:

> . . . wiped off many newspaper pages and television screens, at a time when women had much to say about events that affected them deeply. The people handling this crisis are men. It is men who perpetrated this

violence and men who organize the response. The power structure is exposed at such times, as the token women slide into the background . . .
(Bunting 2001: n.p).

What Bunting articulates is a frustration that women's already fragile place at the news table is instantly rescinded when 'really serious' events need to be reported, and women's complex involvement in and relationship to war, is summarily reduced to mere victimhood, weakly in thrall to the murderous whims of men (Del Zotto 2002). The actions of women soldiers are rarely reported and the complacency that has descended upon the corps of journalists over atrocities such as suicide bombers can still be pierced when a bomber is revealed as female, at which point journalists crank out the routine stereotypes about aberrant women (Naylor 2001; Carter and Weaver 2003). In April 2004, when photographs showing the abuse of Iraqi prisoners at Abu Ghraib prison began circulating in the global news media, it was the horror of an alleged *woman* perpetrator – Lynndie England – which captured the media's attention, as much as the nature of the abuse itself. How could a woman do such things, these newsmen asked, appearing to believe that the male sex has the monopoly on humiliation, whereas a quick glance through history would soon reveal the bloodthirsty nature of women warriors, from Boadicea onwards.

Even sections of the media themselves have begun to recognize gender representation as problematic and have undertaken their own studies in order to recognize and respond to criticism. For example, research undertaken by the Dutch public sector broadcaster, NOS (1995), pointed to a number of subtle ways in which news media treat women differently to men: women are far more likely to be described by their first name rather than title; women are more likely to be addressed in familiar terms; men are often brought on after women to reinforce or validate the points they made; and women are more likely to be questioned about their emotions or private circumstances (see also Michielsens 1991). In another study of itself, members of the Women in Journalism group (see later), argued that, '. . . it seems clear that sometimes news desks go onto auto-pilot, trotting out clichés and stereotypes when, in fact, the woman in the story before them is unique' (Christmas 1996: 11). Admittedly, these studies are more than 10 years old, but there's absolutely no reason to believe that things have changed significantly over the past decade as the more contemporary work on news content cited above makes clear. But some countries are taking gender issues more seriously than others. For example, as a consequence of the publication of the Gender and Media Baseline Study in 2003, the South African News Editors Forum (SANEF) agreed at their AGM that they would make renewed efforts to improve the representation of women in their media, and thus far, workshops and discussions have taken place in several key newsrooms across South Africa.[3] However, a certain amount of cynicism must be allowed here, since a similar declaration was made by European broadcasters in 1995 and, as someone who attended that event, I would argue that the pace of change since then has been *extremely* slow.[4]

Women in the boyzone: gender and news industries

Despite over 30 years of sex equality legislation in Britain (and elsewhere), women's occupation of very senior posts within British news industries is still rare. The direction of media policy and the decisions to determine the nature and orientation of media content remain firmly in the hands of men and even where women have been successful in climbing the greasy professional pole, they are subject to scrutiny about their morals and their behaviour. When Eve Pollard become the first woman editor of a mid-market newspaper – the *Sunday Express* – she was described as a 'killer bimbo' who knew how to use her bosom as a cosh (Dougary 1994: xiii). In interviews I carried out with women journalists in South Africa in 2003, there were clear anxieties about how women's internal promotion would be viewed by their colleagues, precisely because a woman's advancement was routinely characterized as the fruits of her sexual labours.

> You find that if a woman gets a job they will say, something else was going on. They don't even look at your work, the first thing that comes to their mind is no, there has to be something else like you've been sleeping with somebody, you're involved in one way or another with somebody and sometimes you really feel, well, OK, I'll do this [go for promotion] but what is going to be the perception of other people? Will they think that I got this because of my own work or will they start talking around and saying all the nasty things that they can say.
>
> (Thandazo)[5]

Most of the studies that have analysed the position of women in media organizations (see Michielsens 1991; Neves 1994; Gallagher 1995; Steiner 1998; Byerly 2001; Joseph 2004a; Melin-Higgins 2004) evidence women's struggles to penetrate the higher echelons of power within news industries, but also show that women are confined to certain jobs and certain beats that have been traditionally viewed as 'women's work', such as education, lifestyle, society and the women's page/programmes. So, they are less likely to be working in news and current affairs than men, or as news reporters and journalists and they make up a small percentage of technical and production staff. Recent US studies by the American Society of Newspaper Editors and the Radio-Television News Directors' Association both show low numbers of women working as reporters and editors (cited in Lauer 2002). There are, of course, exceptions, and some women occupy very senior positions, including some within mainstream British publications such as the *Guardian* (Sheila Fitzsimmons, Executive Editor), the *Daily Telegraph* (Corinna Honan, Assistant Editor; Sue Ryan, Managing Editor) and the *News of the World* (Rebekah Wade, Editor), but the occupation of these positions is still notable for their infrequency.[6]

Traditional feminist analyses have argued that news content has always focused on the *male*stream, on what interests and concerns men, and that the low numbers of women, as editors, anchors, news readers and reporters simply reflects their subordinate place in the real world. Even in developing areas such as eNews, women are still not reaching executive positions in any numbers: researchers at the Annenberg Public Policy Center (2002) found that, across telecommunications and electronic commerce industries, women comprise 13 per cent of the top executives, and 9 per cent of those sit on boards of directors. This is a dispiriting picture given that, as Rush (2001) points out, women and men graduate from journalism programmes, at least in the US, in equal numbers, leading us to ask, what happens to the women? Part of the answer is that the long hours, smoke-filled, pub culture, which is a routine part of journalism practice, often sits awkwardly with a lifestyle that includes spending time with family and friends, so that for many women (and some men), the work-life balance becomes irrevocably tipped in favour of getting out.

The (relative) absence of women from political news reporting is another disappointing feature of the mainstream mediascape and corresponds with their low numbers in jobs which carry decision-making responsibilities. In *Women in Journalism*'s report of gender and media employment, they found that although women are now routinely appointed to senior roles (although mostly below editor level), 'leader writing [editorials] and political writing remain stubbornly male enclaves' (Christmas 1997: 12). Martin's work on women's careers within the broader information sector comes to similar conclusions (S. Martin 2002). And those few women journalists who are allowed to cover the politics beat do so at a cost. Joanna Coles who writes for the *Guardian*, was one of the journalists on Labour's campaign bus during the 1997 elections, and likened these journeys to a minor stag party, with male colleagues leering at pornographic material on their laptops, sharing cans of lager and sniggering whenever a woman happened to wander down the bus towards them (Coles 1997). That picture is probably equally accurate today, except that buses now have wireless technology so porn is constantly available.

In some areas of news, however, there are considerably more women than in previous decades. The revolution in journalism practice that has been brought about by developments in media and communications technology and the increasingly global nature of mainstream media have forced a reconsideration of the relationship of news to gender. It is clear that the 1990s and into the millennium have witnessed a cultural shift, where a more intimate mode of audience address – witness Channel 5 newscasters' casual leaning against a low bench to deliver the news rather than the more traditional image of man-behind-desk – together with a more tabloid style of journalism has made news both more intimately human (see Beasley 1993; Holland 1998; Van Zoonen 1998), but also more trite. Part of that shift has seen more women in front-of-house roles, especially as news presenters, but do more women in the newsroom signify a step forward on the road to gender equality? One might argue, on the contrary, that the inclusion of attractive young women in front of the camera is simply a cynical ploy (by male managers) to make the news more visually pleasing by appropriating women's bodies to sell the news – woman as commodity, again. As Arthurs has argued, 'more women in the [televisual] industry is not enough: there need to be more women with a politicised understanding of the ways in which women's subordination is currently reproduced and with the will to change it' (Arthurs 1994: 100). The logic of Arthurs' argument can be seen clearly by considering what changes, if any, took place at the *Sun* after Rebekah Wade took over as editor. None were immediately apparent in terms of content, style or orientation and it certainly did not become more women- or family-friendly, nor was the notorious 'page 3 girl' pensioned off. Thus Wade's sex is no guarantee of a different mode of being, thinking, working: we learned that lesson the hard way, from Margaret Thatcher.

Women journalists themselves are often rather ambivalent about pursuing a feminist or even a woman-focused journalism. In a recent small-scale study of British women journalists, three-quarters of the sample disagreed profoundly with the statement: 'I try to do journalism from a feminist perspective', although half the sample agreed strongly with the statement: 'Gender in journalism is important because women and men bring different perspectives to their work.' Nearly 60 per cent agreed strongly with the statement: 'More women in senior positions will have a positive impact on the career prospects of women journalists', although only 40 per cent agreed strongly with the statement: 'More women in journalism would make media output more woman-friendly' (Ross 2001). Clearly, then, there are very different views on being female and working in the news industry. Some studies, which look at, say, the extent to which women journalists are more likely to seek out women sources for stories, argue that women media practitioners *do* make a difference (for example, see Liebler and Smith 1997: Zoch and VanSlyke Turk 1998; Lavie and Lehman Wilzig 2003), but my own work suggests, in concert with Arthurs' (1994), that gender on its own is not enough to provoke a culture shift in the newsroom. Even where there *is* a will for change from within, exogenous factors such as a harsher economic climate that threatens the bottom line, can stall or even reverse those tentative shifts (Aldridge 2001).

Gender and culture in the newsroom I – heavy hierarchy

The power to determine the nature and direction of news media content remains firmly in the hands of men: political men who make the news and media men who write about it, the latter at the invitation of the former. The journalist Joanna Coles (1997) suggests that the atmosphere at a typical press conference resembles that of a boys' public school, where a few clever girls have been allowed into the sixth form. The men on the platform address the journalists in their midst by their first names: 'Yes, Simon, do you have a question? Chris? Andrew?' The few women in the press corps are not similarly encouraged with such intimacy, still less invited to put their question. The kinds of stories, perspectives and interests we see and read about in the news media reflect the kinds of social and economic relations that exist in news organizations themselves, as locations of news production. The culture of the newsroom thus provides a strongly gendered context in which the traditional power plays of economic relations – men on top and women underneath – are played out in alarmingly conventional, sex-stereotyped ways. These power relations at the micro level are further confirmed and consolidated at the macro level when ownership and control of news media are explored (Carter, Branston and Allan 1998; M. Martin 2002; Byerly 2004). In the 1960s, the decade that witnessed the flowering of a vibrant and assertive grassroots political movement campaigning on a number of human rights issues, the feminist campaigner Donna Allen (1968) was warning against the dangers of media conglomeratization. Those warnings are still pertinent today and perhaps even *more* urgent now, as the relaxation of competition law enables cross-media ownership on an unprecedented scale, leaving the door open for even fewer men to control the global media stage.

The media, and television in particular, perform a significant function in agenda setting, involved in the promotion of a continuous circuit of meaning (Miller *et al.* 1998). If the point of theory is to provide alternative explanations of our social world, then the purpose of a critical feminist media theory (see McLaughlin 1993) is to question what passes for knowledge and, in this case, to expose a newsroom ethos which masquerades as 'routine' journalistic practice but is actually irrevocably masculine and trivializes women's contributions and experiences. Some studies (see for example Melin-Higgins 2004) suggest that women journalists use strategies of incorporation to combat the prevailing masculine and macho norms which pervade newsrooms by becoming 'one of the boys'. On the other hand, many women working in news industries have decided to opt out of mainstream journalism in order to find a better space in which to express themselves and satirical feminist magazines such as *Spare Rib* and the Scottish magazine *Harpies and Quines* have been part of the result.

Gender and culture in the newsroom II – fighting back

Increasingly, women in news industries are strategizing for change. For example, in late March 2002, more than 60 feminist demonstrators gathered outside the offices of the Federal Communications Commission in Washington, DC, to protest against the FCC decision to further relax regulations governing media mergers and acquisitions in the cable and television industries (Byerly 2004). The demonstration was organized by a grassroots coalition, which included long time media activist Jennifer Pozner who recently formed Women in Media and News (WIMN), Terry O'Neill, vice president of National Organization for Women (NOW), Media Tank and American Resurrection.

In the UK, the *Women in Journalism* group, formed in 1997, grew out of a bottom-up demand for women to be more effectively represented at senior level in newspapers and magazines, and has since evolved into a forum for women in journalism at all levels. Since it began, its regular seminars and parties offer opportunities for women to discuss career issues with their peers as well as providing occasions for networking and have become major events in the media calendar. Seminar topics have included: making a difference (how words can change lives); writing the big book; the Internet for journalists; and the art of the real life interview.[7]

In India, the Network of Women in Media held its second national conference in January 2004 in Mumbai (Joseph 2004b), and among the issues women discussed there was the desirability of networking among themselves. Out of that conference came a series of recommendations for action including the setting up of an NWMI listserv/Egroup to facilitate communication across the country, supplementing the role of the existing Web site. The suggestion of a printed newsletter for the benefit of those with limited access to the Internet was also considered and a decision taken to explore the idea further, starting with a one-off publication providing information about the network(s), which could be translated into different languages by local groups.

These few examples give a taste of the kinds of strategizing with which women are increasingly involved, taking control of their professional lives by finding strength in solidarity and working for change. But successful media women can still be casually undermined by sexist reporting. When Janet Street-Porter became the (albeit short-lived) editor at the *Independent on Sunday* in 1999, in the face of considerable hostility from her fellow professionals, she used her new position to respond to her critics in her trademark style: 'Guys, guys. Calm down, I can take a joke. But it is a little disappointing to be taken for a goggle-eyed harridan with big teeth and no brain after spending 30-odd years in journalism' (Street-Porter 1999: 2).

More recently, when BBC Radio 4 was named as Station of the Year in the Sony Radio awards 2004, the *Independent* ran a serious interview with the station controller, Helen Boaden. Boaden has had a career of 'firsts', having been the first woman appointed as Head of Current Affairs at the BBC (in 1998) and the first woman Controller at BBC Radio 4 (in 2000) since Monica Sims in 1978. Given her experience, why then is the otherwise straight interview headlined 'Radio's Golden Girl' (Burrell 2004)? Perhaps the copy-editor was simply casting around for a suitably celebratory phrase, but then again, perhaps not . . .

▌ Notes

1   For an excellent, if rather dated, account of the media's fascination with reporting sexual crimes, see Soothill and Walby (1991).
2   http://www.genderlinks.org.za.
3   Personal interview with Judy Sandison, SABC, 8 June 2003; e-mail correspondence with Judy Sandison, 10 May 2004.

4   EU/EBU conference: Reflecting diversity: The challenge for women and men in European Broadcasting, June, London, 1995.
5   Personal telephone interview with Thandazo (not her real name), a black woman journalist who works for a major newspaper, 18 June 2003.
6   At least, they occupied these positions at the time of writing, June 2004.
7   www.leisurejobs.net/wij/index.cfm (accessed 13 February 2004).

▌References

Aldridge, M. (2001) Lost Expectations? Women Journalists and the Fall-out from the 'Toronto Newspaper War', *Media, Culture and Society*, 23(5): 607–24.

Allan, S. (1999) *News Culture*. Buckingham: Open University Press.

Allen, D. (1968) Up Against the Media. *The Liberated Voice* (July) http://www.wifp.org/donnaallenbeforewifp.html (accessed 10 February 2004).

Annenberg Public Policy Center (2002) *No Room at the Top?* Philadelphia, PA: University of Pennsylvania.

Arthurs, J. (1994) Women and Television, in S. Hood (ed.) *Behind the Screens*. London: Lawrence & Wishart.

Beasley, M. H. (1993) Newspapers – Is There a New Majority Defining the News? In P. J. Creedon (ed.) *Women in Communication*, second edition, Newbury Park: Sage.

Burrell, I. (2004) 'Radio's Golden Girl', *Independent*, 1 June.

Bunting, M. (2001) Special Report: Terrorism in the US. *Guardian*, 20 September, www.guardian.co.uk/analysis/story/0,3604,554794,00.html (accessed 4 February 2004).

Byerly, C. M. (2001) The Deeper Structures of Storytelling: Women, Media Corporations and the Task of Communication Researchers, *Intersections*, 1(2): 63–8.

Byerly, C. M. (2002) Gender and the Political Economy of Newsmaking: a Case Study of Human Rights Coverage, in E. R. Meehan and E. Riordan (eds) *Sex and Money: Feminism and Political Economy in the Media*. Minneapolis, MN: University of Minnesota Press.

Byerly, C. M. (2004) Women and Media Concentration, in R. R. Rush, E. C. Oukrup and P. J. Creedon (eds) *Seeking Equity for Women in Journalism and Mass Communication: a 30-Year Update*, Mahwah, NJ: Lawrence Erlbaum Associates.

Cann, D. and Mohr, P. B. (2001) Journalist and Source Gender in Australian Television News, *Journal of Broadcasting and Electronic Media*, 45(1): 162–74.

Carter, C., Branston, G. and Allan, S. (eds) (1998) *News, Gender and Power*. London: Routledge.

Carter, C. and Weaver, C. K. (2003) *Violence and the Media*. Basingstoke: Open University Press.

Christmas, L. (1997) *Chaps of Both Sexes? Women Decision-Makers in Newspapers: Do They Make a Difference?* London: Women in Journalism.

Christmas, L. (1996) *Women in the News: Does Sex Change the Way a Newspaper Thinks?* London: Women in Journalism.

Coles, J. (1997) Boy Zone Story, *Guardian*, 28 April.

Del Zotto, A. C. (2002) Weeping Women, Wringing Hands: How the Mainstream Media Stereotyped Women's Experiences in Kosovo, *Journal of Gender Studies*, 11(2): 141–50.

Dougary, G. (1994) *The Executive Tart and Other Myths: Media Women Talk Back.* London: Virago.

European Commission (1999) *Images of Women in the Media.* Brussels: EC.

Gallagher, M. (1988) *Women and Television in Europe.* Brussels: Commission of the European Communities.

Gallagher, M. (1995) *An Unfinished Story: Gender Patterns in Media Employment* (Reports and Papers on Mass Communication 110). Paris: UNESCO Publishing.

Holland, P. (1998) The Politics of the Smile: 'Soft News' and the Sexualisation of the Popular Press, in C. Carter, G. Branston and S. Allan (eds) *News, Gender and Power.* London and New York: Routledge.

Joseph, A. (2004a) Working, Watching and Waiting: Women and Issues of Access, Employment and Decision-making in the Media in India, in K. Ross and C. M. Byerly (eds) *Women and Media: International Perspectives.* Oxford: Blackwell Publishing.

Joseph, A. (2004b) NWMI's Second National Meeting, http://www.nwmindia.org/ (accessed 9 February 2004).

Kitzinger, J. (2004) Media Coverage of Sexual Violence Against Women and Children, in K. Ross and C. Byerly (eds) *Women and Media: International Perspectives.* Oxford: Blackwell Publishing.

Lauer, N. C. (2002) Studies Show Women's Role in Media Shrinking. Women's Enews, www.womensenews.org (accessed 11 February 2004).

Lavie, A. and Lehman-Wilzig, S. (2003) Whose News? Does Gender Determine the Editorial Product? *European Journal of Communication,* 18(1): 5–29.

Lemish, D. (2004) Exclusion and Marginality: Portrayals of Women in Israeli Media, in K. Ross and C. Byerly (eds) *Women and Media: International Perspectives.* Oxford: Blackwell.

Liebler, C. and Smith, S. (1997) Tracking Gender Differences: a Comparative Analysis of Network Correspondents and their Sources, *Journal of Broadcasting and Electronic Media,* 41 (winter): 58–68.

McLaughlin, L. (1993) Feminism and the Public Sphere, *Media, Culture and Society,* 15(4): 599–620.

McLaughlin, L. (1998) Gender, Privacy and Publicity in 'Media Event Space', in C. Carter, G. Branston and S. Allan (eds) *News, Gender and Power.* London and New York: Routledge.

McNair, B., Hibberd, M. and Schlesinger, P. (2003) *Mediated Access: Broadcasting and Democratic Participation in the Age of Mediated Politics.* Luton: University of Luton Press.

Martin, M. (2002) An Unsuitable Technology for a Woman? Communication as Circulation, in E. R. Meehan and E. Riordan (eds) *Sex and Money: Feminism and Political Economy in the Media.* Minneapolis, MN: University of Minnesota Press.

Martin, S. (2002) The political economy of women's employment in the information sector, in E. R. Meehan and E. Riordan (eds) *Sex and Money: Feminism and Political Economy in the Media.* Minneapolis, MN: University of Minnesota Press.

Media Watch (1995) *Global Media Monitoring Project: Women's Participation in the News.* Ontario: Media Watch.

Melin-Higgins, M. (2004) Coping with Journalism: Gendered Newsroom Culture in Britain, in M. de Bruin and K. Ross (eds) *Gender and Newsroom Cultures: Identities at Work.* Cresskill, NJ: Hampton Press.

Michielsens, M. (1991) *Women in View: How Does BRTN Portray Women?* Brussels: BRTN.

Miller, D., Kitzinger, J., Williams, K. and Beharrell, P. (1998) *The Circuit of Mass Communication: Media Strategies, Representation and Audience Reception in the Aids Crisis.* London: Sage.

Naylor, B. (2001) Reporting Violence in the British Print Media: Gendered Stories, *Howard Journal of Criminal Justice*, 40(2): 180–94.

Neves, H. (1994) Unpublished plenary address to the Prix Niki conference, March, Lisbon.

Norris, P. (1997) Women Leaders Worldwide: a Splash of Color in the Photo Op., in P. Norris (ed.) *Women, Media and Politics.* Oxford: Oxford University Press.

NOS Gender Portrayal Department (1995) *Interviewtechnieken in acualiteitenprogramma's (Interview Techniques on Male and Female Guests in Dutch Current Affairs Features).* Hilversum: NOS.

Ross, K. (2001) Women at Work: Journalism as En-gendered Practice. *Journalism Studies* 2(4): 531–44.

Ross, K. (2002) *Women, Politics, Media: Uneasy Relations in Comparative Perspective.* Cresskill, NJ: Hampton Press.

Ross, K. (2004) Political Talk Radio and Democratic Participation: Caller Perspectives on *Election Call. Media, Culture and Society*, 26(6): 785–801.

Rush, R. R. (2001) Three decades of women and mass communications research: the ratio of recurrent and reinforced residuum hypothesis (r^3) revisited. Paper presented at Donna Allen Memorial Symposium, Freedom Forum, Roslyn, VA.

Soothill, K. and Walby, W. (1991) *Sex Crime in the News.* London: Routledge.

Steiner, L. (1998) Newsroom Accounts of Power at Work, in C. Carter, G. Branston and S. Allan (eds) *News, Gender and Power.* London: Routledge.

Street-Porter, J. (1999) Editorial. *Independent on Sunday*, 11 July.

Van Zoonen, L. (1998) One of the Girls? The Changing Gender of Journalism, in C. Carter, G. Branston and S. Allan (eds) *News, Gender and Power.* London & New York: Routledge.

Women in Journalism (1999) *Real Women: The Hidden Sex.* London: WiJ.

Women's Broadcasting Committee (1993) *Her Point of View.* London: WBC and Bectu.

World Association of Christian Communication (2000) *Global Media Monitoring Project 2000.* London: WACC.

Zoch, L. M. and VanSlyke Turk, J. (1998) Women Making News: Gender as a Variable in Source Selection and Use, *Journalism and Mass Communication Quarterly*, 75(4): 762–75.

22

Gendered news practices

Examining experiences of women journalists in different national contexts

Minelle Mahtani

- What is the relationship between journalism and masculinist practices?
- Do women journalists experience newsroom culture differently from men journalists?
- How do women journalists challenge prevailing definitions of power in their day-to-day professional lives?

This chapter investigates the experiences of women journalists and the challenges they face in a variety of international sites, ranging from Mumbai, Toronto, Sydney and Melbourne. Drawing from open-ended, qualitative interviews with women journalists, I will suggest that while we are witnessing an increase in the number of women entering the field of journalism (Walsh-Childers *et al.* 1996), women journalists continue to face systemic gender discrimination – discrimination that is remarkably similar, despite the different cities where interviews were conducted. I will contend that newsroom dynamics reflect pervasive patterns of masculinism, where women's subordination is recirculated and reproduced despite differences in geography, language and culture. Such masculinist practices appear to be broadly internationalized and localized within the particular newsroom sites identified in this study.

This brief snapshot of the experiences of women journalists in a variety of locales suggests that it is premature to celebrate the dawning of a new era where we are witnessing an increase in the number of women working in journalism. Instead, these interviews reveal that, in spite of these increases, women face complex forms of gender discrimination, which limit their ability to contribute fully to their respective media outlets. Paying particular attention to the kinds of women who are increasingly hired in these newsrooms, I propose that hiring practices reveal systemic patterns of gender subordination, which, if remain unchallenged, have significant ramifications that directly correspond with women journalists' lack of visibility and power – both in the newsroom and of their representation in the media.

Research in the arenas of sociology, feminist theory, and journalism studies have explored the relationship between gender and journalism (Henry and Tator 2004; Gauntlett 2002; Aldridge 2001; Women in Journalism 1999; Carter, Branston and Allan 1998, Baehr and Gray 1996). Such examinations demonstrate a significant effort to consider the role of gender, sexuality, media and performativity. However, few studies have engaged in transnational examinations of the day-to-day experiences of women journalists who are multiply situated in a variety of newsrooms around the world. How do their respective geographies and locations influence their understanding of their experiences in the newsroom? How does their embodied presence in the newsroom influence and challenge masculinist norms reverberating within this particular site of media production? This chapter will examine these questions by suggesting that choices for varied representations of a wide array of marginalized groups in news coverage are made within the rigid restraints of a gendered hierarchy in the newsroom, and remain remarkably similar, despite changes in geography due to the infrastructure of the production of news discourse.

▎Masculinism, objectivity and journalism

Journalism has come to reflect a paragon of progressive liberalism, tolerance, fairness and the search for truth. The world of journalism has often been characterized by these ideas, where the notion of objectivity has anchored the philosophical underpinnings of reporting (see Zelizer and Allan 2002 for critiques). In this section, I will address the problematic nature of such claims by pointing out how masculinism – an ideology that reinforces and justifies continued male domination – structures these imagined forms of journalism's virtues.

According to the standards of objectivity, journalists' personal experiences and life histories ought to be irrelevant and left at the door in the process of news gathering. Their personal histories should not enter into their work. Their identities should not matter. The celebration of objectivity as a standard for newswriting forces journalists to erase themselves from their stories, distance themselves from their subjects, and adopt a consistent pattern of cultural neutrality. However, despite what we would like to believe, news reporting is not fair, democratic nor objective in nature (Alterman 2003; Schecter 2003; Robinson 2002). A CBS news manager once said in an infamous anecdote, 'Our reporters don't cover stories from their point of view. They are presenting them from nobody's point of view.' Such a quote reveals the kind of fallacies upon which journalism has been based. News stories do not emerge from nowhere. Assuming otherwise alleviates journalists' responsibility from considering self-reflexive approaches to journalism, as well as assuming that journalists' personal and professional geographies and experiences never mix. The reality is that journalists, despite popular sentiment, never truly stand outside the communities they cover (Henry and Tator 2002; Mahtani 2001a; Fleras and Kunz 2001). Nonetheless, superficial understandings of democracy, neutrality, balance and fairness govern news-gathering processes, as if transparent neutrality should – and can – exist. The insistence that reporters identities and experiences can be made irrelevant, and that all good reporters leave their racialized, gendered and classed identities at home before they leave to investigate a news story continue to have a tremendous impact on journalists, but it has particular ramifications for women journalists.

The feminist geographer Kim England has suggested that research is a process, not just a product, and that part of that process is reflecting on, and learning from, past experiences (England 1994). Our own identities, whether we like it or not, always play a role in the acquisition of material and the ways we, as academics, literally 'report' our stories. I would suggest that the same can be said about news construction and production. The demand for disembodied objectivity – as if such a thing could ever exist – has specific implications for women journalists. Feminist theorists have insisted that modern political and moral theories have depended upon a binary opposition between reason and rationality – understood traditionally as masculine, versus emotion and desire – designated as feminine. As Gillian Rose has pointed out, rationality has been associated with a universal masculinity, and the subjectivity associated with women is not seen as objective or rational (Rose 1993). Thus, non-rational or non-objective forms of feminine knowledge are relegated to the private sphere, as unimportant or as too uninteresting to be considered truly 'newsworthy'.

The assignment of the female body to the private, and the male body to the public, has also effectively shown how women have been positioned as 'out of place'. This assignment of women to the private realm has consequences in the world of news gathering as well. According to the mythology, women are simply unable to transcend their bodies or their personal involvement with others – and thus they cannot 'write' their way out of their bodies in the same way that men can. This has had a particularly resonance in the world of journalism, where 'women's stories' are still seen as those that focus on the personal, domestic, and the home.

Equating masculinism and objectivity has forced many women journalists to attempt to adopt more masculine traits in the field of journalism in order to become more successful – by wearing particular kinds of clothing (three piece suits, not short skirts) or acting in a way that is seen as traditionally male (Mahtani 2001b). The embedding of masculinity within the newsroom might thus be seen as a lengthy, complicated, complex social and often political process, often marked by gendered performances (Butler 1990).

Masculinized newsroom practices encourage rationality and objectivity, influencing newsroom culture in particular ways, as the following interviews will illustrate. Masculine values and interests permeate the newsroom culture in ways that are often invisible and systematic, leading to ostracization for many women who dare to deviate from those social gendered codes that are sanctioned. Even the language of news reflects masculinist leanings – a story is 'killed', 'if it bleeds, it leads', 'I need a spear for that story'. What are the implications of a masculinist newsroom culture for women journalists – and how do they counter the production and exchange of meanings that are reproduced and recirculated in their respective newsrooms?

Interviews

To consider these questions, I interviewed women journalists working in Mumbai, Toronto, Sydney and Melbourne in 2002. The majority of women interviewed were found through word of mouth. As an ex-journalist myself, I had contact with a number of women who work in the field and 'put the word out' that I was searching for other women to speak to about their experiences as a journalist. It is important to note that my own status as an ex-journalist played a significant role in the acquisition of interview material. I was a national television news producer in Toronto for five years, and that experience created a 'paradoxical space' (Rose 1993). For example, at times during the interviews, women journalists would cock their head, and smile, saying 'well, you know what I mean, Minelle', when in fact I had no idea what they were saying. However, the interviewee assumed that I understood what she was saying. At other times, women journalists would say, 'Well, that's the kind of thing, I'm telling you, because you've been there, I don't think others would understand . . .' thus allowing me access to stories that they may not have otherwise told me. Such experiences forced me to consider the importance of self-reflexivity throughout the gathering of interview material and to continually contemplate my own role in the acquisition of narratives.

For this chapter, I draw from a pool of 20 interviews with women journalists conducted between the years 2000 and 2004. I asked women journalists questions related to their jobs and their day-to-day experiences in their newsrooms and related to their career paths and culture of news production practices. All interviews were tape recorded and transcribed. The women were employed in a variety of journalist arenas, including print, radio and television. The women cited here worked at major daily newspapers, radio stations and various television networks in Mumbai, Toronto, Sydney and Melbourne, including, but not limited to, the *Sydney Morning Herald*, Melbourne's the *Age*, the *Special Broadcasting Service* (Australia's multilingual and multicultural radio and television services), the *Times of India*, the *Canadian Broadcasting Corporation* (CBC) radio and television networks, and the *Toronto Star*, among other media organizations. A few of the women interviewed (two out of twenty) were freelancers. The women ranged in age from 26 to 56, although most of them had worked in journalism for at least 8 years at the time of the interview. All the names employed are pseudonyms and I do not identify where each woman worked, as almost all the women expressed concern that they could be 'outed' by what they had said during the interview.

Before launching into the interview material, it is important to note that this chapter is selectively drawing on such material for purposes of illustration. The chapter is not meant to be comprehensive in scope – rather, it is utilized in this context to provide a glimpse into the day-to-day lives of women journalists in various global cities. Thus, although it is impossible to draw significant generalizations from this data, it is nevertheless useful for the purposes of identifying conceptual issues deserving of future enquiry into the issues facing women and news production. In the rest of the chapter, I explore some of the themes that resonated throughout the interviews, specifically related to gender discrimination in the workplace of many women journalists. I begin with an examination of women's relationship to their positions in the newsroom.

'Yes, the news is different when I write it': women's relationship to their jobs as journalists

Almost all of the women interviewed readily suggested that their own status as a woman influenced the way the told stories as a journalist. Many of the women journalists in this study explained that their gendered identities played a pivotal role in how they carried out their job. Rachel, a 55-year-old radio host in Melbourne focused on her ability to be 'silent' during the interview as a way of drawing out interviewees – a theme that emerged among many interviews as being traditionally feminine:

> My day-to-day reality at work now is sort of partly journalism, partly politics. Because I said, I told you I was elected deputy staff elected director of the [network]. I think . . . if you believe the silence of it all . . . women are good at communicating, we're good at empathizing; we're good at getting people to talk. So, unconsciously probably my role as a woman is quite important in my job, in my daily job . . . I think it's my job to make . . . to bring out the ideas of the people I'm interviewing. Not necessarily to make them look good but if they are good then that's why I want to talk to them. It's not really about how clever I am and how cute I am or how seductive I am or something like that. So probably a bit of self-effacement as a woman compared to a man, that might come in handy in actually making good programmes.

Karla, a 35-year-old newspaper reporter in Melbourne, insisted that women offered a varied viewpoint on news coverage. However, she pointed out that such perspectives were not necessarily valued in her workplace. Indeed, this was a similar theme that came up in interviews in different locales. Interviews in various cities revealed that gender discrimination in story assignments occurred regularly. Several women journalists explained that there were significant obstacles to their ability to alter prevailing news paradigms as Karla suggests:

I think that woman actually do often have quite a different perspective on what's interesting or important about the news. It doesn't fit with the male norm view and therefore we are often dismissed, out of hand. It's not quite that we are belittled actively so much as just ignored. And they just go their own way.

Karla went on to explain that very few women were in positions of power at her newspaper. Women who were in more senior roles tended to dominate the 'lifestyle' sections of the paper or what are seen to be traditionally more 'feminine' arenas of the newspaper – those stories that were seen as less rational, objective and more emotional. As has been suggested by others (see Walsh-Childers *et al.* 1996), hard news stories tend to go to men whereas soft news stories are often assigned to women journalists. Several women insisted that the plum assignments (often seen as hard news stories) were awarded to men and that story assignments were distributed solely on the basis of gender, primarily because of the lack of women in senior positions at their media outlets. Karla explained that there were few women in positions of power at her place of employment and that most women were employed in what was considered the 'soft' news arena:

> There are virtually no women in serious gate-keeping roles at [my paper]. I think at last count we had something like twenty-eight section editors and I think one or two were women. And they were editors of the sections like Epicurean – the food section.

Many women interviewed suggested that gender discrimination was a significant problem, especially in relation to women in positions of power in their newsroom. Several women clearly feel discriminated against in regards to their ability to occupy senior level positions in their workplace. For example, in my interview with Tara, a 45-year-old television producer in Toronto, she emphasized that women were often segregated into particular kinds of positions – namely, covering 'lifestyle' stories – and doors to other areas – including areas like 'investigative journalism' – were rarely open to them:

> Despite the fact that there are many women who work in this [newsroom], the reins of power lie with the men. There are more women executive producers and managers than ever before. But there are still departments where women are still in a distinct minority, and are not encouraged to enter.

In the next section, I will suggest that a certain representation of 'woman' is promoted in the newsroom – the 'safe and attractive' woman, a non-threatening presence who serves to increase the numbers of women in the newsroom without necessarily challenging the status quo.

The 'safe and attractive woman' – hiring women who do not challenge men in authority

Several women journalists in this study questioned whether or not an increased number of women journalists in the newsroom in fact challenged pervasive forms of masculinist practices present in their workplace. Many newsrooms will now cite the growing number of women employed through details on their Web sites, highlighting the so-called successes of gender parity in their respective newsrooms. However, such figures are misleading. In interviews, women pinpointed that there was a particular kind of hiring on the increase – hiring of what I will call 'the safe and attractive woman'. Many women journalists interviewed explained that some women enacted particular kinds of performances in order not to subvert prevailing paradigms of power. Rachel presented a particularly dismal portrait of the dynamics of the newsroom, suggesting that some women in her workplace who were recently hired deliberately chose not to challenge masculinist perspectives:

> This organization I'm working at the moment, which is run by a kind of Caligula figure, that he's surrounded himself with women at top management levels in order that he doesn't have a lot of alpha males trying to challenge him for his own position. This is my suspicion, because I think that the kind of women that he is surrounding himself with are women who will not challenge him. They are really happy to be running things but in fact they're doing his bidding. That's not a real great advance for women, I don't think. It looks good on the numbers, but it doesn't mean anything in practice.

Karla echoed many of Rachel's concerns, suggesting that men working in positions of power in the newsroom surrounded themselves both with women who would not challenge their positions and were also considered attractive:

> Basically it seems to me the sort of women they like to have around are beautiful women who will accept their world view and move with it and just do things when and where they need to be done. The same things goes for the men here, they tend to like beautiful men too, or men at least who see things the way they see them.

Karla also explained that some women who do work in 'hard news' stories are often seen as merely following or carrying out story ideas that are initially suggested by men on the assignment desk:

> They do have women on the news desk, but they tend to be in what I call handmaiden roles. So they're women who are smart and capable and very good administrators and they're used to implement the male editors' ideas. And it seems to me they don't actually have much input themselves.

Lack of mentoring: why young women leave journalism

The relative absence of women who would challenge prevailing mascu-linist viewpoints in the newsroom and in stories tended to be a significant theme that dominated interviews. Karla focused on the lack of resources available to young women who were coming up the ranks at her paper. She lamented that many young women starting in journalism confronted the glass ceiling early on in their careers, and moved on to other creative professions, like screenwriting, marketing, advertising, publishing or other areas of the arts, revealing a lack of support for young women in journalism:

> Younger women often come to me and say, 'There are no role models. I can see I've got no future here'. And our brightest young women are routinely dropping back, going to something on the night desk and finding other things to do. They go back to university. They start writing cinema scripts. They decide to put their creative energy into something other than their journalism because they feel like there are not going to get anywhere here. And they don't make a fuss. They don't talk to our managers about their disheartenment. It happens silently. And so the men are completely unaware of it. So a part of it is about women self-selecting to drop out because they feel that the environment is so unsympathetic. In terms of femininity, some women have found their femininity very well and actually it's more of a problem to not be feminine.

The silence that shrouds this process is of particular interest. Karla's emphasis on the fact that these women 'don't make a fuss' or 'talk to . . . managers about their disheartenment' demonstrates the very real challenges that these women face when confronted with systemic gender biases in their newsroom. Rather than making a concerted attempt to challenge these biases, Karla suggests that these women choose to drop out completely to find their own way to be successful outside of the oppressive newsroom dynamics. Many of the women journalists interviewed suggested that these processes tend to be invisible to senior management, who do not envision these 'dropouts' as a problem, as Karla pointed out:

> It's really clear to me that management has no sense at all that this is a problem for the product. I think that's the first step. We've tried to do various things from committees within the paper and through the years on . . . and they have been really strong and resistant. And it's a world-view thing. I mean it actually makes sense to me, if patriarchy is a system of ideas – okay? What is going to be the last organization to change? The organization that generates the ideas. Do you see what I mean? The problem is that they don't see that it's a problem. They think it might be – if it's a problem at all it's a problem maybe for some of the women. But even then they discount that and say 'Really there's all these people over here doing really well look at how it used to be?' So I think there's a

fair chance that it is not going to get fixed. I have to tell you I think it's not going to change.

Women journalists interviewed spoke not only of women's experiences in the newsroom but also about the role of younger men journalists in newsrooms. They explained that younger men who are employed within their media outlets are not necessarily more willing to challenge gender discrimination. It was suggested by Karla earlier in the interview that there were hopes associated with the employ of younger men within her newsroom, as it was (erroneously) assumed that these men would be less entrenched within the system and more willing to confront discrimination in the newsroom. However, Karla suggested that this was not the case at her own paper:

> And even with some of the younger men I see coming through who don't have the sort of sensitivities and antagonisms towards women and women's power that the older men do, they still don't see that there are any gender issues in the paper. They think everything is hunky dory. So until they see it as their problem that is impacting on the success of product, nothing is going to change.

Expectations of audience played a key role for women, who told me that their news organizations had a very clear idea for whom they were writing – and that their target demographic was not women. Karla explained that her paper specifically aimed to relate their news coverage to men, and that had implications for her as a writer as well as her perspective on her paper's ability to reach out to new, varied audiences:

> I would say that we write for a very conservative middle-aged male audience, which is fine if they are a big enough audience to support the circulation we need, but it's not. And that I think until they open themselves up to alternative ways of looking at the world generally, we are going to have a stuffy product that most young people are going to find utterly irrelevant. I mean we are just so out of touch with young people it's extraordinary.

| Examples of successful networking

In contrast to the interviews conducted in Australia, many of the women journalists in India explained that they had strong support networks to provide them with the help they needed to be successful as journalists. When I asked Australian women journalists if there were support groups for women journalists I often found that I was looked at blankly or questioned if such groups existed in other cities. In contrast, responses in India were strikingly different. In my interview with Kiirti, a 45-year-old newspaper columnist in Mumbai, I was told that there were regular meetings for women journalists. However, interestingly, these meetings were not seen as 'women's meetings' but rather meetings for journalists more generally – but no men were present:

> I think in Bombay we're lucky. I meet other women journalists at the press club once a month. The fact that we are women journalists I think is a kind of coincidence or an accident or we don't sit and discuss women journalists' problems, we discuss journalists' problems.

There was resistance from many members of the group interviewed to see themselves as 'feminists' working within a 'feminist' group. Several women insisted that they were not part of an 'active' women's movement; rather, they saw their participation within these groups as a personal rather than political objective. Another woman, Priya, a 31-year-old freelance journalist working in Mumbai, explained her own position:

> I have never been involved in women's issues. So yeah, all these women you would probably find I am sure would be happy to call themselves feminists. I must say that recently I met someone who says that she doesn't want to call herself a feminist any longer. In fact I wrote a piece about it, because I think those who were feminist like some who were leftist have become a bit disillusioned. I guess I never was in that sense a part of the women's movement actively.

Opportunities for change?

Despite citing examples of systemic discrimination in various newsrooms, many women were optimistic about the possibility for change. While it is clear that several women journalists understand newsroom policies and practices as intrinsically gendered, almost all the interviewees insisted that there were many opportunities for senior management to consider where they could effectively challenge prevailing paradigms of masculinism. Miranda, a 45-year-old newspaper editor for a daily Sydney paper, explained that there were ways that newsrooms could develop a more equitable and open arena for women which would effectively confront systemic gender discrimination in her newsroom:

> I mean you know basically, there's a million ways they could do it. They could promote more women to senior positions, actually listen to them and take their ideas on board. You know, all those things newspapers don't do because they're medieval lords with victims, and they have absolute power.

At the very core of Miranda's narrative is a discussion of power – how it is circulated, re-invoked and permeates newsroom culture. Until power dynamics between women and men journalists are unveiled, made visible, discussed and then challenged, only then will we begin to witness a change in the experiences of women journalists.

This chapter has emphasized through interviews that women journalists in various cities believe they experience newsroom culture differently from men journalists. Many women interviewed explained that there were many ways that gender discrimination could be challenged in their respective workplaces. It is clear from the interviews that women experience varied forms of gender discrimination in newsrooms in various workplace settings in a number of cities worldwide. This indicates that these experiences are not place-specific but rather represent a global scenario occurring in newsrooms that are remarkably similar in regards to gendered professional practices.

Traditionally, successful news gathering has been garnered by a series of imperatives which hold objectivity, fairness and equality in high esteem. Unfortunately, these interviews suggest that there remain forms of inequity and discrimination occurring in newsrooms in a variety of international contexts. For many women interviewed in this study, their place within the newsroom culture was framed through an experience of otherness that relied upon gendered stereotypes of 'woman' – a positioning that relegated them to particular kinds of jobs within the newsroom.

Systemic gender discrimination is a regular way of life for women journalists in cities ranging from Toronto, Sydney, Melbourne and Mumbai. Despite increasing numbers of women entering the world of journalism, the journalistic world continues to be structured by gendered inequities that must be addressed if our representations of women in the news truly hope to be democratic and inclusive.

▌ References

Aldrige, M. (2001) Lost Expectations? Women Journalists and the Fall-out from the 'Toronto Newspaper War', *Media, Culture and Society*, 23(5): 607–24.

Alterman, E. (2003) *What Liberal Media?* New York: Basic Books.

Arthurs, J. (1994) Women and Television, in S. Hood (ed.) *Behind the Screens*. London: Lawrence & Wishart.

Baehr, H. and Gray, A. (eds) (1996) *Turning it On: A Reader in Women and Media*. London: Arnold.

Butler, J. (1990) *Gender Trouble*. London: Routledge.

Carter, C., Branston, G. and Allan, S. (1998) *News, Gender and Power*. London: Routledge.

England, K. (1994) Getting Personal: Reflexivity, Positionality and Feminist Research, *The Professional Geographer*, 46(1) 80–9.

Fleras, A. and Kunz, J. (2001) *Media and Minorities: Representing Diversity in a Multicultural Canada*. Toronto: Thompson Educational Publishing.

Gautlett, D. (2002) *Media, Gender and Identity*. London: Routledge.

Henry, F. and Tator, C. (2002) *Discourses of Domination: Racial Bias in the Canadian English-Language Press*. Toronto: University of Toronto Press.

Henry, F. and Tator, C. (2004) Discrediting the Minister and Her Message: What the Media Did to Hedy Fry! Unpublished paper available from F. Henry, York University, Toronto, Ontario.

Mahtani, M. (2001a) Representing Minorities: Canadian Media and Minority Identities, *Canadian Ethnic Studies*, 33(3): 99–133.

Mahtani, M. (2001b) Mapping the Meanings of 'Racism' and "Feminism" among Women Television Broadcast Journalists in Canada', in F. W. Twine and K. Blee (eds) *Feminism and Anti-Racism: International Struggles*. New York: New York University Press, pp. 349–67.

Robinson, P. (2002) *The CNN Effect: The Myth of News, Foreign Policy and Intervention*. London: Routledge.

Rose, G. (1993) *Feminism and Geography*. London: Polity.

Schechter, D. (2003) *Weapons of Mass Deception: How the Media Failed to Cover the War on Iraq*. New York: Prometheus Books.

Shohat, E. and Stam, R. (2003) *Multiculturalism, Postcoloniality and Transnational Media*. New Brunswick: Rutgers University Press.

Walsh-Childers, K., Chance, J. and Herzog, K. (1996) Women Journalists Report Discrimination in Newsrooms, *Newspaper Research Journal*, 17(3–4): 68–87.

Women in Journalism (1999) *Real Women: The Hidden Sex*. London: WiJ.

Zelizer, B. and Allan, S. (eds) (2002) *Journalism After September 11*. London and New York: Routledge.

PART V

Journalism and the public interest

23

Subterfuge as public service

Investigative journalism as idealized journalism

Michael Bromley

- Is investigative journalism 'the pinnacle of journalism'?
- Is it no more than an excuse to snoop and spy?
- Why is the public hardly ever asked what it thinks about undercover journalists?
- Have investigative journalists squandered the legacy of Watergate?

By the beginning of the twenty-first century, investigative journalism was seen to be in retreat (notably but not exclusively, in the US, UK, Canada and Australia – Bernt and Greenwald 2000; Haxton 2002; Hencke 2001; Malarek 1998). A commonly held explanation for this was the advance of ' "lifestyle" stories, trivia, scandal, celebrity gossip, sensational crime, sex in high places, and tabloidism' as a function of the process of the further commercialization of the media (Bromley 1998; Ehrlich 2000; Hickey 1998). Another was the development of 'splurge' journalism – the instant, sweeping coverage of major events – which left little scope to establish 'a foundation of accumulated research or comprehension' (Woolfinden 1996). Behind both of these positions lay the spectre of the intensification of concentrations of media ownership, which journalists themselves believed 'chilled' the atmosphere for investigative reporting (Foot 1999: 86; Haxton 2002: 22–4; Schultz 1998: 53–4). By 2001, the Independent Television Commission (2002: 33) reported, investigative journalism was a rarity on British commercial television, marginalized on the minority interest Channel Four. Moreover, one of the practitioners of investigative reporting was not a journalist at all, but the comedian Mark Thomas (Collins 2000).

Where reporting in an investigatory style continued, it was accused of being without substance – journalism that amounted only to 'digging up dirt' (Rogers 2001; Williams 1998: 249–51); an 'exposure journalism' reliant on 'stinging' the rich and famous (de Burgh 2000: 19–21), or serving the political-economy and ideological interests of media owners (Linklater

1993: 18–19). In television, investigative journalism was expected to contribute to 'the rush for ratings' (O'Carroll 2000; Reeves 2000); to initiate controversy, to generate publicity, and to be seen as glamorous. Investigative journalists were projected as 'stars' (BBC 2000: 2; O'Sullivan 1999). The series *MacIntyre Undercover*, the most expensive current affairs programme in the history of the BBC, was promoted in 1999 as a response to 'fiercely aggressive and growing competition' from commercial television (O'Sullivan 1999; Salmon 1999). Broadcast on BBC1, the channel where the controller argued 'there's been too much factual material', it contributed to a schedule intended to be 'truly popular' (Salmon 2000). The eponymous investigative journalist, Donal MacIntyre acknowledged that his role was in part to assist the BBC in 'develop[ing] a brand' (quoted O'Sullivan 1999).[1]

BBC news and current affairs executives unselfconsciously privileged journalism that was populist, 'exciting and original', and had 'impact' (Tomlin 2000, 2001), whereas investigative journalism, it was argued even by its practitioners, was 'often complicated ... unentertaining and inconclusive' (Tom Bower cited Spark 1999: 17). It was proposed not only that for television, 'Truth is important, but not quite so important as keeping the audience tuned in', but even that television was 'incapable of being made congruent with the discipline of truth-telling in all its complexity, tedium and dread minutiae' (Young 1990: 14–15). The Australian version of *60 Minutes*, although laying claim to a catalogue of 'bullet-dodging, cult-busting, criminal-unearthing, scandal-exposing and celebrity-probing', was also criticized for sensationalism, trivialization and chequebook journalism (Jackson 2004). In the US 'investigative journalism', and especially the hidden camera and 'sting' operations of undercover reporting, were mobilized to boost television audiences. Consultants engaged to advise news executives on consumer preferences told reporters that 'good' journalism was determined by looks and sound, while all other qualities were far less important.[2] Investigative reporting was hybridized with the publicizing of individual, often highly personal, issues and complaints, so that so-called investigative units incorporated elements which hardly resembled journalism at all.[3]

Finally, investigative journalism was highly dependent on public support. Relying heavily on a sense of 'objective' muckraking, which sometimes shaded towards the greater engagement characteristic of campaigning or crusading, though within strictly defined and understood parameters (Stein 2001: 250–1, 254–5), investigative journalists asserted a moral advocacy on behalf of their imagined audiences. In US television news programmes they were found to be more prominent, more active and more assertive than reporters working on more tabloid, magazine shows (Grabe *et al.* 1999). They were described as 'ethical gladiators' (Stein 2001: 266–7). Nevertheless, these programmes also made their sources visible and voluble, even though they continued to be drawn from a rather narrow élite. By comparison, the newer type of news magazine show subordinated both reporters and sources to visual story telling (Grabe *et al.* 1999).

Justification for investigative reporting was derived from its purposes –

whether that was 'to bring about positive change in existing laws or to expose wrongdoing' (Greenwald and Bernt 2000: 4); or to uncover something that was previously undisclosed (Investigative Reporters and Editors cited in Armao 2000: 43); or 'to discover the truth, and to identify lapses from it' (de Burgh 2000: 9); or to enlighten the public to empower it (Leigh 2000). Investigative reporting proceeded from the *a priori* assumption that 'The job of the investigative journalist is to find something wrong and expose it, [and that] he or she is a positive force for change . . .' (Boyd 2001: 29). This became not merely a question of applying 'forensic skills to what we have been told' as a form of scrutiny, but of assuming the role of moral arbiters – as 'unlicensed sentinels of public morals sneaking into positions to monitor behavior in bedrooms and offices' (de Burgh 2000: 67–70; Ettema and Glasser 1998: 3–4; Stephens 1997: 242). Literal examples of this abounded. In 2003 the [London] *Daily Mirror* planted a journalist in the Royal household (supposedly to demonstrate security failures), which produced photographs of

> the royal breakfast table, complete with flowers, cereals in Tupperware boxes and a plate of fruit . . . the Duke of York's room with a touching message to 'Daddy' embroidered on a pillow . . . [and] the décor in the Wessex's 'stylish bathroom'.
>
> (Lamont 2003)

In pursuing this kind of investigation, journalists were constrained by the 'publicity test', by which they were compelled to justify their actions, and have them accepted, in a wider public domain. Ultimately, it was this 'public court' that sat in judgement on how journalists conducted themselves, and to which those abused by investigative reporting could appeal (Jackson 1992: 106–10). The Australian television journalist Jenny Brockie (in *The Media Report* 2003) argued, 'I think it's something the public really has to decide, whether it believes that public interest is so important . . . I think people have to decide where they want to draw the lines on these questions . . .'

The crudest test of public support was simple popularity, and in the era of mass democracy, some courts – for example, in the UK – accepted that the size of newspaper sales or television audiences of itself provided evidence of 'public interest' (Lamont 2003). On the other hand, in the US scrutiny of investigative reporting focused on tactics, techniques and motives ('the process of reporting') rather than accuracy and 'public interest'. The 'public interest' defence appeared to be weakened in the face of 'a growing backlash against caught-you-in-the-act journalism' (de Burgh 2000: 10; Paulson 1999). Not all of the questionable motives were journalistic. 'Investigative reporting is a costly and trendy enterprise used by publishers and broadcasters to build their audiences' (Leff *et al.* 1986: 300). An 'affinity' has been identified 'between serious-minded investigative news and sensation-minded tabloid news'. Sensationalism, human interest, scoops and gossip characterized the more 'aggressive' reporting of the later nineteenth-century as journalism and the media sought to define and supply, through the contrivance of the exposé, that which was popular (Edge 2000: 103–4, 117; Wiener 1996: 62–5).

As a result, investigative reporting could look like mere 'stunts' (Holland 2001: 80–1; Kovach and Rosenstiel 2001: 122), and appear indistinguishable from entertainment – or even be displaced by entertainment shows with a critical edge (Collins 2000). This left the way open to suspicions that investigative journalism was not used just to further the commercial or ideological interests of the media and their owners – 'to boost . . . ratings by having something which is likely to attract attention' (Longstaff in *The Media Report*, 2003; White 2000); but equally at times may be suppressed where it embarrassed or compromised the media with potentially damaging effects on their profitability or power (Armao 2000: 45–6). A senior British journalist observed that 'The exercise of "investigative journalism" rarely extends to the relationships of journalists with each other, with politicians or with proprietors' (Walker 2000: 237). One student of journalism ethics asked, 'What "value" has investigative reporting based on deceit *and* the deliberate objective to profit financially in the marketplace?' (Berry 2000: 33; emphasis added).[4] Consequently, the arguments for undertaking and publishing (and, equally, for *not* undertaking and *not* publishing) investigations might be either those stated, or some hidden 'real reasons' (Dufresne 1991).

On the other hand, in a world increasingly concerned with establishing and maintaining universal standards of human rights, organizations ranging from the United Nations and the European Court of Human Rights to Article 19 promoted investigative journalism as a major mechanism for exposing wrong doing and guaranteeing justice (Article 19 n.d.). Organizations welcomed and encouraged undercover exposés of 'evils' that they were established to combat – for example, the sexual exploitation of children (White and Holman 1996). Moreover, the International Freedom of Expression Exchange pointed out that in most areas of the world journalists were more likely to be the *victims* of surveillance at the hands of states (see www.ifex.org).

Investigative journalism involved striking a delicate balance between the social responsibility, watchdog role of the media; human rights, including the right to free speech; the public interest (measured at least in part by simple popularity); commercial imperatives, and the ethical behaviour of journalists. Going back to the late seventeenth century, investigative journalism was linked with the rational, democratizing movements of, and the emergence of public opinion in, the modern era (Armao 2000: 36; de Burgh 2000: 29–32; Kovach and Rosensteil 2001: 113). Ettema and Glasser (1998: 11) argued that when the balance was correctly achieved, investigative journalism 'maintains and sometimes updates consensual interpretations of right and wrong, innocence and guilt'. The abiding archetypal image was of muckraking journalists like Ida Tarbell painstakingly assembling her 'careful documentation' of John D. Rockefeller's corrupt Standard Oil (Chambers 1980: 118–19; Dorman 2000; Newton 1999: 142–5).

Journalists and investigative reporting

Journalists and editors remain the most insistent advocates of the news media as the Fourth Estate: watching, questioning, analysing and informing, often despite the opposition of their managers who would prefer a more compliant, more entertaining and less critical approach (Schultz 1998: 6).

Investigative journalism embodied the core of this ideology. Surveying journalists in Australia, Haxton (2002: 33) found them to be 'passionate' about the value of investigative journalism as 'a central pillar of social responsibility theory and the watchdog role'. Investigative journalism was identified as 'without question, the news media's most precious asset' (Malarek 1998: 45), and 'the pinnacle of journalism' (Tanner 2002: xix). Emphasis was laid on the 'major triumphs' of exposing malfeasance in the White House or the effects of thalidomide (Griffiths 1992: 452; Randall 1996: 87–8). Journalists tended to underscore the humdrum nature of investigative journalism, which prioritized 'detailed research' in archives, records and documents (Northmore 1994a: 327, 336). The Watergate case, Bob Woodward told an international conference of investigative journalists in 1991, involved 'the most basic kind of empirical, methodical police reporting' (cited Lashmar 1993: 33). Investigative journalism, it was asserted, 'is old-fashioned, hard-nosed reporting' (Greene 1991: viii); indeed, 'only more so' (Protess *et al.* 1991: 5). Thus, investigative journalism validated journalism as a whole.

Despite the view of one British investigative reporter that 'Investigative journalism . . . has little if anything to do with body microphones, hidden cameras, paid informants or other cloak and dagger stuff' (Northmore 1994b: 50), it has made 'heroes' out of journalists (Shepard 2000). As a result:

> The thirst for fame, truly, as much as adding to the sum of human knowledge, is the ingredient which drives the young investigative journalist on because ever since Woodward and Bernstein became rich and famous we have all known, deep down, that the craft offers that tantalising prospect – to be righteous, to get the bad guy, and to be a hero in a Hollywood movie played by Robert Redford or Dustin Hoffman.
>
> (Greengrass 1996: 67)

Furthermore, investigative journalists tended to view the 'public interest' as a taken-for-granted concept, and to concentrate instead on *how* this interest was served. Some argued that two wrongs made a right (Franklin 1991), and that subterfuge could be justified where those being investigated were guilty of abusing public trust, and this made it impossible to scrutinize them in any other way (Steele 1995). As the British television undercover journalist Adam Holloway put it, 'Yes, we lied, but we got the truth' (quoted in Dugdale 1993). Others believed that practising deception by default, or passive deception, made them less culpable than if they lied openly (Harris

1992: 71–2), or there was less offence if the deception was 'minor' (Fallows 1997: 49).

The public and investigative reporting

Relatively little is known about public attitudes to the ways in which journalists work. Surveys conducted in the US showed a persistent double majority – both for investigative journalism, and generally against surreptitious reporting techniques, particularly where they were believed to be 'unethical, dishonest and sleazy'.[5] The key to balancing one against the other appeared to be motive – where journalism strove to serve the public interest, the public was more tolerant (Opt and Delaney 2000: 94–5). It was this 'public interest' test that conferred on journalism the moral right to seek out wrongdoing with, it would appear, whatever (lawful) means were necessary (Schudson 1995: 162–3). Yet even in the era of the American muckrakers at the beginning of the twentieth century, the views of journalists and the public on how the public interest was to be served were diverging (Thornton 1995). This situation seemed not to alter much: in the 1990s many investigative journalists valued their work because it 'makes things change' (Opt and Delaney 2000: 84), a thread that Schudson (1995: 164–5) argued ran through all investigative journalism. In its concerns, the public seemed to remain remarkably consistent over more than 80 years: it looked to investigative journalism primarily as a source of information (Opt and Delaney 2000: 95).

The public, in whose name such reporting was practised, seemed to become less persuaded that the ends justified the means (Anon 1998). From the 1960s investigative journalism was more closely associated with 'deception and underhanded means' of gathering information, including undercover surveillance, theft and sting operations (Winch 2000: 126). Reporters like Tom Renner, of *Newsday*, were remembered admiringly by journalists for working 'deep and dirty' (Investigative Reporters and Editors n.d.). Two of the most significant acts of journalism of the time, the publication of the Pentagon Papers in the US and *The Times*'s exposure of police corruption in London, relied, respectively, on theft and 'bugging' (Daniel 2000: 14; de Burgh 2000: 48; Doig 1997: 192). A new type of investigative television show, such as *60 Minutes* in the US (begun in 1968), and *World in Action* (1963) in the UK more regularly used hidden cameras (de Burgh 2000: 58, 232; Coffey 1993: 90–1). Working undercover became routine for many investigative journalists (Dashiell 2000: 179–80; Ettema and Glasser 1998: 2, 37–9).

If the fortunes of investigative journalism, as has been suggested, were closely linked to public demands for, and expectations of social change, and estimations of the effective location and beneficial use of power; if adversarial, 'aggressive' reporting was regarded as a brake on government – equally, restrictions on reporting freedoms were seen as a way of curbing excessive media power (Aucoin 1995; de Burgh 2000: 68; Doig 1997: 190; Opt and Delaney 2000). Given public perceptions of the extent of contemporary media power (Opt and Delaney 2000), the persistence of investigatory journalism techniques appeared to be 'contradictory', and sustained by public interest only in sex, 'sleaze' and sensation (de Burgh 2000: 55, 61). Notwithstanding how commonplace the use of certain reporting techniques may have been, distinctions needed to be drawn, therefore, between the quantity of so-called investigative journalism, and its quality (Ehrlich 2000: 103ff).

Declining public confidence and interest in journalism (for examples, see Kovach and Rosenstiel 2001: 10; Worcester 1998: 47) suggested not merely, as many media have interpreted the trend, that journalism no longer amused the public the way it used to, but perhaps, more crucially, that it no longer performed the function of keeping people informed that was expected of it. There was evidence that when this was perceived to happen, public support of journalists using more extreme investigative techniques waned; and when it was suspected that the public interest had been suborned by the media's own self-interests there was even hostility towards such ways of reporting. It was surely hardly revolutionary to suggest that journalism concerned itself centrally with disclosure and openness; that journalism was a process whereby information was revealed (de Burgh 2000: 33–4; DeFleur 1997: vii, 9–10), and that this made investigative journalism popular.

Idealization of investigative journalism

Media organizations, such as local television stations in the US, believed they could exploit the public appeal of spy cam reports, and perhaps they even valued the *caché* of labelling packages 'investigative' – but without accepting the presumption that aggressive, adversarial reporting targeted the sources of power in society to reveal 'the reality of outrageous civic vice and, by implication, the possibility of enhanced virtue in the conduct of public affairs' (Ettema and Glasser 1998: 7). In these circumstances, undercover journalism could seem uncomfortably close to either prurient peeping or secret police operations, both of which mocked the very public morality investigative reporting was supposed to be informing (Greenslade 1999). This situation represented the conflicts evident in the idealization of investigative journalism. Idealization is taken here to indicate the tendency to abstract, and to exaggerate the supposed advantages or ignore the perceived deficiencies of, a phenomenon. This draws in turn on the analysis of Marx and Engels (1988: 58–9), which proposed that idealization 'explain[ed] practice from the idea'.

For journalists, investigation was no less than 'real journalism' (Bernstein cited in Carter and Allan 2000: 133). More than the apogee of practice, it embraced the ideology of freedom of the press, and formed a crucial element in journalists' claim to professionalism – as 'scientific researchers' bound by facticity and objectivity (Longstaff in *The Media Report* 2003; Newton 1999: 143). It involved the heroic 'exposure, by whatever means, of someone doing something unethical, immoral or downright illegal . . . [of] conmen, criminals and the downright evil who blight all our lives' (Alford 1999: 3). Largely absent from such accounts were the 'irrelevant trivia' that consistently accompanied investigative reports, and the (self-)glorification of investigative journalists (Lamont 2003; Newton 1999: 142). The tension with media organizations, driven by over-arching commercial concerns, to privilege celebrity, gossip and sensationalism – what Berstein (cited in Carter and Allan 2000: 134) called a 'sleazoid info-tainment culture' – was self-evident. More intriguing, however, was the apparent disjuncture with public idealization of investigative journalism (Newton 1999: 144).

What evidence there was pointed to the public idealizing investigative journalism as a means of overcoming information deficits; raising the information threshold, and presenting unambiguous evidence around discrete, short-term issues. Presentational techniques – packaging and production values, as well as personalization – seemed to be essential accompaniments that made plain facts noteworthy (Lamont 2003; Leff *et al.* 1986: 311–13). On the other hand, as we have seen, disdain for, or even open hostility towards, investigative methods employed by journalists often overrode beliefs in press freedom. Not much suggested that the public shared the inclination to locate investigative journalists in the higher reaches of the pantheon of journalism.

Conclusion

The contradictory ways in which investigative journalism was idealized betokened a broader contestation around the meaning and purpose of journalism as a whole. This approach suggested, however, that the issues were not binary – information or entertainment; serious or trivial; objective or subjective; facts or comment; accuracy or misinformation; freedom of expression or censorship; democracy or demagoguery – but were arrayed over a complex matrix of sometimes complementary, sometimes antagonistic ideals. How journalism, as a quasi-autonomous occupation; the media, as enterprises; and the public (including audiences and consumers) interacted in imagining journalism attracted the attention of a number of cultural studies scholars (for two notable examples, see Bourdieu 1998 and Hartley 1996). Their intervention served to intensify, rather than ameliorate, polar oppositions, however. Given its exalted status within journalism, investigative journalism provided a fastness from which one side of the equation could be rigorously defended (Bromley 2004). Journalism as practised in the mainstream media may have been going to the dogs, but 'real' journalists knew how to salvage it, seemed to be the argument (Carter and Allan 2000: 133, 137–9).

This position relied on making a case for the suborning of investigative journalism. The resources – training, time, money, legal advice, institutional support – were withheld, or investigative stories remained unpublished, 'for commercial reasons' (Donovan 2002; Kennedy and Morgan 2001; Morgan

2001a). The concept of investigation was conflated with 'salacious details of ... sexual activities' that the director of the UK Press Complaints Commission argued actually threatened to undermine 'three centuries of good, old-fashioned British investigative journalism' (cited Morgan 2001a). Such material was gathered through 'nefarious activities' rather than the skills of journalism – 'digging out facts', 'toothcombing through documents' and 'trailing slippery customers' (Crossley 2001; Donovan 2002; Greenslade 2002; Morgan 2001b; Panton 2001; Snell 2001). Investigative journalism represented a confrontation between the 'culture of journalism ... and the culture of money and profit' inherent in the media (Kalb 2001). As such, because 'The folklore that surrounds investigative reporting closely resembles the American ideal of popular democracy' (Protess *et al.* 1991: 3), those who opposed it were denying democratic rights.

Yet it could be argued that investigative journalism over-privileged the characteristics of journalism – experience as a reporter, 'the contacts built up over years', and 'missionary zeal', rather than subjective expertise (Negrine 1993: 11–13; Williams 1978: xii–xiii). Journalists viewed investigative work as a supreme challenge to information supply restrictions and manipulation, which reduced publics to spectators (Bird 2000: 216; Waisbord 2001). Nevertheless, before anxiety about the super-commercialization of the media reached the fever pitch it attained in the late 1990s, it was argued that this project of mobilization, which put the public centre stage, had already been supplanted by a 'coalition model', in which investigative journalists connected more directly with policy makers, by-passing the public (Protess *el al.* 1991: 249–54). Notwithstanding the rhetoric of investigative journalism, journalists were poorly trained and inexpert as expositors; too wary of 'political advocacy' to facilitate debate and, in any event, unable to distinguish between the two roles, inhibiting their ability to promote 'social action [for] public good' (Garnham 1990: 110–12).

Investigative journalism may have provided journalists with a rallying-point, around which to range the ideology of journalism – 'the lifeblood of any democracy' (Nelson Mandela cited Tyson 1993: 410); but it connected only tangentially with a public that idealized it substantially differently. Aggressive and adversarial, investigative journalism was based on reporting ('the reprocessing of existing discourse' in the form of 'the reality of outrageous civic vice') and agenda setting ('the possibility of enhanced virtue in the conduct of public affairs'), whereas public expectations were of the dissolution of journalistic authority and the framing of information – what Hartley has called 'direct communicative democracy' in redactional form (Ettema and Glasser 1998: 7; Hartley 2000: 41, 44–5). (Re)assertions of the worth in democracies of authorial investigative journalism and the heroism of investigative journalists betrayed an internal referencing that posited investigative work, incomprehensively to any wider public, as 'the sexiest form of journalism' (Downs 2002: 15; Killick 2000).

The continued use of reporting that appeared to rely on investigative techniques may be regarded as a way of legitimating a range of activities as journalism. Media organizations sought to mobilize investigative journalism to meet their own demands for marketable, sensationalist and populist content. This was made more possible by journalism's own indeterminacy over defining what investigative journalism was, and its weak sense of professionalism. As MacIntyre said of his experiences, 'Journalism is too small or too distant a word to cover it. It is theatre; there are no second takes. It is drama – it is improvisation, infiltration and psychological warfare.'

Notes

1   At the *Sunday Times*, executives recognized, too, that Insight was a useful 'brandname' (Doig 1997: 206).
2   I am indebted for much of the information in this section to a number of people with knowledge of and experience in local television news operations in Detroit whom I interviewed between October 2000 and March 2001.
3   Among television stations in Detroit in 2000–1, WJBK-2 (Fox) co-joined the Problem Solvers team with a 'Hall of Shame' feature; WDIV-4 (an NBC affiliate) had The Defenders and 'Ruth to the Rescue', and WXYZ-7 (ABC) The Investigators and 'Call for Action'.
4   Perhaps the classic case is that in which the supermarket chain Food Lion challenged the US television network ABC over the making of a hidden camera *Prime Time Live* report. The case involved not only litigation but also a retaliatory public relations campaign (see Sitrick 1998: 111–16; Winch 2000: 127–30).
5   For example, a 1997 survey in the US found that 29 per cent approved of paying informers for information, 31 per cent approved of not identifying oneself as a reporter, and 42 per cent approved of the use of hidden cameras and microphones. By comparison, 52 per cent approved of using un-named sources (see ASNE Journalism Credibility Project posted at www.asne.org/works/jcp/jcpmain.htm: accessed 22 February 2000).

References

Alford, D. (1999) Would You Care if I Had a Beard? *Guardian* Media, 31 May: 2–3.
Anon (1998) A message about reporting methods: make no mistake, *Hidden Cameras/Hidden Microphones: At the Crossroads of Journalism, Ethics and Law*. Washington, DC: Radio-Television News Directors Foundation. Posted at www.pointer.org. Accessed 5 April 2000.
Armao, R. (2000) The History of Investigative Reporting, in M. Greenwald and J. Bernt (eds) *The Big Chill: Investigative Reporting in the Current Media Environment*. Ames: Iowa State University Press, pp. 35–49.
Article 19 (n.d.) Freedom of expression and investigative journalism. Posted at www.article19.org. Accessed 22 February 2001.
Aucoin, J. L. (1995) The re-emergence of American investigative journalism, 1960–1975, *Journalism History*, 21(1). Accessed 10 May 2000.
BBC (2000) Summary of the Annual Report and Accounts 1999/2000. London: BBC.
Bernt, J. and Greenwald, M. (2000) Enterprise and Investigative Reporting in Metropolitan Newspapers: 1980 and 1995 compared, in M. Greenwald and

J. Bernt (eds) *The Big Chill: Investigative Reporting in the Current Media Environment*. Ames: Iowa State University Press, pp. 51–79.

Berry, D. (2000) Trust in Media Practices: Towards Cultural Development, in D. Berry (ed.) *Ethics and Media Culture: Practices and Representations*. Oxford, Focal Press, pp. 28–53.

Bird, S. E. (2000) Audience Demands in a Murderous Market: Tabloidization of US Television News, in C. Sparks and J. Tulloch (eds) *Tabloid Tales: Global Debates over Media Standards*. Lanham, MD: Rowman & Littlefield, pp. 213–28.

Bourdieu, P. (1998) *On Television and Journalism*, trans. P. P. Feguson. London: Pluto.

Boyd, A. (2001) *Broadcast Journalism: Techniques of Radio and Television News*, fifth edition. Oxford: Focal Press.

Bromley, M. (1998) The 'Tabloiding' of Britain: the 'Quality' Press in the 1990s, in H. Stephenson and M. Bromley (eds) *Sex, Lies and Democracy: The Press and the Public*. Harlow: Longman, pp. 25–38.

Bromley, M. (2005) One Journalism or Many? Confronting the Contradictions in the Education and Training of Journalists in the United Kingdom, in K. W. Y. Leung, J. Kenny and P. S. N. Lee (eds) *Global Trends in Communication Research and Education*. Cresskill, NJ: Hampton Press.

Carter, C. and Allan, S. (2000) 'If it Bleeds, it Leads': Ethical Questions about Popular Journalism, in D. Berry (ed.) *Ethics and Media Culture: Practices and Representations*. Oxford: Focal Press, pp. 132–53.

Chambers, J. W. (1980) *The Tyranny of Change: America in the Progressive Era, 1900–1917*. New York: St Martin's Press.

Clarkson, W. (1990) *Dog Eat Dog: Confessions of a Tabloid Journalist*. London: Fourth Estate.

Coffey, F. (1993) *'60 Minutes': 25 Years of Television's Finest Hour*. Los Angeles: General Publishing.

Collins, M. (2000) Stand-up, Be Counted, *Guardian* Media, 31 January: 2–3.

Crossley, J. (2001) Sticking to the Story, *Press Gazette*, 17 May. Posted at www.pressgazette.co.uk. Accessed 22 April 2002.

Daniel, D. K. (2000) Best of Times, and Worst of Times: Investigative Reporting in Post-Watergate America, in M. Greenwald and J. Bernt (eds) *The Big Chill: Investigative Reporting in the Current Media Environment*. Ames: Iowa State University Press: pp. 11–33.

Dashiell, E. (2000) For Mainstream Audiences Only: Investigative Reporting on Minorities, Gays and Lesbians and Women, in M. Greenwald and J. Bernt (eds) *The Big Chill: Investigative Reporting in the Current Media Environment*. Ames: Iowa State University Press, pp. 177–96.

de Burgh, H. (ed.) (2000) *Investigative Journalism: Context and Practice*. London: Routledge.

DeFleur, M. (1997) *Computer Assisted Investigative Reporting: Development and Methodology*. Mahwah, NJ: Lawrence Erlbaum.

Doig, A. (1997) The Decline of Investigatory Journalism, in M. Bromley and T. O'Malley (eds) *A Journalism Reader*. London: Routledge, pp. 189–213.

Donovan, P. (2002) Justice Loses its Appeal, *Press Gazette*, 14 February. Posted at www.pressgazette.co.uk. Accessed 22 April 2002.

Dorman, J. (2000) Where are Muckraking Journalists Today? *Nieman Reports*, Summer: 55–7.

Downs, H. (2002) Foreword, in C. Jensen (ed.) *Stories that Changed America: Muckrakers of the Twentieth Century*. New York: Seven Stories, pp. 15–16.

Dufresne, M. (1991) Judgment Call: to Sting or Not to Sting? *Columbia Journalism Review*, May/June. Posted at www.cjr.org. Accessed 23 February 2000.

Dugdale, J. (1993) Beyond *Candid Camera, Guardian* Media, 29 March: 14–15.

Edge, M. (2000) And 'The Wall' Came Tumbling Down in Los Angeles, in M. Greenwald and J. Bernt (eds) *The Big Chill: Investigative Reporting in the Current Media Environment*. Ames: Iowa State University Press, pp. 197–210.

Ehrlich, M. C. (2000) Not Ready for Prime Time: Tabloid and Investigative TV Journalism, in M. Greenwald and J. Bernt (eds) *The Big Chill: Investigative Reporting in the Current Media Environment*. Ames: Iowa State University Press, pp. 103–20.

Ettema, J. S. and Glasser, T. L. (1998) *Custodians of Conscience: Investigative Journalism and Public Virtue*. New York, Columbia University Press.

Fallows, J. (1994) *Breaking the News: How the Media Undermine American Democracy*. New York: Pantheon.

Franklin, J. (1991) Using Deceit to Get the Truth: When There's Just No Other Way, *FineLine: The Newsletter on Journalism Ethics* 3(9). Posted at www.journalism.indiana.edu. Accessed 20 March 2000.

Foot, P. (1999) The Slow Death of Investigative Journalism, in S. Glover (ed.) *The Penguin Book of Journalism: Secrets of the Press*. London: Penguin, pp. 79–89.

Garnham, N. (1990) The Media and the Public Sphere, in F. Inglis (ed.) *Capitalism and Communication: Global Culture and the Economics of Information*. London: Sage, pp. 104–14.

Grabe, M. E., Zhou, S. and Barnett, B. (1999) Sourcing and Reporting in News Magazine Programs: *60 Minutes* versus *Hard Copy, Journalism and Mass Communication Quarterly* 76(2). Accessed 14 June 2001.

Greene, R. W. (1991) Foreword, in J. Ullmann and J. Colbert (eds) *The Reporter's Handbook: An Investigator's Guide to Documents and Techniques*, Second edition. New York: St Martin's Press, pp. vi–xi.

Greengrass, P. (1996) Did They Do a Deal with Faust? *British Journalism Review* 7(1): 65–8.

Greenslade, R. (1999) Shut Your Trap, *Guardian* Media, 27 September, pp. 2–3.

Greenslade, R. (2002) Fraternal Feuding, *Press Gazette*, 7 March. Posted at www.pressgazette.co.uk. Accessed 22 April 2002.

Greenwald, M. and Bernt, J. (eds) (2000) *The Big Chill: Investigative Reporting in the Current Media Environment*. Ames: Iowa State University Press.

Griffiths, D. (ed.) (1992) *The Encyclopedia of the British Press, 1492–1992*. London: Macmillan.

Harris, N. G. E. (1992) Codes of Conduct for Journalists, in A. Belsey and R. Chadwick (eds) *Ethical Issues in Journalism and the Media*. London: Routledge, pp. 62–76.

Hartley, J. (1996) *Popular Reality: Journalism, Modernity, Popular Culture*. London: Arnold.

Hartley, J. (2000) Communicative Democracy in a Redactional Society: the Future of Journalism Studies, *Journalism: Theory, Practice and Criticism*, 1(1): 39–48.

Haxton, N. (2002) The Death of Investigative Journalism, in S. Tanner (ed.) *Journalism: Investigation and Research*. Frenchs Forest, NSW: Longman: pp. 20–36.

Hencke, D. (2001) No News is Bad News, *Guardian*, 5 March. Posted at www.mediaguardian.co.uk. Accessed 5 March 2001.

Hickey, N. (1998) Money Lust, *Columbia Journalism Review*, July/August. Posted at www.cjr.org. Accessed 17 July 1998.

Holland, P. (2001) Authority and Authenticity: Redefining Television Current Affairs, in M. Bromley (ed.) *No News is Bad News: Radio, Television and the Public*. Harlow: Longman, pp. 80–95.

Independent Television Commission (2002) *Putting Viewers First: Annual Report for 2001*. London: ITC.

Investigative Reporters and Editors (n.d.) The Arizona Project. Posted at www.ire.org.html. Accessed 24 September 2001.

Jackson, J. (1992) Honesty in Investigative Journalism, in A. Belsey and R. Chadwick (eds) *Ethical Issues in Journalism and the Media*. London: Routledge, pp. 93–111.

Jackson, S. (2004) *60 Minutes* that has Lasted 25 Years, *The Australian* Media, 12 February, p. 20.

Kalb, M. (2001) Media Coverage from Scandal to Crisis. Transition to Governing Project, Wohlstetter Conference Center, Washington DC, 14 November.

Kennedy, P. and Morgan, J. (2001) *Express* Watchdog Panel Backs Desmond Regime, *Press Gazette*, 29 March. Posted at www.pressgazette.co.uk. Accessed 22 April 2002.

Killick, M. (2000) The Truth is Out There, The Rolls Royce 2000 Lectures. Cardiff, Centre for Journalism Studies, Cardiff University. Posted at www.cf.ac.uk. Accessed 14 April 2004.

Kovach, B. and T. Rosenstiel (2001) *The Elements of Journalism: What Newspeople Should Know and the Public Should Expect*. New York: Crown.

Lamont, D. (2003) Her Cereal's Safe from Us, *Guardian*, 24 November. Posted at http://media.guardian.co.uk. Accessed 1 December 2003.

Lashmar, P. (1992) A Fraudster's Charter, *British Journalism Review*, 3(4): 40–3.

Lashmar, P. (1993) Outsiders – In From the Cold, *British Journalism Review*, 4(1): 32–6.

Leff, D. R., Protess, D. L. and Brooks, S. C. (1986) Crusading Journalism: Changing Public Attitudes and Policy-making Agendas, *Public Opinion Quarterly*, 50(3): 300–15.

Leigh, D. (2000) Global Disclosure, *MediaGuardian*, 31 January. Posted at www.media.guardian.co.uk. Accessed 11 September 2001.

Linklater, M. (1993) An Insight into Insight, *British Journalism Review*, 4(2): 17–20.

Malarek, V. (1998) What it Takes to Be an Investigative Reporter, in D. Logan (ed.) *Journalism in the New Millennium*. Vancouver: Sing Tao School of Journalism, pp. 44–56.

Marx, K. and Engels, F. (1988) *The German Ideology*, C. J. Arthur (ed.). New York: International Publishers.

Morgan, J. (2001a) 'Scottish papers behind new law on drugs and children', Press Gazette (22 February). Posted at www.pressgazette.co.uk

Morgan (2001b) PressWise Backs Judge's Kiss-and-tell Clampdown, *Press Gazette*, 15 November. Posted at www.pressgazette.co.uk. Accessed 22 April 2002.

Negrine, R. (1993) *The Organisation of British Journalism and Specialist Correspondents: A Study of Newspaper Reporting*. Discussion Paper in Mass Communication no. MC93/1. University of Leicester, Centre for Mass Communication Research.

Newton, E. (ed) (1999) *Crusaders, Scoundrels, Journalists: The Newseum's Most Intriguing Newspeople*. New York and Toronto: The Freedom Forum Newseum.

Northmore, D. (1994a) Probe Shock: Investigative Journalism, in R. Keeble (ed.) *The Newspapers Handbook*. London: Routledge, pp. 319–36.

Northmore, D. (1994b) Knowing Where to Look, *British Journalism Review*, 5(1): 47–51.

O'Carroll, L. (2000) *Newsnight*'s Paedophile Scoop Sees Ratings Soar, *Guardian Unlimited*, 21 November. Posted at www.mediaguardian.co.uk. Accessed 21 November 2000.

Opt, S. K. and Delaney, T. A. (2000) Public Perceptions of Investigative Reporting, in M. Greenwald and J. Bernt (eds) *The Big Chill: Investigative Reporting in the Current Media Environment*. Ames: Iowa State University Press, pp. 81–102.

O'Sullivan, T. (1999) Who's Exposing Who? *Guardian Unlimited*, 21 November. Posted at www.guardianunlimited.co.uk. Accessed 8 September 2000.

Panton, J. (2001) A new opposition?, *Press Gazette*, 15 November. Posted at www.pressgazette.co.uk. Accessed 22 April 2002.

Paulson, K. A. (1999) Food Lion Verdict Reversal has Lessons for Both Sides, *Free!* November. Posted at www.freedomforum.org. Accessed 22 February 2000.

Protess, D., Cook, F. M. L., Doppelt, J. C., Ettema, J. S., Gordon, K. T., Leff, D. R. and Miller, P. (1991) *The Journalism of Outrage: Investigative Reporting and Agenda Building in America*. London: Guilford Press.

Randall, D. (1996) *The Universal Journalist*. London: Pluto Press.

Reeves, I. (2000) MacIntyre Under Fire, *Press Gazette*, July. Posted at www.pressgazette.co.uk. Accessed 5 March 2001.

Rogers, D. (2001) Lack of Investigative Journalism on TV Criticised, *Guardian*, 18 January. Posted at www.mediaguardian.co.uk. Accessed 23 March 2001.

Salmon, P. (1999) Speech Launching the BBC 1 Autumn Schedule (10 August), BBC News Release. Posted at www2.kw.bbc.co.uk. Accessed 2 September 2000.

Salmon, P. (2000) Contribution to a Chat Session on BBC Online (8 August). Posted at www.bbc.co.uk. Accessed 10 September 2001.

Schudson, M. (1995) *The Power of News*. London: Harvard University Press.

Schultz, J. (1998) *Reviving the Fourth Estate: Democracy, Accountability and the Media*. Melbourne: Cambridge University Press.

Shephard, A. C. (2000) Local heroes, *American Journalism Review* (December). Posted at www.ajr.org. Accessed 25 May 2002.

Sitrick, M. S. (1998) *Spin: How to Turn the Power of the Press to Your Advantage*. Washington DC: Regnery.

Snell, R. (2001). Paper presented to the *Public Right to Know* conference, Australian Centre for Independent Journalism, University of Technology Sydney, 25 October. Posted at www.journalism.uts.edu.au/acij. Accessed 22 April 2002.

Spark, D. (1999) *Investigative Reporting: A Study in Technique*. Oxford: Focal Press.

Steele, B. (1995) Deception/Hidden Camera Checklist, Poynter Institute Handout (February). Posted at www.pointer.org. Accessed 5 April 2000.

Stein, S. R. (2001) Legitimating TV Journalism in *60 Minutes*: the Ramifications of Subordinating the Visual to the Primacy of the Word, *Critical Studies in Mass Communication*, 18(3): 249–69.

Stephens, M. (1997) *A History of News*. Forth Worth, TX: Harcourt Brace.

Tanner, S. (2002) Introduction, in S. Tanner (ed.) *Journalism: Investigation and Research*. Frenchs Forest, NSW: Longman: xix–xxvi.

The Media Report (2003) Australian Broadcasting Corporation, Radio National (30 October). Transcript posted at www.abc.net.au. Accessed 5 November 2003.

Thornton, B. (1995) Muckraking Journalists and their Readers: Perceptions of Professionalism, *Journalism History*, 21(1). Accessed 10 May 2000.

Tomlin, J. (2000) 'Original Journalism' is Key for BBC Current Affairs Boss, *Press Gazette* (July). Posted at www.pressgazette.co.uk. Accessed 5 March 2001.

Tomlin, J. (2001) Weekly Magazine Show Planned by Sambrook, *Press Gazette*, 5 March. Posted at www.pressgazette.co.uk. Accessed 5 March 2001.

Tyson, H. (1993) *Editors Under Fire*. Sandton, South Africa: Random House.

Waisbord, S. (2001) Why Democracy Needs Investigative Journalism, *Global Issues* 6(1). Posted at http://usinfo.state.gove. Accessed 24 April 2002.

Walker, D. (2000) Newspaper Power: a Practitioner's Account, in H. Tumber (ed.) *Media Power, Professionals and Policies*. London: Routledge, pp. 236–46.

White, A. and Holman, K. (1996) Prime Time for Children: Media, Ethics and Reporting of Commercial Sexual Exploitation of Children. Paper presented on behalf of UNICEF to the World Congress Against Commercial Sexual Exploitation of Children, 15 June. Posted at www.childhub.ch. Accessed 20 March 2000.

White, M. (2000) Humbug, *Guardian*, 23 October. Posted at www.media.guardian.co.uk. Accessed 2 November 2000.

Wiener, J. H. (1996) The Americanization of the British press, 1830–1914, in M. Harris and T. O'Malley (eds) *Studies in Newspaper and Periodical History: 1995 Annual*. Westport, CT: Greenwood, pp. 61–74.

Williams, K. (1998) *Get Me a Murder a Day! A History of Mass Communication in Britain*. London: Arnold.

Williams, P. N. (1978) *Investigative Reporting and Editing*. Englewood Cliffs, NJ: Prentice-Hall.

Winch, S. P. (2000) Ethical Challenges for Investigative Journalism, in M. Greenwald and J. Bernt (eds) *The Big Chill: Investigative Reporting in the Current Media Environment*. Ames: Iowa State University Press, pp. 121–36.

Woolfinden, B. (1996) Fast and Loose, *MediaGuardian*, 12 August, p. 13.

Worcester, R. M. (1998) Demographics and Values: What the British Public Reads and What it Thinks of its Newspapers, in H. Stephenson and M. Bromley (eds) *Sex, Lies and Democracy: The Press and the Public*. Harlow: Longman, pp. 39–48.

Young, H. (1990) Can Television Tell the Truth? *British Journalism Review*, 2(1): 11–16.

24

Opportunity or threat? The BBC, investigative journalism and the Hutton Report

Steven Barnett

- Why is investigative journalism in trouble?
- What is the role of the BBC in promoting a healthy journalistic culture?
- Why did the BBC's story about WMD create such a furore?
- In what ways were the conclusions of Lord Hutton's report misguided?
- What are the repercussions for BBC journalism and the BBC itself?

It has been described by several commentators as the gravest crisis in the BBC's history, threatening not just its reputation for impartial and reliable journalism, but its structure, funding and even its very existence. It has also been described as a defeat for journalism and a victory for politicians and government manipulation. It is certainly true that the abrupt departure of both its Chairman and Director General is unprecedented even in the most fraught circumstances of previous BBC confrontations with governments.

Nevertheless, as I shall try to show in this chapter, the furore surrounding the BBC's reporting of intelligence service concerns over the government's stated reasons for going to war with Saddam Hussein, the suicide of David Kelly – the weapons expert and main BBC source – and the subsequent verdict of Lord Hutton's report into the circumstances of Kelly's death has left the BBC and its journalism less damaged than many believed in the immediate aftermath. While the events themselves were cataclysmic for the BBC as well as tragic for David Kelly and his family, there are important lessons to be learned for investigative journalism in general and about the role of the BBC in particular. As the events recede and we can start to take a broader perspective of their significance, it may even be possible to argue that the final outcome will be benign for the BBC.

▌Investigative journalism under threat

The fundamental premise of this chapter is that a vigorous journalistic culture – and in particular challenging investigative journalism – is vital to a healthy democracy. Without it, executive or corporate wrongdoing will not only continue but can eventually corrupt the body politic. I believe that this process of investigative journalism – of breaking important stories rather than simply reporting or recycling public relations handouts – is under serious threat. Conceptually, it is possible to identify six reasons.

First there is the process of corporate consolidation and globalization. The number of independent newsgathering businesses is diminishing in proportion to the growth of huge multinationals such as the Disney Corporation, AOL-Time Warner and News Corporation. These corporations have little to gain from rattling the cages either of other businesses or government, not least because they will frequently seek political approval for proposed mergers or acquisitions. A newspaper or TV channel is less likely to be interested in breaking stories that might embarrass the very government from which it is seeking permission to expand its business activities.

Second, in the cut-throat world of global competition there is more pressure to reduce expenditure and more emphasis on maximizing profits. Investigative journalism is the most expensive and riskiest form of reporting, partly because it is labour intensive and partly because by its very nature it can sometimes result in no story.[1] Today's news gatherers are more financially constrained, and therefore find it easier to spend a diminishing budget on chasing celebrities or the Royal Family.

The third and related reason is the increased competition for viewers and readers. In a fragmented, multi-channel world, there is more pressure to go for populist stories that will attract or retain viewers. American news bulletins are now notorious for their virtual absence of international coverage, and my own research suggests that at least in some bulletins there are indications of similar trends in the UK (Barnett *et al.* 2000). This tabloidization thesis also applies to the press, where stories about footballers' affairs or the royal princes are more likely to attract 'casual' readers than any revelations about government improprieties.

Fourth, there are diminishing opportunities for learning the essential skills for this kind of reporting. Training courses have been cut, and on-the-job learning opportunities are in decline as investigative programmes are removed from the schedules or have their budgets cut. The shift towards a freelance culture means fewer journalists steeped in the investigative tradition or with the requisite expertise.

Fifth, the decline in serious journalism has been in inverse proportion to the rise of public relations, which is now a lucrative and attractive career for good working journalists. In the words of Ian Hargreaves, himself both a former newspaper editor and a former director of BBC news and current affairs:

'The fear among journalists is that they no longer have the resources to counter the increasingly sophisticated munitions of their traditional enemy: that journalism is being hung out to dry by the not-so-hidden persuaders.'

(Hargreaves 2003: 180)

The PR bandwagon has now extended to the public sector, where local authorities, NHS trusts and hospitals, police forces and even some of the bigger voluntary and campaigning groups have extensive PR operations.

Finally, the biggest public sector expansion in PR is political: the professionalization of media relations within the political parties and particularly, under New Labour, within government. Labour imported its methods of political communication from the campaign trail to government, and routinely employ a number of methods (as do governments around the world) to promote favourable stories and discourage unfavourable ones. There is nothing new in this principle, but the professionalism and sheer weight of resources devoted to media relations means that there is almost certainly a greater risk of a 'chilling effect' on independent journalism through government pressure than ever before.

The role of BBC journalism

Arising from this analysis, there are four main reasons for the BBC's essential role in contributing to a vibrant journalistic culture in Britain.

First, the BBC is not subject to the globalizing and profit-making pressures of private corporations. There are no shareholders demanding that costs be cut in expensive areas of programming that cannot demonstrate a decent return on investment. Although there has always been pressure on the BBC to demonstrate that it spends money efficiently, the BBC's abiding commitment is to high quality, accurate and impartial journalism and therefore to investing the necessary resources to sustain it.

Second, because the BBC has a predictable source of revenue, it can afford to invest in expensive programming over the long term. While a sudden downturn in advertising revenue, sponsorship or subscriptions force commercial broadcasters to respond with immediate budget cuts, particularly in the less popular programming areas like current affairs, the BBC can take a longer view.

Third, the BBC has the advantage of economies of scale. Because its journalism operates across radio, television and online as well as on the World Service, and because part of its public service responsibility is to include news and current affairs throughout its schedules, its news operation dwarfs anything offered by its rivals. This allows the BBC to keep more foreign news bureaux, more foreign and domestic correspondents and cover more local news through its regional radio stations than any other broadcaster.

Finally, because of its public service ethos, the BBC can resist the entertainment lure of news that increasingly afflicts commercial stations. It still has to find a sometimes uncomfortable compromise between making news 'accessible' to viewers while not surrendering to the more trivializing or sensationalist tendencies of some of its rivals, and critics are still apt to accuse the BBC of 'dumbing down'. But the BBC is in a position to resist the diet of Hollywood and crime stories that dominate American bulletins.

The corollary of these advantages of public funding and public service journalism is the greater susceptibility to pressure and interference from government sources. However robust and independent the institution itself and the individuals in charge of its journalism, in the age of professionalized political communication a publicly funded institution will be more vulnerable to government attempts at lobbying and bullying than an entirely commercial one. The story of the BBC's report on the government's Iraq intelligence dossier, and the cataclysmic events that followed, is one that embodies the very public nature of the BBC, its funding and its ethos.

Context for the WMD story

Throughout its history the BBC has been in conflict with governments of all colours. These tensions are particularly acute at times of war when potential loss of life means the stakes are higher and governments' reputations are more vulnerable. So the BBC expected government pressure before and during the war in Iraq, and in April 2003 the BBC director general Greg Dyke made it clear that the BBC would resist:

> Far from backing off when this country is at war – as some politicians would like – there's no more important time to hold governments to account . . . Our job is to reflect the concerns and anxieties of the country and the public. Politicians should not be concerned by tough questioning, if their decision to go to war is the right one they have nothing to fear from scrutiny.
>
> (Dyke 2003)

Dyke had more reason than most of his predecessors to be quite so unequivocal. Before he was appointed as Director General, Dyke was revealed to have donated £50,000 to the Labour Party. Senior executives at the BBC found it untenable that anyone with known party affiliations should be appointed to the job that constitutionally oversaw all BBC journalism. One wrote to the then Chairman, Sir Christopher Bland: '[Greg Dyke] may or may not be a candidate who would find favour with you, but in the event of his selection the cloud of political suitability would henceforth hang over the office' (Wyatt 2003: 21).

The perceived problem was exacerbated by the appointment of a Chairman, Gavyn Davies, who also had close links to Labour. His wife ran the office of the Chancellor of the Exchequer, Gordon Brown, and Davies had been the co-author of a government appointed study on the future of BBC funding in 1999. This combination of a Chairman and Director General with close personal links to the government was one of the undercurrents in the events to follow and was to have unfortunate – and counter-intuitive – consequences.

Six months before the war started, on 24 September 2002, the government published an intelligence dossier entitled: *Iraq's Weapons of Mass Destruction: the Assessment of the British Government*. It formed the basis on which the government hoped to persuade the British public that Saddam Hussein was a dangerous tyrant who was a threat to the Western world. Not only did he have weapons of mass destruction (WMD) at his disposal, but chemical weapons could be launched within 45 minutes of an order being given. That day's London *Evening Standard* ran the headline '45 minutes to attack'; the next day's *Sun* led with 'He's got 'em . . . let's get him'.

Nevertheless, the government faced a great deal of popular hostility to its belief that Britain should ally itself to America's military offensive. On 15 February 2003, between 1 million and 2 million people gathered for an anti-war demonstration in London, the largest in the country's history. Tony Blair was acutely aware of the risk he was taking in alienating his voters. In this febrile atmosphere, he and his Cabinet colleagues argued passionately that the existence of WMD made Saddam Hussein's Iraq a real and present danger.

By 1 May, military operations were over and the allied occupation of Iraq was complete. No WMD were fired at troops, none were discovered as the occupying forces advanced, and none have been found to date. The Americans constituted an Iraq Survey Group, detailed to comb the country to find evidence of WMD. On 23 January 2004 Dr David Kay, head of the group, resigned and explained the following week to the Senate armed services committee that he no longer wanted to search for Iraqi WMD because 'I don't think they existed' (Freedland 2004: 353).

With the formal military campaign declared over and no evidence of any WMD discovered, some of the more inquisitive journalists began to probe behind the stark government warnings that they not only existed but constituted a major threat. One journalist, Andrew Gilligan, was the defence correspondent of the BBC's *Today* programme on Radio 4 and had reported from Iraq on the conduct of the war. On 22 May he met David Kelly, an old contact, who was a weapons inspector and regarded as one of the country's leading experts on weapons of mass destruction in Iraq.[2]

Although the precise details of what Kelly said to Gilligan on 22 May will never be known, few deny the general gist: that changes had been made to strengthen intelligence material that had first appeared in traditionally dry and qualified terms, and that those changes had come after interventions from Downing Street. In the words of one media commentator:

> In essence, Kelly was suggesting that the basis on which the British
> government had taken the country to war was false, that it had pulled

the wool over the eyes of the electorate, and that the intelligence community was . . . unhappy about it.

(Wells 2004a: 31)

What followed became an object lesson, for students of journalism as well as the BBC, in different approaches to professional journalistic standards and a fascinating insight into the relationship between government and the BBC.

▎The WMD story and its aftermath

Andrew Gilligan's story was scheduled for the Today programme of 29 May. At 06.07 in the morning, while most of the programme's listeners were still asleep, Gilligan introduced his story for the first time:

> What we've been told by one of the senior officials in charge of drawing up that dossier was that, actually the government probably knew that that 45-minute figure was wrong, even before it decided to put it in . . . Downing Street, our source says, ordered a week before publication, ordered it to be sexed up, to be made more exciting and ordered more facts to be er, to be discovered.

The allegation of a deliberate and premeditated lie, orchestrated by Downing Street, was – as Gilligan was later to admit himself – further than he should have gone. For his next broadcast, at 7.32, he said only that the 45-minute claim was 'questionable' – although the problem was compounded by an assertion by presenter John Humphrys that the September dossier was 'cobbled together at the last minute'. For most newspapers, particularly those with an anti-war agenda, this might have been a minor slip. For the BBC, it was much more serious both in terms of its reputation for accuracy and professionalism, and in terms of its relationship with the government.

Other BBC journalists who were following the story also found Kelly a useful source but were more circumspect in how they used his information. Following up the story for BBC television's *Ten O'clock News* that night, Gavin Hewitt said only that he had spoken to one of those consulted on the dossier and that 'in the final week before publication, some material was taken out, some material put in. His judgement: spin from No. 10 did come into play.' And Susan Watts, BBC *Newsnight*'s science correspondent, had interviewed Kelly the previous year and went back to him in the light of Gilligan's story. She reported for *Newsnight* that her source believed the use of the 45-minute claim was 'a mistake'. She also said: 'He talks of the government seizing on anything useful to the case, including the possible existence of weapons being ready within 45 minutes.' Each of the three BBC journalists had located David Kelly independently, without knowing they had spoken to the same source. Each used his material in a subtly different way.

It is conceivable that, after a flurry of furious letters, this particular row may have subsided. Gilligan, however, fuelled the row with an article in the *Mail on Sunday* three days later where he recorded what his source replied when asked how the transformation of the dossier happened. He wrote: 'The answer was a single word. Campbell.' This reference to Alastair Campbell, the government's communications strategy director and widely perceived as Blair's most influential adviser, turned a generalized row about government and the intelligence services into something altogether more personal.

Over the next two weeks there followed an exchange of letters between Campbell and Richard Sambrook, the BBC's director of news, in which Sambrook made it clear that the BBC was standing by its reports and would not apologize. On 25 June, Campbell gave evidence to the Foreign Affairs Select Committee (FASC) accusing the BBC of telling lies and demanding an apology. Sambrook himself responded with a highly unusual appearance on the following day's *Today* programme, saying 'We have nothing to apologise for.'

By this time, Kelly had come forward and told his superiors that he had met with Gilligan. Although denying that he could have been the source of the story, it was an admission that gave the government – and Campbell – more ammunition. Through some judicious briefing by the Ministry of Defence, Kelly's name was published in three newspapers on 10 July. Five days later, Kelly was called to give evidence himself to the FASC where he denied that he could have been the source for either Gilligan or Susan Watts' report. Watts, however, had recorded her interview which was a clear record of Kelly saying what she subsequently reported. Two days later, on 17 July, Kelly took his own life. The Prime Minister immediately ordered an independent judicial inquiry, headed by Lord Hutton, into the circumstances surrounding Kelly's death.

An analysis of Hutton's conclusions

Lord Hutton's report, published on 28 January 2004, was almost a complete vindication for the government and disastrous for the BBC.[3] He accepted the government's position that 'nothing should be stated in the dossier with which the intelligence community were not entirely happy'. It was not improper for John Scarlett, the head of the Joint Intelligence Committee, to take into account drafting suggestion from Downing Street. The furthest Hutton was prepared to go was to acknowledge the possibility that Scarlett and the JIC may have been 'subconciously influenced' by the Prime Minister's desire to 'have a dossier which . . . was as strong as possible in relation to the threat posed by Saddam Hussein's WMD'.

For this reason, Gilligan's allegation of 'sexing up' was, concluded Hutton, unfounded because it would have been interpreted as meaning that the dossier had been 'embellished with intelligence known or believed to be false or unreliable, which was not the case'. Moreover, the BBC's editorial system, which allowed the unscripted 6.07 broadcast was 'defective' and BBC management failed to investigate properly the government's complaints about the 6.07 broadcast or to draw the governors' attention to a lack of support in Gilligan's notes for his most serious allegations. The governors failed to give 'proper consideration' to whether there was validity to the government's complaints or to recognize fully that this was not incompatible with their duty to protect the independence of the BBC. The governors were to be criticized for 'failing to make more detailed investigations' into whether Gilligan's allegations could be supported.

This was worse than the worst scenario that the BBC had anticipated, and Chairman Gavyn Davies had no hesitation in tendering his immediate resignation. It was agreed that Greg Dyke would also offer his resignation at the emergency governors' meeting the following day, expecting that this would be turned down. In the event, partly because Davies was not there to defend him, Dyke's resignation was accepted. A few days later, Gilligan resigned.

Hutton's conclusions were met with a mixture of astonishment and condemnation. Some commentators accused him of a deliberate government whitewash, while others felt he was simply naïve about the normal conduct of journalism. And although the government certainly emerged better than expected, a closer analysis of the evidence presented to Hutton – rather than his own narrow interpretation of the evidence – tells a much healthier story about the state of BBC journalism and its future. There are essentially three reasons.

First, there is no question that BBC journalists had discovered a legitimate story of huge public significance: that within the intelligence services there were real doubts about the strength of the information published in the September dossier, which was the basis on which Britain went to war with Iraq.[4] Brian Jones, who was head of a scientific section of the Defence Intelligence Analysis Staff and heavily involved in the production of the dossier, told Hutton that he felt Iraq's chemical and biological weapons capabilities 'were not being accurately represented in all regards in relation to the available evidence'. He also talked about 'influence from outside the intelligence community' (Evidence: 219–20).

Jones' concerns were supported by a former UN weapons inspector and current member of the Iraq survey group, known for security reasons only as Mr A. He told Hutton of a perception that 'the dossier had been round the houses several times in order to try to find a form of words which would strengthen certain political objectives' (Evidence: 221–2). In an e-mail to David Kelly on 25 September 2002, following a meeting about the dossier, he wrote that 'you and I should have been more involved in this than the spin merchants of this administration' (Evidence: 223).

Second, there was also no question about Kelly's status as a senior and reliable source. Patrick Lamb, deputy head of the Counter Proliferation Department, told the inquiry about Kelly's expertise on Iraq and the fact that senior officials would trust information from him over information contained in documents. He also made it clear that Kelly was intimately involved in preparation of the dossier: 'At all times we would show the text to David and we would very much rely on his expertise and knowledge, as the source and person who could verify the accuracy of what we were producing' (Evidence: 93).

Third, there was no question that changes had been made to the dossier after – and almost certainly as a result of – discussions with Number Ten advisers. Five days before publication, the draft dossier read: 'Intelligence indicates that as part of Iraq's military planning Saddam is prepared to use chemical and biological weapons *if he believes his regime is under threat*' (emphasis added). In an e-mail, the Prime Minister's chief of staff Jonathan Powell warned that this supported the argument that Iraq did not pose a CBW threat and 'we will only create one if we attack him. I think you should redraft the para' (Evidence: 274). The final version changed the word 'prepared' to 'willing' and omitted the qualification.

The so-called '45-minute' claim was also picked out by Kelly as a cause for concern in his interview with Susan Watts, not least because it was emphasized in the preface signed by the Prime Minister. The claim that Iraqi forces could deploy chemical and biological weapons within 45 minutes of an order to do so was widely interpreted to mean long-range missiles, which could therefore be fired on enemy countries, including British bases in Cyprus. It emerged during questioning that this applied only to short-range battlefield weapons, which would only be used in self-defence.

It is important, given the furore that followed, to remember that this was a story broken by and followed up by BBC journalists who were not afraid – indeed, in Gilligan's case he had a specific brief – to challenge the government. But it did need careful handling – not because of potential government repercussions, but because the reputation and tradition of BBC journalism required a more robust standard of journalistic evidence than is required on most newspaper desks.

It was not handled sufficiently carefully by Gilligan, particularly in the unscripted 6.07 interview. He himself confessed to the Hutton inquiry that the allegation that Downing Street inserted the 45-minute claim knowing it was wrong was 'the kind of slip of the tongue that does happen often during live broadcasts' (Evidence: 246). For any journalist accusing the Prime Minister of taking the country to war on a deliberately false premise, that would be regarded as unprofessional. For a BBC journalist on the most high profile radio programme in the BBC's repertoire, it was unforgivable. There were many BBC journalists at the time who were apprehensive that the BBC was intent on defending itself for a story that they believed had been taken one step too far.

As the row escalated, Gilligan's lack of scrupulous care was compounded within the BBC by two other factors. First, there had been what director of Richard Sambrook called a 'very high volume' of complaints from Downing Street in the run-up to and during the conduct of the war. While expected at times of high tension, it heightened the BBC's sense of being the target for persistent and hostile government attacks. This hostility was exacerbated by Alastair Campbell's evidence to the Foreign Affairs

Committee on 28 June, which chairman Gavyn Davies said in his evidence to Hutton was 'an almost unprecedented attack on the BBC . . . he accused the BBC of having followed an anti-war agenda before, during and after the Iraqi conflict' (Evidence: 187–8). The complaint lodged by Campbell following Gilligan's broadcast must therefore be seen in the context of scores of similar complaints – by phone, fax and e-mail – from Downing Street as the political pressure mounted.

Second, the scale of this hostility, combined with Davies' and Dyke's personal backgrounds as Labour sympathizers, made them all the more determined to demonstrate their independence. In an e-mail to governors in advance of their emergency meeting on 29 June, Davies wrote:

> I remain firmly of the view that, in the big picture sense, it is absolutely critical for the BBC to emerge from this row without being seen to buckle in the face of government pressure . . . This, it seems to me, really is a moment for the governors to stand up and be counted.
>
> (Evidence: 285)

While an admirable sentiment, it is possible that a Chairman who felt less politically conflicted might have taken some time to interrogate management on the provenance and robustness of the story in question.

In other words, as the BBC conceded, it made mistakes. That Hutton decided to focus almost entirely on those mistakes and ignore the wider context should not obscure the fact that a publicly funded broadcaster, with both a Chairman and Director General alleged to have pro-government sympathies, pursued a politically explosive story of immense public interest in the face of unremitting government pressure. That it could do so was not just a measure of its impartiality, but also its resources.

Neither of its two rivals, ITN or Sky News, had the same contacts or resources. ITN, after a series of cuts and redundancies, no longer has the resources to pursue difficult political stories with vigour and determination. And it is difficult to believe, given that Sky News is ultimately owned by Rupert Murdoch, that a story of such political sensitivity would have been pursued within the News International stable with the same vigour. While Sky News is rightly seen as a high quality and impartial service, it is less certain that its journalists would willingly pursue such a contentious and potentially explosive anti-government story in the knowledge that their employer was fervently pro-war and pro-government.

The repercussions and the future

In the immediate aftermath of the Hutton Report, there was a great deal of anguished predictions about the future of the BBC and its journalism – that the institution itself would find it hard to recover, and that its journalism would inevitably be cowed in the face of such comprehensive criticism. There were three areas in which commentators voiced serious concerns about the BBC's future. In all three, it is possible to show cause for much greater optimism once the immediate crisis subsided.

The first was BBC journalism, and concerns that the post-Hutton recriminations would result in a more conservative, fact-gathering approach to reporting. Certainly, in the immediate shadow of Hutton and the two resignations, there was a greater sense of caution. Senior managers were distracted by an internal inquiry designed to discover what editorial mechanisms had failed and could be improved, and journalists felt under greater pressure to ensure that any stories that were uncomfortable for the government were properly and securely sourced and where necessary referred upwards. This process of tighter editorial control was no worse than other occasions where the BBC had faced enormous upheavals, and probably less severe than the traumas that followed the sacking of director general Alasdair Milne in 1986 (Barnett and Curry 1994; Leapman 1986).

There is, however, a deeply rooted journalistic culture within the BBC that places enormous value on impartiality, professionalism and above all independence. In an astonishing display of solidarity, 10,000 BBC staff each paid £5 to pay for a full-page newspaper advertisement expressing their dismay at the departure of Greg Dyke. It read in part: 'Greg Dyke stood for brave, independent and rigorous journalism that was fearless in its search for the truth. We are resolute that the BBC should not step back from its determination to investigate the facts in pursuit of the truth' (Wells 2004b: 333). Four months later, the BBC flagship programme *Panorama* ran a hard-hitting programme about the lack of readiness of London's emergency services in the event of a terrorist attack on London, in the face of bitter criticism from the Home Secretary David Blunkett. There is no evidence that, compared to its main rivals, the BBC has become 'softer' on the government.

Moreover, Hutton's one-sided conclusions made it more difficult for the government to complain too loudly about unfair coverage: even its friends were concerned about a public backlash that sympathized with the BBC's treatment in the face of perceived aggression and bullying by government strategists.

The second area of concern was BBC management. With both a Chairman and a Director General to be replaced, there were widespread fears that the government would use this opportunity to appoint a chairman with whom it found favour – not necessarily of the 'right' political persuasion, but someone who would espouse a more cautious journalistic philosophy. The deputy chairman, Richard Ryder, who took over from Davies, caused consternation by apologizing unreservedly for BBC 'mistakes'. It was also Ryder who, at a governors' meeting, had suggested that reporting rather than discovering facts may be the more appropriate approach for the BBC.

In fact, and partly because the government did not want to face accusations of cronyism, the populist and widely respected broadcaster Michael Grade was appointed. This was significant because of Grade's reputation: he would not be prepared to preside over a smaller, downsized BBC and can be expected to champion not just the BBC's independence but its continued scale and vitality. Furthermore, his appointment of Mark Thompson as director general – a former *Panorama* and news editor – cemented the feeling that the BBC again had a first-class leadership team that would be just as robust in resisting government pressure as their predecessors. They had the added advantage of coming without the baggage of any known political sympathies.

This links directly to the third area, the coming review of the BBC's charter. The BBC's current Royal Charter expires at the end of 2006 and, as in previous years, the government has initiated a review of the funding and structure of the BBC. This was seen by some as an opportunity for the government to 'bring the BBC to heel', perhaps by proposing abolition of the licence fee or the privatization or break-up of the BBC.

With a government Green Paper not due until early 2005, it is too early to say what proposals will be advanced. However, Culture Secretary Tessa Jowell has spoken at every opportunity of the importance of maintaining a 'strong and independent' BBC, and there appears to be little appetite within government circles for dismantling or restructuring the BBC. On the contrary, a report commissioned by the Conservative Party on the BBC's future – which recommended radical plans to turn it over to subscription funding – was coolly received by the government and is unlikely even to be embraced by the Conservative opposition (Elstein *et al.* 2004). Similar arguments and proposals put forward by an influential government adviser have also been conspicuously ignored by the government (Cox 2004).

Despite concerns that the government might want to extract revenge for the BBC's mishandling of the WMD story, in fact there is probably more sympathy within government circles for a publicly funded BBC of real cultural significance than there was within the Conservative government of the 1980s. The problem for both the government and the BBC will be arguing the case for sustained public funding in a multi-channel era, against growing opposition from powerful media conglomerates. Once again, it is arguable that the government will feel it necessary to protect the BBC, partly to avoid accusations of exacting revenge for the Gilligan story.

The one area in which change is almost certain, and where problems were certainly illuminated by the Gilligan affair, is BBC governance. Hutton drew particular attention to the inability of the governors properly to execute their regulatory role of holding management to account. As we have seen, Davies in particular was intent on defending the BBC against government attack. But the contradictory roles within the governing board – having to act as both champions and regulators of the BBC – were particularly exposed and will be subjected to intense scrutiny during the charter review period. Even the BBC's most fervent supporters agree that change in this area is not necessarily an evil and may well strengthen its institutional hand.

In summary, there is no convincing evidence that the BBC has been substantially weakened either institutionally or journalistically. Its critical role as upholder of the public interest, as a seeker after new facts as well as an accurate and impartial reporter has been demonstrated and upheld, and the perceived 'whitewash' of the Hutton Report has, if anything, made it easier for the BBC to pursue a robust investigative journalistic culture. Those who fear for the BBC's independence sometime confuse two very different imperatives: the need to maintain the highest possible journalistic standards in terms of accuracy, impartiality and fairness and its vulnerability to intervention and pressure from government. There are times when abiding by a strict code of professional journalistic standards to uphold the former can easily be misconstrued as giving into the latter. For the moment at least, there is no indication that the BBC is any more susceptible to government pressure in the light of Hutton than it has been in the aftermath of clashes with powerful governments in the past.

Notes

1   When the Thames TV programme *This Week* established in 1988 that three alleged IRA terrorists shot dead by the SAS in Gibraltar may have been summarily executed, the resulting programme took months of painstaking research for a one-hour documentary which eventually embroiled the channel in a massive and expensive row with the Conservative government of the day.

2   Gilligan had been the *Sunday Telegraph*'s defence correspondent before being recruited in 1999 by the then editor of the *Today* programme, Rod Liddle. Liddle was concerned that too much of the BBC's defence reporting relied on government spin and press briefings, and Gilligan's role was to be more investigative and challenging. Before his posting to Iraq, he had gone undercover to buy anti-personnel landmines in contravention of the 1998 Landmines Act and obtained a series of damning leaked official reports about Britain's performance in the Kosovo war. His reporting was not comfortable for the government, but was precisely part of the BBC's independent 'watchdog' function.

3   The following quotations are taken from 'Lord Hutton's summary of his conclusions' in Rogers (2004: 309–22).

4   Where quotations are sourced to 'Evidence', they are taken from 'The Evidence Day by Day' in Rogers (2004: 90–296).

References

Barnett, S., Seymour, E. and Gaber, I. (2000) *From Callaghan to Kosovo: Changing Trends in British Television News 1975–1999*. London: University of Westminster.

Barnett, S. and Curry, A. (1994) *The Battle for the BBC*. London: Aurum Press.

Cox, B. (2004) *Free for All? Public Service Television in the Digital Age*. London: Demos.

Dyke, G. (2003) Speech given to the University of London Goldsmiths College Journalism Symposium, 24 April.

Elstein, D., Cox, D., Donoghne, B., Graham, D. and Metzger, S. (2004) (Broadcasting Policy Group), *Beyond the Charter: the BBC after 2006*. London: Premium Publishing.

Freedland, J. (2004) 'Tugging back the Veil' in S. Rogers (ed.) *The Hutton Inquiry and its Impact*. London: Politicos.

Hargreaves, I. (2003) *Journalism: Truth or Dare*. Oxford: Oxford University Press.

Leapman, M. (1986) *The Last Days of the Beeb*. London: Hodder & Stoughton.

Rogers, S. (ed.) (2004) *The Hutton Inquiry and its Impact*. London: Politico's.

Wells, M. (2004a) 'The Story of the Story' in S. Rogers (ed.) *The Hutton Inquiry and its Impact*. London: Politico's.

Wells, M. (2004b) 'Bring Back Greg' in S. Rogers (ed.) *The Hutton Inquiry and its Impact*. London: Politico's.

Wyatt, W. (2003) *The Fun Factory: A Life in the BBC*. London: Aurum Press.

25

Journalism, media conglomerates and the Federal Communications Commission

Oliver Boyd-Barrett

- Do US Administrations barter business opportunities for media support?
- Can US news media perform a public service watchdog role?
- Is ownership of US news media too concentrated?
- Were the FCC's 2003 deregulation proposals designed to serve special interests or the public good?

In June 2003, the five members of the US Federal Communications Commission (FCC) voted 3–2 (three Republicans, two Democrats) in support of changes to rules governing media ownership – changes that would probably intensify media merger and acquisition activity. The precise wording was not available either to Congress or to the public in advance of the vote. Chairman Michael Powell resisted calls for a delay to the vote, as he would later resist attempts to delay implementation of the changes (Ahrens 2003b).

George Bush appointed Michael Powell shortly after Bush acceded to the US presidency in 2001. Michael was son of Secretary of State Colin Powell who, three months before the June vote, prosecuted what critics believe was an illegal war of invasion and occupation of Iraq, on the false pretexts that Iraq had stockpiled weapons of mass destruction, and was a threat to the US. Mainstream media support for the war was almost unanimous, uncritical and enthusiastic (but later more reserved, in face of evidence of Administration duplicity, Iraqi chaos, evidence of torture of Iraqis by US military and prison guards, and increased terrorism worldwide) (Boyd-Barrett 2003a). I believe we should ask whether, in 2002–3, media giants bartered their support for Bush's 'total spectrum dominance' policy in return for regulatory changes that would facilitate business acquisitions in lucrative media markets. Was their later (muted) criticism of the war a reaction to heated congressional resistance to the changes? Or was their initial support an accidental outcome of shared ideology between sectors of the US establishment? Were media proprietors and executives interested players rather than guardians of public interest?

In this chapter, I explore what the 2003 FCC proposals reveal about media conglomerates, the implications for journalism in general and the 2004 presidential election. I explore whether the proposals intensified processes of deregulation typified by the 1996 Telecommunications Act. Such processes, promoted in the name of *competition*, facilitated *consolidation*, and media conglomeration, though it has benefits, is undemocratic. But smallness, in itself, serves the public little better. Journalism faces an enduring, pervasive crisis in its relationship to capitalism and democracy, most acutely apparent when citizens are in gravest danger. Several such moments were encountered in the period 2000–4.

The FCC proposals

The FCC was established by the 1934 US Communications Act to regulate the broadcasting industry. It established broadcasting as a commercial enterprise – one that should also serve the public interest. The concept of 'public interest' was defined vaguely and gradually, through case law (Corn-Revere and Carfveth 2004). From the 1980s up to and including the 1996 Telecommunications Act, the FCC has reduced restrictions on business initiative in the interest of promoting competition.

Continuing this trend towards 'deregulation', the FCC in 2003 voted to allow a single multi-station television provider to reach a maximum of 45 per cent of American TV households (previously 35 per cent) (Ahrens 2003b). Because an anachronistic existing provision required the FCC to count as one every two viewers of UHF stations (TV channels 14 and above) a single company technically could now reach 90 per cent of viewers. Another proposal allowed a single company to own two (in some cases, three) stations in the same town, in all but the smallest markets; and to own a combination of newspapers, radio and television stations in the same community. Many towns might now see a single company own both the town's only newspaper and the top TV station. The FCC left unchanged the cap for radio stations, but revised the method for defining boundaries of a local market, in an effort to close a loophole permitting a single company to own all the radio stations in some cities. It did not oblige companies such as Clear Channel or Infinity Broadcasting, who had acquired stations under older rules, to sell their holdings. Application of new rule changes was to be guided by a controversial, strictly quantitative 'diversity index'.

The FCC proposals impinged directly on issues of diversity: diversity of values, viewpoints, perspectives and sources available to the public in informational and entertainment media products.

Public and congressional reaction

A preponderance of prior comment from close to a million people opposed further deregulation. This included a broad range of non-governmental organizations such as the AFL-CIO, the Leadership Conference on Civil Rights, National Rifle Association, the National Organization for Women, national associations of Hispanic and Black journalists, the Consumers Union, the Consumers Federation of America and the United States Conference of Catholic Bishops (Ahrens 2003a). Of the 18,000 public statements filed electronically, 97 per cent opposed more concentration. Even CNN founder Ted Turner complained: 'There's really five companies that control 90 per cent of what we read, see and hear. It's not healthy' (Deggans 2003). In the run-up to voting, the FCC had met privately with the heads of major media corporations 71 times, but only five times with opposition groups. During 1995–2003, FCC members had enjoyed $2.8 million of corporate largesse, including dozens of trips to Las Vegas and London.

Most opponents argued that further deregulation was against the 'public interest' (Null 2003; Tourtellotte 2003). Michael Powell had publicly ridiculed this concept, imitating his predecessor in the Reagan years, Mark Fowler, who had declared television no different in principle to a kitchen toaster. Commissioner Democrat Jonathan Adelstein described the FCC's decision as 'remarkable, unprecedented and bad' (Ahrens 2003a; Bartash 2003; Boehlet 2003). The proposals encountered unanticipated Congressional resistance. Senate and House enacted measures to disallow their implementation. Among other things, politicians were leery of ceding to conglomerates greater influence over the local media that served their own constituencies. Having first threatened to veto attempts to roll back the regulations, the White House forced a compromise, raising the cap to 39 per cent – less than the proposed 45 per cent, but high enough that Fox (News Corp) and Viacom could retain acquisitions that had lifted them above the previous 35 per cent ceiling. Although the 39 per cent cap was now consolidated into law, a Federal Appeals Court in September 2003 imposed a 12-month moratorium on implementation of FCC changes, while it investigated the implications of cross-ownership and duopoly-related transactions (McChesney and Nichols 2003; Stolberg 2003). The Appeals Court, reporting in June 2004, as this book went to press, rejected the FCC's justifications for the changes.

Although it is still too early to judge whether the court's verdict will represent the end of the matter (unlikely, in this author's opinion), the proposals themselves and the interests that they served, provide a window through which it is possible to discern the political-economic dynamics behind media regulation and media concentration in the US.

▍ What were the proposals 'really about?'

The *real* debate – if there was one (Powell scheduled only one official hearing, one hour long, and declined to attend nine semi-official hearings, some of them personally organized by FCC Democrat Michael Copps) – arguably had little to do with public interest (Nichols 2003; Nichols and McChesney 2003). What it *did* have to do with was whether and how the wealth of local television stations (many enjoying profit rates of 40 per cent – higher in the big cities) could be (re-)distributed among corporate media. On one side were lined the networks, pleading poverty, supported by large newspaper chains anxious to acquire or increase holdings of local television and radio in their own markets. On the other were affiliate or independent television chains, gripping tightly to their golden-egg geese. These were supported by independent television and movie producers, fearing the proposals would reduce clients for their products, homogenize content, and weaken their leverage over fees; and by advertisers, worrying that consolidation would encourage conglomerates to raise fees and force advertisers to buy packages rather than specific slots. The National Association of Broadcasters (NAB) opposed lifting the ceiling on audience reach, but supported cross-ownership measures, since many local television members wanted to acquire neighbouring stations and newspapers.

The discourse of debate framed networks as independent of other players. Yet apart from 126 local television stations they already owned (enhancing their leverage as programme suppliers to stations they did *not* own), the four networks were smallish components of larger conglomerates, specifically Disney (ABC), General Electric (NBC), News Corporation (Fox) and Viacom (CBS), participating in joint ventures with others such as AOL-Time Warner, AT&T and Microsoft. Thus the networks were incorporated alongside cable channels, satellite services, Hollywood studios, theatres, theme parks and publishing houses, within converged corporate environments.

The conglomerates had been nurtured by deregulation measures of the 1980s and 1990s. These had increased the national audience share a single broadcast network could reach; introduced cross-ownership between newspapers and broadcasters in some markets; lifted restrictions on networks' ownership of local television and of programming; relaxed the separation of telephony from broadcasting, and of 'common carrier' from content provider; and removed obligations on broadcasters for fairness, equal time and balance. Deregulation initiated intensive consolidation (for sources on US media conglomerates and related data in this chapter, see Alexander *et al.* 2004; Bagdikian 2004; Croteau and Hoynes 2001; Herman 1998; McChesney 2000, 2004).

Public interest assessment

Chairman Powell had argued that the FCC was obliged by the terms of the 1996 Telecommunications Act to review media regulations once every two years, and that the Act required him to valorize market competitiveness above all other considerations (Powell 2003). Further, the US Court of Appeals for the DC circuit in 2002 challenged the legality of the FCC's ownership restrictions, and called for stronger, empirical methodologies for determination of market diversity. Powell contended there was no risk that a market free-for-all would cause unhealthy consolidation. With the development of cable, satellite, Internet and mobile wireless, there was bandwidth for everybody; older regulations intended to ensure equitable division of a scarce resource were unnecessary and anti-competitive.

Channels of communication had vastly increased in numbers – the combined result of new technologies and deregulation. But Powell overlooked the extent to which these had been 'conglomerized'. Increasing numbers of outlets do not compensate for concentration of ownership *across* media categories, delivering consumers' time and expenditure to a handful of giants. Media conglomerates were now so powerful, and the costs of market entry so high, that they drowned out alternative voices by means of acquisition strategy, superior production and marketing resources.

There was more diversity in 2003 than in 1963, but market share continued to be dominated by a (shrinking) handful of suppliers. Existing diversity was more apparent than real: everywhere, content was increasingly homogenized and commercialized.

In 2003, the six most influential sources of news on network and cable systems were owned by five conglomerates (AOL Time Warner, Disney, General Electric, News Corporation and Viacom). Forty per cent of cable systems were controlled by two corporations, Comcast and AOL Time Warner. Direct-to-home satellite delivery was completely controlled by two corporations, Echostar and News Corporation (DirecTV). Of 25 top-rated cable channels, 20 were at least one-third owned by one of the five media behemoths. Media corporations, generally, hunted the advertiser-prized 18–34-year-old male demographic. In radio, Clear Channel and Viacom (Infinity) reached 42 per cent of listeners and raked in 45 per cent of revenues; Clear Channel was part owner of Hispanic Broadcasting Services, soon to be acquired by Univision, which, with NBC's Telemundo, commanded the US Hispanic market. More than 90 per cent of daily newspapers enjoyed local monopolies, serving over 70 per cent of newspaper readers.

Ownership of newspapers and television stations fell from 1,500 in the 1970s to 600 and could fall to 300 under the new regulations. Hollywood majors took in over 80 per cent of movie revenues (Wasko 2004) and dominated production and distribution. In 1992, independent Hollywood created 16 new TV series, but only one in 2002. The radical potential of Public Broadcasting Service (PBS) stations had been neutralized or reversed by miserly governmental financing and dependence on corporate sponsorship.

Even on the Internet, the same major corporations controlled the most popular Web sites and sources of news (which in turn relied heavily on news agencies AP and Reuters). The top 20 Internet news sites were controlled by major conglomerates. Even industry insider, Barry Diller, worried that cable and phone companies, as ISPs, would become principal gateways to the Internet at the cost of censorship and higher prices (Moyers 2003). Local telephony was largely controlled by Baby Bell monopolies, themselves consolidating under the leadership of Verizon and SBC, resistant to market entry by long-distance operators. Computer manufacture, components, servers and software, and control of the 'Internet backbone' were all heavily consolidated (Boyd-Barrett 2004a).

Networks complained they had lost market share to cable and satellite (FAIR 2003). Yet in contrast with single alternative channels, their *programming* was still the most popular on cable and satellite. Fox, as part of News Corporation, was integrated with cable and satellite channels. All networks sold productions to cable and satellite channels, and advertisers depended mainly on networks to reach *national* audiences. Unlike their cable and satellite competitors, however, advertising was networks' main source of revenue. Networks complained about the 'compensation' they paid affiliate local stations for using their airspace. Owning these stations, they claimed, would allow them cost-cutting efficiency and synergy. They moaned about increasing costs of producing popular television series like *Friends*. They were irritated when affiliate stations used their (restricted) right to 'pre-empt' network with local programming. Networks threatened that without enhanced profitability through ownership of more television stations, they could not justify expenditure on 'quality' programming or their purchase of rights to sports events for free 'over-the-air' dissemination. They would have to restrict quality programming to cable and satellite. Powell supported their pleas, in the interest, he claimed, of the remaining 15 to 25 per cent of television homes that still received free terrestrial television (James 2003).

To explain weakening profitability, networks and their parent conglomerates could look to their acquisition fever of the 1990s, that had been stimulated by relaxation of ownership restrictions in the 1996 Telecommunications Act and was financed by high levels of debt. Debt intensified commercialization and put pressure on consumer prices. A crisis of profits and share value ensued, leading to sell-offs and divestitures, thus mocking the original rationale for acquisitions.

Critics argued that network (or other non-local) acquisition of local stations would reduce diversity of opinion and de-localize news in markets where most people turned to television for local news (Safire 2003). Remaining independents would have less leverage to 'pre-empt' network programming or promote local shows. The impact of press/television cross-ownership would be similar. It might lead to savings (and loss of jobs) where operations were pooled, and might give conglomerate owners leverage to raise advertising rates. Critics claimed that efficiencies, synergies and profit should not be the primary concern of the FCC. The campaign for deregulation, they claimed, was about increasing stock options and salaries for

CEOs, repeating the cycle of corruption that had helped trigger economic recession. The FCC's primary concern should derive instead from the public's First Amendment rights to diversity of perspective and viewpoint, essential to democracy. FCC defenders retorted that in markets where cross-ownership already existed – 'grandfathered' from previous regulatory regimes – news quantity and quality had improved. Yet the absence of diverse, critical viewpoints following 11 September 2001 or in the lead-up to the invasion of Iraq, and journalists' own confessions of self-censorship and pressure from advertisers or parent corporations (Croteau and Hoynes 2001), suggested such improvements were marginal.

Issues of size and journalistic quality

Local television was no panacea for problems of conglomerate journalism, even though local news remained a highly profitable advertising-driven business. Few who opposed consolidation of media wanted an extension of practices associated with local television (chronicled by the Project for Excellence in Journalism 2004): reactive and superficial coverage, homogeneity in look and feel, preference for immediacy rather than storytelling, localism (76 per cent of stories), dominance of crime news (24 per cent of stories, followed by accidents, bizarre events, fires and catastrophes – 12 per cent, human interest – 10 per cent, politics – 10 per cent), extremely brief news reports (70 per cent less than a minute), little investigative reporting (7 per cent of stories), one-sided reporting (in 60 per cent of stories involving disputes), minimal independent political coverage (why reduce the motivation of politicians to advertise?) and emphasis on branding over content. There was growing reliance on stories that did not require a correspondent (for example corporate video news releases). Weather was the main reason why viewers tuned in. Even the claim to localism was increasingly bogus, as where newsrooms serviced multiple stations ('centralcasting'), using anchors or presenters that were not local, showing packages designed for several markets. Newsrooms were expected to do more with less, increasing the hours of news with the same or lower budgets. Three-quarters of stations had assigned beats, but many of these were part-time. Stations owned by local owners with only one or two stations were vanishing.

The public had come to expect that large media would provide programming that required substantial investment, including services of national and global news. Yet in practice big media were undependable guardians of public interest. Not only did they not maintain adequate resources for gathering and delivery – they failed to protect the public interest on occasions of critical importance, including coverage of the presidential election of 2000, the terrorist attacks of 11 September 2001, the subsequent invasion of Afghanistan, and the US invasion and occupation of Iraq in 2003 (Boyd-Barrett 2003b).

The 2004 Project for Excellence in Journalism (PEJ) found that media did not command public confidence in their credibility and impartiality. Fifty-nine per cent of the public thought news organizations were biased. Only 59 to 66 per cent of citizens considered their newspapers and network news services were believable. People were increasingly distrustful of giant corporations of the sort that owned news media.

❙ Relative decline of television news

Although still the 'most watched and influential news outlets in America', networks' news ratings fell 34 per cent from 1993 to 2003 and 59 per cent since 1969, while the median age of viewers increased to 60. (Most data in this section come from the 2004 PEJ report.) Early evening local news' combined share had also begun to decline, slipping from 50 per cent to 41 per cent between 1997 and 2004. Once-celebrated network news magazine programmes now appeared less regularly, accounting for only one-fifth of the hours of programming in 2003 that they did in 1997, and earning 48 per cent less revenue. They could no longer be said to cover major news of the day, but specialized in lifestyle and behaviour, consumer news and entertainment. Their economic usefulness as a cheap genre (half the cost of drama) had been superseded by 'reality' shows.

Coverage of government in 2003 (18 per cent of all network stories) was half that of 1987, even less on morning news. News divisions had become small, unprofitable components of larger broadcasting corporations that themselves yielded only between 5 per cent and 35 per cent of the revenues of their multi-media or conglomerate parents. Once regarded as prestigious loss leaders that kept regulators off the backs of parent corporations, news divisions were increasingly judged in terms of profits returned. In an era of costly international conflicts, networks were severely challenged. Network news was increasingly pitched towards younger audiences with less serious, more consumer-oriented coverage that appealed to advertisers, and interrupted by more commercials (over 30 minutes in 2 hours). News divisions experienced numerous staff reductions, forcing fewer and less experienced correspondents to produce the same number of stories or more. The number of correspondents featured on air during the average evening newscast fell by over a third between 1986 and 2004. Each network once had 15 overseas bureaus, but now had around six, some of them staffed by freelancers. Fewer minutes were dedicated to news, down from 21 to 18.7 in 30-minute nightly newscasts from 1991 to 2002.

Did other news sources compensate for this decline? Cable had eaten away at network audience share but audiences for nightly network newscasts in 2003 were 12 times higher than prime-time audience for cable. The median age of cable news audiences was marginally lower than that for network news (as 'young' as 52.4 in the case of MSNBC). The quality, reliability and seriousness of such news left much to be desired, according to the PEJ report. Sixty-two per cent of cable news was conducted in 'live' mode, most of it in the form of interviews, usually by anchors. The reporter's role on cable was often confined to live reporter 'stand-ups', taking the emphasis away from edited stories and de-emphasizing reporting as such. Most cable news was something close to a 'first draft'. Talkativeness and telegenicity outweighed traditional journalism skills such as writing, editing, cultivating sources and writing to pictures. Cable news was less adequately sourced than either network news or newspapers. The PEJ report identified a 'Fox effect' – 'using fewer people to produce news by focusing on fewer topics doing fewer edited stories and airing more live reports'.

With the exception of national newspapers *USA Today*, the *New York Times* and the *Wall Street Journal*, the percentage of Americans reading newspapers has been shrinking since 1970; since 1990 shrinkage has been absolute – despite an increasing population – across most age and demographic groups. Newspapers remained attractive to advertisers, supplying 80 per cent of revenues, and offered more reporters, editors and news-gathering capacity than other media. But the top 7 per cent of the nation's newspapers commanded 55 per cent of total circulation. Newspapers have experienced a net drop in staff and resources. In 2002, newspapers had 2,200 fewer newsroom employees than in 1990. Staff reductions often followed buy outs, disproportionately affecting experienced, higher salaried reporters and editors, while workloads increased and budget cuts hit training, travel and resources for investigative or in-depth reporting.

One in two Americans in 2003 went online; between half and two-thirds of these used online news sources some of the time. Internet news sites attracted younger consumers more readily than other news media. Some major news sites were not yet breaking even, and revenues represented a small fraction of overall revenues of parent corporations. A handful of major companies dominated. Time Warner controlled two of the top four news sites. Close to half of the most popular Web sites were owned by one of the ten largest media companies, and four were owned by a single company, which also earned most of the revenue. Internet journalism still largely comprised material from 'old' media. Only one-third of lead articles on major sites came from the organizations' own staffs, and most of the material was not even original to the Web. A large percentage of lead pieces, 42 per cent, comprised unedited wire stories, mainly from AP and Reuters, while a further quarter comprised partly edited or supplemented wire stories.

Betrayal of public interest

Corporatization, conglomeration and commercialization do not adequately account for failures of mainstream media to serve the public on issues of unprecedented global importance in the period from 2000 to 2004, failures that arguably amount to criminally negligent collusion by mainstream media. I do not argue there was *no* media coverage of any of the following, but that the issues were shunted to one side, dealt with irresolutely, sporadically, one-sidedly (or often not at all), without persistence, curiosity, insight, passion, or a modicum of justifiable outrage on behalf of a wronged and misled public.

Media coverage of the 2000 US presidential election failed to communicate to the public the darker side of the Bush dynasty: service to Nazi and communist regimes; involvement in scandals such as Bay of Pigs, Iran-Contra and BCCI; connections to intelligence and defence communities; the feudal antics of Yale's Skull and Bones; Bush junior's experiences with alcohol, drugs, insider trading and born-again Christianity; the family's ties with Saudi elites; his prostration before big business interest; disregard and contempt for environmental issues; and lack of compassion (Boyd-Barrett 2003a). What about the 'neoconservative' cabal, plotting from the first Gulf War if not from the Reagan years, what it could do if and when a "new Pearl Harbor" might handily present itself? Its very existence, intellectual roots in elitist and Machiavellian ideas, penetration of both Bush Administrations, ties with greater-Israel lobbies as well as the Christian right, think-tank camouflage such as Project for a New American Century and American Enterprise Institute, came as a complete surprise from 2002 for most of the public. None of this had to wait upon such revelations as Kevin Phillips' account of the Bush Dynasty in 2003. Criminal aspects of the Florida 2000 election, exposed in British media by Greg Palast (2002) even before the close of the election, were covered only many months later in US mainstream media, off-handedly, in inside pages. And although by mid-2004 the subject of corruptible, paperless voting machines – largely operated by a right-wing oligopoly acting without the restraint of vetting or licensing by regulatory authorities – had finally commanded at least three editorials in the *New York Times*, its appearance on the media agenda was too little, too late.

The terrorist attacks of 11 September 2001 raised swarms of complex, disturbing questions (Boyd-Barrett 2003b; Griffin 2004). Among other things these pertained to prior and precise warnings, both internal to the Administration and externally from overseas' intelligence services, the failure of standard operating procedures for the interception of hijacked planes, piggybacking of the attacks on simulated anti-terrorist exercises, contradictions in evidence concerning such things as the presence of firearms on board the airliners, expert speculation that the planes were guided by remote control, pre-9/11 speculative bets on Wall Street, and a plethora of other concerns, any one of which would have occupied newspaper front pages of a normally functioning democracy for months on end. The search for culprits of the anthrax murders was a related thread that few media even bothered to try to follow; none dared wonder whether a *system* rather than an individual might be at its root. With occasional, half-hearted exceptions, media passively and timidly waited upon inadequate and contaminated systems of formal investigation such as the joint intelligence committee report of 2003 and the Kean commission of 2004. Media timidly played along, first with the preposterous notion that the overthrow of the Taliban was a rational or even useful response to the attacks of 11 September (most of the hijackers were Saudi, most of the money that financed them was Saudi, the Taliban were the creation of Pakistan in alliance with Saudi Arabia and the US, and purported hijackers had been under the noses of international and domestic intelligence agencies for several months). Then for several months they ignored issues of oil, strategic interest and US military bases in Central Asia; they failed to investigate other possible culprits of 11 September, roundly ignored evidence that the invasion of Afghanistan had been planned for October 2001 well *before* the attacks of 11 September, and then, when the hideous farce of retribution had been executed, meekly chronicled the Administration's long-planned preparations for invasion and occupation of Iraq, buying into every lie spewed out by the Administration, even while alternative media were unpacking and exposing such lies, often on the very days they were uttered.

Resource issues cannot explain such failures, because even shoestring Web operations run by intelligent, curious, open-minded individuals provided a better service on many issues than the mainstream press, simply because their authors read books, studied overseas sources, both mainstream and alternative, and brought to their enquiries some independent, critical, historical and political understanding. Herman and Chomsky's (1988) propaganda model certainly speaks to the problem of mainstream media, but falls short. The model identifies news 'filters' of media ownership, dependence on advertising, standard journalistic procedures, fear of flak, and shared media-establishment ideological blinkers at the root of mainstream media ineptitude and collusion. It purports to be non-conspiratorial but then fails to investigate how, if ownership is an important factor, owners manage in such a timely and uniform manner, without bidding, to identify and mutually agree to serve the key strategic objectives of the military-industrial complex. The model does scant justice to penetration of media by the omnipresent and well resourced intelligence communities, and by other special interests. But it provides a framework that helps make sense of one-off studies. In her study of media coverage of weapons of mass destruction, Susan Moeller (2004) charts how media routinely became stenographers for the Administration, but then blames this on such factors as the inverted pyramid style of reporting with its presumption that authoritative sources be awarded pride of first mention, determining what statements and 'frames' are foregrounded. This accords with sociological charting of media prioritizing of authoritative sources and with agenda-setting theory, but it does not answer how such an unsatisfactory and dangerous *modus operandum* could have been perpetuated by a self-acclaimed critical, professional community, were it not that the system well serves elites, and that they know it does.

Towards a watchdog journalism

What must happen to preserve public communications space from further corporate colonization? First, there must be a sustained, coordinated and publicized effort by non-governmental and credible media monitors to expose the daily abuses of the communication privileges so recklessly awarded by government to media behemoths, of corporate media incompetence in protecting the public interest against the imperatives of commercial profit and political venality, and of corporate complicity with plutocratic elites. We need a rainbow coalition of non-profits, artists, intellectuals and educators to campaign tirelessly on behalf of alternative, non-mainstream sources of news and entertainment, and for the reform of mainstream media. We need rogue members of the plutocracy who may be prevailed upon to help finance the development of new voices and channels within the mainstream. The long-term goal for reformists must be a communications universe within which all voices are heard, with equal opportunity for all experiences and visions to be represented. Even more crucial, the goal must be a new *culture* of civil governance, and of government-people communication through the media – one that reflects the values and practices not of the very rich, nor of the corporations, nor of religious fundamentalists, but of the people. One measure of effectiveness, among many others, in this reformed communications environment, will be the willingness, capacity, intellectual and moral leadership of media in creating agendas that have a demonstrable relevance to real local and global problems that affect ordinary people and whole societies alike, regardless of, or perhaps specifically in opposition to, the claims and agendas of politicians, military, corporations and plutocratic classes.

Postscript

On 17 June 2004, the Senate voted to repeal the FCC's rule changes of June 2003. Prospects for a similar vote in the House of Representatives had been resisted by Congressional leaders. A week later, the US Court of Appeals for the Third Circuit in Philadelphia, which, as has been seen, had temporarily stayed the FCC changes in 2003, voted 2–1 to remand them for further consideration, on the grounds that the evidence and logic presented did not justify the changes as serving the public interest (see Labaton 2004; Rintels 2004; Squeo and Flint 2004, principal sources for what follows).

The Court did not dispute the FCC's right to ease ownership limitations, but said it had to do so in a way that was not 'arbitrary and capricious' – which it said had occurred in this case. Ironically, this language recalled that of the DC Circuit Court in 2002, which, in adjudicating complaints then lodged by Fox Television and other media giants, and in the spirit of the

1996 Telecommunications Act, which had required the FCC to review ownership rules every two years, ruled that the decision of the FCC that year to *maintain* existing restrictions on ownership had been 'arbitrary and capricious'. FCC's Michael Powell called the Philadelphia result 'chaotic', and said the state of media law was now 'clouded and confused'.

The Appeals Court ruled that the FCC should fix flaws in its diversity index, which the FCC had used to determine the new local cross-ownership rules. The Court cited as an 'essential flaw' the FCC argument that different media outlets make an equal contribution to diversity and competition regardless of their market share. It questioned the FCC's decision to exclude cable television outlets in determining the number of voices in a local area, while including Internet ones. The Court proposed a new definition of local radio markets that would generally prevent larger radio clusters by rejecting distinctions between AM and FM stations in determining market identities.

The Court did not review the national audience-reach cap on potential US television households any one company can reach with its stations (leaving it to stand at 39 per cent, the compromise struck between Congress and the White House). (Industry sources have indicated they will push for caps that are based on actual rather than potential viewership.) The Court affirmed the FCC's decision to lift an existing ban on allowing the same entity to own a local newspaper and radio or television station in the same market.

The Court placed a temporary halt on all the FCC's new media ownership rules until it had a chance to review new ones to be crafted by the FCC. The FCC's options were either to rewrite the rules or take the case to the Supreme Court: either approach might take a year or more.

The Court's decision was celebrated by groups such as the Media Access Project, the Caucus for Television Producers, Writers and Directors; Center for Creative Voices in Media; Center for Digital Democracy; Consumer Federation of America; Consumers Union, Center for Creative Voices in Media; Parents' Television Council; and the National Council of Churches, as well as by FCC Commissioner (democrat) Michael J. Copps (2004) who said that it was time 'for the FCC to start over and come up with a set of rules to encourage localism, diversity and competition in the broadcast media instead of always waving the green flag for more big-media consolidation'. He further noted that without sustained grassroots input the FCC commissioners could 'come back with rules that are almost as bad for media democracy as the ones that Congress and the Courts have rejected'.

▌References

Ahrens, F. (2003a) Unlikely Alliances Forged in Fight over Media Rules, *Washington Post*, 16 May.

Ahrens, F. (2003b) FCC Releases its New Media Ownership Rules, *Washington Post*, p. E01.

Ahrens, F. (2003c) Senate Move to Block New Media Ownership Rules, *Washington Post*, 16 July.

Alexander, A., Owers, J., Carveth, R., Hollifield, C. and Greco, A. (2004) *Media Economics. Theory and Practice*, third edition, Mahwah, NJ: Lawrence Erlbaum.

Bagdikian, B. (2004) *The New Media Monopoly*. Boston: Beacon Press.

Bartash, J. (2003) FCC grilled on media ownership rules, CBS Marketwatch.com, 4 June.

Boehlet, E. (2003) Congress to Big Media: Not so Fast, Salon.com, July.

Boyd-Barrett, O. (2003a) Imperial News for the New Imperialism, *Third World Resurgence*, N.151–2, pp. 44–8.

Boyd-Barrett, O. (2003b) Doubt Foreclosed: US Mainstream Media and the Attacks of 11 September 2001, in D. Demers (ed.), *Terrorism, Globalization and Mass Communication*, pp. 3–33. Spokane, WA: Marquette Books.

Boyd-Barrett, O. (2004a) Cyberspace, Power and Globalization. Paper presented to the annual conference of the *International Communication Association*, New Orleans, 31 May.

Boyd-Barrett, O. (2004b) Understanding: The Second Casualty, in S. Allan and B. Zelizer (eds) *Reporting War: Journalism in Wartime*. London and New York: Routledge.

Cooper, M. (2003) *Media Ownership and Democracy in the Digital Information Age*. Stanford, CA: Center for Internet and Society, Stanford Law School.

Copps, Michael (2004) Corporate Media and Local Interests Downsizing the Monster, *San Francisco Chronicle*, 19 July.

Corn-Revere, R. and Carveth, R. (2004) Economics and Media Regulation, in A. Alexander, J. Owers, R. Carveth, C. Hollifield and A. Greco (eds), *Media Economics: Theory and Practice*, third edition, pp. 49–67. Mahwah, NJ: Lawrence Erlbaum.

Croteau, D. and Hoynes, W. (2001) *The Business of Media*. Thousand Oaks, CA: Pine Forge Press.

Deggans, E. (2003) Diverse Critics Fight FCC on Media Ownership Rules, *St. Petersburg Times*, 29 April.

FAIR (2003) Will the FCC help big media get even bigger? *Fair.org*, 20 May.

Griffin, D. (2004) *The New Pearl Harbor: Disturbing Questions about the Bush Administration and 9/11*. Northampton, MA: Olive Branch Press.

Herman, E. (1998) *The Global Media: The Missionaries of Global Capitalism*. London: Cassell Academic.

Herman, E. S. and Chomsky, N. (1988) *Manufacturing Consent: The Political Economy of the Mass Media*. New York: Pantheon.

James, F. (2003) FCC Chief Warns of Future Shock. *Chicago Tribune*, 7 September.

Labaton, S. (2004) Court Orders Rethinking of Rules Allowing Large Media to Expand, *New York Times*, 25 June.

McChesney, R. (2000) *Rich Media, Poor Democracy: Communication Politics in Dubious Times*. New York: New Press.

McChesney, R. (2004) *The Problem of the Media: US Communication Politics in the Twenty-First Century*. New York: Monthly Review Press.

McChesney, R. and Nichols, J. (2003) Up in Flames. *The Nation*, 17 November.

Moeller, S. (2004). *Media Coverage of Weapons of Mass Destruction*. College Park, MD: Center for International and Security Studies at Maryland.

Moyers, B. (2003) Barry Diller Takes on Media Regulation. *NOW with Bill Moyers*, 28 April.

Nichols, J. (2003) FCC Rejects Public Interest. *The Nation*, 3 June.

Nichols, J. and McChesney, R. (2003) Public Be Damned. *The Nation*, 3 June.

Null, B. (2003) Diverse critics fight FCC on media ownership Rules. *St. Petersburg Times*, 29 April.

Palast, G. (2002) *The Best Democracy that Money Can Buy*. London: Pluto Press.

Powell, M. (2003) New Rules, Old Rhetoric. *New York Times*, 28 July.

Project for Excellence in Journalism (2004) *The State of the News Media 2004: An Annual Report on American Journalism*. New York: Colombia University School of Journalism.

Rintels, J. (2004). Michael Powell Lays an Egg. MediaChannel.org, 29 June.

Safire, W. (2003) Localism's Last Stand. *New York Times*, 17 July.

Squeo, A. M. and Flint, J. (2004) Court Bars Media-Ownership Rules. *Wall Street Journal*, 25 June, p. A3.

Stolberg, S. (2003) Media Ownership Deal Reached, Clearing Way for Big Spending Bill. *New York Times*, 25 November.

Tourtellotte, B. (2003) Major Media Players Square Off On FCC Rule Change. *Reuters*, 28 April.

Wasko, J. (2004) *How Hollywood Works*. Thousand Oaks, CA: Sage.

26

News in the global public space

Ingrid Volkmer

- How do you describe 'foreign' journalism in the global public space?
- What is the relationship between a 'national' and 'sub'-national news audience?
- How do you define the responsibility of news organizations operating in this transnational era?

The worldwide dimension of news and political communication has undergone tremendous changes since the mid-1980s. Various factors have contributed to this transformation. One of the key factors is the increase in satellite capacity and, as a result, the decrease of satellite leasing costs. Based on this development, multinational corporations are able to distribute their programmes transnationally while, at the same time, ever smaller companies (even so-called 'grassroot' ones) can afford to use satellite platforms for their programme delivery. Based on these new structures, moreover, we are facing an increasing diversity of 'global' news flow. New analytical concepts are thus required so as to help us better understand the consequences for news journalism in this transnational era.

In addition to the familiar major Western broadcasters and agencies delivering their programmes worldwide, such as CNN's international channel (CNNI) and the BBC's World Service Television (BBC-WS-TV), there are also transnational news channels. These channels began to appear in the mid-1980s. Examples include the Arab news channel, Al Jazeera, based in Qatar, and ZEE-TV, a highly successful channel targeting the expatriate Indian community worldwide. In addition to channels such as these, which have already built substantial audience bases worldwide, a variety of small 'grassroots' stations have emerged. They tend to be supported by organizations – even individual entrepreneurs – which distribute audience-specific programmes within this new global infrastructure of news flows. By and large, these developments tend to be overlooked by those approaches that automatically assume that globalization is necessarily associated with media imperialism.

An evaluation of new approaches to worldwide political communication reveals that the broad 'coordinates' of the global public are slowly being defined. One example is the obvious impact of transnational media on public opinion and, because of this, on governmental policy processes. This phenomenon was initially described as 'media diplomacy' and attributed to the BBC's and Voice of America's (VOA's) international influence. More recently, however, CNN's powerful role in a variety of international political crises (see Robinson 2002, 2001; Neuman 1996; Rawnsley 1996, Seib 1996) has redefined 'media diplomacy' in the context of 24-hour news channels. The so-called 'CNN factor' is held to represent the impact of these channels on policy makers and their decisions, for instance in conjunction with humanitarian crises. At the same time, other approaches discern the emergence of new political communication platforms (Tehranian 1999) in conjunction with 'soft power' approaches to 'public' diplomacy (see Nye 2003). Cunningham and Sinclair (2001), for example, discuss new transnational 'diasporic' cultures and identities, which means the creation of 'ethnic minority' political communities within the scope of any one nation. Similarly, Curran and Park (2000) have called for media studies to be 'de-Westernized' within a new global arena in order to compare better the effects of globalization of media on different national systems.

These are important new concepts. However, in my view, they should be integrated into an overall theoretical approach to political communication within this new globalized framework. I argue that the diversity – as well as the density – of the transnational political sphere and its different forms in times of 'peace' and times of 'crisis' can only be detected if these phenomena

Table 26.1: Examples of transnationally available channels providing political information and news

Type of channel	Name	Target audience
Commercial	CNNI	Interested in Western viewpoints
Public service/Commercial	BBC World Service Television	Interested in Western viewpoints
State funded/Commercial	Al Jazeera	Arab communities and those interested in Arab viewpoints
Commercial	ZEE TV	Indian communities
State funded	CCTV 4	Chinese communities
Public service	RAI	Italian communities
State funded	Channel Sun	Korean communities
State funded	ARY Digital	Korean communities
State funded	STN TV Somali TV Network	Somali communities

are viewed from a global perspective. Such a theoretical approach recognizes the 'global whole', that is, it detects certain 'formats of connectivity' that help us to distinguish between conventional concepts of a national/statist public sphere, which are based on the assumption of nation/statehood, and the 'global public space', which represents a new extra-societal political territory.[1]

The German philosopher Jürgen Habermas has made a profound contribution to analyses of the role of the 'public sphere' as a communication space and, with it, the emergence of a new societal power vacuum for the bourgeois class in Europe (Habermas 1992).[2] His work on the political role of a public sphere within European national contexts, published in German in 1962, has greatly influenced all subsequent debates about the 'public' as a political construct. However, we should keep in mind that, in his analysis, the term 'public' is closely tied to very specific processes of 'modern' nation building, which have taken place in a very unique way in Europe. Such a European-type national 'public' is, in his theory, located *between* the State (the government) and 'the people'; or, in other words, between statist institutions and shared subjectivities in civil society. Habermas (1992) argues that the original 'medium' of public debate was the 'public use of reason', which has since been transformed by media formats into the manufactured 'spin' of so-called 'public' opinion management (Habermas 1992: 105). In Habermas's view, the mass media – with their commercialized and 'mass' market approaches – effectively operate as a forum for a pseudo public. They mimic debates in talk shows, as well as televised 'discussions', and relegate wider public issues and debates into segregated, increasingly isolated, private spheres.

The global public space, in contrast, is composed not only of a variety of 'publics' (which originate in cultures and traditions of diverse societies) but also, increasingly, transnational individuals and communities making use of global institutions. That is to say, when examining the global or transnational level, it is possible to identify a variety of national or statist 'publics' convening around new communication institutions. In so doing, they establish discourses, which are not necessarily 'rational' (at least in Habermas's sense) but which initiate varying engagements with 'global reasoning'. Typically they invoke notions of a cosmopolitan (in Kant's sense) citizenship, as well as religious worldviews, to say nothing of ideological standpoints from different global perspectives.

Whereas in times of modern nation building, the public sought to establish democratic institutions *within* the nation, the 'global public space' consists of very particular 'institutions' (transnational news media) which cohere as elements of a newly formed 'global public'. Exactly for this reason, the role and meaning of political media is quite different from that envisaged in Habermas's theory. In global public space, news media are viewed as being 'actors' and 'reflectors' of worldwide political developments, creating 'representations' of the world, which shape *Weltanschauung*. Approaches to global public space view transnational media (television, Internet) in this sense as 'public' institutions, which nevertheless create their own 'public' platforms of discourses. In this sense, then, the 'global public' is to be counterpoised against the nation/state. Still, it is not to be located between the government and 'the people', as in Habermas's analysis, but rather *beyond* the nation/state in a new transnational extra-societal territory, in an unstructured new supra- and subnational open space.

From networks of 'relativity' to networks of 'connectivity'

A review of the transnational media infrastructure of the last two decades reveals that specific 'networks' have shaped very particular notions of the 'global public space'. In this time, the available news media infrastructure has created certain modes of 'connectivity'.

McLuhan's metaphor of a 'global village' was the first substantial attempt to explain the profound impact of internationalization on various worldwide dispersed societies, which were shown to be exposed to the *same* signals and messages. McLuhan's vision was strongly influenced by the first worldwide distribution of news and political events, the first 'live' coverage distributed worldwide. Although this and other metaphors attributed to McLuhan are commonly used to describe globalization processes, it is important to bear in mind that, in this era, 'live' satellite feeds did not target households directly, as they do in many world regions today. Rather, 'live' coverage was fed into newsrooms of national/statist broadcasters, who then – following the usual 'gatekeeping' procedures – edited these international 'live' events for their domestic news audience. Just to give one example: Algerian Television, which covered the 'live' event of the moon landing, provided commentary on Armstrong's arrival on the moon's surface in local frames. The 'live' coverage was associated with comments made by Algerian television, namely that Armstrong was hearing the voice of the Muezzin while taking his first steps. In this way, this global event was 'domesticated' for local Islamic audiences in a manner that provided a religious framework for this unique scientific achievement (Volkmer 1998).

In terms of political communication, the 'world' became internationalized. However, from today's view, this was so only in a very limited – or, as the example above suggests, 'domesticated' – sense; that is, in accordance with the networks constitutive of the 'political world news zones'. These world news zones were created via networks of relativity in McLuhan's era, which means that world events and other international events were viewed from the point of view of a nation. National news media provided, in this sense, the 'frame' of analysis and, in so doing, defined 'foreign' news in relation to their own national agenda. This was the same era, of course, when continental news pools were also being founded, such as Eurovision, providing news footage for Western European nations and Asiavision in Asia (see, for example, Boyd-Barrett and Rantanen 1999). It could be argued that even the whole news infrastructure, which means the infrastructure of news agencies, was effectively based on this 'relativity' concept.

In the nineteenth century, news agencies had operated along the lines of colonial powers. Reuters covered the Commonwealth world regions, Agence France Presse reported on francophone Africa, and so on. Throughout the 1970s, a range of issues regarding the global imbalances characteristic of information flow were raised time and again by developing nations in various UNESCO debates. The established routes of information flow were criticized for framing nation/states of the South in 'dependency' formats – thereby shaping worldview stereotypes – primarily because of the harmful influence of these routes for local journalism. As Stevenson and Cole (1984: 48) observes:

> An important consideration in the flow of news from news agency – largely, but not exclusively Western – to media system is the degree to which the agency material influences the local editor. To use the popular term, it is often argued that the wire services set the media agenda by telling local editors (and their readers, in turn) what part of the world and what issues they should think about, even if the big news agencies do not influence directly how the news is presented.
>
> (Stevenson and Cole, 1984: 48)

Of course, so-called international information within these 'networks of relativity' was dominated by the West, especially Western news sources.

In the early 1990s, sociological debates suggested a new globalization paradigm, which emphasized the contradictory processes of diversification underpinning globalization. During this period, new media – especially satellite – institutions were formed, many of which easily circumvented the former gatekeeping functions of national/statist media. These institutions were able to directly target dispersed regional audiences worldwide, through cable outlets, programme cooperation arrangements and direct-to-home satellite distribution. These distribution modes have established new network types, which could be described as networks of 'connectivity' (as opposed to former 'networks of relativity').

One of the first media institutions within this new sphere of connecting networks was CNN, which provided a uniquely diversified global programme by directly targeting households with 'local' as well as 'global' newsfeeds. CNNI, as the international outlet of CNN, quickly challenged the former 'networks of relativity', with their clear structures of 'deadline-defined' newsfeeds, by providing a constant news flow. As one CNN journalist remarked when talking about the initial events of the first war in the Persian Gulf in 1991:

> I remember being down in the newsroom when we first heard that Baghdad was being bombed and, you know, this group of people in Atlanta knew it maybe two minutes before the world knew it . . . The world knew it because of CNN, and I think that's the journalistic accomplishment that's probably the most striking'.
>
> (cited in Volkmer 1999: 146)

This constant flow of news has increased immediacy at the same time as it has decreased the proximity of events through eyewitness, 'breaking news' reporting. New journalistic styles were packaged and offered as a news agency type subscription directly to a variety of local broadcasters world-wide. It is not surprising, then, that when CNNI emerged as a 'global news leader' it had begun to replace former 'relativity' models of local/national news with new attempts to create a global news platform. One such example is 'World Report', where broadcasters from around the world submit 'their' view of a story (see Flournoy 1992; Volkmer 1999).

Thus in the mid-1990s, the unique global news platform provided by formats such as 'World Report' had already begun to transform former 'relativity' models of 'foreign' journalism, and with them the 'domestication' of international news for national audiences. These innovations helped to establish CNNI as an institution of political information for transnational policy. A platform that is still used today, in the Internet age, by heads of state to make announcements 'to the world' or to offer rare interviews, such as with Saddam Hussein. The former President of Liberia, Charles Taylor, used CNN to proclaim his resignation to the (Western) world but also to the US administration simultaneously.

Within these networks of connectivity, therefore, diversity continues to be enhanced by new structures of particularism and universalism. To clarify, particular media target transnational communities around issues such as democracy, women's rights, ecology and so forth. In so doing, they increasingly undermine the national/statist public sphere, even to the extent of destabilizing familiar distinctions between the 'internal' and the 'external' (Robertson 1992: 16). At the same time, one could also argue that while former globalization processes tended to homogenize global culture, the network approach polarizes globalization, by enforcing authenticity and identity.

Public spheres, in my view, are partially merging into a global public space, finding new ways to 'connect'. It is worth pointing out, however, that within the transnational infrastructure of political media, the term of the public sphere (or even global public sphere, for that matter) can be misleading, at least to the extent that it is narrowly restricted to the nation as a social and political 'connectivity' structure. The global public space, in contrast, forms a new transnational dimension for political communication, one that influences national/statist political spheres. Here again, Al Jazeera stands as a useful example. Even where it is received through illegal satellite dishes, it has an impact on political discourses in Arab countries.

Supra- and subnational infrastructures : self-referential spaces of connectivity

Transnational media as institutions of the global public space also operate in a supranational mode, which means that they engage dispersed emigrants living in countries around the world. These individuals, more often than not, continue to feel some sense of attachment to the 'public' cultures of their former societies. Despite various cultural and political embeddings, these subnational 'publics' reveal a common ground of connectivity. As Castells argues, the 'network society is based on the systemic disjunction between the local and the global for most individuals and social groups' (Castells 1996: 11). In a transnational context, media take the role of re-organizing these 'disjunctured' individuals and social groups in diverse types of 'self-referential' spaces and connectivity modes.

Political flows refine 'meaning' in a new transnational parallelism, that is, in both supra- and subnational dimensions, with important implications for Castells' (1996) notion of 'identity' within the network society. And yet, the role that the media play as self-referential institutions – that is, as support systems for identity formation (individual and communal) and communication in the global public space – has not been properly recognized in international communication theory. Whereas the Internet provides interactive spaces and very specific types of information, transnational television channels operate along the lines of altogether different connectivity models. These so-called 'fragmented media flows' have been discussed as 'diasporic' media (Cunningham 2001), and are often defined as 'global narrowcasting of polity and culture'. Alternatively, following Gitlin's (1998) terminology, they become subnational 'sphericals' or, after Hartley and McKee (2000), 'semiospheres'. Overall, these approaches have led to interesting debates about new media-supported identities (see, for example, Cunningham and Sinclair 2001). However, it can be argued that the infrastructure of the advanced network society has developed various 'connectivity modes', which are coordinates of the global public space.

Spaces of community

One such mode, connecting the internationally dispersed national community, can be described as spaces of community. Examples include, for instance, the Chinese state channel CCTV4, which is available on all continents but also on NHK World TV, the global Japanese channel of the national Japanese broadcaster, as well as on Thai TV. CCTV4 gathers information from Chinese state television so as to provide a 'Chinese perspective' for English-language audiences worldwide. These national community media distribute the political worldview of the country of origin within the global space, for instance, to the Chinese population in Europe, the US and the Americas. Other examples for this model are original national/statist channels associated with a variety of Arab countries, which are aired in Europe, such as Jordan TV. ARIRANG, from Seoul, is distributed in North and South America, Europe and Asia, PTA Armenia, Europe/ Africa and Asia. Two Iranian channels, IRIB 1 and 2, are available in Europe, the US and Asia. Fox News from the US can be received via satellite in Europe and the Middle East, as well as in Japan.

This model of 'spaces of community' will be even further developed in the years to come when, for instance, China and France launch a worldwide 24-hour news channel. The goal of these national/statist news channels is to make the Chinese and French political viewpoints of world events globally available.

Whereas these channels are national/statist channels, that is, international outlets of domestic media intended to serve as a 'bridge' to political debates in their home countries, a second model can be described as Spaces of Supranational Community. These channels are not of national/statist origin, but instead have been established particularly for the supranational community. One example is NITV, an Iranian channel, aired from Los Angeles. NITV's goal is to connect Iranians living around the world so as to target the political sphere in Iran from 'outside'. That is to say, the channel attempts to influence political activities directly in Iran, although its signal can be received in Iran only with illegal satellite dishes. Drawing on new modes of supranational connectivity, this channel shows the potential power of the global public space on national/statist policy, a dimension of political power far beyond the conventional term of 'media diplomacy'.

Spaces of microspheres

Within the de-territorialized global public space, new information platforms seem most likely to appear during times of world crises. Whereas during the first war in the Persian Gulf, CNN established itself as a powerful news monopoly, today the role of CNN in world crisis journalism – while still highly relevant – does not enjoy the same degree of dominance. In conjunction with 11 September 2001, new transnational crisis platforms emerged as competing news sources, such as Al Jazeera.

Western media tend to describe Al Jazeera as an 'Arab voice' in the global news flow, but from the viewpoint of Arab audiences, living in places such as North America and in Europe, Al Jazeera is just one element in a variety of transnational Arab channels. Indeed, it is one element in what is an expanding transnational Arab 'microsphere', which has only become visible for Western audiences with the leading role of Al Jazeera in the context of 11 September 2001 coverage and the war in Afghanistan. Where previously it was the case that transnational channels attempted to approach a broad worldwide audience, these 'microsphere' spaces operate within a particular political, cultural or otherwise specified transnational 'microsphere space.

Currently one of the most recognized 'microsphere' spaces has been formed around Arab worldwide communities for quite some time. Besides Al Jazeera, which tends to be a somewhat 'liberal' voice within the Arab media world, other transnational Arab channels have been established since the early 1990s. Examples include MBC, the Middle East Broadcasting Centre, which operates out of London, UK. MBC was, in fact, the first transnational Arab television channel, and typically takes a conservative angle in its news reporting. In this context, Al Jazeera's goal can be seen as one of trying to counterbalance conservative Arab state channels. It has already transformed journalism (with 'live' interviews, call-in shows and so forth) in the Arab world 'from outside' as a transnationally operating channel.

Al Jazeera's approach to journalism is considered to be very controversial in the Arab world. At one time or another, it has offended various governments in the region who do not share its news agenda. Kuwait, for example, has shut down Al-Jazeera's local office, calling the station's broadcast hostile, as has Jordan. Jordan even recalled its ambassador from Qatar. Reasons for these moves are mainly domestic; for instance, the reason for Jordan's reaction was a talk show that examined Jordan's relations with Israel prior to their 1994 peace treaty. Other examples include Saudi Arabia, which also withdrew its ambassador from Qatar, reportedly in response to a report on Al Jazeera, in which the Founder of the Kingdom of Saudia Arabia was criticized.

Spaces of microspheres, as suggested above, assume a particular prominence in times of world crisis, when these fragmented 'flows' gain intensity and provide 'authentic' feedback and information within the global public space (see also Volkmer 2002). This was obvious when Al Jazeera's English language Web site, launched *in response* to CNN's site competing for the English-speaking world audience, was hijacked several times by US hackers during the war in Iraq. Over the course of several weeks, this information war revealed its potential for further radicalization. Whenever Al Jazeera posted photos of civilian victims, the site was hijacked and these images were replaced by varying US images, such as a US flag and the phrase 'let the freedom bell ring'. In general, though, depending on the location of Arab audiences and the availability of satellite 'footprints', other channels also operate within this microsphere.

Interestingly, Al Jazeera's success (the channel reaches 44 million people) within the Arab world – together with suspicions aroused by its 'liberal' journalism – have led to another transnational channel within this de-territorialized space. Al Arabya currently competes directly with Al Jazeera. This news channel was launched by MBC in February 2003, just before the formal declaration of hostilities in Iraq. In the months leading up to the war, CNN began to participate in this transnational Arab microsphere via an Arab language Web site. Moreover, Arab audiences in Europe have access to some 20 Arab state channels, which are distributed in their original format on the satellite system Eutelsat. Furthermore, the US State Department has recently launched the radio station Sawa and a magazine to target the 18–35-year-olds in this microsphere.

While the Arab microsphere is the most advanced worldwide, others are also beginning to emerge. Mention has been made above about Chinese efforts, but here it is also important to mention a further microsphere organized for the benefit of the largest expatriate group worldwide, Indians. ZEE TV offers primarily entertainment and music programmes. In the US, for example, ZEE TV also uses English subtitles in order to target local audiences (see Thussu 2000: 198).

Spaces of discourse

The infrastructure of political media in the global public space also affects national/statist political spheres on various levels, not least by engendering spaces for subnational discourse. The inflow of transnational media has altered journalistic formats, helping to establish new forms of 'coorientation'. Whereas in 1992, when a survey among journalists of public service stations in Europe revealed that they watched CNN so as to see 'what is going on in the world', today it is more likely that media sources such as Al Jazeera will serve as indicators of worldwide news relevance. The impact of these inflows on domestic news agendas is deserving of careful attention.

In media environments that are tightly controlled by the State in terms of content inflow, such as the Arab nations, but also to a lesser extent Russia and China, these 'spaces of discourse' are continuously monitored. If required, news content is censored and satellite distribution is interrupted and jammed. In places such as the US, where 'international news' tends to revolve around the activities of US activities and interests abroad (even the domestic feed of CNN is largely limited to US bilateral activities), so-called 'foreign' channels, such as BBC America, are shaping the national news agenda. 'Our news agenda is different,' a leading BBC journalist claims. 'We're like the outsider looking through the window, and that can be of immense value to US audiences' (cited in Burt 2003: 2). US media groups, he adds, 'don't want their news coverage to upset the Bush administration as it ponders long-waited media ownership reforms.' In contrast, the BBC 'aims to exploit that trend, arguing that there is an appetite for "long form" journalism: a mixture of news and detailed analysis whether from Basra or Berlin.' The BBC is planning to launch a 24-hour news channel in the US. Meanwhile, other subnational programme formats have been developed for Spanish-speaking citizens, which is the largest minority group (37 million households) in the country. The NBC network acquired Telemundo, a Spanish channel, in October 2002.

In other parts of the world, such as India, new domestic news channels have been launched in order to counterbalance the inflow of transnational channels, such as CNN and the BBC. In India, Doordarshan, the national Indian broadcaster, has started a 24-hour news channel. In Europe, Euronews has been launched to provide an alternative European worldview to CNN.

▌Global connectivity and the search for meaning

Given these connectivity modes, it seems that the global public space is by no means 'universal' or 'cosmopolitan', but rather quite the opposite – that is, increasingly 'particular' and 'fragmented'. It is not an open, 'homogenizing' territory, but nor is it one where terms of 'world citizenship' and 'global civil society' are without meaning. In my view, the global public space is less 'public' than 'private', based on transnational media, on the one hand, and on lifeworlds, on the other. Both of these 'bases' are connected in various connectivity modes, which produce self-referential 'reality' and 'meaning'.

Whereas in Habermas's theory of the public sphere, 'meaning' is defined by the nation-state, the search for meaning in the network society is located on the lifeworld level. Lifeworlds are penetrated by a variety of opposing and multi-perspective political global news flows, which compose individual news agendas and notions of *Weltanschauung* (that is, in a philosophical sense, 'world perception') about how we perceive and view the world. These are important issues, because we coordinate our 'action' and 'participation' based on these notions.

Never before have living room 'lifeworlds' been so directly encroached upon by transnational political media, via terrestrial, cable and satellite television. As Castells suggests, 'civil societies shrink and disarticulate because there is no longer continuity between the logic of powermaking in the global network and the logic of association and representation in specific societies and cultures' (Castells 1996: 11). He argues that the search for meaning 'takes place then in the reconstruction of defensive identities around communal principles' (Castells 1996: 11). In other words, it is to be found in the dynamics of 'connectivity' between the supra- and the sub-national, that is, between the global public space and the lifeworld. As Kumar argues in the context of India and Pakistan, ' "network" societies too are "transitional", as much as societies in transition can have many of the characteristics of a "network society"' (Kumar 2003: 42).

In my view, however, the relationship between the global public space and the lifeworld is of vital significance. In state-controlled media environments, such as Iran, where satellite dishes are officially prohibited and are hidden 'behind a window or amidst some specially arranged plants and flowers in the backyard' (Mass 2003: 12), opposing inflows of political communication allow people to overcome official state worldviews. The outside, that is, transnational viewpoint (articulated via CNN, MBC, Al Jazeera and so forth) serves as a more reliable source of 'meaning' (and even 'reality' in the sense of 'what really happens') and provide the reference frame for the 'inside' view, that is, statist media or government announcements. In market-based pluralist models (such as the US), as well as public service broadcasting (such as in the UK) environments, the inflow of opposing transnational media increases pressure on lifeworlds in the search for meaning and 'world orientation'. As an Egyptian living in the US states:

'You can't believe any station . . . When you watch al-Jazeera, you see what they do to the people, not what the army is doing. Al-Jazeera shows the bad side of America. CNN shows you the bad side of the Iraqi government. I watch CNN – nobody gets killed. I watch al-Jazeera – it's like a tragedy' (cited in Roumani 2003).

The inflows of political information create a new dialectic process on the lifeworld level, which provides the reference frame for 'world' meaning. Based on the political relevance of this dialectic on the lifeworld level, crisis communication could in future be radicalized. During the war in Iraq, we have already eyewitnessed such a 'radicalization potential' with the continuous hijacking of Al Jazeera's English language Web site. Another example is CNN's attempt to show both sides of the Palestinian suicide attacks. When CNN aired an interview with parents of one suicide bomber in the US, Israel threatened CNN in Atlanta to remove CNNI's signal from the satellite in Israel. No country is immune from these types of disputes, and they promise to grow in intensity in the years to come. It is a task and responsibility of communication and media studies to address these new developments, and to build a new framework for global communication.

▌Notes

1 In the context of this discussion, I prefer to distinguish between 'national' and 'statist' political spheres. Whereas the national political sphere is based on a common ground of 'the nation' and a common identity of 'the people', the statist political sphere could be based on political authority and governmental influence (for instance in authoritarian states).

2 Although Habermas has modified some of his arguments in recent years, his basic analysis has been developed in the 1960s under the impression not only of an increasing influence of mass media but also of the post-World War II transformation of various Western nations from traditional to mass societies consumption (Riesman 1970). A transformation process, in which the mass media also played an important, mainstreaming role.

▌References

Boyd-Barrett, O. and Rantanen, T. (eds) (1999) *The Globalization of News*. London: Corwin Press.

Burt, T. (2003) Trust me, I'm British, *Financial Times*, 19 July, W1/W2.

Cardoso, F. H. (n.d.) UN debate on global civil society, see http://www.un.org/reform/pdfs/cardosopaper13june.htm.

Castells, M. (1996) *The Rise of the Network Society*. Oxford: Blackwell.

Clausen, L. (2003) *Global News Production*. Copenhagen: Copenhagen Business School Press.

Cunningham, S. (2001) Diasporic Media and Public Sphericules, in K. Ross (ed.) *Black Marks: Minority Ethnic Audiences and Media*. Aldershot: Ashgate, pp. 177–94.

Cunningham, S. and Sinclair, J. (eds) (2001) *Floating Lives: The Media and Asian Diasporas.* Lanham, MD: Rowman & Littlefield.

Curran, J. and Park, M.-J. (eds) (2000) *De-Westernizing Media Studies.* London and New York: Routledge.

Flournoy, D. (1992) *CNN World Report: Ted Turner's International News Group.* London: John Libbey.

Gitlin, T. (1998) Public Sphere or Public Sphericules? in T. Liebes and J. Curran (eds) *Media, Ritual and Identity.* London: Routledge, pp. 175–292.

Habermas, J. (1992) *The Structural Transformation of the Public Sphere.* Cambridge, MA: MIT Press.

Hartley, J. and McKee, A. (2000) *The Indigenous Public Sphere: The Reporting and Reception of Aboriginal Issues in the Australian Media.* Oxford: Oxford University Press.

Kumar, K. (2003) India and Pakistan: From Transitional to Network Societies? *Development,* 46(1): 41–8.

Lasica, J. D. (2002) Blogging as a Form of Journalism, in R. Blood (ed.) *We've Got Blog. How Weblogs are Changing our Culture.* Cambridge, MA: Perseus, pp. 163–70.

Maass, M., Riviera, D. and Hofman, A. (2005) Mexico, in: I. Volkmer (ed.) *News in Public Memory.* New York: Peter Lang.

Neuman, J. (1996) *Lights, Camera, War: Is Media Technology Driving International Politics?* New York: St Martin's Press.

Nye, J. (2003) *The Paradox of American Power: Why the World's Only Superpower Can't Go It Alone.* Oxford: Oxford University Press.

Robinson, P. (2001) Theorizing the Influence of Media on World Politics: Models of Media Influence on Foreign Policy, *European Journal of Communication,* 16(4): 523–44.

Robinson, P. (2002) *The CNN Effect: The Myth of News, Foreign Policy and Intervention.* London and New York: Routledge.

Rawnsley, G. D. (1996) *Radio Diplomacy and Propaganda: The BBC and VOA in International Politics.* London: Macmillan.

Riesman, D. (1970) *The Lonely Crowd.* New York: Yale University Press.

Roumani, R. (2003) One War, Two Channels, *Columbia Journalism Review,* section 'Voices', online edition http://www.cjr.org/year/03/3/roumani.asp May, June.

Seib, P. (1996) *Headline Diplomacy: How News Coverage Affects Foreign Policy.* Westport, CT: Praeger.

Stevenson, R. L. and Cole, R. (1984) Patterns of Foreign News, in R. L. Stevenson and D. L. Shaw (eds) *Foreign News and the New World Information Order.* Ames, Iowa: The Iowa State University Press, 44–47.

Tehranian, M. (1999) *Global Communication and World Politics: Domination, Development and Discourse.* Boulder, CO: Lynne Rienner.

Thussu, D. (2000) *International Communication: Continuity and Change.* London: Arnold.

Volkmer, I. (1998) 'Hic et nunc' von Nachrichtengenerationen: Überlegungen zu der Kategorie des 'Da-seins' aus der Sicht globaler Phänomenologie, in Hug, T. (ed.) *Technologiekritik und Medienpädagogik. Zur Theorie und Praxis kritisch-reflexiver Medienkommunikation.* Hohrengehren: Schneider.

Volkmer, I. (1999) *News in the Global Sphere. A Study of CNN and Its Impact on Global Communication.* Luton: University of Luton Press.

Volkmer, I. (2002) Journalism and Political Crises in the Global Network Society, in B. Zelizer and S. Allan (eds) *Journalism After September 11.* London and New York: Routledge, pp. 235–46.

27

Journalism and the war in Iraq

Howard Tumber

- Was Gulf War II a turning point for the Fourth Estate?
- Can an embedded journalist be impartial and objective?
- Is the safety of non-embedded or independent journalists becoming seriously compromised?

Scholars and journalists can often be precipitate in claiming contemporary events as crucial turning points in history. Alas communication researchers are not immune from being seduced into exaggerating the relative importance and possible effects of events. So what critical issues for journalism did Gulf War II (2003) produce? Was the war a turning point for the Fourth Estate or merely the continuation of particular political, economic, cultural and technological trends?

A number of studies have analysed various aspects and produced important and interesting insights into the news media coverage. Reassessments of new digital technologies, 24-hour news, propaganda, media bias and framing, news sources and the marginalization of dissent, have been made in the light of Gulf War II. However, in the main these analyses reveal trends evident in recent and past conflicts rather than highlighting uniqueness (see for example Allan 2004; Aufderheide 2004; Bromley 2004; Couldry and Downey 2004; Iskandar and El-Nawawy 2004; Kellner 2004; Lewis and Brookes 2004; Moeller 2004; Rantanen 2004; Reese 2004).

Within the profession itself, Nik Gowing, BBC World journalist and main presenter, has frequently highlighted how the proliferation of new media technologies is blurring the distinctions between the media and the private citizen. The ubiquitous use of camcorders, digital cameras and computers is enabling large numbers of people to capture events, causing concern for both governments and military, as well as for news organizations. The security forces are finding it harder to 'hide' their activities and this is having an effect on military doctrine, strategy and practice. Governments are facing a new propaganda war against terrorist and guerrilla groups who now have the means to manipulate and spread images, while broadcasters are facing considerable challenges in deciding which images to broadcast – especially when they come from unknown and unverifiable sources. Correcting the impact of unreliable reports or faked images is very tricky and can leave the broadcaster in a vulnerable position (Gowing 2004).

But what are the issues arising out of Gulf War II that journalism itself has subsequently introspectively reviewed? Two stand out: the embedding of over 500 journalists with military units; and the physical safety of news organization personnel.

Embedding

The embedding of more than 500 journalists with the military was one of the most talked-about developments of the media coverage of Gulf War II. Unlike the Falklands conflict in 1982, when journalists were 'embedded' with the British Task force almost by accident, this time there was a deliberate plan set out by the US Department of Defense in consultation with news organizations for journalists to be 'situated' with various parts of the military. The strategy behind this 'innovation' had been developing for some time.

Ever since the Vietnam War, governments and military have tried different methods of 'controlling' and 'managing' the media. The belief that television had somehow 'lost the war' in Vietnam led to the view that stricter controls over the media were necessary in order to contain information and ultimately win the battle for the hearts and minds of the public. The information policy adopted by the British government and the military during the Falklands, based on the myth of Vietnam, was poorly organized and lacked planning. There was an absence of agreed procedure or criteria, no centralized system of control and no coordination between departments (see Morrison and Tumber 1988: 189–90). During the Falklands conflict, the battle for public opinion was fought under the guise of 'operational security', an all-embracing term used as an excuse for delaying and censoring information and disseminating misinformation (see Morrison and Tumber 1988: 189).

Military and defence officials in the US, noting the experience of the Falklands conflict, adopted in various forms the uses of both military and civilian minders, the stationing of reporters in military units and pooling arrangements. In the 1980s discussions took place between news organizations and the Pentagon in order to establish some ground rules for cooperation. The first 'test' for improved relations occurred in the invasion of Grenada, known as operation 'Urgent Fury'. However, rather than setting a tone for harmonious relations between the military and the media, it provoked outcry from news organizations as more than 600 reporters were left stranded in Barbados unable to report what was occurring in Grenada.

It was to be two days (when all the 'action' was over) before journalists arrived on the island. The military had been logistically unresponsive to the needs of news organizations. The intense criticism that followed led to the United States Joint Chiefs of Staff setting up a commission, headed by General Winant Sidle, to look into future media operations. One of the main recommendations proposed that a national media pool should be created to cover future operations where full media access was not available. These proposals were implemented during Operation Earnest Will in the Persian Gulf (1988) and then in Panama (1989) when US troops were engaged. This latter operation proved a disaster for the 'new' pooling system because Dick Cheney, then Secretary of Defense, obstructed the mobilization of the pool and journalists were unable to cover the engagement (Tumber and Palmer 2004: 2).

By the time of Gulf War I in 1991, journalists covered military events via organized pools and formal briefings. They were restricted in their travel movements and had to subject their copy to formal security review. The problem for the military became a logistical one of how to cope with hundreds of reporters flocking to the region. *Ad hoc* press pools were organized, but many journalists decided to ignore them and move about independently. The outcome was frustration for news organizations and continuing bewilderment for the military about how journalists operate. Whereas the military is all about order and cooperation, journalism is competitive, fragmented and often anarchic. When the two cultures clash the result is often antipathy to – and confusion about – one another. The experience and lessons of the Falklands should have been a blueprint for the military in future conflicts. Instead, a misinterpretation of how journalists operate meant that it was to be 20 years before an organized 'embedding' process was fully implemented.

Embedding is not a 'new' phenomenon though. Versions of it were used in World War II, and in Vietnam. In more recent times, following the deeply unpopular pool system adopted in the Persian war, variations were used in Haiti in 1994, Somalia in 1992–5 and in Bosnia in 1995 (see Porch 2002). However, before the embedding in Gulf War II, military-media relations went through a further downturn during the Kosovo campaign (1999) to remove Yugoslavian troops from the region. This was a conflict where journalists had little access to the province and relied on the military for information about the bombing campaign. For the invasion in Afghanistan (2001), many editors, bureau chiefs and correspondents regarded the Pentagon's reporting rules as some of the toughest ever (see Hickey 2002). The main grievances focused on the lack of reasonable access to land and sea bases from which air attacks on Taliban positions were launched and the restrictions on access to information emanating from the Pentagon. The news organizations at one stage even received an apology from Victoria Clarke, Assistant Secretary of Defense for Public Affairs and chief spokesperson at the Pentagon (Tumber and Palmer 2004: 3).

In the arrangements for media facilitation in Gulf War II, the most important innovation was the large-scale presence of journalists on the battlefield, embedded in military units. The embedding process was an organized strategy planned well in advance of the conflict by the Pentagon in consultation with news organizations. No one, least of all the journalists and their news organizations, relished the idea of a return to the pool system or the sole reliance on official briefings employed in previous wars. Many of the journalists expressed apprehension about the embedding process, particularly about the ability to maintain their impartiality. Others embraced the opportunity to go to the front line while the news organizations looked forward to continuous live broadcasting. A second concern to emerge in the days following the invasion was that the embedded journalists were only providing a snapshot of the war. Both US and UK governments complained that the public was receiving a distorted picture of the conflict (Tumber and Palmer 2004: 7).

The administration of the embedded process was based on a plan of allocating places to news organizations not individual reporters. This made it difficult for freelancers to gain accreditation unless they were contracted to a news organization. It also enabled the US Department of Defense to 'control' the process more easily through possible sanctions on news organization for 'misbehaviour' on the part of their correspondents.

The journalists embedded with the troops were given special procedures and guidelines for how they could operate. Journalists and news organizations were required to sign documents complying with the rules set out at the beginning about what they could or could not report. For example, no details were to be reported about future operations, no private satellite telephones or cell phones, no travelling in their own vehicles while in an embedded status, no photography showing the level of security or showing an enemy prisoner of war or detainee's face, nametag or other identifying feature. Reporters also had to agree to honour news embargoes that could be imposed to protect operational security (Tumber and Palmer 2004: 16)

The initial enthusiasm of news organization editors for the embedded reporters was very marked because the process allowed reporting virtually in real time with no censorship from the military, although sandstorms and rapid troop movements had caused a few delays. The Pentagon's agreement to allow large numbers of journalists to be embedded with the troops enabled news organizations and outlets not normally on the Pentagon's top priority list to gain access to the war. It gave smaller, locally based newspapers a presence in the conflict and a prestigious 'we were there' with their audiences, something that was rare in previous conflicts (Tumber and Palmer 2004: 19).

The process of embedding started off with a wave of enthusiasm from both the military and the news organization but it was not long before tensions began to emerge. Some journalists were frustrated that they were embedded with units that were not seeing any action. As a consequence some left their units or were told to leave by their news organizations. For the larger news organizations who had other journalists working independently of the embedding process this was not as great a problem as it was for some of the smaller ones who did not have the resources to base reporters all over the conflict area. Some journalists complained about their reliance on military communications for sending their copy back.

Another major issue to arise was the safety of the journalists. Those embedded with the troops could rely on the protection of their units with the risk, like that of their military protectors, of injury or death. But there was also the potential problem of capture and if that happened whether they would be regarded as prisoners of war under the protection of the Geneva Convention or treated as spies and therefore not entitled to the same protections. For those operating independently of the military ('unilaterals', as they came to be called) the dangers were all too obvious. Not only did the military often treat them as second-class citizens compared with the embeds, namely by refusing access, transport and communications, but many of them were killed or injured in the conflict (see Tumber and Palmer 2004: 7).

An interesting collection of accounts of the embedding process in Gulf War II is contained in an edited collection of accounts by journalists. As Katovsky and Carlson (2003) suggests in the introduction, some of the reporters confessed to the attraction of the adrenaline rush, whereas others remained haunted by their experiences. Some of them crossed the line of objectivity by donning military gear, including weapons, and on occasions pointed out snipers (Katovsky and Carlson 2003: xix).

As governments and military become more adept at refining the embedding process, the critical issue for journalists, when reporting on future conflicts, is how to operate in a manner that protects and maintains their professional integrity. Members of the US Army War College's Centre for Strategic Leadership, having discussed future scenarios, have made the recommendation that permanent embedding be established within the military, thereby following examples set by police departments, sports teams and political campaigns (Tumber and Palmer 2004: 60). Apart from the cost to news organizations that this may entail, the possibilities of compromising objectivity would be considerably raised. When journalists are embedded with the military their future becomes intimately entwined with that of the soldiers they are accompanying. The possibility of remaining detached diminishes appreciably and the professional values that 'normally' ensure a protective armour for the journalist can be compromised as an environment of professional uncertainty develops.

The safety of journalists

Gulf War II was critical in highlighting issues around the safety of journalists. In its August 2004 news release the International News Safety Institute (INSI) reported 50 news personnel killed so far in Iraq, either through hostilities or so-called 'friendly fire' accidents. According to the Committee to Protect Journalists (CPJ), 17 journalists or media staff were killed or died covering the war in Iraq in the first six weeks (March/April 2003). The high death toll has led to concerns that Gulf War II could spell the end of the independent witnessing of war. The unexplained killings of seven journalists by coalition forces in four separate incidents in Basra and Baghdad provoked unprecedented outrage among journalists around the world. The International Federation of Journalists (IFJ) was very critical of a military and political culture that led to astonishing complacency and neglect over the safety of journalists. 'The impulse to monitor, control, and manipulate the information process had led to a casual disregard of journalists' rights to work safely and to report independently' (IFJ 2003a). Figures from the IFJ show that the levels of killings of journalists in Gulf War II were unprecedented. Over the 21 years of war in Vietnam between 1954 and 1975, some 63 journalists were killed. In the Iraq conflict, the casualty rate among media staff was higher than in any other conflict and, in proportion to the numbers present, even higher than it was among soldiers of the coalition (IFJ 2003a; see also Tumber and Palmer 2004: 36).

IFJ reports show that 1,100 journalists and media staff were killed in the line of duty over the 12 years leading up to the report (IFJ 2003b). These deaths do not just occur under hostile regimes and in war zones. The majority of journalists killed are local ones targeted because of their reporting of organized crime, drugs and arms deals. The casualties are not confined to one or two areas in the world. IFJ reports identify killings in 38 countries. These numbers indicate that the physical safety of media workers is under increasing threat and consequently the pressure on media organizations to create a safety framework that will safeguard the lives of their employees is intensifying (see Tumber 2002a).

The need for safety measures is becoming a major issue in war reporting. The deaths of two journalists in Sierra Leone in May 2000 led many news organizations (Reuters, The Associated Press, CNN, BBC, ITV and the big American networks) to sign a code of practice on safety (Owen 2001). The International Code of Practice for the safe conduct of journalists requires media organizations to provide risk-awareness training, social protection (life insurance), free medical treatment and protection for freelance or part-time employees. It also requires public authorities to respect the rights and physical integrity of journalists and media staff (IFJ 2000). Although this Code of Practice was accepted by some leading media organizations, an industry-wide response that would enable all media workers to benefit from risk-awareness training has not yet been established. The broadcasters and agencies have kept their pledge to extend training to all of their local stringers and 'fixers' but the newspapers have not made a similar commitment so far. Furthermore, the deaths of journalists killed in Gulf War II have led to more urgent demands for a better understanding of the reasons behind those deaths (Tumber and Palmer 2004: 37).

Apart from the killings in Gulf War II, journalists received threats, and experienced expulsions, detentions and confiscation of equipment. The attacks on reporters were not confined to Iraq and surrounding countries. Reports from Madrid and Cairo told of journalists being attacked while covering anti-war protests (IFJ 2003a). Philip Knightley (2003) described the Iraq war as the one 'when journalists seemed to become a target'. John

Simpson, the BBC world affairs editor, who was injured in a 'friendly fire' incident, blamed the deaths of many of the journalists on the 'ultimate act of censorship'. Simpson believes that the system of embedding meant that journalists operating independently of the US and British troops became potential targets (Tumber and Palmer 2004: 39).

The problems for journalists reporting from Baghdad, for example, started before the invasion when in February 2003 Iraq decided to expel 69 journalists. On 17 March there were 450 journalists present in Baghdad, according to NBC estimates, but by 20 March, through a combination of expulsions and withdrawals by news organizations, only 150 remained (IFJ 2003a). A number of news organizations pulled their Baghdad correspondents and photographers out of Baghdad because they were concerned that their reporters would be targets of Iraqi reprisals and would be used as human shields (Tumber and Palmer 2004: 42).

The safety considerations for journalists based in hostile environments can lead to compromises by news organizations over editorial integrity. One example of this arose subsequent to the war and involved CNN, one of the few organizations to remain in Baghdad during Gulf War I. The chief news executive of CNN, Eason Jordan, wrote an opinion piece in the *New York Times* in April 2003 stating that over the previous 12 years CNN had buried a series of deeply damaging stories about the brutality of Saddam Hussein's regime. The reason for burying the stories was ostensibly to protect the lives of Iraqis, particularly those who were working for CNN. According to Jordan, during 13 trips to Baghdad to lobby the government to allow the news network's bureau to remain open and to arrange interviews with Iraqi leaders, he had become increasingly disturbed about what he heard and saw but that could not be reported because it might jeopardize staff. According to reports, in the mid-1990s for instance, an Iraqi CNN cameraperson was abducted and tortured by the secret police because they believed Jordan worked for the CIA. CNN said Jordan had been in Baghdad long enough to know that telling the world about the torture of one of its employees would almost certainly have led to his death and would have put his family and co-journalists at serious risk. Jordan also stated that at other times stories went unreported because of the risk to non-CNN Iraqis. Jordan recounted that in 1995 Saddam's eldest son, Uday, had informed him that he was going to assassinate two of his brothers-in-law who had defected. Jordan stated that he was aware that he couldn't report it because he was unsure whether Uday would have responded by killing the Iraqi translator. Jordan maintained that he could not report it because he feared that Uday might retaliate by killing the Iraqi translator. He added that there were also other disturbing stories, told to him by Iraqi officials, that could only now be revealed. He was accused of compromising CNN's journalistic mission in order that the network could continue to report from Iraq (Tumber and Palmer 2004: 42–3).

In defence of his position, Jordan informed his staff that Saddam Hussein's brutality was already well documented and his decision to tell all only after the downfall of the regime had saved innocent lives. CNN had reported on Iraq's human rights record from outside the country instead. He pointed out that CNN was expelled from Iraq six times, most recently just three days into the war when reporters such as Christiane Amanpour and Brent Saddler were thrown out (Fletcher 2003; see also Tumber and Palmer 2004: 42–3).

In Gulf War II, one of the most widely covered incidents involving the deaths of journalists occurred at the Palestine Hotel in Baghdad. On 8 April 2003, a Spanish TV cameraperson and a Reuters cameraperson were killed and four others wounded when US troops fired on the Palestine Hotel, the base for most of the Western media in Baghdad. On the same day an Al-Jazeera cameraperson died when a bomb hit the TV station's office in the city. Abu-Dhabi TV was also hit that day which, in effect, meant that the US military had attacked – whether by design or accident – all the main Western and Arab media headquarters in the space of just one day (Tumber and Palmer 2004: 45).

Chris Cramer, the president of CNN international networks, and the honorary president of the International News Safety Institute, stated:

> As we all feared, this conflict has become the worst ever for our profession. Each and every day, journalists and media professionals are being killed and injured at an alarming rate. Unlike the military, they are all there voluntarily and I hope the public appreciate the risks they're taking to cover the crisis.
>
> (cited in Byrne 2003)

Cramer has long been a champion of journalist safety and recently attacked the old culture of news gathering, in which any display of emotion or psychological anguish was a potential threat to one's career. Cramer argued that employers should allow journalists to display emotion, especially when they were just back from a war zone, 'people should be allowed to do their laundry and their head laundry too' (Hodgson 2001; see also Tumber 2002a).

The initial explanation by US military officials for the attack at the Palestine Hotel was that one of the tanks had fired on the building in response to sniper and rocket fire. General Buford Blount, commander of the US Third Infantry Division in Baghdad, told Reuters: 'The tank was receiving small arms fire from the hotel and engaged the target with one tank round.' In addition US military officials said that the Al-Jazeera office that was hit was a mistake (cited in IFJ 2003a). Following the attacks on the Palestine Hotel in Baghdad, representatives of editors in 115 countries wrote to Donald Rumsfeld, to condemn the 'inexcusable' and 'reckless' American attack. Leaders of unions representing thousands of US journalists also wrote to the Defense Secretary (see IFJ 2003a).

Johann Fritz, the director of the Vienna-based International Press Institute, and vice chair Richard Tait, a former ITN editor in chief, told Rumsfeld that the IPI believed the US could have been in breach of the Geneva Convention when one of its tanks opened fire on the Palestine Hotel. The attack on the hotel was fully investigated by the Committee to Protect Journalists (CPJ 2003). Their report detailed the incident, including statements from eyewitnesses, and found that: 'There is simply no evidence to support the official US position that US forces were returning hostile fire from the Palestine Hotel. It conflicts with the eyewitness testimony of numerous journalists in the hotel.' The report ended by demanding a full inquiry (Tumber and Palmer 2004: 44).

The Pentagon inquiry into the affair, released in a two-page summary at the end of August 2003, exonerated the US military of any responsibility. It claimed that the soldiers responsible had determined that an Iraqi 'hunter-killer' team was using a spotter in the hotel to fire at them and that they were well within the rules of military engagement in responding. The summary was widely condemned by the IFJ as a 'cynical whitewash' for glossing over false claims by US officials and press staff immediately after the attack that troops were fired on from the hotel (IFJ 2003a: 28).

One way forward for the protection of journalists was set out at the launch of the International News Safety Institute in May 2003. Three new laws were proposed that would enhance respect for media independence in war reporting and deliver transparent and extensive investigation whenever journalists were the victims of violence.

1 To establish an international framework for the independent investigation of killings of journalists and media staff. This must include the capacity to call witnesses and to obtain information from all relevant sources of information.

2 To make the deliberate targeting of journalists and media staff an explicit crime punishable under international law.

3 To make the failure to provide adequate protection to journalists or to act in any way that recklessly endangers the lives of media staff or leads to the death of journalists or media staff an explicit crime under international law (IFJ 2003a).

The wider implication of these incidents is very serious for the reporting of future conflicts. If armies, terrorists and assassins target journalists in order to prevent independent reporting and witnessing of events, the public will undoubtedly suffer from the absence of reliable information. Journalists are becoming increasingly vulnerable to physical and verbal attack. If the embedding process is widely repeated, journalists run the risk of becoming identified with the military units they accompany, leading to possible attack and/or capture by enemy armies. Should reporters retain the status of 'unilaterals' they run the risk of attack or lack of protection by both sides. Both groups run the risk of accusations of spying. Freelancers are the most vulnerable because in addition to the dangers experienced by 'embeds' and 'unilaterals', they do not enjoy the same protection (such as equipment, training and insurance) from news organizations as do the staffers (Tumber and Palmer 2004: 46).

The process of embedding journalists with the military and the safety of journalists in conflict situations are clearly linked. Since 1999 sections of the profession and parts of the industry have begun to take the latter very seriously. But if the public is to be well informed about the actions of its governments and military in future wars, then continual vigilance by the Fourth Estate will be essential if it is to operate effectively.

▎References

Allan, S. (2004) The Culture of Distance: Online Reporting of the Iraq War, in S. Allan and B. Zelizer (eds) *Reporting War*. London: Routledge.

Aufderheide, P. (2004) Big Media and Little Media: the Journalistic Informal Sector during the Invasion of Iraq, in S. Allan and B. Zelizer (eds) *Reporting War*. London: Routledge.

Bromley, M. (2004) The Battlefield is the Media: War Reporting and the Formation of National Identity in Australia – from Belmont to Baghdad, in S. Allan and B. Zelizer (eds) *Reporting War*. London: Routledge.

Byrne, C. (2003) Iraq – the Most Dangerous War for Journalists. Available at http://media.guardian.co.uk/iraqandthemedia/story/0,12823,932496,00.html.

Couldry, N. and Downey, J. (2004) War or Peace? Legitimation, Dissent, and Rhetorical Closure in Press Coverage of the Iraq War Build-up, in S. Allan and B. Zelizer (eds) *Reporting War*. London: Routledge.

CPJ (2003) Twenty-seven Journalists Killed in 2003. Committee to Protect Journalists, Available at http://www.cpj.org/killed/killed03.html#unconfirmed. Accessed 30 October 2003.

Fletcher, K. (2003) CNN's Secret News Agenda. *Daily Telegraph*, 18 April.

Gowing, N. (2004) Power of the Media, http://www.britischebotschaft.de/en/news/events/nik_gowing.htm.

Hickey, N. (2002) Access Denied, Columbia Journalism Review. Available at http://www.Cjr.org, January/February.

Hodgson, J. (2001) Let Reporters Show Emotion. Available at http://www.media.guardian.co.uk/attack/story/0,1301,596093,00.html, 19 November.

IFJ (2000) International Code of Practice for the Safe Conduct of Journalism. IFJ Report on Media Casualties in the Field of Journalism and Newsgathering. Available at http://www.ifj.org.

IFJ (2003a) Justice Denied On the Road To Baghdad. Available at http://www.ifj.org, October.

IFJ (2003b) Press Freedom and Safety. Available at http://www.ifj.org/default.asp?Issue=PRESSFREEDOM&Language=EN. Accessed 28 October 2003.

Iskandar, A. and El-Nawawy, M. (2004) Al-Jazeera and War coverage in Iraq: the Media's Quest for Contextual Objectivity, in S. Allan and B. Zelizer (eds) *Reporting War*. London: Routledge.

Katovsky, B. and Carlson, T. (2003) *Embedded: The Media at War in Iraq: An Oral History*. Guilford, CT: The Lyons Press.

Kellner, D. (2004) The Persian Gulf TV war revisited, in S. Allan and B. Zelizer (eds) *Reporting War*. London: Routledge.

Knightley, P. (2003) Psyops: The Battle for our Hearts and Minds, *Guardian*, 2 April.

Lewis, J. and Brookes, R. (2004) How British Television News Represented the Case for the War in Iraq, in S. Allan and B. Zelizer (eds) *Reporting War*. London: Routledge.

Moeller, S. D. (2004) A Moral Imagination: the Media's Response to the War on Terrorism, in S. Allan and B. Zelizer (eds) *Reporting War*. London: Routledge.

Morrison, D. E. and Tumber, H. (1988) *Journalists at War*. London: Sage.

Owen, J. (2001) Training Journalists to Report Safely in Hostile Environments, *Nieman Reports*, 55(4): 25–7. The Neiman Foundation For Journalism At Harvard University.

Porch, D. (2002) No Bad Stories, http://www.Nwc.navt.mil/press/review/2002/winter/art5-w02.

Rantanen, T. (2004) European News Agencies and their Sources in the Iraq War Coverage, in S. Allan and B. Zelizer (eds) *Reporting War*. London: Routledge.

Reese, S. D. (2004) Militarised Journalism: Framing Dissent in the Gulf Wars, in S. Allan and B. Zelizer (eds) *Reporting War*. London: Routledge.

Tumber, H. (2002a) Reporting Under Fire, in B. Zelizer and S. Allan (eds) *Journalism After September 11*. London and New York: Routledge.

Tumber, H. (2002b) Sources, the Media and the Reporting of Conflict, in E. Gilboa (ed.) *The Media and International Conflict*. New York: Transnational Publishers, pp. 135–52.

Tumber, H. and Palmer, J. (2004) *Media at War: The Iraq Crisis*. London: Sage.

Index